Praise for the First Edition

"An easy-to-read book and a great way to get up to speed with Clojure."
— **Craig Smith, Suncorp**

"A broad but thorough overview of the current state of the art in this exciting new language."
— **Tim Moore, Atlassian**

"Down-to-earth and thorough, just what you need to get building real-world applications."
— **Stuart Caborn, BNP Paribas**

"I love the inclusion of testing and web topics!"
— **Chris Bailey, HotelTonight**

"An insightful look at Clojure and its unique position in the JVM family of languages. A good read for anyone trying to 'get' Clojure."
— **Jason Rogers, MSCI Inc.**

"Don't just learn Clojure—learn how to build things with it."
— **Baishampayan Ghose (BG), Qotd, Inc.**

"Explains functional programming with Java."
— **Doug Warren, Java Web Services**

"It shows what you can get mixing the power of Java libraries with a pragmatic functional language."
— **Federico Tomassetti, Politecnico di Torino**

"A very approachable text and a great introduction to Clojure and Lisp."
— **Kevin Butler, HandyApp, LLC**

"Brings together the features of Clojure and shows how they can be used cohesively to implement a number of engineering solutions. Each solution is stunningly simple and elegant. I highly recommend this book."
— **A.B., Amazon reviewer**

T0197974

Clojure in Action
Second Edition

AMIT RATHORE
FRANCIS AVILA

MANNING
SHELTER ISLAND

For online information and ordering of this and other Manning books, please visit
www.manning.com. The publisher offers discounts on this book when ordered in quantity.
For more information, please contact

>   Special Sales Department
>   Manning Publications Co.
>   20 Baldwin Road
>   PO Box 761
>   Shelter Island, NY 11964
>   Email: orders@manning.com

Manning Publications Co.
20 Baldwin Road
PO Box 761
Shelter Island, NY 11964

Development editor: Karen Miller
Technical development editors: Andrew Luly, Michael Williams
Copyeditor: Jodie Allen
Proofreader: Linda Recktenwald
Technical proofreader: Joe Smith
Typesetter: Dennis Dalinnik
Cover designer: Marija Tudor

ISBN: 9781617291524
Printed in the United States of America
1 2 3 4 5 6 7 8 9 10 – EBM – 20 19 18 17 16 15

contents

preface to the second edition   xi
preface to the first edition   xiii
acknowledgments   xvi
about this book   xviii

1 Introducing Clojure   1

1.1   Clojure: What and why?   1

*Clojure: A modern Lisp   2 ▪ Clojure: Pragmatic functional
programming   3 ▪ Clojure on the JVM   6*

1.2   Language basics   7

Lisp syntax   7 ▪ Parentheses   9

1.3   Host interoperation: A JVM crash course   10

*Java types, classes, and objects   11 ▪ The dot and new
operators   12 ▪ Threads and concurrency   13*

1.4   Summary   14

2 Clojure elements: Data structures and functions 16

2.1 Coding at the REPL 16

Clojure REPL 17 ▪ "Hello, world!" 19 ▪ Looking up
documentation using doc, find-doc, and apropos 20
A few more points on Clojure syntax 21

2.2 Clojure data structures 24

nil, truth, and falsehood 24 ▪ Characters and strings 24
Clojure numbers 25 ▪ Symbols and keywords 26
Lists 27 ▪ Vectors 29 ▪ Maps 31 ▪ Sequences 33

2.3 Program structure 34

Functions 34 ▪ The let form 35 ▪ Side effects with do 37
Reader macros 38

2.4 Program flow 39

Conditionals 39 ▪ Logical functions 41 ▪ Functional
iteration 44 ▪ Threading macros 50

2.5 Summary 54

3 Building blocks of Clojure 55

3.1 Metadata 56

Java type hints 58 ▪ Java primitive and array types 59

3.2 Java exceptions: try and throw 60

3.3 Functions 62

Defining functions 62 ▪ Calling functions 69
Higher-order functions 70 ▪ Writing higher-order functions 73
Anonymous functions 76 ▪ Keywords and symbols 77

3.4 Scope 80

Vars and binding 80 ▪ The let form revisited 85
Lexical closures 86

3.5 Namespaces 87

ns macro 87 ▪ Working with namespaces 90

3.6 Destructuring 91

Vector bindings 91 ▪ Map bindings 93

3.7 Reader literals 95

3.8 Summary 97

4 Multimethod polymorphism   98

4.1   Polymorphism and its types   98

Parametric polymorphism   99 ▪ *Ad hoc polymorphism   99*
Subtype polymorphism   101

4.2   Polymorphism using multimethods   103

Life without multimethods   103 ▪ *Ad hoc polymorphism*
using multimethods   103 ▪ *Multiple dispatch   106*
Subtype polymorphism using multimethods   108

4.3   Summary   114

5 Exploring Clojure and Java interop   116

5.1   Calling Java from Clojure   117

Importing Java classes into Clojure   117 ▪ *Creating*
instances   118 ▪ *Accessing methods and fields   119*
Macros and the dot special form   120 ▪ *Helpful Clojure*
macros for working with Java   122 ▪ *Implementing interfaces*
and extending classes   125

5.2   Compiling Clojure code to Java bytecode   126

Example: A tale of two calculators   126 ▪ *Creating Java classes*
and interfaces using gen-class and gen-interface   129

5.3   Calling Clojure from Java   133

5.4   Summary   134

6 State and the concurrent world   135

6.1   The problem with state   136

Common problems with shared state   136
Traditional solution   137

6.2   Separating identities and values   139

Immutable values   140 ▪ *Objects and time   140*
Immutability and concurrency   142

6.3   Clojure's way   143

Immutability and performance   143 ▪ *Managed references   144*

6.4   Refs   145

Creating refs   145 ▪ *Mutating refs   145* ▪ *Software*
transactional memory   148

6.5   Agents   150

Creating agents   150 ▪ *Mutating agents   151* ▪ *Working with*
agents   152 ▪ *Side effects in STM transactions   155*

6.6   Atoms   155
Creating atoms   155 ▪ *Mutating atoms   156*

6.7   Vars   157
Creating vars and root bindings   157 ▪ *Var bindings   158*

6.8   State and its unified access model   159
Creating   159 ▪ *Reading   159* ▪ *Mutation   159*
Transactions   160 ▪ *Watching for mutation   160*

6.9   Deciding which reference type to use   161

6.10   Futures and promises   162
Futures   162 ▪ *Promises   163*

6.11   Summary   164

7   **Evolving Clojure through macros   166**

7.1   Macro basics   167
Textual substitution   167 ▪ *The unless example   168*
Macro templates   171 ▪ *Recap: Why macros?   176*

7.2   Macros from within Clojure   177
comment   177 ▪ *declare   177* ▪ *defonce   178*
and   178 ▪ *time   179*

7.3   Writing your own macros   180
infix   180 ▪ *randomly   180* ▪ *defwebmethod   181*
defnn   183 ▪ *assert-true   184*

7.4   Summary   185

8   **More on functional programming   186**

8.1   Using higher-order functions   187
Collecting results of functions   187 ▪ *Reducing lists of
things   189* ▪ *Filtering lists of things   191*

8.2   Partial application   192
Adapting functions   193 ▪ *Defining functions   196*

8.3   Closures   197
Free variables and closures   197 ▪ *Delayed computation
and closures   198* ▪ *Closures and objects   199*
An object system for Clojure   202

8.4   Summary   215

9 Protocols, records, and types 217

9.1 The expression problem 218

Setting up the example scenario 218 ▪ A closer look at the expression problem and some potential solutions 222 Clojure's multimethods solution 223

9.2 Examining the operations side of the expression problem 225

def-modus-operandi 225 ▪ detail-modus-operandi 226 Tracking your modus operandi 227 ▪ Error handling and trouble spots in this solution 233

9.3 Examining the data types side of the expression problem with protocols 234

defprotocol and extend-protocol 234 ▪ Defining data types with deftype, defrecord, and reify 239

9.4 Summary 245

10 Test-driven development and more 247

10.1 Getting started with TDD: Manipulating dates in strings 248

First assertion 248 ▪ month-from and year-from 251 as-string 252 ▪ Incrementing and decrementing 253 Refactor mercilessly 255

10.2 Improving tests through mocking and stubbing 256

Example: Expense finders 256 ▪ Stubbing 257 Mocking 260 ▪ Mocks versus stubs 261 Managing stubbing and mocking state 264

10.3 Organizing tests 265

The testing macro 266 ▪ The are macro 266

10.4 Summary 267

11 More macros and DSLs 268

11.1 A quick review of macros 269

11.2 Anaphoric macros 270

The anaphoric if 270 ▪ The thread-it macro 273

11.3 Shifting computation to compile time 276

Example: Rotation ciphers without macros 276 Making the compiler work harder 279

11.4   Macro-generating macros   281

Example template   282 ▪ Implementing make-synonym   282
Why macro-generating macros   285

11.5   Domain-specific languages   286

DSL-driven design   286 ▪ User classification   289

11.6   Summary   299

Conclusion   301

appendix   Installing Clojure   302

index   307

preface to the second edition

Many new arrivals to Clojure—including Amit Rathore, the primary author of *Clojure in Action*—come from the world of enterprise software. Theirs is a world of staticly typed, object-oriented, rigid languages tied to enormous ecosystems of tools, frameworks, and libraries designed to introduce looser coupling among components and ever-changing business requirements. This is the Java and C# world of dependency injection, servlet containers, XML configuration, and code generation. Because Clojure runs on Java it is a natural choice for people seeking to escape the complexity of their world without completely leaving the good and familiar behind. The scary and unfamiliar aspects of Clojure for enterprise software developers are its dynamic typing and first-order functions, but the appeal of Clojure is liberation from incidental complexity and static typing, while still being able to use their old code when they need to.

I did not come to Clojure from this world: I came from the Wild West of web development. This is a crazy world of dynamically typed programming languages such as PHP, Javascript, Python, and Ruby. Some of these languages were originally created with little or no thought to their suitability for large projects and hastily evolved new features and workarounds to adapt to this use. Many of their practitioners—including myself—have no computer science training and probably started their careers by messing around with HTML to give a web presence to their day job. Their programming knowledge, like the languages they use, was hastily acquired as the demands on their web presence grew. Unlike in the enterprise software world, dynamic typing, automatic type coercion, and late binding are the norm, first-class functions are common, and object-orientation is not a bedrock assumption. There are still large ecosystems of frameworks and libraries, but they are not as discipline-enforcing and configuration-oriented as in enterprise software development. For web developers, the scariest thing about Clojure is the specter of enterprise software lurking behind it—in a word: Java. For enterprise developers, Clojure's Java heritage is a feature; to web developers, it's a bug.

If you come from the web developer world, I'm here to tell you not to be afraid of Java. Much enterprise software complexity is compile-time: static types, verbose code, and lots of XML configuration. I didn't have those problems. But web development's complexity in popular web development languages is run-time: the weak typing and extreme dynamism and mutability that make programs difficult to reason about. This is the incidental complexity I was searching for a better answer to when I found Clojure, and I was skeptical of Java too. I heard the Java EE stories, saw the enormous class files and the FactoryFactoryInterfaces. How, I wondered, could Clojure manage software complexity better when it is built on Java, the most notoriously rigid, brittle, and complex software stack there is? And how am I supposed to balance all those parentheses?

Clojure occupies a middle ground between the undisciplined web development world, where codebases are difficult to change safely, and the excessive ceremony in the enterprise software world, where codebases are verbose and difficult to comprehend. Clojure encourages more discipline on my programs than when I was writing PHP, but this is a discipline with no downside: your code is still as succinct (if not more) as what you used to write; you can easily and painlessly take advantage of many niceties of the Java ecosystem, like sane package management and jar-based deployment; and thanks to the JVM your application will probably run faster, too!

Clojure benefited me even before I wrote it professionally. Internalizing Clojure's philosophy of simplicity and immutability helped me recognize the root causes of the complexity I was encountering in other languages and manage that complexity better. I now write Clojure (and ClojureScript) for a living and, yes, there's still plenty of incidental complexity in my software, but it's easier to see and far more manageable, and I'm building things I would never have dreamed of building in PHP or even Python.

The first edition of this book was instrumental in sending me down the Clojure path I walk today. So I am honored to have had a hand in this second edition, and I hope it can help you tame the software complexity in your life, too. And don't be afraid of the Java, or the parentheses! They're really quite tame.

FRANCIS AVILA

preface to the first edition

I can tell you how much I enjoy being a geek. I can tell you how fascinated I was with the punch cards my dad showed me back in 1985. I can tell you how I got my first computer when I was seven. And I can tell you that I've loved programming since 1989. I can tell you a great many things about all that, but I'm not sure how interesting they'd be.

Instead, let me tell you about my quest for an answer of sorts. There's been one issue about our industry that has continued to puzzle me over the years: Why is it that no software project is ever as simple as it seems? Why is it that no project ever comes out on time and on budget? Why are there always bugs? Why doesn't it ever quite do what was intended? And why is it always so hard to make changes to the software? No matter how clean the slate is when a project starts, why does it always become a big ball of mud?

Almost everyone acknowledges the problem, and they seem to accept the status quo. Most of our industry deals with it by adding buffers to schedules and budgets, and by accepting mediocre software. Isn't there a better way?

This book is not the answer, not by a long shot. But it is part of my exploration of the way forward. It is my notion that better tools can help us create better software.

This raises the obvious question: what is a better tool? Better at what? I believe the answer is that a better tool is one that helps manage complexity better. After all, complexity is one of the root causes for the state of things in our world. Indeed, Fred Brooks wrote about complexity in a paper as early as 1986. He drew a distinction between essential complexity and accidental complexity. Essential complexity is inherent in the problem domain, whereas accidental complexity is introduced by things external to the problem domain. For example, in a software project that deals with fil-ing taxes, complexity that arises from convoluted tax-codes is part of the domain, and hence essential. Any complexity that arises from, say, employing the rather intricate visitor pattern, is accidental.

So let me rephrase my statement: a better tool helps us minimize accidental com-plexity. It lets us do our job as best as we can, while getting out of the way. And great tools go beyond that; they give us leverage. They let us amplify our effectiveness as designers and programmers, without introducing problems of their own. The Lisp programming language was designed to be just such a tool. And Clojure is an amaz-ingly well designed Lisp.

Every programmer who stumbles onto Lisp has a story, and mine is similar to many. I started my professional career with Java, and eventually ran into a wall with what I could create with it. I started exploring dynamic languages and they felt more expressive and malleable. Mostly, I enjoyed using Python and Ruby, and wrote several nontrivial applications with them. I was working at a company called ThoughtWorks at the time, and I had a lot of like-minded colleagues to work with. Eventually, one of them turned me onto Common Lisp. The more I read about the language, the more I began to realize how primitive other languages were. I used Common Lisp on a few personal projects, but never did anything major with it; it did however have a pro-found effect on my code in all the other languages I was using, and I kept looking for an opportunity to use a Lisp on a real-world project.

I finally got my chance in 2008. I had moved to the Bay Area in California, and ended up joining the founding team of a startup named Runa. In true Silicon Valley tradition, our first office was in the founder's garage. We wanted to disrupt the world of eCommerce with Runa. The idea was to collect lots of data, use machine-learning techniques to make sense of it all, and then present personal deals to select shoppers in real-time. And in order to do all that, we had to overcome serious tech-nological challenges. The system needed to handle thousands of requests a second. It needed to handle several terabytes of data a day. It needed to be scriptable via a set of high-level, declarative DSLs. It needed to support hot code-swaps so it could be updated on the fly. It needed to run on the cloud, and it needed to be entirely API-driven. And we had to build it without much in the way of resources; we were an engineering team of three.

With these kinds of constraints, we needed a language that gave us leverage. So we turned to this new language called Clojure. It was a modern, functional language that ran on the JVM. It also promised to solve the problems inherent in concurrent, multi-threaded code. And it was a Lisp!

I was the architect at this startup, and am now the VP of Engineering. I staked the success of our future on this new (pre-release at the time) programming language cre-ated by someone who I had never heard of before. But everything I read about it reso-nated with me; all the pieces fit. We've been using Clojure ever since with incredible success. Our team has grown over the past three years, but it's still about an order of magnitude smaller than other teams at similar companies. I suspect they're using plain old Java. If nothing else, the past three years have upheld my belief that tools matter, and that some are far superior to others.

When we started out, I used to think of Clojure as our secret weapon—but the Clojure community is so strong and supportive that making it an open secret seemed like a much better idea. I started the Bay Area Clojure User Group, and we've now got hundreds of members. I like to think there are dozens of people who have come to our meetings, liked what they heard, and decided to use Clojure on their own projects.

In that same spirit, I wrote this book to share my experience with Clojure with you. It's my hope that I can convince some of you to look beyond the parentheses to what is possible with a Lisp in general, and with Clojure specifically. I hope you find this book useful and enjoyable.

AMIT RATHORE

acknowledgments

We'd like to thank everyone at Manning Publications who helped get this book off the ground, including Erin Twohey and Michael Stephens for offering us the opportunity to work on a revised edition of *Clojure in Action;* Karen Miller for thoroughly reviewing the manuscript in development; Joseph Smith for his expert technical editing; and Kevin Sullivan, Jodie Allen, Linda Recktenwald, and Mary Piergies for guiding the book through production.

We'd also like to thank the reviewers who read the chapters numerous times during development and who provided invaluable feedback: Bruno Sampaio Alessi, David Janke, Fernando Dobladez, Gary Trakhman, Geert Van Laethem, Gianluigi Spagnuolo, Jeff Smith, Jonathan Rioux, Joseph Smith, Justin Wiley, Palak Mathur, Rick Beerendonk, Scott M. Gardner, Sebastian Eckl, and Victor Christensen.

Thanks also to our MEAP (Manning Early Access Program) readers, who posted comments and corrections in the Author Online forum. We appreciate your interest and support.

Finally, we'd like to thank the prophet of immutability, Rich Hickey, for creating Clojure and encouraging us to program more simply.

Amit Rathore

Writing a book while working on a startup (and having your first child) is definitely not a recipe for relaxation! I would never have managed to get through both editions without the support of my incredibly patient wife, Deepthi. There were times when I just hit a blank wall and her encouragement is all that kept me going. Thanks, sweetheart, I could never have done this without you!

I would also like to thank my parents who started me down this path all those years ago. I grew up in India at a time when computers were these fantastical things, out of reach for most people. They took a loan to buy me a computer, instead of buying their first car, and without that I wouldn't be here today. So thanks a million, Mom and Dad!

I also want to acknowledge Ravi Mohan, who in 2001 pointed me to Lisp and to Paul Graham's essays. Thanks for showing me the way! And, I guess, thanks also to Paul Graham, who is an inspiration to many of us.

Thanks to the folks at Runa, for letting me work on this book. Ashok Narasimhan, the founder, was extremely supportive of the whole effort. The rest of my colleagues were also very supportive. Specifically, I'd like to thank Kyle Oba and George Jahad for their feedback and encouragement.

Finally, I'd like to give special thanks to Siva Jagadeesan who has supported me throughout this effort in so many ways, and to Franics Avila, for stepping up and helping update the book for the second edition.

Francis Avila

First of all, I would like to thank Amit Rathore, whose first edition of *Clojure in Action* was important for my own introduction to Clojure three years ago. Though I have remodeled and redecorated, the original sturdy columns are yours and remain the true foundation of this book.

I must also thank my wife, Danielle, who encouraged me to accept Manning's offer to coauthor the second edition, patiently endured long nights with our newborn daughter while I wrote, and offered another pair of proofreading eyes. Thank you for your love and support in spite of my strange obsession with parentheses.

I also thank Breeze EHR, the tiny startup which three years ago first plunged me into the wild and wonderful world of production Clojure. I thank especially Tyler Tallman, the founder, heart, and soul of the company, who rescued me from the PHP mines. And I'm sorry for being a curmudgeon every time you share an exciting new idea with me.

about this book

A lot has changed in the software engineering world since 2011 when the first edition of this book was published. Clojure had just released version 1.3 and the community was hard at work on 1.4. The ThoughtWorks technology radar had just advanced Clojure from "assess" to "trial" (https://www.thoughtworks.com/radar/languages-and-frameworks/clojure). Adventurous programmers and software companies were starting to take notice, but building a major project in Clojure was still a hard sell. Now, late in 2015, Clojure is an established feature of the programming landscape. Even household names like Walmart and Consumer Reports—companies not known for exotic tastes—are using Clojure at the very core of their businesses (http://cognitect.com/clojure#successstories). Clojure is now so well established that it is no longer on the ThoughtWorks radar at all.

Even where Clojure itself is still considered fringe, its core ideas—immutability and functional programming—have pollinated and borne fruit. Datomic, a Clojure-inspired immutable database, is seeing greater adoption. Java 8 now has lambdas: anonymous inline functions designed for higher-order functional programming. And there are now multiple immutable data structure libraries to choose from in many different programming languages. These ideas have even sparked revolutions in Javascript through synergies between Clojurescript (only just released in October 2011!) and Facebook's React UI framework. Immutability and functional programming are now firmly mainstream ideas.

In response to these shifts in culture, the second edition of *Clojure in Action* has narrowed its focus and broadened its audience. More and more programmers outside of the Java ecosystem have heard of Clojure and are interested in learning about it, so we expanded the introductory chapters, assumed less about the reader's knowledge of Java, and more brightly highlighted Clojure's philosophical tenants, which can be practiced beneficially in *any* language. With an explosion in popularity has come an explosion of different libraries and online tutorials for common programming tasks. Therefore we removed the hands-on chapters that dealt with the particulars of connecting to databases, building web services, and the like. All of these chapters have aged poorly as libraries and alternative approaches have grown, and if we were to rewrite them to use modern tools and techniques they would no doubt be out of date before publication. Thankfully, it is no longer difficult to find up-to-date documentation on how to use Clojure in any software engineering subfield.

Stated simply, it is no longer as necessary to evangelize Clojure quite as much as we did in the first edition. If you are reading this book, you probably already know it is a mature and powerful general-purpose functional language inspired by Lisp and built on the JVM. You've already heard stories of small Clojure teams building powerful distributed systems in a fraction of the time taken by much larger teams using other languages. You're reading this book because you want to learn how Clojure made this possible, and how you can do it, too.

How to use this book

Learning Clojure can be quite a leap for a lot of programmers. The drastically different syntax, the move from imperative to functional programming, immutability, the macro system ... these can be daunting. This book takes a slow and steady approach to learning the language and the various pieces. It assumes no prior experience with Lisp or with any functional programming language. It starts out with the absolute basics and slowly layers on the different features of the language in a way to make it all fit together in an intuitive manner. It takes a first-principles approach to all the topics, first explaining why something needs to be done a certain way, and only then talking about the Clojure way.

Once you get past the basics, the book introduces features, concepts, and techniques necessary for larger, "serious" Clojure programs written by multiple people. You'll see how to manage mutable state effectively, leverage higher-order functional programming at scale, create polymorphic types and abstractions while balancing expressivity and performance tradeoffs, write test-driven Clojure, and write domain-specific languages. To get the most out of the book, we've assumed you're familiar with an OO language like Java, C++, Ruby, or Python, but no background in Java, Lisp, or Clojure is required.

Roadmap

This book consists of 11 chapters, highlights of which are described below.

Chapter 1 is a high-level overview of the language and its three pillars: functional programming with immutable data structures, lisp syntax, and interoperability with Java.

Chapter 2 introduces the REPL (read-evaluate-print loop, which is Clojure's command prompt shell) and gets you started writing Clojure code. It includes a survey of function definition, flow control, and the built-in data structures.

Chapter 3 is about visiting the more exotic features of Clojure: metadata (data annotating other data), exception handling, higher order functions (functions as parameters to other functions), two sets of scoping rules (lexical and dynamic), namespaces to organize your code, a destructuring syntax to pull parts of nested data structures into variables easily and concisely, and finally reader literals which are a way to add new literal syntax to your code. A lot of this will be different from what you may be used to, but at the end of this chapter, you'll be able to read and write most simple Clojure programs.

Chapter 4 discusses the three basic kinds of polymorphism and what each looks like in Clojure using multimethods. If you're coming from the Java/C++ world, this is going to be quite different. Clojure's multimethods are an extremely open-ended way to implement polymorphic behavior, and they give control of method dispatch directly to the programmer.

Chapter 5 covers how Clojure embraces the JVM. No programming language can succeed without a strong set of libraries, and Clojure neatly sidesteps this problem. It makes it trivial to use any Java library in your programs, giving you instant access to the thousands of battle-tested frameworks and libraries available. It also lets you continue to benefit from your previous investment in the Java stack. In this chapter you will learn how to use Java code from Clojure, how to use Clojure code from Java, and how to write Clojure that defines or extends Java classes.

Chapter 6 explains Clojure's approach to state management and concurrency and its four basic concurrency primitives. Again, this is a fresh take on the problem of mutable state. Clojure sports extremely efficient immutable data structures and implements a database-like STM system (software transactional memory). This combination lets the language offer built-in support for correct, safe, and lock-free concurrency. This is a big deal! Your programs can take advantage of multiple cores without any of the problems associated with traditional multi-threaded code.

Chapter 7 looks at yet another feature of Clojure that is different from most other programming languages. This is the macro system (not to be confused with C macros and the like). Clojure essentially provides language-level support for code generation. It has a hook in its runtime that allows programmers to transform and generate code any way they like. This is an incredibly powerful feature that blurs the line between the language designer and an application programmer. It allows anyone to add features to the language.

Chapter 8 dives deep into the functional programming paradigm and how to leverage the higher-order functions introduced in chapter 3. You'll create your own versions of the core higher-order functions: `map`, `reduce`, and `filter`. You'll also get a thorough understanding of partial application and currying of functions. Finally, you'll build your own OOP system on top of Clojure, and will lay to rest the concern about how Clojure relates to the OO paradigm. In fact, you'll not think of OO in the same way again.

Chapter 9 deals with the expression problem and builds upon the study of polymorphism in chapter 4. You'll first review what this age-old problem is, and then you'll use Clojure multimethods to solve it in an elegant fashion. Then, we'll show you a more limited but better performing solution after introducing another constellation of Clojure features: protocols, records, and types.

Chapter 10 shows how you can raise your productivity level significantly by combining the process of writing test-driven code with the Clojure REPL introduced in chapter 2. It also addresses mocking and stubbing functions to enable better unit-testing tactics.

Chapter 11 is the last chapter and focuses on advanced macros and DSLs and builds upon what you will learn in chapter 7. This will bring you full circle: we started out in search of a tool that minimizes accidental complexity. Clojure allows you to bend the programming language to your will through the macro system, and this chapter takes a deeper dive into this feature. You'll design an internal DSL that will serve as an example of how you can use DSLs to drive core business logic in your Clojure applications.

Code conventions and downloads

All code in the book is presented in a `fixed-width font like this` to separate it from ordinary text. Code annotations accompany many of the listings, highlighting important concepts. In some cases, numbered bullets link to explanations that follow the listing.

Please see the appendix for instructions on how to download and install Clojure. You will find the full code for all the examples in the book available for download from the publisher's website at manning.com/books/clojure-in-action-second-edition.

Author Online

The purchase of *Clojure in Action, Second Edition* includes free access to a private forum run by Manning Publications where you can make comments about the book, ask technical questions, and receive help from the authors and other users. You can access and subscribe to the forum at manning.com/books/clojure-in-action-second-edition. This page provides information on how to get on the forum once you're registered, what kind of help is available, and the rules of conduct in the forum.

Manning's commitment to our readers is to provide a venue where a meaningful dialogue between individual readers and between readers and the authors can take place. It isn't a commitment to any specific amount of participation on the part of the authors, whose contributions to the book's forum remain voluntary (and unpaid). We suggest you try asking the authors some challenging questions, lest their interest stray!

The Author Online forum and the archives of previous discussions will be accessible from the publisher's website as long as the book is in print.

About the cover illustration

On the cover of *Clojure in Action, Second Edition* is "A woman from Sinj," a town in Croatia about 30 kilometers north of Split. The illustration is taken from a reproduction of an album of Croatian traditional costumes from the mid-nineteenth century by Nikola Arsenovic, published by the Ethnographic Museum in Split, Croatia, in 2003. The illustrations were obtained from a helpful librarian at the Ethnographic Museum in Split, itself situated in the Roman core of the medieval center of the town: the ruins of Emperor Diocletian's retirement palace from around AD 304. The book includes finely colored illustrations of figures from different regions of Croatia, accompanied by descriptions of the costumes and of everyday life.

Sinj is located in the Dalmatian region of Croatia and women's costumes in Dalmatia consist of layers of clothing worn over more clothing: a white blouse, skirt, or tunic is most common, with a colorful, embroidered apron decorated with complicated geometric patterns and fringes worn on top, as well as a red vest and black coat with colorful stitching added to stand out from the white blouse underneath. Jewelry consists mainly of beads worn around the neck or silver coins added as adornments to the costume. Both men and women wear a red or white pillbox cap (called a *bareta* or *crvenkapa*), with a white veil attached to the women's cap, like in the illustration on this cover.

Dress codes and lifestyles have changed over the last 200 years, and the diversity by region, so rich at the time, has faded away. It is now hard to tell apart the inhabitants of different continents, let alone of different hamlets or towns separated by only a few miles. Perhaps we have traded cultural diversity for a more varied personal life—certainly for a more varied and fast-paced technological life.

Manning celebrates the inventiveness and initiative of the computer business with book covers based on the rich diversity of regional life of two centuries ago, brought back to life by illustrations from old books and collections like this one.

Introducing Clojure

This chapter covers

- Clojure as a Lisp
- Clojure as a functional programming language
- Clojure hosted on the Java virtual machine (JVM)
- Key features and benefits of Clojure

> Any sufficiently complicated C or Fortran program contains an ad hoc, informally specified, bug-ridden, slow implementation of half of Common Lisp.
>
> —Philip Greenspun (http://philip.greenspun.com/research/)

1.1 Clojure: What and why?

Clojure is a simple and succinct programming language designed to leverage easily both legacy code and modern multicore processors. Its simplicity comes from a sparse and regular syntax. Its succinctness comes from dynamic typing and functions-as-values (that is, functional programming). It can easily use existing Java libraries because it's hosted on the Java virtual machine. And, finally, it simplifies multithreaded programming by using immutable data structures and providing powerful concurrency constructs.

1

This book covers Clojure version 1.6. In the first few chapters you'll learn the fundamentals of Clojure: its syntax, building blocks, data structures, Java interoperability, and concurrency features. As we progress beyond the basics, you'll learn how Clojure can simplify larger programs using macros, protocols and records, and higher-order functions. By the end of this book you'll understand why Clojure is traveling a rare path to popularity and how it can transform your approach to developing software.

Clojure's strengths don't lie on a single axis. On the one hand, it's designed as a hosted language, taking advantage of the technical strengths of platforms like the JVM, Microsoft's Common Language Runtime (CLR), and JavaScript engines on which it runs, while adding the "succinctness, flexibility, and productivity" (http://clojure.org/rationale) of a dynamically typed language. Clojure's functional programming features, including high-performance immutable data structures and a rich set of APIs for working with them, result in simpler programs that are easier to test and reason about. Pervasive immutability also plays a central role in Clojure's safe, well-defined concurrency and parallelism constructs. Finally, Clojure's syntax derives from the Lisp tradition, which brings with it an elegant simplicity and powerful metaprogramming tools (http://clojure.org/rationale).

Some of these points may elicit an immediate positive or negative reaction, like whether you have a preference for statically or dynamically typed languages. Other language design decisions may not be entirely clear. What is a functional programming language and is Clojure like other ones you may have seen? Does Clojure also have an object system or provide design abstractions similar to mainstream object-oriented (OO) languages? What are the advantages and disadvantages of hosting the language on an existing VM?

The promise of Clojure's synthesis of features is a language that's composed of simple, comprehensible parts that not only provide power and flexibility to writing programs but also liberate your understanding of how the parts of a language can fit together. Let no one deceive you: there are many things to learn. Developing in Clojure requires learning how to read and write Lisp, a willingness to embrace a functional style of programming, and a basic understanding of the JVM and its runtime libraries. We'll introduce all three of these Clojure pillars in this chapter to arm you for what lies ahead in the rest of the book: a deep dive into an incredible language that's both new and old.

1.1.1 *Clojure: A modern Lisp*

Clojure is a fresh take on Lisp, one of the oldest programming language families still in active use (second only to Fortran). Lisp isn't a single, specific language but rather a *style* of programming language that was designed in 1958 by Turing award winner John McCarthy. Today the Lisp family consists primarily of Common Lisp, Scheme, and Emacs Lisp, with Clojure as one of the newest additions. Despite its fragmented history, Lisp implementations, including Clojure, are used for cutting-edge software systems in various domains: NASA's Pathfinder mission-planning software, algorithmic trading at hedge funds, flight-delay prediction, data mining, natural language processing, expert systems, bio-informatics, robotics, electronic design automation, web development, next-generation databases (http://www.datomic.com), and many others.

Clojure belongs to the Lisp family of languages, but it doesn't adhere to any existing implementation exclusively, preferring instead to combine the strengths of several Lisps as well as features from languages like ML and Haskell. Lisp has the reputation of being a dark art, a secret weapon of success, and has been the birthplace of language features like conditionals, automatic garbage collection, macros, and functions as language values (not just procedures or subroutines; http://paulgraham.com/lisp.html). Clojure builds on this Lisp tradition with a pragmatic approach to functional programming, a symbiotic relationship with existing runtimes like the JVM, and advanced features like built-in concurrency and parallelism support.

You'll get a practical sense of what it means for Clojure to be a Lisp when we explore its syntax later in this chapter, but before we get bogged down in the details, let's consider the other two pillars of Clojure's design: Clojure as a functional programming language hosted on the JVM.

1.1.2 Clojure: Pragmatic functional programming

Functional programming (FP) languages have seen an explosion in popularity in the last few years. Languages like Haskell, OCaml, Scala, and F# have risen from obscurity, and existing languages like C/C++, Java, C#, Python, and Ruby have borrowed features popularized by these languages. With all of this activity in the community, it can be difficult to determine what defines a functional programming language.

The minimum requirement to be a functional language is to treat functions as something more than named subroutines for executing blocks of code. Functions in an FP language are *values*, just like the string "hello" and the number 42 are values. You can pass functions as arguments to other functions, and functions can return functions as output values. If a programming language can treat a function as a value, it's often said to have "first-class" functions. All of this may sound either impossible or too abstract at this point, so just keep in mind that you're going to see functions used in new, interesting ways in the code examples later in this chapter.

In addition to functions as first-class values, most FP languages also include the following unique features:

- Pure functions with referential transparency
- Immutable data structures as the default
- Controlled, explicit changes to state

These three features are interrelated. Most functions in an FP design are *pure*, which means they don't have any side-effects on the world around them such as changing global state or doing I/O operations. Functions should also be *referentially transparent*, meaning that if you give the same function the same inputs, it will always return the same output. At the most elementary level, functions that behave this way are

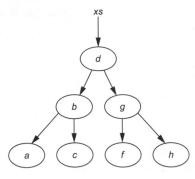

Figure 1.1   Representation of a tree of values called xs. Used with permission from https://commons.wikimedia.org/wiki/ File:Purely_functional_tree_before.svg.

simple, and it's simpler and easier[1] to reason about code that behaves consistently, without respect to the implicit environment in which it runs. Making immutable data structures the language default guarantees that functions can't alter the arguments passed to them and thus makes it much easier to write pure, referentially transparent functions. In a simplistic sense, it's as if arguments are always passed by value and not by reference.

"Hold on," you might say, "passing arguments by value and copying data structures everywhere is expensive, and I need to *change* the values of my variables!" Clojure's immutable data structures are based on research into the implementation of performant, purely functional data structures designed to avoid expensive copying.[2] In theory, if you make a change to an immutable data structure, that change results in a brand-new data structure, because you can't change what's immutable. In reality, Clojure employs *structural sharing* and other techniques under the hood to ensure that only the minimum amount of copying is performed and that operations on immutable data structures are fast and conserve memory. In effect, you get the safety of passing by value with the speed of passing by reference.

Persistent data structures can't be changed, but the diagrams in figures 1.1 and 1.2 demonstrate how one might "edit" a persistent tree. The tree *xs* shown in figure 1.1 consists of immutable nodes (circled letters) and references (arrows), so it's impossible to add or remove a value from tree *xs*. But you could create a new tree that shares as much of the original tree *xs* as possible. Figure 1.2 demonstrates how you can add a new value *e* by creating a new set of nodes and references in the path to the root of the tree (d', g', f') that reuse old nodes (*b*, *a*, *c*, and *h*), resulting in the new persistent tree *ys*. This is one of the basic principles underlying Clojure's persistent data structures.

---

[1] See the talk "Simplicity Ain't Easy" to understand the unique role *simplicity* has in Clojure's design considerations: http://youtu.be/cidchWg74Y4. For a deeper but more abstract and less Clojure-centric presentation of the easy-versus-simple distinction, watch "Simple Made Easy" by Clojure's creator Rich Hickey: http://www.infoq.com/presentations/Simple-Made-Easy.

[2] Chris Okasaki, *Purely Functional Data Structures*, 1996. Download thesis at http://www.cs.cmu.edu/~rwh/theses/ okasaki.pdf.

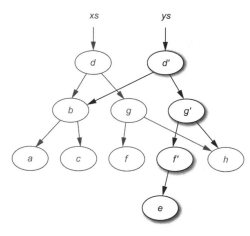

Figure 1.2 Representation of new tree ys. Used with permission from https://commons.wikimedia.org/wiki/ File:Purely_functional_tree_after.svg.

Things in your programs change, though. Most programming languages have variables that serve as named pieces of state that you can change at any time. In Clojure, the story is more controlled and better defined. As a fact, *values* like the number 42 can't change; 42 is 42, and subtracting 2 from 42 doesn't change the number 42 but, rather gives a new value of 40. This truth extends to all values, not just numbers. On the other hand, if you have a variable acting as the *identity* for something in your program that has the value 42 initially assigned to it, you might want to assign a new value to that variable at some later point in your program. In this case a variable is like a container into which you may put different values at different times. In a multithreaded, concurrent world, your programming language should provide you assurances about how those changes take place, and Clojure does just that.

Clojure lets you change the values variables hold but with well-defined semantics regarding *how* and *when* the changes take place. If you have one variable and you want to change its value, Clojure lets you do that atomically, so you're certain that if multiple threads of execution are looking at a variable's value, they always get a consistent picture, and that when it changes it does so in a single, atomic operation.[3] If you need to change *multiple* variables together as a unit, Clojure has a separate facility using its software transactional memory (STM) system to change multiple variables as part of a transaction and rollback changes if they don't all complete as expected. If you need to change a variable but want that change to happen on a separate thread of execution so it doesn't block the main thread of your program, Clojure provides facilities for that as well. All of these are built into the core of the

---

[3] In this case, "atomic" is a synonym for "indivisible." If an operation is atomic, then no other operations can interfere with the underlying state while it's being changed. If any other processes attempt to get the state of a variable during an atomic operation, they simply get the last value of the variable before the atomic operation began. In the case of other processes attempting to change the underlying state during an atomic operation, they're held off until the atomic operation is complete.

language, making concurrency so easy you have to work to make your programs *not* support it.[4]

Functional languages are often judged by their functional "purity," or strict adherence to the theoretical underpinnings of functional programming language design. On the one hand, Clojure's default use patterns encourage pure functional programming: immutable data structures, higher-order functions and recursion that take the place of imperative loops, and even a choice between lazy or eager evaluation of collections. On the other hand, Clojure is pragmatic. Even though most problems can be solved using immutable data structures and functional programming patterns, certain tasks are more clearly modeled with mutable state and a more imperative approach. Clojure provides constructs with well-defined semantics for sharing state and changing it over time as we've just described. In addition, Clojure also doesn't require the developer to annotate code that causes side-effects, whether they be changes to state, printing to the screen, or network I/O, as some "purer" functional programming languages require.

Another part of Clojure's pragmatism stems from its hosted design. When necessary, you can always drop down to the host platform and use Java APIs directly from Clojure, with all of the performance (and pitfalls) that come from coding directly in Java.

1.1.3 *Clojure on the JVM*

Clojure was designed as a *hosted* language. Whereas most programming language projects combine a language design with an accompanying runtime platform for that language, Rich Hickey, Clojure's creator, decided to focus on Clojure-the-language and rely on existing VMs for the runtime platform. He began his work on the JVM, but Clojure has since spread to the CLR with interoperability with the .NET ecosystem (Clojure-CLR), as well as to browser and server-side JavaScript engines (ClojureScript).

Rich made this decision with the best kind of engineering laziness in mind (http://blog.codinghorror.com/how-to-be-lazy-dumb-and-successful/). The JVM is a mature, ubiquitous platform with a myriad of third-party libraries. The canonical HotSpot JVM implementation is open source and sports an advanced just-in-time (JIT) compiler with choice of garbage collectors, maintaining competitive performance with "native" runtimes for a variety of use cases.[5] By taking these features for granted as part of the underlying runtime host, the Clojure community is free to focus its time on a solid language design and higher-level abstractions instead of reinventing the VM wheel (and the bugs that come with it).

From a business perspective, relying on existing VMs lowers the risk of introducing Clojure. Many organizations have existing architectures and personnel expertise tied

---

[4] For those already familiar with Clojure, note that we use the term *variable* loosely at this point to introduce Clojure's unique handling of values, identities, and underlying state and how those all change over time. We'll cover the specifics of Clojure's concurrency constructs in a later section using Clojure's precise terminology.

[5] A fine starting point for an overview of JVM performance characteristics is the Wikipedia article on Java performance at http://en.wikipedia.org/wiki/Java_performance.

to the JVM or the CLR and the ability to introduce Clojure as part of a larger Java or C# application is a powerful selling point. Clojure compiles down to bytecode on the JVM and Common Intermediate Language (CIL) on the CLR, meaning that it participates as a first-class citizen of the VMs it runs on.

On the other hand, Clojure intentionally doesn't shield you from the host platform on which it runs. To be effective in Clojure on the JVM, you'll have to learn about its runtime environment, including the following at a minimum:

- Java's core `java.lang.*` classes and their methods
- The JVM's threading/process model
- How the JVM finds code to compile on its *classpath*

We'll introduce these minimum Java and JVM concepts in this chapter and more advanced topics as we encounter them, so you don't need to put this book down and study Java first. If you're interested in working with Clojure on the CLR or a JavaScript engine, you'll need to have an equivalent understanding of those platforms to use Clojure on them effectively.

Now that you have a high-level understanding of Clojure as a functional Lisp on the JVM, let's get started writing some Clojure code to bring these concepts to life.

1.2 Language basics

It's impossible to separate the Lisp, functional programming, and JVM features of Clojure. At every step they play on each other and tell a compelling software development story, but because we have to start somewhere, tackling the syntax on the page is a good place to start.

1.2.1 Lisp syntax

Clojure's syntax is derived from its Lisp roots: lots of parentheses. It's alien to most developers with experience in languages with Algol-inspired syntax like C, C++, Java, Python, Ruby, Perl, and so on. Because it's so foreign, there are some tricks we'll employ for getting over the parenthesis hump:

- Initially ignore the parentheses.
- Consider how other languages use parentheses.
- See parentheses as "units of value" or *expressions*.
- Embrace the parentheses.

To convince you that initially ignoring the parentheses is okay, let's take our first look at some example code:

```
(get-url "http://example.com")
```

If you guessed that this makes an HTTP request for the URL http://example.com, you're correct. The `get-url` function isn't defined in Clojure by default, but it makes for a nice self-describing function name, and we'll use this as one of our main examples once we get past the basics. Let's look at some code examples that use built-in Clojure functions and see their output:

```
(str "Hello, " "World!")
;; Result: "Hello, World!"
; (A Semi-colon starts a code comment which continues
; to the end of the line.)
```

The str function stands for "string" and concatenates its arguments into a single output string. Other languages generally use an operator like +. What would it look like to concatenate several strings with operators?

```
"Hello from " + "a language " + "with operators";
# Result: "Hello from a language with operators"
```

This is called *infix notation* because you put the operator *in between* each string that you're concatenating. As a Lisp, Clojure uses *prefix notation* for all of its functions and even things that look like operators, so if you need to concatenate more than two strings, you just keep passing arguments to the str function:

```
(str "Hello from " "Clojure with " "lots of " " arguments")
;; Result: "Hello from Clojure with lots of arguments"
```

And if you need to do arithmetic, the same principle holds:

```
(+ 1 2)
;; Result: 3

(+ 1 2 3)
;; Result: 6
```

These examples demonstrate two advantages of Clojure's approach. First, there's no difference between functions and operators because Clojure *doesn't have operators*. There's no system of operator precedence to memorize. The forms str and + are both regular Clojure functions; one just happens to have a nonalphabetic character as its name. Second, because you don't need to interleave operators between arguments, it's natural for these kinds of functions to take an arbitrary number of arguments (called *variable arity*), allowing you to add more arguments without fear of forgetting to put an operator in between each one.

In the preceding examples, you can safely ignore the parentheses, but let's step up the difficulty. If you needed to do more than one operation, you might write the following in a language that uses operators for arithmetic:

```
3 + 4 * 2
```

In a language with operators you'd need to remember the precedence of the + and * operators, but you can make this unambiguous regardless of language by surrounding expressions with parentheses:

```
3 + (4 * 2)
# Result: 11
```

By not having operators, Clojure makes that level of explicitness a requirement:

```
(+ 3 (* 4 2))
;; Result: 11
```

Let's break that down expression by expression.

The outermost function is +, which has two arguments: 3 and the form (* 4 2). You know what 3 is all about, so let's solve the (* 4 2). If you call the multiplication function * with arguments of 4 and 2, you get 8. Let's write the expression again, solving the (* 4 2) step first, bolding the important parts to call your attention to them:

```
(+ 3 (* 4 2))
(+ 3 8)
;; Result: 11
```

Now you have the + function with two simple arguments and the sum is obviously 11. Although leveraging operators and their precedence rules makes writing such mathematical expressions more concise in other languages, Clojure makes calling functions completely consistent across the language.

Now that you've seen some parentheses in action, let's stop ignoring them for a moment and understand their primary purpose.

1.2.2 Parentheses

Lisp's use of parentheses is its secret syntactic weapon, but we're not going to delve into their deeper purpose right now. For the sake of reading and writing your first Clojure programs, we're going to say that parentheses serve two purposes:

- Calling functions
- Constructing lists

All of the code so far has shown examples of the first purpose—to call functions. Inside a set of parentheses, the first language form is always a function, macro, or special form, and all subsequent forms are its arguments. Figure 1.3 is a simple example of this use of parentheses. We'll cover what macros and special forms are as we encounter them, but for now you can think of them as functions that get special treatment.

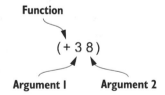

Figure 1.3 Parentheses for calling functions

Start training your brain to associate left parenthesis with function invocation. That left parenthesis is like a phone being held up to the function's ear, getting ready to call it with the rest of the items up to the matching right parenthesis. It will become increasingly important to have this association firmly planted in your mind once we start looking at higher-order functional programming patterns. Also remember that arguments to functions won't always be simple values but, as in the earlier examples, will be nested expressions—see figure 1.4 for an example.

The second use of parentheses is at once the most common and the least noticeable—to construct lists. On the one hand, Clojure has literal syntax for collections other than lists, and idiomatic Clojure programs use all of the collection types based on their different performance strengths. Clojure isn't as list-centric as other Lisps, in part because it provides literal syntax for these other types of collections. On the other hand, at the meta level, your entire Clojure program is a series of lists: the very source code of your program is interpreted by the Clojure compiler as lists that contain function names and arguments that need to be parsed, evaluated, and compiled. Because the same language features are available at both

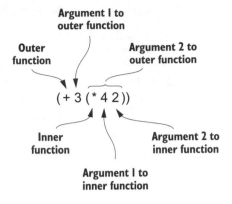

Figure 1.4   Nested parentheses for calling functions

the lower compiler levels and in your normal program code, Lisp enables uniquely powerful meta-programming capabilities. We'll delve into the significance of this fact when we discuss Clojure macros in later chapters, but for now let's take a tour of Clojure's essential data structures and collection types so we can read realistic code examples.

You've now seen Clojure's essential syntax: parentheses that contain functions (or special things that act like functions) and their arguments. Because parentheses are the containers for all expressions in the language, you edit your Clojure code by arranging these expressions like building blocks, each one a little self-contained world of functionality that results in a consistent value and can be placed anywhere in your program where that value is required. Moreover, this consistency in parenthetical syntax means IDEs and text editors can provide *structural editing* for moving expressions around easily, meaning you never have to make sure your open and close parentheses are matched. As you spend more time writing Clojure, we highly recommend learning some of these tools in your development environment of choice, so that Clojure's parentheses become an advantage and not a hindrance.

1.3   *Host interoperation: A JVM crash course*

Clojure doesn't hide the host platform on which it's implemented from the programmer. In this book we'll focus on the canonical JVM implementation of Clojure, but the principles of interoperation with the host, usually just called *interop*, are common to all of the platforms that Clojure targets. Because Clojure embraces its host platform instead of trying to hide it, you *must* learn the basics of Java and the JVM to be able to code in Clojure.

Java is three distinct pieces that were designed and shipped together: a language, a virtual machine, and a standard library. Parts of Clojure are written in Java the language, but Clojure itself doesn't use it. Instead, Clojure code is compiled directly to bytecode for the JVM to run. Clojure also requires you to use the standard library for many basic functions. Because the standard library was written in and for Java the language, some basic knowledge of Java the language will help you make better use of Java the library.

In many cases Clojure uses Java types and the standard library directly. For example, strings in Clojure are Java String objects and literal numerals are Java Long objects, and Clojure's collections implement the same collection interfaces implemented by Java collections. Reusing Java types and interfaces has the added benefit that *Java* code can use *Clojure* types (such as its immutable data structures) seamlessly.

Sometimes Clojure wraps Java library features with functions of its own, like many of the functions in Clojure's `clojure.string` namespace that delegate to methods in Java's `String` class. But often there's no Clojure wrapper and you'll need to call Java methods directly. For example, Clojure doesn't implement regular functions for mathematical methods like abs[olute], exp[onent], log, sin, cos, and tan found in the `java.lang.Math`[6] class, which therefore need to be invoked via the Java interop syntax we introduce later in this section.

Let's briefly review Java's types, classes, and object system, so that we can make sense of what it means for Clojure code to interoperate with Java.

1.3.1 Java types, classes, and objects

Java is an object-oriented language based on a class hierarchy with single inheritance. In addition to classes, common behaviors can be grouped into *interfaces*, which act as simple outlines of method signatures that classes that implement the interface must support.[7] Only one public class or interface can be defined in a single file, and those files must be placed in directories that are on Java's classpath. The Java classpath is akin to C's search path or Ruby's `$LOAD_PATH` in that it's a collection of directories that the Java compiler will search when looking for files to compile as part of your program. The fully qualified name of a Java class or interface consists of its package name followed by the name of the class or interface being defined; for example, Java's `Math` class is situated in the `java.lang` package. This allows individual classes to share the same name (for example, `Math`) as long as they aren't in the same package and thus have a unique full name when loaded into the JVM (for example, `java.lang.Math` vs. `com.mycompany.Math`).

What does all of this have to do with Clojure? All of the classes located in Java's `java.lang` package are imported by default in all Clojure programs, so that you can refer to things like `String` and `Integer` without having to type out `java.lang.String` and `java.lang.Integer`. Many Clojure data structures (especially collections) implement

---

[6] API documentation for the `Math` class can be found at http://docs.oracle.com/javase/7/docs/api/java/lang/Math.html.

[7] Java 8 introduced default methods for interfaces. Because, as of this writing, Clojure currently targets Java 6 as its minimum target version, we'll continue to treat interfaces as simple method contracts without default implementations.

Java interfaces, so Java libraries that expect objects that implement those interfaces will accept Clojure data structures as arguments. All Clojure collections, for example, implement `java.lang.Iterable` or `java.util.Collection`, whereas only some implement `java.util.List` or `java.util.Map`, depending on their purpose.

Like the Java compiler, the Clojure compiler expects to find your Clojure source code on the Java classpath and also expects that the full name of a namespace be unique. Appendix A covers the particulars of how projects are organized on the file system, how the classpath is set up, and how to invoke the Clojure compiler.

The flip side to having to learn some Java basics is that you get access to a plethora of mature, battle-tested Java libraries that you can consume seamlessly from your Clojure programs: Joda Time provides correct date and time manipulation; JDBC drivers expose a common API for communicating with different databases; Jetty is an advanced embeddable web server; Bouncy Castle has a convenient API for working with Java's cryptographic features; Selenium WebDriver lets you test web applications by controlling real web browsers programmatically; and the various Apache Commons libraries provide miscellaneous utilities that act as an extended Java standard library. In addition to application libraries, you can use all of the built-in tools for monitoring the performance of the JVM, as well as external profilers like VisualVM, YourKit, and profilers-as-a-service like New Relic to gain a deeper understanding of how your Clojure applications run.

Having described all the wonderful features you have access to via Java interop, we still haven't discussed how to access them from Clojure. How does Clojure differentiate between regular Clojure code and code that does Java interop? The first part of this answer is the dot operator.

1.3.2 *The dot and new operators*

The dot operator—written as a literal `.`—forms the basis for Java interop. When seen by itself after an opening parenthesis, it should be read as "in the scope of A do B with arguments…." For example:

```
(. Math PI)
;; Result: 3.141592653589793
(. Math abs -3)
;; Result: 3
(. "foo" toUpperCase)
;; Result: "FOO"
```

To accommodate the fact that, outside of Java interop, the first form in a Clojure expression is a function, macro, or special form, Clojure provides some syntactic sugar to make this code more idiomatic.

The first two examples deal with static members of the `Math` class and can be rewritten like this:

```
Math/PI;; Result: 3.141592653589793
(Math/abs -3)
;; Result: 3
```

Fields and methods that are *static* (defined on the class and not on instances of the class) are accessed with a forward slash. In the Java Math class, PI is a static field and not a method, so it doesn't need to be invoked (using parentheses) to return a value. But abs is a method, so it must still be invoked with parentheses.

The third example is an instance method invocation: it calls the toUpperCase method of the string instance "foo". This example can be rewritten as follows to make it look more like a function call:

```
(.toUpperCase "foo")
;; Result: "FOO"
```

To create instances of classes, you can use the new operator or a trailing dot to indicate that the class's constructor should be called:

```
(new Integer "42")
;; Result: 42
(Integer. "42")
;; Result: 42
```

The trailing dot here, the leading dot for instance fields and methods, and the forward slashes for static fields and methods are all syntactic conveniences. During Clojure's macro expansion phase of compiling code, the trailing dot expands to use the new special form, and the others expand to the standalone dot form demonstrated at the beginning of this section, so they're all literally equivalent by the time your Clojure code is evaluated.

The dot operator only provides a doorway for consuming Java APIs. We'll cover other advanced topics of Java interop that involve extending Java's class system in later chapters. More importantly, we'll explore the powerful design abstractions that Clojure provides *in spite of* the underlying object-oriented nature of its host platform as we work through programs in later chapters. Before closing out this chapter, we should touch on one more aspect of the JVM that's central to Clojure's mission: the JVM model for threads and concurrency.

1.3.3 *Threads and concurrency*

A thread represents program execution. Every program, regardless of programming language, has at least one main thread or process in which the application code is being evaluated. In addition to this main application thread, language runtimes generally provide a way to start new, separate threads of execution. The default runtimes for Ruby and Python, for example, provide lightweight or "green" threads that are managed completely by the runtime itself. JVM threads map directly to native system threads, which means they can take advantage of multiple CPU cores "for free" by letting the operating system manage scheduling threads and delegating to CPUs. By engaging all available cores on a machine using native threads, the JVM provides genuine and performant parallelism.

In an application with a single thread of execution, the program is evaluated serially, and it's relatively simple to understand when objects are created, changed, and destroyed based on the flow of the program. But when introducing additional threads of execution that are running at the same time as the main thread, issues of concurrency have to be dealt with. If you have state (a variable) that can be accessed from multiple threads simultaneously, how can you be sure that two threads aren't attempting to make changes to that state at the same time? Are you certain that changes to the state can be performed atomically, such that no other threads see a corrupt "in progress" state for a variable that's being changed during a program's execution?

Although Java has all the tools necessary to write safe concurrent programs with shared mutable state, in practice it's extremely difficult to write such programs correctly. Having spent years writing such programs himself in Java and other languages, Rich Hickey implemented a set of concurrency constructs in Clojure that not only allow for correctness but also enforce it at the language level.

By virtue of the fact that Clojure's core data structures are all immutable, the issue of shared *mutable* state becomes largely moot. When some mutable state is required, Clojure provides concurrency data structures called *vars*, *atoms*, *refs*, and *agents* that have clearly defined semantics for how to change the underlying state they reference. Furthermore, Clojure always allows fast access to the value of these data structures—even if they're in the middle of being changed by another thread—by maintaining a snapshot of the old values during changes. For use cases that need only parallel exccution but not shared state, Clojure provides futures and promises similar to other languages but implemented using JVM threads and not bound to any particular callback as is common in languages like JavaScript.

Instead of comparing all of the specific features of each concurrency construct in the abstract or listing all the functions that deal with parallel execution here, we'll continue exploring these topics in more depth with code examples in later chapters.

1.4   Summary

We've completed our transit around the three basic pillars of Clojure: functional programming with immutable data structures, Lisp syntax, and host interop. You now know the absolute basics of reading Lisp and Java interop code, and we can continue to explore Clojure's functions and data structures and worry about the underlying platform only when the need arises.

The most difficult aspect of learning Clojure for most developers isn't the syntax of Lisp or the idiosyncrasies of the JVM platform. The truly mind-bending part of coding in Clojure comes from the shift from an imperative mindset (prevalent in most mainstream languages) to a functional programming approach to program design. Much of your time in the beginning will be spent wondering how to accomplish things in Clojure that you can already do easily in your imperative language of choice. In our experience, people often spend more time unlearning complex idioms from other languages than they do learning the simple, flexible, and composable parts that make up the Clojure language.

The chapters that follow will cover Clojure's core data structures and APIs in detail using code examples that demonstrate the strengths of Clojure's language design. By the end of the next chapter, you'll have the skills to set up your own Clojure projects and write small- to medium-size programs.

Clojure elements: Data structures and functions

This chapter covers
- Clojure's core data structures
- Clojure functions
- Program flow with Clojure

In the previous chapter, you read about some features of the Clojure language that make it interesting. You saw *some* code, but it probably looked a little alien. It's now time to set that right. This chapter and the next address the basics of writing code in Clojure. This one will give an overview of the various data structures that make up the core of the language and walk you through the fundamentals of the structure and flow of Clojure programs. By the end of the next chapter, you'll be able to read most Clojure code and write your own programs.

2.1 Coding at the REPL

Unlike many other languages, Clojure doesn't have to be typed into files and compiled all at once. Instead, you can interactively build a working program an expression at a time and try out code immediately. This form of interactive development is possible through the read-evaluate-print loop (REPL). It's an interactive shell similar to those provided by languages such as Ruby and Python. In this section we'll introduce you to interacting with a live Clojure environment through the REPL, which will enable you to follow along with the lessons in this chapter and the next. We encourage you to read these chapters near a REPL, copy the examples, explore different approaches, and try some code of your own and see what happens.

If you haven't already done so, get a Clojure REPL up and running—see appendix A for instructions. (If you don't want to wait, go to http://www.tryclj.com.)

2.1.1 *Clojure REPL*

Clojure programs are usually not all typed out in one go. In fact, these days, programs in most languages are often written using test-driven design (TDD). This technique allows the programmer to build up a larger program from smaller units of tested code. Doing this keeps programmer productivity high because the focus is always on one piece of the program at any given time. You write the test for something, write just enough code to make the test pass, and repeat the process. This style of development also has the added benefit of leaving behind a set of regression tests that can be used later. It ensures that as the program is modified and enhanced, nothing breaks existing functionality.

Clojure code can also be written with a TDD approach; indeed, it often is. The Clojure REPL adds a fantastic tool that allows you to be even more productive than when using plain TDD. This combination of using the REPL alongside the typical TDD style results in far shorter code-test-debug cycles.

The REPL prompt (the text behind the cursor that waits for keyboard input) is the name of the active namespace followed by the > symbol. When you first start the REPL, you'll see the following prompt:

```
user>
```

As this prompt shows, Clojure puts you into the default namespace of user. You can type Clojure code at this prompt. When you finish typing in a form (a single valid expression, also called a symbolic expression or s-expression)[1] and press Enter, the Clojure *reader* accepts the stream of characters from the prompt (or any other source) and converts it into Clojure data structures. The data structures are *evaluated* to produce the result of the program, which is usually another data structure. The Clojure printer attempts to *print* the result in a format that can be read back by the reader. Finally, Clojure *loops* back and waits for more input.

---

[1] If you want to be super-pedantic, there's a distinction between "form" and "expression." A form is a single readable unit, such as a number, a pair of matched quotation marks for a string, or a pair of matched parentheses. Forms are what matter when reading. An expression is something with a value, such as a data structure. Expressions are what matter when evaluating. This distinction between forms and expressions, reading and evaluating, is another symptom of Lisp's nonsyntax as explained in chapter 1: it's possible to read forms without knowing how to evaluate them as expressions!

Let's look at a concrete example of REPL interaction:

```
user> (+ 1 2)                    ⟵⎤ Type this part
=> 3
user> (def my-addition (fn [operand1 operand2] (+ operand1 operand2)))
=> #'user/my-addition
user> (my-addition 1 2)
=> 3
user> (my-addition 100 30)
=> 130
user> (+ 1 2) "Two forms on one line!"
=> 3
=> "Two forms on one line!"
```

Lines starting with => are the printed values of the expression evaluated on the previous prompt. The first expression adds 1 and 2. The second expression defines a namespace-qualified global user/my-addition, which contains an addition function. That funny-looking #'user/my-addition is a var (created and returned by def). A var is a named, mutable container that holds a value, in this case the addition function. You'll learn more about vars later. For now, just know that if you want to save the value of an expression to refer to it later, use (def variable-name "value to save").

The third and fourth expressions invoke the newly defined addition function and return the results. There's no explicit "return" from the function—the value returned from a function is always the last expression evaluated in the function.

Notice from the final three lines that the REPL isn't run per prompt or per line but *per form*. Clojure reads until it sees a complete form, then evaluates and prints, and then if there are still characters in its buffer it reads another form, evaluates, and prints. The REPL will not prompt the user for more input until it runs out of complete forms to read (which is exactly what happens when Clojure is reading code out of a file instead of from the prompt).

Functions like my-addition are usually created first in the REPL and then tested with various inputs. Once you're satisfied that the function works, you copy the test cases into an appropriate test file. You also copy the function definition into an appropriate source file and run the tests. At any time you can modify the definition of the function in the REPL by redefining it, and your tests will run using the new definition. This is because the REPL is a long-running process with the various definitions present in memory. That means that functions using any such redefined functions will exhibit the new behavior.

Various editors can integrate with the REPL and provide convenient ways to evaluate code from inside files being edited. This kind of integration further increases the productivity of the REPL-based TDD cycle. (Chapter 10 has much more detail on testing and TDD using Clojure.)

Now that you're somewhat comfortable interacting with a Clojure environment via the REPL, it's time for you to write some more code. We'll begin with the traditional "Hello, world!" program, and before ending the section, we'll address a few more points about Clojure syntax.

2.1.2   *"Hello, world!"*

Let's get started with a simple program. To keep with tradition, we'll examine a program that prints "Hello, world!" as shown here:

```
user> (println "Hello, world!")
Hello, world!
=> nil
```

Pretty simple, right? But there are still a few points to note. First, notice that "Hello, world!" was printed on a line by itself, with no => in front of it, and that a second line says nil. What's going on? The function println is unusual (well, for Clojure) because it's a side-effecting function: it prints a string to standard-out and then returns nil. Normally you want to create *pure* functions that only return a result and don't modify the world (for example, by writing to the console). So the Hello, world! line was printed during the REPL's *evaluation* phase, and the => nil line was printed during the REPL's *print* phase.

From now on we'll omit the user> prompt and begin result lines with ;=> if there's no ambiguity between return values and printed side effects. This is a convention designed to facilitate easy copy-pasting of Clojure code into files and REPLs.

MAGIC REPL VARIABLES

There are also four magic REPL variables that you should keep in mind to save you some typing as you experiment in the REPL: *1, *2, *3, and *e. These variables hold the value of the last, second-last, and third-last successfully read forms (that is, the lines starting with =>) and the last error. Each time a new form is evaluated successfully, its value is put in *1, and the old *1 moves to *2, and the old *2 moves to *3. For example:

```
"expression 1"
;=> "expression 1"
"expression 2"
;=> "expression 2"
*1
;=> "expression 2"
*3
;=> "expression 1"
"a" "b" "c"
;=> "a"
;=> "b"
;=> "c"                          Save "a"
*3                               for later
;=> "a"
(def a-str *1)     ◁──────┘      a-str contains value
;=> #'user/a                     that was in *1.
a-str              ◁──
;=> "something else"             Becomes new
"something else"   ◁──────       value of *1
;=> "something else"
a-str              ◁────┐  Still "a"
;=> "a"
```

If there's an error, the number variables stay the same and the error is bound to *e:

```
())
;=> ()
RuntimeException Unmatched delimiter: )  clojure.lang.Util.runtimeException
(Util.java:221)
*1
;=> ()
*e
;=> #<ReaderException clojure.lang.LispReader$ReaderException:
java.lang.RuntimeException: Unmatched delimiter: )>
```

Before moving on to the various topics planned for this chapter, let's look at a couple of facilities provided by Clojure that can help with the learning process itself.

2.1.3 *Looking up documentation using doc, find-doc, and apropos*

Thanks to a feature of Clojure called metadata, all functions have documentation available at runtime, even in the REPL. You'll learn more in chapter 3 about adding documentation to functions you define yourself and about custom metadata, but before we introduce these concepts formally, we'll review a family of functions you can use to search for and read Clojure documentation as you explore in the REPL: doc, find-doc, and apropos.

DOC

Clojure provides a useful macro called doc that allows you to look up the documentation associated with any other function or macro. It accepts the name of the entity you're trying to learn about. Here's an example:

```
user> (doc +)
-------------------------
clojure.core/+
([] [x] [x y] [x y & more])
  Returns the sum of nums. (+) returns 0.
```

Note that it prints not only the documentation string but also what arguments can be passed to the function or macro. The line ([] [x] [x y] [x y & more]) is the argument specification. Each pair of square brackets describes a possible way of calling the function. For example, the + function can be called in any of the following ways:

```
(+)                      No arguments: []
;=> 0
(+ 1)                    One argument: [x]
;=> 1
(+ 1 2)                  Two arguments: [x y]
;=> 3
(+ 1 2 3)                Two or more arguments:
;=> 6                    [x y & more]
(+ 1 2 3 4 5 6 7 8)      Two or more arguments:
;=> 36                   [x y & more]
```

The & symbol in a function argument specification means "and any number of optional arguments." Functions like this are called *variadic* functions. You'll learn more about using and defining variadic functions in chapter 3.

FIND-DOC

The find-doc function accepts a string, which can be a regular expression (regex) pattern. It then finds the documentation for all functions or macros the names or associated documentation of which match the supplied pattern. Although doc is useful for when you know the name of the function or macro you want to look up, find-doc is useful if you aren't sure of the name. Here's an example:

```
user> (find-doc "lazy")
------------------------
clojure.core/concat
([] [x] [x y] [x y & zs])
  Returns a lazy seq representing the concatenation of...
------------------------
clojure.core/cycle
([coll])
  Returns a lazy (infinite!) sequence of repetitions of...
... more results
```

These two forms, doc and find-doc, are quite useful at the REPL when you want to quickly look up what a function does or you want to find the right options. You may see a lot of functions and documentation you don't understand yet, but rest assured we'll cover it all eventually.

APROPOS

A related function is apropos, which works very similarly to find-doc but prints only the names of the functions that match the search pattern. Here's an example:

```
user=> (apropos 'doc)
(find-doc doc *remote-javadocs* javadoc add-remote-javadoc add-local-javadoc
*local-javadocs*)
```

2.1.4 A few more points on Clojure syntax

In chapter 1, we discussed the unique, parentheses-heavy syntax that Clojure employs. We examined why it exists and what it makes possible. Before we start examining the various constructs of the Clojure language, let's cover a few more key points about Clojure syntax:

- Prefix notation
- Whitespace and comments
- Case sensitivity

PREFIX NOTATION

Clojure code uses *prefix notation* (also called *polish notation*) to represent function calls. For those who are new to Lisp, this definitely takes a little getting used to, especially when it comes to using math functions such +, /, *, and the like. Instead of writing 1 + 2,

Clojure represents this evaluation as `(+ 1 2)`. Prefix notation is less familiar than the mathematical form we all learned at school.

Regular functions, on the other hand, don't have this problem. In a language such as Ruby, you'd call an `add` function as follows:

```
add(1, 2)
```

If you look closely, this is also prefix notation because the name of the function appears first, followed by arguments. The advantage of prefix notation for functions is that the function always appears as the first symbol, and everything else that follows can be treated as arguments to it. The Clojure version moves the parentheses (and drops the unnecessary comma, because whitespace is sufficient to delimit the arguments):

```
(add 1 2)
```

In most languages, mathematical functions like addition and subtraction are special cases built into the language as operators to make it possible to represent math in the more familiar in-fix notation. Clojure avoids this special case by not having any operators at all. Instead, math operators are just Clojure functions. All functions work the same way, whether they're math related or not.

By avoiding special cases and relying on the same prefix notation for all functions, Clojure maintains its regularity and gives you all the advantages that come from having no syntax. We discussed this aspect of the language in some detail in chapter 1. The main advantage we talked about was that it makes it easy to generate and manipulate code. For example, consider the regular way in which Clojure structures the conditional cond form (you can think of this as a set of if-then-else clauses in other languages):

```
(def x 1)
;=> #'user/x
(cond
    (> x 0)  "greater!"        .
    (= x 0)  "zero!"
    (< x 0)  "lesser!")
;=> "greater!"
```

This is a nested list, and it contains an even number of expressions that appear in pairs. The first element of each pair is a test expression, and the second is the respective expression that's evaluated and returned if the test expression succeeds. Generating such a simple list is easy, especially when compared to a case statement in a language like Java.

This is the reason Clojure uses prefix notation, and most programmers new to this way of calling functions will get used to it in no time. Now, let's discuss two more aspects of writing Clojure code: whitespace and comments.

WHITESPACE
As you've seen, Clojure uses parentheses (and braces and square brackets) to delimit fragments of code. Unlike languages such as Ruby and Java, it doesn't need commas

to delimit elements of a list (such as a vector or arguments passed to a function). You can use commas if you like, because Clojure treats them as whitespace and ignores them. So the following function calls are all equivalent:

```
(+ 1 2 3 4 5)
;=> 15
(+ 1, 2, 3, 4, 5)
;=> 15
(+ 1,2,3,4,5)
;=> 15
(+ 1,,,,,2,3 4,,5)
;=> 15
```

Although Clojure ignores commas, it sometimes uses them to make things easier for the programmer to read. For instance, if you have a hash map like the following

```
(def a-map {:a 1 :b 2 :c 3})
;=> #'user/a-map
```

and ask for its value at the REPL, the Clojure printer echoes it with commas:

```
user> a-map
{:a 1, :c 3, :b 2}
```

The results are easier to read, especially if you're looking at a large amount of data. By the way, if you're wondering why the ordering of the key-value pairs is different, it's because hash maps aren't ordered, and the Clojure printer doesn't print them in any specific order. It makes no difference to the actual hash map, just how it looks after being printed. We'll talk more about hash maps in this chapter. Now let's look at comments.

COMMENTS

Like most Lisps, single-line comments in Clojure are denoted using semicolons. To comment out a line of text, put one or more semicolons at the beginning. Here's an example:

```
;; This function does addition.
(defn add [x y]
  (+ x y))
```

HOW MANY SEMICOLONS? As an aside, some folks use the following convention relating to comment markers. Single semicolons are used when the comment appears after some program text. Double semicolons are used, as shown previously, to comment out an entire line of text. And finally, triple semicolons are used for block comments. These are just conventions, of course, and you're free to decide what works for you.

Clojure provides a rather convenient macro that can be used for multiline comments. The macro is called comment, and here's an example:

```
(comment
  (defn this-is-not-working [x y]
    (+ x y)))
;=> nil
```

This causes the whole s-expression to be treated as a comment. Specifically, the `comment` macro ignores forms passed in and returns `nil`.

As a final note on syntax, let's address case sensitivity.

CASE SENSITIVITY

Like the majority of modern programming languages (including Java), Clojure is case sensitive. This is *unlike* most Lisps, however, which are usually not case sensitive.

Now that we've covered Clojure syntax, you're ready to learn about writing programs in the language. We'll begin by surveying the built-in data structures Clojure makes available and the functions that manipulate them. Then you'll learn how to fill those functions with definition and control-flow forms, such as `let`, `if`, `when`, `cond`, `loop`, and others.

2.2   Clojure data structures

In this section, we're going to explore the various built-in data types and data structures of Clojure. We'll start with the basic characters and strings, and end with Clojure sequences.

2.2.1   nil, truth, and falsehood

You've seen these in action in the last several pages, so let's run a quick recap. Clojure's `nil` is equivalent to `null` in Java and `nil` in Ruby. It means "nothing." Calling a function on `nil` may lead to a `NullPointerException`, although core Clojure functions try to do something reasonable when operating on `nil`.

Boolean values are simple. Everything other than `false` and `nil` is considered true. There's an explicit `true` value, which can be used when needed.

2.2.2   Characters and strings

Clojure characters are Java characters (unsigned 16-bit UTF-16 code points). Clojure has a reader macro, the backslash, which can be used to denote characters, like \a or \g. (There are other reader macros; you'll learn more about reader macros in section 2.3.4.)

Clojure strings are Java strings. They're denoted using double quotes (because a single quote is a reader macro, which as you saw earlier means something else entirely). For this reason, it's useful to know the API provided by the Java `String` class. Some examples are

```
(.contains "clojure-in-action" "-")
```

and

```
(.endsWith "program.clj" ".clj")
```

both of which return what you'd expect: `true`. Note the leading periods in `.contains` and `.endsWith`. This is Clojure syntax for calling a nonstatic Java method, and chapter 5 focuses entirely on Java interop.

2.2.3 *Clojure numbers*

The basics of Clojure numbers are easy: most of the time the numbers you'll be using in Clojure are 64-bit integers (Java primitive longs) or 64-bit floating-point numbers (Java primitive doubles). When you need a bigger range, you can use big integers (arbitrary-precision integers) or big decimals (arbitrary-precision decimals).

Clojure also adds another less-common type of number: the ratio. Ratios are created when two integers are divided such that they can't be reduced any further. For example, executing the code (/ 4 9) returns a ratio 4/9. Table 2.1 summarizes Clojure numbers.

Table 2.1 Syntax of Clojure numbers

Type	Casting function	Range and implementation	Syntax examples	Contagiousness
Integer	Long	Signed 64 bits (Java long)	Base 10: 42 Base 16: 0x2a 0x2A 0X2a (case of letters never matters) Base 8: 052 (leading zero) Any base from 2 to 36: 2r101010 10r42 36r16 Negative numbers: -42 -0x2a -052 -36r16	0 (Lowest)
Big integer	bigint	Infinite (like a Java BigInteger, but actually a clojure.lang.BigInt)	Base 10: 42N Base 16: 0x2aN Base 8: 052N Note: XrX syntax of normal integers isn't supported!	1
Ratio	rationalize	Infinite: big integer numerator and denominator	1/3 -2/4	2
Big decimal	bigdec	Exact decimal number of arbitrary magnitude, good for financial calculations (Java BigDecimal)	2.78M 278e-2M +0.278E1M	3
Floating point	double	IEEE-794 double-precision floating point (Java double)	2.78 278e-2 +0.278E1	4 (Highest)

When different number types are mixed together in the same arithmetic operations, the number type with the highest "contagiousness" will "infect" the result with its type. Here's an illustration of this principle:

```
(+ 1 1N)
;=> 2N
```

```
(+ 1 1N 1/2)
;=> 5/2
(+ 1 1N 1/2 0.5M)
;=> 3.0M
(+ 1 1N 1/2 0.5M 0.5)
;=> 3.5
```

There's one more subtlety of Clojure integers. Sometimes an arithmetic operation on integers can produce a result too large to represent as a Clojure integer (that is, in 64 bits)—this is called *overflow*. The only possible arithmetic operations that can overflow in Clojure are adding, subtracting, and multiplying integers (dividing integers produces a ratio if the division is out of range). Normally when an overflow occurs Clojure throws a `java.lang.ArithmeticException`. If you'd like Clojure to autopromote the result to a big integer instead, you should use a set of alternative math functions: `+'`, `-'`, `*'`, `inc'` (increment), and `dec'` (decrement). Note that these are spelled like their normal, nonoverflowing counterparts except for a single quote at the end. Here's an example:

```
user> (inc 9223372036854775807)
ArithmeticException integer overflow  clojure.lang.Numbers.throwIntOverflow
(Numbers.java:1424)
user> (inc' 9223372036854775807)
;=> 9223372036854775808N
```

2.2.4 *Symbols and keywords*

Symbols are the identifiers in a Clojure program, the names that signify values. For example, in the form `(+ 1 2)` the `+` is a symbol signifying the addition function. Because Clojure separates reading and evaluating, symbols have two distinct aspects: their existence in the program data structure after reading and the value that they resolve to. Symbols *by themselves* are just names with an optional namespace, but when an expression is evaluated they're replaced with the value they signify.

It's easy to have an intuitive sense of what a valid symbol looks like, but their syntax is difficult to explain precisely. Basically, a symbol is any run of alphanumeric characters or the following characters: `*!_?$%&=<>`. But there are a few restrictions. Symbols can't start with a number; if they start with `-`, `+`, or `.`, they can't have a number as the second character (so they aren't confused with *number* literals); and they can optionally have a single `/` in the middle (and nowhere else!) to separate the namespace and name parts.

Here are some representative examples of valid symbols: `foo`, `foo/bar`, `->Bar`, `-foo`, `foo?`, `foo-bar`, and `foo+bar`. And here are some invalid attempts at symbols: `/bar`, `/foo`, and `+1foo`.

In a program, symbols normally resolve to something else that isn't a symbol. But it's possible to treat a symbol as a value itself and not an identifier by *quoting* the symbol with a leading single-quote character. The quote tells the reader that the next form is literal data and *not* code for it to evaluate later. Notice the difference:

```
arglebarg
CompilerException java.lang.RuntimeException: Unable to resolve symbol:
arglebarg in this context.
'arglebarg
;=> arglebarg
```

In the first example the symbol arglebarg isn't bound to anything, so an attempt to evaluate it throws an error. The second example is evaluating the symbol arglebarg itself as a value.

Essentially what's happening when you quote a symbol is you're treating the symbol as *data* and not *code*. In practice you'll almost never quote symbols to use them as data because Clojure has a special type specifically for this use case: the *keyword*. A keyword is sort of like an autoquoted symbol: keywords *never* reference some other value and *always* evaluate to themselves. Keyword syntax is almost like symbol syntax, except keywords always begin with a colon. Here are some examples of keywords: :foo, :foo/bar, :->foo, and :+. You'll end up using keywords very often in your Clojure code, typically as keys in hash maps and as enumerated values.

You can construct keywords and symbols from strings using the keyword and symbol functions, which take a string of the name and optionally a string of the namespace. Likewise, you can examine keywords and functions using the name and namespace functions. For example:

```
(keyword "foo")
;=> :foo
(symbol "foo" "bar")
;=> foo/bar
(name :foo/bar)
;=> "bar"
(namespace :foo)                    No namespace
;=> nil                             part returns nil.
(name "baz")                        name returns
;=> "baz"                           strings unchanged.
```

We've discussed all the scalar Clojure types. Let's now talk about some Clojure collections.

2.2.5 *Lists*

Lists are the basic collection data structure in Clojure. If you're familiar with lists from other languages, Clojure lists are singly linked lists, meaning that it's easy to go from the first to the last element of a list but impossible to go backward from the last to the first element. This means that you can only add or remove items from the "front" of the list. But this also means that multiple different lists can share the same "tails." This makes lists the simplest possible immutable data structure.

Use the list function to create a list and the list? function to test for list types:

```
(list 1 2 3 4 5)
;=> (1 2 3 4 5)
(list? *1)
;=> true
```

Use the `conj` function to create a new list with another value added to it:

```
(conj (list 1 2 3 4 5) 6)
;=> (6 1 2 3 4 5)
```

The `conj` function is the generic "add an item to a collection" function in Clojure. It always adds an item to a collection in the fastest way possible for that collection. So on lists `conj` adds to the beginning, as you saw, but with other collections it may add to the end or even (for unordered collections) nowhere in particular. You'll see more of `conj` when we look at the other collection types.

   `conj` can take multiple arguments; it will add each argument to the list in the order in which it is supplied. Note that this means it will appear in the new list in the *reverse* order, because lists can grow only from the front:

```
(conj (list 1 2 3) 4 5 6)
;=> (6 5 4 1 2 3)                              ⟵  **Same as**
(conj (conj (conj (list 1 2 3) 4) 5) 6)       **previous**
;=> (6 5 4 1 2 3)
```

You can treat a list like a stack, too. Use `peek` to return the head of the list and `pop` to return the tail:

```
(peek (list 1 2 3))
;=> 1
(pop (list 1 2 3))                            **Head of an empty**
;=> (2 3)                                     **list is nil.**
(peek (list))                    ⟵
;=> nil
(pop (list))                                  **Tail of an empty list**
IllegalStateException Can't pop empty list    **is an exception.**
clojure.lang.PersistentList$EmptyList.pop (PersistentList.java:183)
```

Finally, you can count the number of items in a list in constant time using the count function:

```
(count (list))
;=> 0
(count (list 1 2 3 4))
;=> 4
```

LISTS ARE SPECIAL

As you learned earlier, Clojure code is represented using Clojure data structures. The list is special because each expression of Clojure code is a list. The list may contain other data structures such as vectors, but the list is the primary one.

   In practice, this implies that lists are treated differently. Clojure assumes that the first symbol appearing in a list represents the name of a function (or a macro). The remaining expressions in the list are considered arguments to the function. Here's an example:

```
(+ 1 2 3)
```

This list contains the symbol for plus (which evaluates to the addition function), followed by symbols for numbers representing one, two, and three. Once the reader reads and parses this, the list is evaluated by applying the addition function to the numbers 1, 2, and 3. This evaluates to 6, and this result is returned as the value of the expression (+ 1 2 3).

This has another implication. What if you wanted to define three-numbers as a list containing the numbers 1, 2, and 3? You can try that:

```
(def three-numbers (1 2 3))
; CompilerException java.lang.ClassCastException: java.lang.Long cannot be
cast to clojure.lang.IFn, compiling:(NO_SOURCE_FILE:1)
```

The reason for this error is that Clojure is trying to treat the list (1 2 3) the same way as it treats all lists. The first element is considered a function, and here the integer 1 isn't a function. What you want here is for Clojure not to treat the list as code. You want to say, "This list isn't code, so don't try to apply normal rules of evaluation to it." Notice you had the same problem with the arglebarg symbol earlier, where you wanted to treat the symbol as data instead of as code. The solution is the same, too—quoting:

```
(def three-numbers '(1 2 3))
;=> #'user/three-numbers
```

In practice you won't use lists for data very often in your Clojure code unless you're writing a macro. The same way that Clojure has a special data type for the symbol-as-data use case (the keyword type), Clojure also has a superpowered counterpart to the humble list that's more appropriate for use as data: the vector.

2.2.6 *Vectors*

Vectors are like lists, except for two things: they're denoted using square brackets, and they're indexed by number. Vectors can be created using the vector function or literally using the square bracket notation:

```
(vector 10 20 30 40 50)
;=> [10 20 30 40 50]
(def the-vector [10 20 30 40 50])
;=> #'user/the-vector
```

Vectors being indexed by numbers means that you have fast random access to the elements inside a vector. The functions that allow you to get these elements are get and nth. If the-vector is a vector of several elements, the following is how you'd use these functions:

```
(get the-vector 2)
;=> 30
(nth the-vector 2)
;=> 30
(get the-vector 10)
;=> nil
```

```
(nth the-vector 10)
IndexOutOfBoundsException    clojure.lang.PersistentVector.arrayFor (Persis-
tentVector.java:107)
```

As shown here, the difference between nth and get is that nth throws an exception if the value isn't found, whereas get returns nil. There are also several ways to modify a vector (that is, return a new one with the change). The most commonly used one is assoc, which accepts the index at which to associate a new value, along with the value itself:

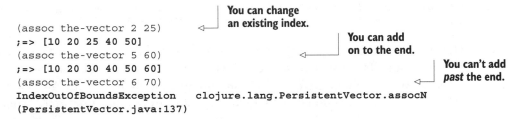

You saw how the conj function works on lists earlier. It also works on vectors. Notice that the new element ends up at the *end* of the sequence this time, because that's the fastest spot on a vector:

```
(conj [1 2 3 4 5] 6)
;=> [1 2 3 4 5 6]
```

peek and pop work, too, and they also look at the *end* of the vector instead of the *beginning* like with lists:

```
(peek [1 2])
;=> 2
(pop [1 2])
;=> [1]
(peek [])
;=> nil
(pop [])
IllegalStateException Can't pop empty vector
clojure.lang.PersistentVector.pop (PersistentVector.java:381)
```

Vectors have another interesting property: they're functions that take a single argument. The argument is assumed to be an index, and when the vector is called with a number, the value associated with that index is looked up inside itself. Here's an example:

```
(the-vector 3)
;=> 40
```

The advantage of this is that vectors can be used where functions are expected. This helps a lot when using functional composition to create higher-level functions. We'll revisit this aspect of vectors in the next chapter.

2.2.7 *Maps*

Maps are similar to associative arrays or dictionaries in languages like Python, Ruby, and Perl. A map is a sequence of key-value pairs. The keys can be pretty much any kind of object, and a value can be looked up inside a map with its key. Maps are denoted using braces. Here's an example of a map using keywords as keys, which, as it turns out, is a common pattern:

```
(def the-map {:a 1 :b 2 :c 3})
;=> #'user/the-map
```

Maps can also be constructed using the `hash-map` function:[2]

```
(hash-map :a 1 :b 2 :c 3)
;=> {:a 1, :c 3, :b 2}
```

Here, `the-map` is a sequence of key-value pairs. The keys are `:a`, `:b`, and `:c`. The values are 1, 2, and 3. Each key-value pair appears in sequence, establishing which value associates with which key. The values can be looked up like this:

```
(the-map :b)
;=> 2
```

The reason this is valid Clojure code is because a Clojure map is also a function. It accepts a key as its parameter, which is used to look up the associated value inside itself. Clojure keywords (like `:a` and `:b`) are also functions: they accept an associative collection, such as a map or vector, and look themselves up in the collection, for example:

```
(:b the-map)
;=> 2
(:z the-map 26)        ◁─┤  Keywords can also
;=> 26                      return a default
                            value if not found.
```

The advantage of both maps and keywords being functions is that it makes function composition more flexible. Both these kinds of objects can be used where functions are needed, resulting in less and clearer code.

Like all Clojure data structures, maps are also immutable. There are several functions that can modify a map, and `assoc` and `dissoc` are the ones commonly used.

---

[2] Map literals and the `hash-map` function aren't exactly equivalent, because Clojure actually has two different map implementations: `hash-map` and `array-map`. Array maps store keys and values in sorted order and perform lookups by scanning instead of hashing. This is faster for small maps, so smaller map literals (approximately 10 keys or less) actually become an array map instead of a hash map. If you `assoc` too many keys to an array map, you'll eventually get a hash map instead. (The opposite is not true, however: a hash map will never return an array map if it gets too small.) Transparently replacing the implementation of a data structure is a common performance trick in Clojure made possible by the use of immutable data structures and pure functions. The `hash-map` and `array-map` functions will *always* return the corresponding structure, regardless of the number of arguments you call them with.

Here's an example of inserting a new key value into a map (except that Clojure returns a new map):

```
(def updated-map (assoc the-map :d 4))
;=> #'user/updated-map
updated-map
;=> {:d 4, :a 1, :b 2, :c 3}
(dissoc updated-map :a)
;=> {:b 2, :c 3, :d 4}
```

Before wrapping up this section, let's look at some rather convenient functions that can make working with maps easy. First, let's look at what you want to accomplish. Imagine you had an empty map, and you wanted to store user details in it. With one entry, the map might look like this:

```
(def users {:kyle {
              :date-joined "2009-01-01"
              :summary {
                :average {
                  :monthly 1000
                  :yearly 12000}}}})
```

Note the use of nested maps. Because maps are immutable, if you wanted to update Kyle's summary for his monthly average, you couldn't simply drill down to the spot on the map and update it in place as you would in most other languages. Instead, you would need to go down to the place you want to change, create the changed map, and assoc the changes into the intermediate maps on your way back up to the root. Doing this all the time would be tedious and error prone.

Fortunately, Clojure provides three functions that make updating nested collections easy. The first one is called assoc-in, and here it is in action:

```
(assoc-in users [:kyle :summary :average :monthly] 3000)
;=> {:kyle {:date-joined "2009-01-01", :summary {:average {:monthly 3000,
:yearly 12000}}}}
```

This is helpful, because you don't have to write a new function to set a new value rather deep in the user's map. The general form of assoc-in is

```
(assoc-in map [key & more-keys] value)
```

If any nested map doesn't exist along the way, it gets created and correctly associated.

The next convenience function reads values out of such nested maps. This function is called get-in:

```
(get-in users [:kyle :summary :average :monthly])
;=> 1000
```

The final function that's relevant to this discussion is called update-in, which can be used to update values in such nested maps. To see it in action, imagine you wanted to increase Kyle's monthly average by 500:

```
(update-in users [:kyle :summary :average :monthly] + 500)
;=> {:kyle {:date-joined "2009-01-01", :summary {:average {:monthly 1500,
:yearly 12000}}}}
```

The general form of update-in is

```
(update-in map [key & more-keys] update-function & args)
```

This works similarly to assoc-in, in that the keys are used to find what to update with a new value. Instead of supplying the new value itself, you supply a function that accepts the old value as the first argument (and any other arguments that you can supply as well). The function is applied to these arguments, and the result becomes the new value. The + function here does that job—it takes the old monthly average value of 1000 and adds it to the supplied argument of 500.

Many Clojure programs use the map as a core data structure. Often, programmers used to objects in the stateful (data) sense of the word use maps in their place. This is a natural choice and works well.

2.2.8 Sequences

A sequence isn't a collection type. Rather, a sequence is an interface (called ISeq) that exposes a "one thing followed by more things" abstraction. This interface is implemented pervasively by Clojure's data structures, functions, and macros. The sequence abstraction allows all data structures to look and act like lists, even if the underlying values are some other collection type (such as a vector or hash map) or are even created lazily as they're needed.

The ISeq interface provides three functions: first, rest, and cons. Here's how first and rest work:

```
(first (list 1 2 3))
;=> 1
(rest (list 1 2 3))
;=> (2 3)
(first [1 2 3])
;=> 1
(rest [1 2 3])
;=> (2 3)
(first {:a 1 :b 2})        Order of items
;=> [:b 2]             ◄──┘ isn't guaranteed.
(rest {:a 1 :b 2})
;=> ([:a 1])               Empty collections
(first [])             ◄──┘ return nil for first.
;=> nil
(rest [])           ◄─┐ Empty collections return an
;=> ()                │ empty sequence for rest.
```

first returns the first element of the sequence like peek does for lists but the same way on all collection types. rest returns the sequences without the first element just like pop does on lists but the same way on all collection types and without throwing an exception for empty things.

cons (short for *construct*) creates new sequences given an element and an existing sequence:

```
(cons 1 [2 3 4 5])
;=> (1 2 3 4 5)
```

cons adds an item to the *beginning* of a sequence (even on vectors) and the original sequence is the "tail" of the new sequence. Notice that this is exactly how conj would work on a list: the sequence abstraction cons uses allows it to act as though all sequential structures it touches are listlike.

Note that the sequence abstraction is usually lazy, meaning that functions like first, rest, and cons don't do extra work to create lists, even though the result *prints* like a list (that is, surrounded by parentheses). Observe:

```
(list? (cons 1 (list 2 3)))
;=> false
```

The sequence abstraction allows everything to *seem* as though real lists were being manipulated but avoids actually creating any new data structures (such as actual lists) or doing any unnecessary work (such as creating items farther down the sequence that are never used).

Now that you have a solid foundation in the data structures of Clojure, it's time to write some programs that use them.

2.3   Program structure

In this section, we'll examine several constructs that are part of the Clojure language. Most of those that we discuss here are categorized as structural forms because they lend structure to the code; they set up local names, allow for looping and recursion, and the like. We'll begin with the most fundamental aspect of structuring Clojure code, namely the function.

2.3.1   Functions

Clojure is a functional language, which means that functions are first-class citizens of the language. For something to be first class, the language should allow them to

- Be created dynamically
- Be passed as arguments to functions
- Be returned from other functions
- Be stored as values inside other data structures

Clojure functions comply with all of these requirements.

If you're used to programming in a language like C++ or Java, this will be a different experience. To start, let's see how to define Clojure functions.

FUNCTION DEFINITION

Clojure offers the convenient `defn` macro, which allows traditional-looking function definitions, such as the following:

```
(defn addition-function [x y]
  (+ x y))
```

In reality, the `defn` macro expands to a combination of calls to `def` and `fn`, where `fn` is itself another macro and `def` is a special form. Here, `def` creates a var with the specified name and is bound to a new function object. This function has a body as specified in the `defn` form. Here's what the equivalent expanded form looks like:

```
(def addition-function
  (fn [x y]
    (+ x y)))
```

The `fn` macro accepts a sequence of arguments in square brackets, followed by the body of the function. The `fn` form can be used directly to define anonymous functions. The `def` form shown here assigns the function created using `fn` to the var `addition-function`.

VARIABLE ARITY

To define functions of variable arity, parameter lists can use the `&` symbol. An example is the addition function from Clojure core, where the parameters are defined as

```
[x y & more]
```

This allows + to handle any number of arguments. Functions are explained in more detail in chapter 3. Now you'll learn about a form that helps in structuring the innards of functions themselves.

2.3.2 The let form

Consider the following function that calculates the average number of pets owned by the previously declared users:

```
(defn average-pets []
  (/ (apply + (map :number-pets (vals users))) (count users)))
```

Don't worry yet about all that's going on here. Observe that the body of the function is quite a long, complex-looking line of code. Such code can take several seconds to read. It would be nice if you could break it down into pieces, to make the intent of the code clearer. The `let` form allows you to introduce locally named things into your code by *binding* a symbol to a value. Consider the following alternate implementation:

```
(defn average-pets []
  (let [user-data (vals users)
        pet-counts (map :number-pets user-data)
        total (apply + pet-counts)]
    (/ total (count users))))
```

apply calls a function with items of a sequence as individual arguments; for example, (apply + [1 2]) is the same as (+ 1 2).

Here, user-data, pet-counts, and total are namespace-less symbols that resolve to specific values but *only* in the scope of the let. Unlike vars created by def, these bindings can't be changed, only shadowed by other bindings in nested scopes. Now the computation is much clearer, and it's easy to read and maintain this code. Although this is a trivial example, you can imagine more complex use cases. Further, the let form can be used to name things that might be needed more than once in a piece of code. Indeed, you can introduce a local value computed from previously named values, within the same form, for instance:

```
(let [x 1
      y 2
      z (+ x y)]
  z)
;=> 3
```

More specifically, the let form accepts as its first argument a vector containing an even number of forms, followed by zero or more forms that get evaluated when the let is evaluated. The value of the last expression is returned.

UNDERSCORE IDENTIFIER

Before moving on, it's worth discussing the situation where you might not care about the return value of an expression. Typically, such an expression is called purely for its side effect. A trivial example is calling println, because you don't care that it returns nil. If you do this inside a let form for any reason, you'll need to specify an identifier in which to hold the return value. The code might look like this:

```
(defn average-pets []
  (let [user-data (vals users)
        pet-counts (map :number-pets user-data)
        value-from-println (println "total  pets:" pet-counts)
        total (apply + pet-counts)]
    (/ total (count users))))
```

In this code, the only reason you create value-from-println is that the let form needs a name to bind the value of each expression. In such cases where you don't care about the value, you can just use a single underscore as the identifier name. Take a look at the following:

```
(defn average-pets []
  (let [user-data (vals users)
        pet-counts (map :number-pets user-data)
        _ (println "total  pets:" pet-counts)
        total (apply + pet-counts)]
    (/ total (count users))))
```

The underscore identifier can be used in any situation where you don't care about the value of something. There's nothing special about the underscore symbol: this is merely a Clojure convention to signal that the programmer doesn't care about the symbol's value and isn't planning to use it later, but syntax requires the programmer to provide a binding symbol.

Although this example works for debugging, it isn't particularly widespread in production code. The underscore identifier will be even more useful when we explore Clojure's destructuring support in the next chapter.

We've covered the basics of the let form. We're going to explore immutability and mutation a lot more, starting in chapter 3. For now, let's continue with learning about the do form.

2.3.3 *Side effects with do*

In a pure functional language, programs are free of side effects. The only way to "do something" is for a function to compute a value and return it. Calling a function doesn't alter the state of the world in any way. Consider the following code snippet:

```
(defn do-many-things []
  (do-first-thing)
  (do-another-thing)
  (return-final-value))
```

In a world without state and side effects, the do-many-things function would be equivalent to this one:

```
(defn do-many-things-equivalent []
  (return-final-value))
```

The calls to do-first-thing and do-another-thing can be eliminated without change in behavior, even without knowing what they do. This is because in a stateless world without side effects, the only thing that "does something" in do-many-things is the last function call to return-final-value, which presumably computes and returns a value. In such a world, there'd be no reason to ever call a series of functions (as shown in the first example), because only the last one would ever do anything useful.

The real world is full of state, and side effects are a necessity. For example, printing something to the console or to a log file is a side effect that changes the state of the world. Storing something in a database alters the state of the world and is another example of a side effect.

To combine multiple s-expressions into a single form, Clojure provides the do form. It can be used for any situation as described previously where some side effect is desired and the higher-order form accepts only a single s-expression. As an example, consider the if block:

```
(if (is-something-true?)
  (do
    (log-message "in true branch")
    (store-something-in-db)
    (return-useful-value)))
```

Normally, because the consequent part of the if form accepts only a single s-expression, without the do as shown here, it would be impossible to get the true case to call all three functions (log-message, store-something-in-db, and return-useful-value).

The do form is a convenient way to combine multiple s-expressions into one. This is a common idiom in macros, and plenty of core Clojure forms are macros that accept multiple forms as parameters and combine them into one using an implicit do. Examples are fn, let, doseq, loop, try, when, binding, dosync, and locking.

Now that you know how to create blocks of code using do, we'll move on to learning about other structural constructs in the remainder of this section. First, though, let's look at exception handling in Clojure.

2.3.4   Reader macros

The Clojure reader converts program text into Clojure data structures. It does this by recognizing that characters such as parentheses, braces, and the like are special and that they form the beginning (and ending) of lists, hash maps, and vectors. These rules are built into the reader.

Other characters are special also, because they signal to the reader that the form that follows them should be treated in a special way. In a sense, these characters extend the capability of the reader, and they're called reader macros. The simplest (and most traditional) example of a reader macro is the comment character (;). When the reader encounters a semicolon, it treats the rest of that line of code as a comment and ignores it. Table 2.2 shows the available reader macros in Clojure.

Table 2.2   Clojure's reader macros and their descriptions

Reader macro character	Description of reader macro
Quote (')	Quotes the form following it, same as (quote)
Character (\)	Yields a character literal
Comment (;)	Single-line comment
Meta (^)	Associates metadata for the form that follows
Deref (@)	Dereferences the agent or ref that follows
Dispatch (#)	#{} Constructs a set #"" Constructs a regex pattern #^ Associates metadata for the form that follows (deprecated by ^) #' Resolves the var for the symbol that follows, same as (var) #() Constructs an anonymous function #_ Skips the following form
Syntax quote (`)	Used in macros to render s-expressions
Unquote (~)	Unquotes forms inside syntax-quoted forms
Unquote splice (~@)	Unquotes a list inside a syntax form, but inserts the elements of the list without the surrounding parentheses

You don't have to understand all of these now: you'll learn about each of these reader macros in the relevant section in the book. For instance, we'll use the last three quite heavily in chapter 7, which examines macros.

Reader macros are implemented as entries in a read table. An entry in this table is essentially a reader macro character associated with the macro function that describes how the form that follows is to be treated. Most Lisps expose this read table to the programmers, allowing them to manipulate it or add new reader macros. Clojure doesn't do this, and so you can't define your own reader macros. Starting with Clojure 1.4, Clojure does let you define your own data literals, something that we'll examine in the next chapter.

In this section, you saw various structural constructs provided by Clojure. In the next section, you'll see forms that control the execution flow of Clojure programs.

2.4 Program flow

Like most other languages, the basics of Clojure are simple to learn, with few special forms and indeed few constructs that control the flow of execution. In this section, we'll begin with conditional program execution, with the if special form and other macros built on top of the if form, and then we'll look at various functional constructs that allow for looping and working on sequences of data. Specifically, we'll consider loop/recur, followed by a few macros that use loop/recur internally to make it convenient to process sequences. We'll close this chapter with a few higher-order functions that apply other functions to sequences of data.

2.4.1 Conditionals

A conditional form is one that causes Clojure to either execute or not execute associated code. In this section, we'll examine if, if-not, cond, when, and when-not. We'll also briefly look at logical functions.

IF

The most basic example of this is the if form. In Clojure, the general form of if looks like this:

```
(if test consequent alternative)
```

This shows that the if form accepts a test expression, which is evaluated to determine what to do next. If the test is true, the consequent is evaluated. If the test is false, and if an alternative form is provided, then it is evaluated instead (otherwise nil is returned). Because the consequent and alternative clauses of the if form can only be a single s-expression, you can use the do form to have it do multiple things. Here's an example:

```
(if (> 5 2)
  "yes"
  "no")
;=> "yes"
```

if is a special form, which means that the Clojure language implements it internally as a special case. In a language that provides the if special form and a macro system, all other conditional forms can be implemented as macros, which is what Clojure does. Let's visit a few such macros.

IF-NOT

The if-not macro does the inverse of what the if special form does. The general structure of this macro is

```
(if-not test consequent alternative)
```

Here, if the test is false, the consequent is evaluated; else if it's true and the alternative is provided, it's evaluated instead. Here's a quick example:

```
(if-not (> 5 2) "yes" "no")
;=> "no"
```

COND

cond allows you to flatten nested trees of if conditions. The general form looks like the following:

```
(cond & clauses)
```

Here's a simple example of using cond:

```
(def x 1)
;=> #'user/x
(cond
    (> x 0)  "greater!"
    (= x 0)  "zero!"
    :default "lesser!")
;=> "greater!"
```

As you can see, the clauses are pairs of expressions, each of the form test consequent. Each test expression is evaluated in sequence, and when one returns true (actually anything other than false or nil), the associated consequent is evaluated and returned. If none returns a truthy value, you can pass in something that works as a true value (for example, the keyword :default), and the associated consequent is evaluated and returned instead.

WHEN

Here's the general form of the when macro:

```
(when test & body)
```

This convenient macro is an if (without the alternative clause), along with an implicit do. This allows multiple s-expressions to be passed in as the body. Here's how it might be used:

```
(when (> 5 2)
  (println "five")
  (println "is")
  (println "greater")
  "done")
```

```
five
is
greater
;=> "done"
```

Note that there's no need to wrap the three functions in the body inside a do, because the when macro takes care of this. You'll find this a common pattern, and it's a convenience that most macros provide to their callers.

WHEN-NOT

when-not is the opposite of when, in that it evaluates its body if the test returns false or nil. The general form looks similar to that of when:

```
(when-not test & body)
```

Here's an example:

```
(when-not (< 5 2)
  (println "two")
  (println "is")
  (println "smaller")
  "done")
two
is
smaller
;=> "done"
```

These are some of the many forms that allow programs to handle different kinds of conditional situations. Except for the if special form, they're all implemented as macros, which also implies that the programmer is free to implement new ones, suited to the domain of the program. In the next section, you'll see a little more detail about writing test expressions using logical functions.

2.4.2 *Logical functions*

Any expression that returns a truthy or falsey value can be used for the test expression in all the previously mentioned conditional forms. To write compound test expressions, Clojure provides some logical operators. Let's examine the logical and first.

and accepts zero or more forms. It evaluates each in turn, and if any returns nil or false, and returns that value. If none of the forms return false or nil, then and returns the value of the last form. and short-circuits the arguments by not evaluating the remaining if any one returns a falsey value. A simple rule to remember the return value of and is that it returns the "deciding" value, which is the last value it had to examine, or true if there are no values. Here are some examples:

```
(and)
;=> true
(and :a :b :c)
;=> :c
(and :a nil :c)
;=> nil
```

```
(and :a false :c)
;=> false
(and 0 "")
;=> ""
```

> Remember, in Clojure only `nil` and `false` are logically false; everything else is true.

`or` works in the opposite way. It also accepts zero or more forms and evaluates them one by one. If any returns a logical true, it returns it as the value of the `or`. If none return a logical true, then `or` returns the last value. `or` also short-circuits its arguments. Here are some examples:

```
(or)
;=> nil
(or :a :b :c)
;=> :a
(or :a nil :c)
;=> :a
(or nil false)
;=> false
(or false nil)
;=> nil
```

Another point of interest is that both `and` and `or` are also macros. This means that they're not built into the Clojure language but come as part of the core library. It also means that you can write your own macros that behave like `and` or `or` and they would be indistinguishable from the language. We'll explore this more in chapter 7.

Finally, Clojure provides a `not` function that inverts the logical value of whatever is passed in as an argument. It *always* returns the exact values `true` or `false`. Here are some examples:

```
(not true)
;=> false
(not 1)
;=> false
(not nil)
;=> true
```

As a relevant side note, Clojure provides all the usual comparison and equality functions. Examples are `<`, `<=`, `>`, `>=`, and `=`. They all work the way you'd expect them to, with an additional feature: they take any number of arguments. The `<` function, for instance, checks to see if the arguments are in increasing order. Here are a couple quick examples:

```
(< 2 4 6 8)
;=> true

(< 2 4 3 8)
;=> false
```

The `=` function is the same as Java's `equals`, but it works for a wider range of objects including `nil`, numbers, and sequences. Note that it's a single `=` symbol and not `==`, which is commonly used in many programming languages.

= (SINGLE-EQUALS) VS. == (DOUBLE-EQUALS)

But Clojure does *also* have a == (double-equals) function that can only compare numbers. The difference between = and == is very subtle. = can compare any two Clojure values but gives unintuitive results when comparing numbers among the three different categories of numbers: integer (including ratio), big decimal, and floating point. Here are some examples:

```
(= 1 1N 1/1)
;=> true
(= 0.5 1/2)
;=> false
(= 0.5M 0.5)
;=> false
(= 0.5M 1/2)
;=> false
```

You're probably scratching your head at those false values! If you're comparing numbers from different classes, you can use == instead, but all arguments *must* be numbers:

```
(== 1 1N 1/1)
;=> true
(== 1/2 0.5M 0.5)
;=> true
1.999999999999999
;=> 2.0
(== 2.0M 1.999999999999999)
;=> true
(== :a 1)
ClassCastException clojure.lang.Keyword cannot be cast to
java.lang.Number   clojure.lang.Numbers.equiv (Numbers.java:206)
(== nil 1)
NullPointerException   clojure.lang.Numbers.ops (Numbers.java:961)
```

Numbers in different categories now compare roughly how you'd expect.

But == isn't a magic wand against floating-point precision and rounding behavior.

All arguments must be numbers or Clojure will throw an exception.

A simple rule of thumb: if you know that *everything* you're comparing is a number *and* you expect different categories of numbers, use ==; otherwise, use =.[3]

These logical functions are sufficient to create compound logical expressions from simple ones. Our next stop in this section is iterations—not strictly the kind supported by imperative languages such as C++ and Java but the functional kind.

---

[3] You may be wondering why Clojure has this wart. Clojure (and Java) has a contract stipulating that values that compare equal have the same hash code. This makes it possible to do extremely fast hash-based equality checks even when comparing large collections against one another. But it's difficult to write a fast hash function that would produce the same value for different number categories. Further, even if they could hash the same, numbers in different categories aren't complete replacements for one another because they have different precision, range, and arithmetic behavior. It would lead to surprising results if a floating-point number were used in place of a big decimal or a ratio. If you want a deeper dive into issues surrounding Clojure's notion of equality, read the document *Equality* by Andy Fingerhut at https://github.com/jafingerhut/thalia/blob/master/doc/other-topics/equality.md.

2.4.3   *Functional iteration*

Most functional languages don't have traditional iteration constructs like for because typical implementations of for require mutation of the loop counter. Instead, they use recursion and function application to process lists of things. We'll start this section by looking at the familiar while form, followed by examining Clojure's loop/recur looping construct. Then we'll examine a few convenient macros such as doseq and dotimes, which are built on top of loop/recur.

WHILE

Clojure's while macro works in a similar fashion to those seen in imperative languages such as Ruby and Java. The general form is as follows:

```
(while test & body)
```

Consider the case where you have a function request-on-queue? that checks to see if a message has arrived on a messaging system you're using and another function pop-request-queue that retrieves such a message. The following shows a way to set up the request-handling loop:

```
(while (request-on-queue?)
  (handle-request (pop-request-queue)))
```

Here, requests will continue to be processed as long as they keep appearing on the request queue. The while loop will end if request-on-queue? returns a value either false or nil, presumably because something else happened elsewhere in the system. Note that the only way for a while loop to end is for a side effect to cause the test expression to return a logically false value (that is, either false or nil).

Now, let's move on to another looping construct—one that's somewhat different from imperative languages, because it relies on what appears to be recursion.

LOOP/RECUR

Clojure doesn't have traditional for loops for iteration; instead, programs can achieve similar behavior through the use of higher-level functions such as map and other functions in the sequence library. The Clojure version of iterative flow control is loop and the associated recur. Here's an example of calculating the factorial of a number n using loop/recur:

```
(defn fact-loop [n]
  (loop [current n fact 1]
    (if (= current 1)
      fact
      (recur (dec current) (* fact current) ))))
```

Return whatever value fact ends up having when current is 1

But if current isn't 1, repeat the loop with current reset to current minus 1 and with fact set to current times fact

Here's the general form of the loop:

```
(loop bindings & body)
```

loop sets up bindings that work exactly like the let form does. In this example, [current n fact 1] works the same way if used with a let form: current gets bound to the value of n, and fact gets bound to a value of 1. Then it executes the supplied body inside the lexical scope of the bindings. In this case, the body is the if form.

Now let's talk about recur. It has similar semantics as the let form bindings:

```
(recur bindings)
```

The bindings are computed, and each value is bound to the respective name as described in the loop form. Execution then returns to the start of the loop body. In this example, recur has two binding values, (dec current) and (* fact current), which are computed and rebound to current and fact. The if form then executes again. This continues until the if condition causes the looping to end by not calling recur anymore.

recur is a special form in Clojure, and despite looking recursive, it doesn't consume the stack. It's the preferred way of doing self-recursion, as opposed to a function calling itself by name. The reason for this is that Clojure currently doesn't have tail-call optimization, though it's possible that this will be added at some point in the future if the Java virtual machine (JVM) were to support it. recur can be used only from tail positions of code, and if an attempt is made to use it from any other position, the compiler will complain. For instance, this will cause Clojure to complain:

```
(defn fact-loop-invalid [n]
  (loop [current n fact 1]
    (if (= current 1)
      fact
      (recur (dec current) (* fact current)))       An illegal
    (println "Done, current value:" current)))      position for
                                                     recur
```

The specific error you'll see is

```
CompilerException java.lang.UnsupportedOperationException: Can only recur
from tail position, compiling:(NO_SOURCE_PATH:5:7)
```

This will tip you off that you have a recur being used from a nontail position of loop, and such errors in code are easy to fix.

As you've seen, loop/recur is simple to understand and use. recur is more powerful and can cause execution to return to any recursion point. Recursion points can be set up, as you saw in the example, by a loop form or by a function form (enabling you to create self-recursive functions). You'll see the latter in action in the next chapter. By the way, another point to note is that by using recur, you're being explicit about where you want the recursion to occur in a tail-recursive manner. This improves the readability of the code.

Now let's look at a few macros that Clojure provides that make it easy to work with sequences without having to use loop/recur directly.

DOSEQ AND DOTIMES

Imagine that you have a list of users and you wish to generate expense reports for each user. You could use the looping construct from the previous section, but instead there's a convenient way to achieve the same effect in the following dispatch-reporting-jobs function:

```
(defn run-report [user]
  (println "Running report for" user))

(defn dispatch-reporting-jobs [all-users]
  (doseq [user all-users]
    (run-report user)))
```

Here, the form of interest is doseq. The simplest form accepts a vector containing two terms, where the first term is a new symbol, which will be sequentially bound to each element in the second term (which must be a sequence). The body will be executed for each element in the sequence and then the entire form will return nil. In this case, dispatch-reporting-jobs will call run-reports for each user present in the sequence all-users.

dotimes is similar. It's a convenience macro that accepts a vector containing a symbol and a number n, followed by the body. The symbol is set to numbers from 0 to (n – 1), and the body is evaluated for each number. Here's an example:

```
(dotimes [x 5]
  (println "X is" x))
```

This will print the numbers 0 through 4 and return nil.

Despite the convenience of these macros, they're not used as much as you'd imagine, especially if you're coming from an imperative background. In Clojure, the most common pattern of computing things from lists of data is using higher-level functions such as map, filter, and reduce. We'll look at these briefly in the remainder of this section.

MAP

Don't be confused by the name here: map the function is different from "map" the data structure! The simplest use of map accepts a unary function and a sequence of data elements. A *unary function* is a function that accepts only one argument. map applies this function to each element of the sequence and returns a new sequence that contains all the returned values, for example:

```
(map inc [0 1 2 3])
;=> (1 2 3 4)
```

Even though this is a common way of using map, it's even more general than this. map accepts a function that can take any number of arguments, along with the same number of sequences. It collects the result of applying the function to corresponding elements from each sequence. If the sequences are of varying lengths, map works through the shortest one:

```
(map + [0 1 2 3] [0 1 2 3])
;=> (0 2 4 6)
(map + [0 1 2 3] [0 1 2])
;=> (0 2 4)
```

◄─┤ **When supplying multiple sequences, each supplies an additional argument to function.**

◄─ **Length of return value is length of shortest sequence.**

In other languages, this would have required much more code: an iteration block, a list that collects the return values, and a condition that checks to see if the list is exhausted. A single call to map does all this.

FILTER AND REMOVE

filter does something similar to map—it collects values. But it accepts a predicate function and a sequence and returns only those elements of the sequence that return a logically true value when the predicate function is called on them. Here's an example that returns only valid expenses that aren't zero in value:

```
(defn non-zero-expenses [expenses]
  (let [non-zero? (fn [e] (not (zero? e)))]
    (filter non-zero? expenses)))
;=> #'user/non-zero-expenses
(non-zero-expenses [-2 -1 0 1 2 3])
;=> (-2 -1 1 2 3)
```

◄─┘ **Notice 0 is gone from sequence.**

remove is the opposite of filter: where filter uses the predicate to decide what to *keep*, remove uses it to decide what to *drop*. You can rewrite the non-zero-expenses function using remove:

```
(defn non-zero-expenses [expenses]
  (remove zero? expenses))
;=> #'user/non-zero-expenses
(non-zero-expenses [-2 -1 0 1 2 3])
;=> (-2 -1 1 2 3)
```

◄─┘ **Notice that you get same result using remove but don't need to create a non-zero? function.**

For several kinds of calculations, you'll need to operate on only those expenses that aren't zero. non-zero-expenses is a function that selects all such values, and it does so in one line of code (three words!).

REDUCE

The simplest form of reduce is a high-level function that accepts a function of arity two and a sequence of data elements. The function is applied to the first two elements of the sequence, producing the first result. The same function is then called again with this result and the next element of the sequence. This then repeats with the following element, until the last element is processed.

Here you'll write the factorial function using reduce:

```
(defn factorial [n]
  (let [numbers (range 1 (+ n 1))]
    (reduce * numbers)))
```

range is a Clojure function that returns a list of numbers starting from the first argument (inclusive) to the second argument (exclusive). For instance:

```
(range 10)
;=> (0 1 2 3 4 5 6 7 8 9)
```

This is why numbers is computed by calling range with 1 and (+ n 1). The rest is easy; you reduce the sequence using the multiply (*) function.

Let's examine how this works when factorial is called with 5:

```
(factorial 5)
;=> 120
```

numbers is set to the result of calling range on 1 and 6, which is the sequence of the numbers 1, 2, 3, 4, and 5. This sequence is what reduce operates on, along with the multiplication function. The result of multiplying 1 and 2 (which is 2) is multiplied by 3 (resulting in 6). That's then multiplied by 4 (resulting in 24), which is finally multiplied by 5, resulting in 120.

If you're ever having trouble visualizing the steps of a reduction, you can replace the reduce function with the reductions function: reduce returns only the final reduced value, but reductions returns a sequence of every intermediate value. You'll rewrite the factorial function to use reductions:

```
(defn factorial-steps [n]
  (let [numbers (range 1 (+ n 1))]
    (reductions * numbers)))
;=> #'user/factorial-steps
(factorial-steps 5)
;=> (1 2 6 24 120)
(factorial 1)
;=> 1
(factorial 2)
;=> 2
(factorial 3)
;=> 6
(factorial 4)
;=> 24
(factorial 5)
;=> 120 #A
(map factorial (range 1 6))
;=> (1 2 6 24 120)
```

Notice that results of factorial steps correspond to results of calling normal factorial with all values from 1 to 5.

Another practical illustration of map and range

reduce is a powerful function, and as shown here, it accomplishes in a single line of code what might require several lines in other languages.

FOR

What book can be complete without mentioning for in the context of iteration? We said earlier that few functional languages have a traditional for construct. Clojure does have for, but it isn't quite like what you might be used to. In Clojure, for is used for list comprehensions, which is a syntactic feature that allows sequences to be constructed out of existing ones. The general form of the for construct follows:

```
(for seq-exprs body-expr)
```

seq-exprs is a vector specifying one or more binding-form/collection-expr pairs. body-expr can use the bindings set up in seq-exprs to construct each element of the list. Consider the following example that generates a list of labels for each square on a chessboard:

```
(def chessboard-labels
  (for [alpha "abcdefgh"
        num (range 1 9)]
    (str alpha num)))
```

The str function concatenates the string values of the arguments passed to it. Now chessboard-labels is a lazy sequence with all 64 labels:

```
chessboard-labels
;=> ("a1" "a2" "a3" "a4" "a5" ... "h6" "h7" "h8")
```

The for seq-exprs can take modifiers :let, :when, and :while. To see an example of :when in use, first consider a function that checks to see if a number is prime:

```
(defn prime? [x]
  (let [divisors (range 2 (inc (int (Math/sqrt x))))      ←┤  Math/sqrt returns
        remainders (map (fn [d] (rem x d)) divisors)]          square root of a
    (not (some zero? remainders))))                            number as a double;
                                                               int is to truncate
                                                               result to an integer.
```

Although there are more efficient ways to test for a prime number, this implementation will suffice for this example. By the way, some is a core function that returns the first logical true value returned when the specified predicate is called with each element of the specified collection. We'll revisit this function shortly. Also, Math/sqrt is code that calls the sqrt static method on the Math Java class. This is an example of Clojure's Java interop, and chapter 5 is dedicated to it.

Now you'll use for to write a function primes-less-than, which returns a list of all primes between 2 and the number passed in:

```
(defn primes-less-than [n]
  (for [x (range 2 (inc n))
        :when (prime? x)]
    x))
```

Notice how you specify a condition in the for form using the :when option. You can test this function:

```
(primes-less-than 50)
;=> (2 3 5 7 11 13 17 19 23 29 31 37 41 43 47)
```

Let's look at another, slightly more complex example. You'll use the prime? function to find all pairs of numbers under, say, a number like 5, such that the sum of each is prime. Here it is:

```
(defn pairs-for-primes [n]
  (let [z (range 2 (inc n))]
    (for [x z y z :when (prime? (+ x y))]
      (list x y))))
```

Now test it out:

```
(pairs-for-primes 5)
;=> ((2 3) (2 5) (3 2) (3 4) (4 3) (5 2))
```

As you can see, Clojure's for is a powerful construct, and it can be used to create arbitrary lists. A great advantage of this feature is that it's almost declarative. For instance, the code in pairs-for-primes reads almost like a restatement of the problem itself.

Our next stop isn't strictly about program flow but about a couple of macros that are useful in writing other functions and macros.

2.4.4 Threading macros

You're going to learn a lot about macros in this book, starting with an introduction to them in chapter 7. From a developer point of view, several macros are extremely useful. You've seen some already, and in this section you'll see two more, which make writing code a lot more convenient and result in more readable code as well. They're called *threading macros*.

THREAD-FIRST

Imagine that you need to calculate the savings that would be available to a user several years from now based on some amount the user invests today. You can use the formula for compound interest to calculate this:

```
final-amount = principle * (1 + rate/100) ^ time-periods
```

You can write a function to calculate this:

```
(defn final-amount [principle rate time-periods]
  (* (Math/pow (+ 1 (/ rate 100)) time-periods) principle))
```

Math/pow returns first argument raised to power of second argument as a double.

You can test that it works by calling it at the REPL:

```
(final-amount 100 20 1)
;=> 120.0
(final-amount 100 20 2)
;=> 144.0
```

This is fine, but the function definition is difficult to read, because it's written inside out, thanks to the prefix nature of Clojure's syntax. This is where the thread-first macro (named ->) helps, as shown in the following code:

```
(defn final-amount-> [principle rate time-periods]
  (-> rate
      (/ 100)
      (+ 1)
      (Math/pow time-periods)
      (* principle))))
```

It works the same, and you can confirm this on the REPL:

```
(final-amount-> 100 20 1)
;=> 120.0
(final-amount-> 100 20 2)
;=> 144.0
```

What the thread-first macro does is take the first argument supplied and place it in the second position of the next expression. It's called thread-first because it moves code into the position of the first argument of the following form. It then takes the entire resulting expression and moves it into the second position of the following expression, and through all of them, until all expressions are exhausted. So when the macro expands in the case of the final-amount-> function, the form looks like this:

```
(* (Math/pow (+ (/ rate 100) 1) time-periods) principle)
```

To be more accurate, the call to Java's Math/pow is also expanded, but we'll explore that in chapter 5. For now, it's enough to see that the expanded form is exactly like the one we manually defined in final-amount earlier. The advantage is that final-amount-> is much easier to write and read. This is an example of how a macro can manipulate code to make it easier to read. Doing something like this is nearly impossible in most other languages.

In the next section, we'll examine a related macro, called thread-last.

THREAD-LAST

The thread-last macro (named ->>) is a cousin of the thread-first macro. Instead of taking the first expression and moving it into the second position of the next expression, it moves it into the last place. It then repeats the process for all the expressions provided to it. Examine a version of the factorial function again:

```
(defn factorial [n]
  (reduce * (range 1 (+ 1 n)))))
```

This is also written in the inside-out syntax, and it isn't immediately obvious what the sequence of operations is. Here's the same function rewritten using the ->> macro:

```
(defn factorial->> [n]
  (->> n
       (+ 1)
       (range 1)
       (reduce *)))
```

You can check that it works by testing it at the REPL:

```
(factorial->> 5)
;=> 120
```

This macro expands the `factorial->>` function to

```
(reduce * (range 1 (+ 1 n)))
```

This ensures that it works the same way as `factorial` defined previously. The main advantage of this macro (similar to the `->` macro) is that it lets developers focus on the sequence of operations, rather than ensuring they're writing the nested expressions correctly. It's also easy to read and maintain the resulting function.

A far more common use of this macro is when working with sequences of data elements and using higher-order functions such as `map`, `reduce`, and `filter`. Each of these functions accepts the sequence as the last element, so the thread-last macro is perfect for the job.

While we're on the topic of threading macros, Clojure 1.5 introduced two related ones called `some->` and `some->>`. These two behave exactly the same as the respective ones we just discussed, but computation ends if the result of any step in the expansion is `nil`.

THREAD-AS

Another threading macro introduced in Clojure 1.5 is thread-as (named `as->`). The threading macros you've seen so far don't give you any control over the position of the previous expression: it is either first or last, depending on which threading macro you use. `as->` is more flexible: you supply it a name, and it will bind the result of each successive form to that name so you can use it in the next. For example:

```
(as-> {"a" [1 2 3 4]} <>
      (<> "a")
      (conj <> 10)
      (map inc <>))
;=> (2 3 4 5 11)
```

First form is bound to name <>; you can use any name.

Can be used anywhere in next form

<> is [1 2 3 4] before this form executes, and becomes [1 2 3 4 10] afterward.

inc increments a number by one.

This may look like magic, but the macro is actually quite simple. This is what the previous example expands to:

```
(let [<> {"a" [1 2 3 4]}
      <> (<> "a")
      <> (conj <> 10)
      <> (map inc <>)]
  <>)
```

The as-> macro is really just a more compact way of chaining a series of let bindings to the same name.

CONDITIONAL THREADING

The final set of threading macros we'll look at were also introduced in Clojure 1.5: cond-> and cond->>. These threading macros are exactly like -> and ->>, except each form is guarded by a conditional (which is *not* threaded) and can be skipped if the conditional is false. Here's an example:

```
(let [x 1 y 2]
  (cond-> []
          (odd? x)              (conj "x is odd")
          (zero? (rem y 3))     (conj "y is divisible by 3")
          (even? y)             (conj "y is even")))
;=> ["x is odd" "y is even"]
```

[] is only threaded through the right form; conditions can't see value being threaded.

Condition is false, so this form is skipped, but threading continues to next pair of forms.

Notice that when the left-hand condition form of a pair is false, the right-hand threaded form is skipped. cond-> is superficially similar to cond because both accept predicate-result pairs, but cond will stop evaluating pairs as soon as it finds a predicate that's truthy, though the cond-> threading macro will evaluate every conditional. cond->> is the same as cond->, except that the form is threaded into the last position like ->> instead of through the first position like ->.

The succinctness of cond-> and cond->> also makes them hard to grasp at first. It may help to see an equivalent implementation that makes more explicit what the predicates are doing and where the threading occurs:

```
(let [x 1 y 2]
  (as-> [] <>
        (if (odd? x)            (conj <> "x is odd")            <>)
        (if (zero? (rem y 3))   (conj <> "y is divisible by 3") <>)
        (if (even? y)           (conj <> "y is even")           <>)))
;=> ["x is odd" "y is even"]
```

The conditional threading macros are handy when you need to build up a data structure based on a large number of other factors, such as building a map of configuration settings or running different map and filter functions conditionally over the same data structure.

In this section, you saw various ways to control the execution flow of Clojure programs. We started off with conditionals and explored the associated logical functions. We then addressed the idea of looping—not directly as imperative for loops do in other languages but through a recursive form and through higher-order functions. Armed with this knowledge, you could write a lot of code without ever missing imperative constructs.

2.5   Summary

This was a long chapter! We started out by getting up and running with the Clojure REPL and then addressed the basics of writing code in the language. Specifically, we addressed forms that structure code, such as functions, let, and looping. We also looked at execution control forms, such as if, when, and cond. We also visited some of the data types and data structures that come built into the language. Understanding these equips you to use and create the right data abstractions in your programs.

Armed with this knowledge, you can probably write a fair amount of Clojure code already. The material from the next chapter, combined with this one, should enable you to write almost any basic program using the core of Clojure. And from there we'll dive into more intermediate concepts.

In the next chapter, we're going to explore more building blocks of Clojure. We'll begin with a deep dive into functions in an attempt to understand Clojure's support for functional programming. We'll also explore the idea of scope and show how to organize your programs with namespaces. Finally, we'll explore a concept somewhat unique to Clojure (well, uncommon in imperative languages such as Java and C++ at least) called destructuring.

Building blocks of Clojure

This chapter covers

- Clojure metadata
- Java exceptions
- Higher-order functions
- Scoping rules
- Clojure namespaces
- Clojure's destructuring feature
- Clojure's reader literals

When people are good at something already (such as a programming language), and they try to learn something new (such as another programming language), they often fall into what Martin Fowler (martinfowler.com/bliki/Improvement-Ravine.html) calls an "improvement ravine." For programming, the *ravine* refers to the drop in productivity experienced when one has to relearn how to do things in the new language. We've all been guilty of switching back to a language we're already good at to get the job done. It sometimes takes several attempts to get over enough of the ravine to accomplish simple things. The next few chapters aim to do that—we'll review the basics of Clojure in more detail. After reading them, you'll be comfortable enough to solve problems of reasonable complexity. We'll also cover most of the remaining constructs of the language, many of which will be familiar to you if you use other common languages.

First, we'll examine metadata, which is a unique way to associate additional data with an ordinary Clojure value without changing the value. Next, we'll show you another piece of Java interop: exception handling and throwing.

Then in the meat of the chapter we'll examine functions in some detail. Lisp was born in the context of mathematics, and functions are fundamental to it. Clojure uses functions as building blocks, and thus mastering functions forms the basis of learning Clojure. We'll then look at how namespaces help organize large programs. These are similar to Java packages; they're a simple way to keep code organized by dividing the program into logical modules.

The next section will examine *vars* (those things created by def) in detail and how to use them effectively. The following section is about destructuring, something that's rather uncommon in most languages. Destructuring is a neat way of accessing interesting data elements from inside larger data structures.

Finally, we'll conclude this chapter by taking a look at reader literals, which will allow you to add your own convenience syntax for data literals. Without any further ado, let's review how Clojure creates and uses functions.

3.1   Metadata

Metadata means data about data. Clojure supports tagging data (for example, maps, lists, and vectors) with other data *without changing the value of the tagged data*. What this means specifically is that the same values with different metadata will still compare equal.

The point of using immutable values instead of mutable objects is that you can easily compare values by their *content* instead of their *identity*. The two vectors [1 2 3] and [1 2 3] are the same even if they have different addresses in computer memory, so it doesn't matter which one your program uses. But in the real world you often need to distinguish between otherwise identical things in meaningful ways. For example, one value may compare equal to another, but it makes a difference if one value came from an untrusted network source or a file with a specific name. Metadata provides a way to add *identity* to values when it matters.

For example, you'll use the tags :safe and :io to determine if something is considered a security threat and if it came from an external I/O source. Here's how you might use metadata to represent such information:

```
(def untrusted (with-meta {:command "delete-table" :subject "users"}
                          {:safe false :io true}))
```

Now the map with keys :command and :subject has a metadata map attached to it with keys :safe and :io. Metadata is *always a map*. Note that the metadata map is attached on the "outside" of the object with metadata: :safe and :io aren't ever added as keys to the original map.

You can also define metadata with a shorthand syntax using the reader macro ^{ }. This example is exactly the same as the previous one except the metadata is added at read time instead of eval time:

```
(def untrusted ^{:safe false :io true} {:command "delete-table"
                                        :subject "users"})
```

The read-time verses eval-time distinction is important: the following example is *not* the same as using vary-meta:

```
(def untrusted ^{:safe false :io true} (hash-map :command "delete-table"
                                                 :subject "users")
```

This associates metadata with the *list* starting with hash-map, not the hash map that a function call produces, so this metadata becomes invisible at runtime.

Objects with metadata can be used like any other objects. The additional metadata doesn't affect their values. In fact, if you were to check what untrusted was at the read-evaluate-print loop (REPL), the metadata won't even appear:

```
untrusted
;=> {:command "delete-table", :subject "users"}
```

As mentioned earlier, metadata doesn't affect value equality; therefore, untrusted can be equal to another map that doesn't have any metadata on it at all:

```
(def trusted {:command "delete-table" :subject "users"})       <--- No metadata
;=> #'user/trusted
(= trusted untrusted)          <--- But still equal
;=> true
```

If you want to examine the metadata associated with the value, you can use the meta function:

```
(meta untrusted)
;=> {:safe false, :io true}
(meta trusted)
;=> nil
```

When new values are created from those that have metadata, the metadata is copied over to the new data. This is to preserve the identity semantics of metadata, for example:

```
(def still-untrusted (assoc untrusted :complete? false))
;=> #'user/still-untrusted
still-untrusted
;=> {:complete? false, :command "delete-table", :subject "users"}
(meta still-untrusted)
;=> {:safe false, :io true}
```

Functions and macros can also be defined with metadata. Here's an example:

```
(defn ^{:safe true :console true
        :doc "testing metadata for functions"}
  testing-meta
  []
  (println "Hello from meta!"))
```

Now try using the `meta` function to check that the metadata was set correctly:

```
(meta testing-meta)
;=> nil
```

This returns `nil` because the metadata is associated with the var `testing-meta` and not the function itself. To access the metadata, you'd have to pass the `testing-meta` var to the `meta` function. You can do this as follows:

```
(meta (var testing-meta))
;=> {:ns #<Namespace user>,
     :name testing-meta,
     :file "NO_SOURCE_FILE",
     :line 1, :arglists ([]),
     :console true,
     :safe true,
     :doc "testing metadata for functions"}
```

You'll learn more about vars and functions later in this chapter.

Metadata is useful in many situations where you want to tag things for purposes orthogonal to the data they represent. Such annotations are one example where you might perform certain tasks if objects are annotated a certain way, such as if their metadata contains a certain key and value. By the way, this may seem similar to Java's annotations, but it's much better. For instance, in Clojure, nearly anything can have metadata, unlike in Java where only classes and methods can have annotations. Sadly, you can't add Clojure metadata to native Java types such as strings.

Clojure internally uses metadata quite a lot; for example, the `:doc` key is used to hold the documentation string for functions and macros, the `:macro` key is set to `true` for functions that are macros, and the `:file` key is used to keep track of what source file something was defined in.

3.1.1 Java type hints

One of the pieces of metadata you may encounter often when making Java method calls from Clojure is a Java type hint, which is stored in the meta key `:tag`. It's used often enough that it has its own reader macro syntax: `^symbol`. Why do you need this?

When you make a Java method call using interop, the Java virtual machine (JVM) needs to know what class defines a method name so it can find the implementation of a method in the class. In Java this is normally not a problem because most types are annotated in the Java code and verified at compile time. Clojure is dynamically typed, however, so often the type of a variable isn't known until runtime. In these cases the JVM needs to use reflection to determine the class of an object at runtime and find the correct method to call. This works fine but can be slow. Here's an example of the problem:

```
(set! *warn-on-reflection* true)          ⟵  Warns you when
;=> true                                       reflection is needed
(defn string-length [x] (.length x))
Reflection warning, reference to field length can't be resolved.
;=> #'user/string-length
```

```
(time (reduce + (map string-length (repeat 10000 "12345"))))
"Elapsed time: 45.751 msecs"
;=> 50000
(defn fast-string-length [^String x] (.length x))          ◄─┐  No reflection
;=> #'user/fast-string-length                                  │  warning
(time (reduce + (map fast-string-length (repeat 10000 "12345"))))
"Elapsed time: 5.788 msecs"
;=> 50000
(meta #'fast-string-length)
;=> {:ns #<Namespace user>, :name fast-string-length, :file "NO_SOURCE_FILE",
     :column 1, :line 1, :arglists ([x])}
(meta (first (first (:arglists (meta #'fast-string-length)))))  ◄─┐  Type hint on
;=> {:tag String}                                                   │  the function
                                                                    │  argument
```

The last line demonstrates how Clojure stores type hints on function arguments: here you inspect the metadata on fast-string-length, get its :arglists (list of the signatures of all a function's arities), and get metadata on the x symbol in the argument list.

Clojure's compiler is pretty smart about inferring types, and all core Clojure functions are already type-hinted where necessary, so it's not that often that you'll need to resort to type hints. The idiomatic approach is to write all your code without type hints and then (set! *warn-on-reflection* true) and keep reevaluating your namespace and adding hints one at a time until the reflection warnings go away. If you concentrate type hinting on function arguments and return values, Clojure will often figure out all the types in the function body for you. You can read all the details of type hinting (including how to hint function return values) in Clojure's documentation at http://clojure.org/java_interop#Java%20Interop-Type%20Hints.

3.1.2 *Java primitive and array types*

Java has some special types called *primitives* that aren't full-fledged objects and that get special treatment by the JVM to increase speed and save memory (http://docs.oracle.com/javase/tutorial/java/nutsandbolts/datatypes.html). They're recognized by their lowercase type names in Java documentation: byte, short, int, long, float, double, boolean, and char. These are sometimes called *unboxed* types because they don't have an object "box" around them or any object methods.[1] Java arrays are fixed-length homogenous containers for other types; they're *also* primitive types, and there's even a different array type for each possible thing the array can hold!

Primitives don't have a pronounceable class name to refer to them, so it's not obvious how to type hint them. Fortunately, Clojure defines aliases for all the primitive types and for all arrays of primitive types: just use a type hint like ^byte for the primitive and the plural form ^bytes for the array-of-primitive.

---

[1] Java will automatically "box" primitive types with a corresponding object wrapper (for example, a long with a java.lang.Long) when you call a method on the primitive. See http://docs.oracle.com/javase/tutorial/java/data/autoboxing.html for details.

But you may occasionally need to type hint an array of Java objects. In this case you need to do some magic to find the strange class name:

```
(defn array-type [klass]
  (.getName (class (make-array klass 0))))
;=> #'user/array-type
(array-type BigDecimal)
;=> "[Ljava.math.BigDecimal;"
(def bigdec-arr
  ^"[Ljava.math.BigDecimal;"
  (into-array BigDecimal [1.0M]))
```

class returns an instance of java.lang.Class representing the class of its argument; Class has a method getName that returns class name as a string.

Type hint with a string name

into-array returns a Java array of a specified type filled with items from a Clojure collection.

Pretty much the only time you'll need to know the class name of an object array is when you're writing classes and interfaces in Clojure that are meant to be used by Java code and you need to accept or return an array of objects. We'll cover this topic in chapter 6.

3.2 *Java exceptions: try and throw*

Java has exceptions, as you've seen, but until now we haven't mentioned how to manipulate them in Clojure. If an expression has the potential to throw an exception, a try/catch/finally block can be used to catch it and decide what to do with it.[2] Suppose you have a function that calculates the average of a collection of numbers:

```
(defn average [numbers]
  (let [total (apply + numbers)]
    (/ total (count numbers))))
```

If you call the average function with an empty collection, you get an exception:

```
(average [])
ArithmeticException Divide by zero  clojure.lang.Numbers.divide
    (Numbers.java:156)
```

Normally you'd check for the empty collection, but you can add a try/catch block to illustrate:

```
(defn safe-average [numbers]
  (let [total (apply + numbers)]
    (try
      (/ total (count numbers))
      (catch ArithmeticException e
        (println "Divided by zero!")
        0))))
;=> #'user/safe-average
```

Exception object is bound to e.

---

[2] If you're familiar with Java, note that Clojure doesn't have checked exceptions. Catching and handling exceptions are always optional in Clojure.

```
(safe-average [])
Divided by zero!
;=> 0
```

The general form of using `try`/`catch`/`finally` is straightforward:

```
(try expr* catch-clause* finally-clause?)
```

The form accepts multiple expressions as part of the `try` clause and multiple `catch` clauses. The `finally` clause is optional. The expressions passed to the `try` clause are evaluated one by one, and the value of the last is returned. If any of them generate an exception, the appropriate `catch` clause is executed based on the type (Java class) of the exception, and the value of that is then returned. The optional `finally` clause is always executed for any side effects that need to be guaranteed, but nothing is ever returned from it. For example:

```
(try
  (print "Attempting division... ")
  (/ 1 0)
  (catch RuntimeException e "Runtime exception!")        RuntimeException
  (catch ArithmeticException e "DIVIDE BY ZERO!")        is a superclass of
  (catch Throwable e "Unknown exception encountered!")   ArithmeticException.
  (finally
    (println "done.")))                                  Throwable is
Attempting division... done.                             most generic
;=> "Runtime exception!"                                 possible
(try                                                     exception type
  (print "Attempting division... ")                      in Java; all
  (/ 1 0)                                                 exception types
  (finally                                                are subclasses of
    (println "done.")))                                  java.lang
Attempting division... done.                             .Throwable.
ArithmeticException Divide by zero   clojure.lang.Numbers.divide
    (Numbers.java:156)
```

finally clause is always executed, even if no exception is thrown.

Not "DIVIDE BY ZERO!" as you expected? See discussion that follows.

If no `catch` clause matches, exception is thrown as normal, but `finally` is still executed.

Notice that the `RuntimeException` catch clause matched, not the `ArithmeticException` clause, even though this exception type is a better match. The reason is that `catch` clauses are tried *in order* and the first possible match is used. `ArithmeticException` is a kind of `RuntimeException`, so the `RuntimeException` test matched and that `catch` clause was executed. You should arrange your `catch` clauses from most specific to least specific exception type to avoid confusion about which clause will match.

Exceptions can be thrown as easily using the `throw` form. In any place where you wish to throw an exception, you can do something like the following:

```
(throw (Exception. "this is an error!"))
Exception this is an error! user/eval807 (NO_SOURCE_FILE:1)
```

throw accepts a `java.lang.Throwable` instance, so any kind of exception can be thrown using it.

That covers the basics of using the `try/catch/finally` form as well as throwing exceptions. This isn't a commonly used feature of the Clojure language because there are several helper macros that take care of many situations where you might need to use this form. You'll see this more in chapter 5.

3.3   Functions

As discussed in chapter 1, Lisp was born in the context of mathematics and is a functional language. A functional language, among other things, treats functions as first-class elements. This means that the following things are true:

- Functions can be created dynamically (at runtime).
- Functions can be accepted as arguments by other functions.
- Functions can be returned from functions as return values.
- Functions can be stored as elements inside other data structures (for example, lists).

You've been creating and using functions for at least a chapter, but we haven't yet fully explored all their features and uses. This section will give you a more detailed look at what functions are and how they work, and you'll see several code examples that illustrate their more advanced uses. We'll begin by defining simple functions, with both fixed and variable number of parameters. After that, we'll examine anonymous functions and a few shortcuts for using them, followed by using recursion as a means of looping. We'll end the section with a discussion on higher-order functions and closures. To get started, let's examine the means that Clojure provides to define your own functions.

3.3.1   Defining functions

Functions are defined using the `defn` macro. The syntax of the `defn` macro is

```
(defn function-name
  doc-string?
  metadata-map?
  [parameter-list*]
  conditions-map?
  body-expressions*)
```

Here, the symbols with a question mark at the end are optional. In other words, although `function-name` and `parameters` are required, `doc-string`, `metadata-map`, and `conditions-map` are optional. Before discussing more details of this structure, let's take a quick look at an example. This example is quite basic; all it does is accept an item cost and the number of items and returns a total by multiplying them together:

```
(defn total-cost [item-cost number-of-items]
  (* item-cost number-of-items))
```

Here, `total-cost` is the name of the new function defined. It accepts two parameters: `item-cost` and `number-of-items`. The body of the function is the form that's the call to the multiply function (`*`), which is passed the same two arguments. There's no explicit return keyword in Clojure; instead, function bodies have an implicit `do` block surrounding them, meaning that the value of the last expression in the function body is returned. By the way, you can just type these examples (and the others in this book) at the REPL to see how they work.

Notice that `defn` is described as a macro. There's a whole chapter on macros coming up (chapter 7), but it's worth mentioning that the `defn` form expands to a `def`. For example, the definition of the previous `total-cost` function is expanded to this:

```
(def total-cost (fn [item-cost number-of-items]
                  (* item-cost number-of-items)))
```

`total-cost` is what Clojure calls a *var*. Note also that the function is in turn created using the `fn` macro. Because creating such vars and pointing them to a function is common, the `defn` macro was included in the language as a convenience.

If you wanted to, you could add a documentation string to the function, by passing a value for the `doc-string` parameter you saw earlier:

```
(defn total-cost
  "return line-item total of the item and quantity provided"
  [item-cost number-of-items]
  (* item-cost number-of-items))
```

In addition to providing a comment that aids in understanding this function, the documentation string can later be called up using the `doc` macro. This is because the `doc-string` is simply syntactic sugar to add the `:doc` key to the function var's metadata that the `doc` macro can then read. To see this, type the following at the REPL:

```
(meta #'total-cost)
;=> {:ns #<Namespace user>, :name total-cost, :file "NO_SOURCE_FILE",
     :column 1, :line 1, :arglists ([item-cost number-of-items]),
     :doc "return line-item total of the item and quantity provided"}
(doc total-cost)
-------------------------
user/total-cost
([item-cost number-of-items])
 return line-item total of the item and quantity provided
;=> nil
```

If you hadn't defined the function with the `doc-string`, then `doc` wouldn't have been able to return any documentation other than the function name and parameter list.

The `metadata-map` is rarely seen outside of macros that define functions, but it's good to know what it means. It's simply another way to add metadata to the defined var. Observe what happens when you use the `metadata-map` field:

Metadata without using ^ {}

```
(meta (defn myfn-attr-map {:a 1} []))
;=> {:ns #<Namespace user>, :name myfn-attr-map, :file "NO_SOURCE_FILE",
     :column 7, :line 1, :arglists ([]), :a 1}
(meta (defn ^{:a 1} myfn-metadata []))
;=> {:ns #<Namespace user>, :name myfn-metadata, :file "NO_SOURCE_FILE",
     :column 7, :line 1, :arglists ([]), :a 1}
(meta (defn ^{:a 1} myfn-both {:a 2 :b 3} []))
;=> {:ns #<Namespace user>, :name myfn-both, :file "NO_SOURCE_FILE",
     :column 7, :line 1, :arglists ([]), :a 2, :b 3}
(meta (defn ^{:a 1 :doc "doc 1"} myfn-redundant-docs "doc 2" {:a 2 :b 3
     :doc "doc 3"} []))
;=> {:ns #<Namespace user>, :name myfn-redundant-docs, :file "NO_SOURCE_FILE",
     :column 7, :line 1, :arglists ([]), :a 2, :b 3, :doc "doc 3"}
```

Notice ^ {} before name

Metadata merged together

Metadata key-value pairs from different metadata sources overwrite each other from left to right.

As you can see, adding metadata to the function name symbol and using a `metadata-map` are exactly equivalent. You can even use multiple ways of defining metadata at the same time: metadata farther to the right (like `doc-string` and `metadata-map`) will overwrite the same keys defined to their left.

Recall the general form of the `defn` macro from earlier. It has an optional `conditions-map`, and you'll now see what it's used for. Consider the following function definition:

```
(defn item-total [price quantity discount-percentage]
  {:pre [(> price 0) (> quantity 0)]
   :post [(> % 0)]}
  (->> (/ discount-percentage 100)
       (- 1)
       (* price quantity)
       float))
```

Here, `item-total` behaves as a normal function that applies a simple formula to the arguments and returns a result. Remember, you saw the thread-last (`->>`) operator in the previous chapter. At runtime, this function runs additional checks as specified by the hash map with the two keys `:pre` and `:post`. The checks it runs before executing the body of the function are the ones specified with the `:pre` key (hence called preconditions). In this case, there are two checks: one that ensures that `price` is greater than zero and a second that ensures that `quantity` is also greater than zero.

Try it with valid input:

```
(item-total 100 2 0)
;=> 200.0
(item-total 100 2 10)
;=> 180.0
```

Now try it with invalid input:

```
(item-total 100 -2 10)
AssertionError Assert failed: (> quantity 0)  user/item-total
```

Note that in this case, the function didn't compute the result but instead threw an `AssertionError` error with an explanation of which condition failed. The Clojure runtime automatically takes care of running the checks and throwing an error if they fail.

Now let's look at the conditions specified by the `:post` key, called the postconditions. The `%` in these conditions refers to the return value of the function. The checks are run after the function body is executed, and the behavior in the case of a failure is the same: an `AssertionError` is thrown along with a message explaining which condition failed. Here's an example of a corner case that you may have forgotten to check for, but luckily you had a postcondition to catch it:

```
(item-total 100 2 110)
AssertionError Assert failed: (> % 0)  user/item-total
```

Now that you've seen how to add preconditions and postconditions to your functions, we're ready to move on. We'll next look at functions that can accept different sets of parameters.

MULTIPLE ARITY

The *arity* of a function is the number of parameters it accepts. Clojure functions can be overloaded on arity, meaning that you can execute a different function body depending on the number of parameters the function was called with. To define functions with such overloading, you can define the various forms within the same function definition as follows:

```
(defn function-name
  ;; Note that each argument+body pair is enclosed in a list.
  ([arg1]      body-executed-for-one-argument-call)
  ([arg1 arg2] body-executed-for-two-argument-call)
  ;; More cases may follow.
)
```

Let's look at an example:

```
(defn total-cost
  ([item-cost number-of-items]
    (* item-cost number-of-items))
  ([item-cost]
    (total-cost item-cost 1)))
```

Here, two arities of the `total-cost` function are defined. The first is of arity 2, and it's the same as the one we defined earlier. The other is of arity 1, and it accepts only the first parameter, `item-cost`. Note that you can call any other version of the function from any of the other arities. For instance, in the previous definition, you call the dual-arity version of `total-cost` from the body of the single-arity one.

VARIADIC FUNCTIONS

We touched very briefly on variadic functions in chapter 2, but now we get the full story. A variadic function is a function with an arity that takes a variable number of arguments. Different languages support this in different ways; for example, C++ has the ellipsis, and Java has varargs. In Clojure, the same is achieved with the & symbol:

```
(defn total-all-numbers [& numbers]
  (apply + numbers))
```

Here, `total-all-numbers` is a function that can be called with any number of optional arguments. All the arguments are packaged into a single list called `numbers`, which is available to the body of the function. You can use this form even when you do have some required parameters. The general form of declaring a variadic function is as follows:

```
(defn name-of-variadic-function [param-1 param-2 & rest-args]
  (body-of-function))
```

Here, `param-1` and `param-2` behave as regular named parameters, and all remaining arguments will be collected into a list called `rest-args`. By the way, the `apply` function is a way of calling a function when you have the arguments inside a list. You'll see this in more detail in section 3.3.2, "Calling functions."

Notice that a variadic function can have other nonvariadic arities, too. (Nonvariadic arities are called *fixed arities*.) The only restriction is that the variadic arity must have at least as many required arguments as the longest fixed arity. For example, the following is a valid function definition:

```
(defn many-arities
  ([]              0)
  ([a]             1)
  ([a b c]         3)
  ([a b c & more] "variadic"))
;=> #'user/many-arities
(many-arities)
;=> 0
(many-arities "one argument")
;=> 1
(many-arities "two" "arguments")
ArityException Wrong number of args (2) passed to: user/many-arities
      clojure.lang.AFn.throwArity (AFn.java:429)
(many-arities "three" "argu-" "ments")
;=> 3
(many-arities "many" "more" "argu-" "ments")
;=> "variadic"
```

RECURSIVE FUNCTIONS

Recursive functions are those that either directly or indirectly call themselves. Clojure functions can certainly call themselves using their names, but this form of recursion consumes the stack. If enough recursive calls are made, eventually the stack will overflow. This is how things work in most programming languages. There's a feature in Clojure that circumvents this issue. You'll first write a recursive function that will blow the stack:

```
(defn count-down [n]
  (when-not (zero? n)
    (when (zero? (rem n 100))
      (println "count-down:" n))
    (count-down (dec n))))
```

rem means remainder of division.

dec means decrement by one.

If you try calling `count-down` with a large number, for instance 100,000, you'll get a `StackOverflowError` thrown at you:

```
(count-down 100000)
count-down: 100000
count-down: 99900
count-down: 99800
...
count-down: 90200
StackOverflowError    clojure.lang.Numbers$LongOps.remainder (Numbers.java:505)
```

You'll now see how to ensure that this doesn't happen.

In the last chapter, you saw the `loop/recur` construct that allowed you to iterate through sequences of data. The same `recur` form can be used to write recursive functions. When used in the "tail" position of a function body, `recur` binds its arguments to the same names as those specified in its parameter list. You'll rewrite `count-down` using `recur`:

```
(defn count-downr [n]
  (when-not (zero? n)
    (if (zero? (rem n 100))
      (println "count-down:" n))
    (recur (dec n))))
```

This now works for any argument, without blowing the stack. The change is minimal because at the end of the function body, `recur` rebinds the function parameter n to (dec n), which then proceeds down the function body. When n finally becomes zero, the recursion ends. As you can see, writing self-recursive functions is straightforward. Writing mutually recursive functions is a bit more involved, and we'll look at that next.

MUTUALLY RECURSIVE FUNCTIONS

Mutually recursive functions are those that either directly or indirectly call each other. Let's begin this section by examining an example of such a case. Listing 3.1 shows a contrived example of two functions, `cat` and `hat`, that call each other. Because `cat` calls `hat` before `hat` is defined, you need to declare it first. When given a large enough argument, they'll throw the same `StackOverflowError` you saw earlier. Note that the `declare` macro calls `def` on each of its arguments. This is useful in cases where a function wants to call another function that isn't defined yet, as is the case with a pair of mutually recursive functions in the following listing.

Listing 3.1   Mutually recursive functions that can blow the stack

```
(declare hat)
(defn cat [n]
  (when-not (zero? n)
    (when (zero? (rem n 100))
      (println "cat:" n))
    (hat (dec n))))

(defn hat [n]
  (when-not (zero? n)
    (if (zero? (rem n 100))
      (println "hat:" n))
    (cat (dec n))))
```

Let's now fix this problem. You can't use `recur` because `recur` is only useful for self-recursion. Instead, you need to modify the code to use a special Clojure function called `trampoline`. To do so, you'll make a slight change to the definition of `cat` and `hat`. The new functions are shown in the following listing as `catt` and `hatt`.

Listing 3.2   Mutually recursive functions that can be called with `trampoline`

```
(declare hatt)
(defn catt [n]
  (when-not (zero? n)
    (when (zero? (rem n 100))
      (println "catt:" n))
    (fn [] (hatt (dec n)))))

(defn hatt [n]
  (when-not (zero? n)
    (when (zero? (rem n 100))
      (println "hatt:" n))
    (fn [] (catt (dec n)))))
```

The difference is so minor that you could almost miss it. Consider the definition of `catt`, where instead of making the recursive call to `hatt`, you now return an anonymous function that when called makes the call to `hatt`. The same change is made in the definition of `hatt`. You'll learn more about anonymous functions in section 3.3.5.

Because these functions no longer perform their recursion directly, you have to use another function to call them. A function that accepts another function as an argument is called a *higher-order function*. The higher-order function you need here is `trampoline`, and here's an example of using it:

```
(trampoline catt 100000)
catt: 100000
catt: 99900
...
catt: 200
catt: 100
;=> nil
```

This doesn't blow the stack and works as expected. Internally, `trampoline` works by calling `recur`. Here's the implementation:

```
(defn trampoline
  ([f]
    (let [ret (f)]
      (if (fn? ret)              ◁─┤ fn? means "Is
        (recur ret)                │ my argument a
        ret)))                     │ function?"
  ([f & args]
    (trampoline (fn [] (apply f args)))))
```

Notice that `trampoline` is a higher-order function that sets up a local recursion point using the `let` form. It executes the function represented by the argument `f` and calls `recur` whenever the return value is itself a function. You could have done this yourself, but conveniently `trampoline` is available to you as part of the core set of Clojure functions.

You've now seen how recursive functions can be written in Clojure. Although using `recur` and `trampoline` is the correct and safe way to write such functions, if you're sure that your code isn't in danger of consuming the stack, it's okay to write them without using these. Now that you've seen the basics of defining functions, let's look at a couple of ways to call them.

3.3.2 Calling functions

Because functions are so fundamental to Clojure, you'll be calling a lot of functions in your programs. The most common way of doing this looks similar to the following:

```
(+ 1 2 3 4 5)
;=> 15
```

Here, the symbol + represents a function that adds its arguments. As a side note, Clojure doesn't have the traditional operators present in other languages. Instead, most operators are defined in Clojure itself, as any other function or macro. Coming back to the previous example, the + function is variadic, and it adds up all the parameters passed to it and returns `15`.

There's another way to evaluate a function. Let's say someone handed you a sequence called `list-of-expenses`, each an amount such as `39.95M`. In a language such as Java, you'd have to perform some kind of iteration over the list of expense amounts, combined with collecting the result of adding them. In Clojure, you can treat the list of numbers as arguments to a function like +. The evaluation, in this case, is done using a higher-order function called `apply`:

```
(apply + list-of-expenses)
```

The `apply` function is extremely handy, because it's quite common to end up with a sequence of things that need to be used as arguments to a function. This is because a lot of Clojure programs use the core sequence data structures to do their job.

As you saw, `apply` is a higher-order function that accepts another function as its first parameter. Higher-order functions are those that accept one or more functions as parameters, or return a function, or do both. You'll now learn a bit more about this powerful concept by looking at a few examples of such functions provided by Clojure.

3.3.3 *Higher-order functions*

As we discussed in the previous chapter, functions in Clojure are first-class entities. Among other things, this means that functions can be treated similarly to data: they can be passed around as arguments and can be returned from functions. Functions that do these things are called higher-order functions.

Functional code makes heavy use of higher-order functions. The `map` function that you saw in chapter 2 is one of the most commonly used higher-order functions. Other common ones are `reduce`, `filter`, `some`, and `every?`. You saw simple examples of `map`, `reduce`, and `filter` in chapter 2. Higher-order functions aren't just convenient ways of doing things such as processing lists of data but are also the core of a programming technique known as *function composition*. In this section, we'll examine a few interesting higher-order functions that are a part of Clojure's core library.

EVERY?

`every?` is a function that accepts a testing function that returns a boolean (such functions are called *predicate* functions) and a sequence. It then calls the predicate function on each element of the provided sequence and returns `true` if they all return a truthy value; otherwise, it returns `false`. Here's an example:

```
(def bools [true true true false false])
;=> #'user/bools
(every? true? bools)                                    true? is a
;=> false                                               predicate function.
```

This returns `false` because not every value in the `bools` vector is true.

SOME

`some` has the same interface as `every?`—that is, it accepts a predicate and a sequence. It then calls the predicate on each element in the sequence and returns the first logically `true` value it gets. If none of the calls return a logically `true` value, `some` returns `nil`. Here's an example, which is a quick-and-dirty way to check if a particular value exists in a sequence:

```
(some (fn [p] (= "rob" p)) ["kyle" "siva" "rob" "celeste"])
;=> true returns true
```

This returns `true` because it returns the first logically `true` value returned by applying the anonymous function to each of the elements of the vector. In this case, the third element of the vector is `"rob"`, and that returns `true`.

CONSTANTLY

constantly accepts a value v and returns a variadic function that always returns the same value v no matter what the arguments. It's equivalent to writing (fn [& more] v). Here's an example:

```
(def two (constantly 2)) ; same as (def two (fn [& more] 2))
                         ; or      (defn two [& more] 2)
;=> #'user/two
(two 1)
;=> 2
(two :a :b :c)
;=> 2
```

two is a function that returns 2, no matter what or how many arguments it's called with.

constantly is useful when a function requires another function but you just want a constant value.

COMPLEMENT

complement is a simple function that accepts a function and returns a new one that takes the same number of arguments, does the same thing as the original function does, but returns the logically opposite value.

For instance, consider a function that checks if the first of two arguments is greater than the second:

```
(defn greater? [x y]
   (> x y))
```

And here it is in action:

```
(greater? 10 5)
;=> true
(greater? 10 20)
;=> false
```

Now, if you wanted to write a function that instead checked if the first of two arguments was smaller than the second, you could implement it in a similar way, but you could also just use complement:

```
(def smaller? (complement greater?))
```

And in use:

```
(smaller? 10 5)
;=> false

(smaller? 10 20)
;=> true
```

It's a convenient function that in certain cases lets you implement one side of logical scenarios and declare the other side as being opposite.

COMP

comp, short for *composition*, is a higher-order function that accepts multiple functions and returns a new function that's a composition of those functions. The computation goes from right to left—that is, the new function applies its arguments to the right-most of the original constituent functions, then applies the result to the one left of it, and so on, until all functions have been called. Here's an example:

```
(def opp-zero-str (comp str not zero?))
```

Here are examples of using this:

```
(opp-zero-str 0)
;=> "false"
```

```
(opp-zero-str 1)
;=> "true"
```

Here, opp-zero-str when called with 1 first applies the function zero? to it, which returns false; it then applies not, which returns true, and then applies str, which converts it to a string "true".

PARTIAL

partial, which is short for *partial application*, is a higher-order function that accepts a function f and a few arguments to f but fewer than the number f normally takes. partial then returns a new function that accepts the remaining arguments to f. When this new function is called with the remaining arguments, it calls the original f with all the arguments together. Consider the following function that accepts two parameters, threshold and number, and checks to see if number is greater than threshold:

```
(defn above-threshold? [threshold number]
  (> number threshold))
```

To use it to filter a list, you might do this:

```
(filter (fn [x] (above-threshold? 5 x)) [ 1 2 3 4 5 6 7 8 9])
;=> (6 7 8 9)
```

With partial, you could generate a new function and use that instead:

```
(filter (partial above-threshold? 5) [ 1 2 3 4 5 6 7 8 9])
;=> (6 7 8 9)
```

The idea behind partial is to adapt functions that accept n arguments to situations where you need a function of fewer arguments, say n-k, and where the first k arguments can be fixed. This is the example you just saw previously, where a two-argument function above-threshold? was adapted to a situation that needed a single-argument function. For instance, you may want to use a library function that has a slightly different signature than what you require and needs to be adapted for your use.

MEMOIZE

Memoization is a technique that prevents functions from computing results for arguments that have already been processed. Instead, return values are looked up from a cache. Clojure provides a convenient `memoize` function that does this. Consider the following artificially slow function that performs a computation:

```
(defn slow-calc [n m]
  (Thread/sleep 1000)
  (* n m))
```

Calling it via a call to the built-in function `time` tells you how long it's taking to run:

```
(time (slow-calc 5 7))
"Elapsed time: 1000.097 msecs"
;=> 35
```

Now, you can make this fast, by using the built-in `memoize` function:

```
(def fast-calc (memoize slow-calc))
```

For `memoize` to do its thing, you call `fast-calc` once with a set of arguments (say 5 and 7). You'll notice that this run appears as slow as before, only this time the result has been cached. Now, you call it once more via a call to `time`:

```
(time (fast-calc 5 7))
"Elapsed time: 0.035 msecs"
;=> 35
```

This is pretty neat! Without any work at all, you're able to substantially speed up the function.

But there's a big caveat to `memoize`: the cache that backs `memoize` doesn't have a bounded size and caches input and results forever. Therefore, `memoize` should only be used with functions with a small number of possible inputs or else you'll eventually run out of memory. If you need more advanced memoization features (such as caches with bounded size or with eviction policies) look at the much more powerful `clojure.core.memoize` library at https://github.com/clojure/core.memoize. These are some examples of what higher-order functions can do, and these are only a few of those included with Clojure's standard library. Next, you'll learn more about constructing complex functions by building on smaller ones.

3.3.4 *Writing higher-order functions*

You can create new functions that use existing functions by combining them in various ways to compute the desired result. For example, consider the situation where you need to sort a given list of user accounts, where each account is represented by a hash map, and where each map contains the username, balance, and the date the user signed up. This is shown in the next listing.

```
(def users
  [{:username      "kyle"
    :firstname     "Kyle"
    :lastname      "Smith"
    :balance       175.00M                    ; Use BigDecimals for money!
    :member-since "2009-04-16"}
   {:username      "zak"
    :firstname     "Zackary"
    :lastname      "Jones"
    :balance       12.95M
    :member-since "2009-02-01"}
   {:username      "rob"
    :firstname     "Robert"
    :lastname      "Jones"
    :balance       98.50M
    :member-since "2009-03-30"}])
(defn sorter-using [ordering-fn]
  (fn [collection]
    (sort-by ordering-fn collection)))
(defn lastname-firstname [user]
  [(user :lastname) (user :firstname)])
(defn balance [user] (user :balance))
(defn username [user] (user :username))
(def poorest-first (sorter-using balance))
(def alphabetically (sorter-using username))
(def last-then-firstname (sorter-using lastname-firstname))
```

Here, users is a vector of hash maps. Specifically, it contains three users representing Kyle, Zak, and Rob. Suppose you wanted to sort these users by their username. You can do this using the sort-by function: it's a higher-order function the first argument of which is a key function. The key function must accept one of the items you're sorting and return a key to sort it by. Let's see this step by step. If you call username on every user, you get every user's name:

```
(map username users)
;=> ("kyle" "zak" "rob")
(sort *1)
;=> ("kyle" "rob" "zak")
```

> Remember, *1 means
> "last result returned
> by REPL."

This is the list that sort-by will see when sorting items. sort-by will sort the items *as if* it were instead sorting a list created by (map key-function items). Putting it all together:

```
(sort-by username users)
;=> ({:member-since "2009-04-16", :username "kyle", …}
     {:member-since "2009-03-30", :username "rob",  …}
     {:member-since "2009-02-01", :username "zak",  …})
```

Notice that the order of users is now Kyle, Rob, and Zack.

But what if you want to create functions that always sort in a specific order, without having to specify an ordering function? That's what the sorter-using function does.

It accepts a key function called `ordering-fn` and returns a function that accepts a collection that it will always sort using `sort-by` and the original `ordering-fn`. Take a look at `sorter-using` again:

```
(defn sorter-using [ordering-fn]
  (fn [collection]
    (sort-by ordering-fn collection)))
```

You define `sorter-using` as a higher-order function, one that accepts another function called `ordering-fn`, which will be used as a parameter to `sort-by`. Note here that `sorter-using` returns a function, defined by the `fn` special form that you saw earlier. Finally, you define `poorest-first` and `alphabetically` as the two desired functions, which sort the incoming list of users by `:balance` and `:username`. This is as simple as calling `sorter-using`, thus:

```
(def poorest-first (sorter-using balance))
```

This is the same as

```
(defn poorest-first [users] (sort-by balance users))
```

Both produce a sequence of users sorted by balance:

```
(poorest-first users)
;=> ({:username "zak",   :balance  12.95M, …}
     {:username "rob",   :balance  98.50M, …}
     {:username "kyle",  :balance 175.00M, …})
```

But suppose you wanted to sort by two criteria: first by each user's last name and then by first name if they share a first name with another user. You can do this by supplying an ordered collection as the sorting key for an item: sequences are sorted by comparing each of their members in order. For example, the `lastname-firstname` function returns a vector of the last then first name of a user:

```
(map lastname-firstname users)
;=> (["Smith" "Kyle"] ["Jones" "Zackary"] ["Jones" "Robert"])
(sort *1)
;=> (["Jones" "Robert"] ["Jones" "Zackary"] ["Smith" "Kyle"])
```

So you can use this to sort the full user records with the `last-then-firstname` function:

```
(last-then-firstname users)
;=> ({:lastname "Jones", :firstname "Robert",  :username "rob",  …}
     {:lastname "Jones", :firstname "Zackary", :username "zak",  …}
     {:lastname "Smith", :firstname "Kyle",    :username "kyle", …})
```

The two functions `username` and `balance` are used in other places, so defining them this way is okay. If the only reason they were created was to use them in the definition of `poorest-first` and `alphabetically`, then they could be considered clutter. You'll see a couple of ways to avoid the clutter created by single-use functions, starting with anonymous functions in the next section.

3.3.5   *Anonymous functions*

As you saw in the previous section, there may be times when you have to create functions for single use. A common example is when a higher-order function accepts another function as an argument. An example is the `sorter-using` function defined earlier. Such single-use functions don't even need names, because no one else will be calling them. Therefore, instead of creating regular named functions that no one else will use, you can use anonymous functions.

You've seen anonymous functions before, even if we didn't call them out. Consider this code snippet from earlier in the chapter:

```
(def total-cost
  (fn [item-cost number-of-items]
    (* item-cost number-of-items)))
```

As we discussed earlier, this code assigns a value to the `total-cost` var, which is the function created by the `fn` macro. To be more specific, the function by itself doesn't have a name; instead, you use the var with the name `total-cost` to refer to the function. *The function itself is anonymous.* To sum up, anonymous functions can be created using the `fn` form. Let's consider a situation where you need a sequence of dates of when your members joined (perhaps for a report). You can use the `map` function for this:

```
(map (fn [user] (user :member-since)) users)
;=> ("2009-04-16" "2009-02-01" "2009-03-30")
```

Here, you pass the anonymous function (which looks up the `:member-since` key from inside the `users` map) into the `map` function to collect the dates. This is a fairly trivial use case, but there are cases where this will be useful.

Before we move on, let's look at a reader macro that helps with creating anonymous functions.

A SHORTCUT FOR ANONYMOUS FUNCTIONS

We talked about reader macros in chapter 2. One of the reader macros provided by Clojure allows anonymous functions to be defined quickly and easily. The reader macro that does this is `#(`.

Here you'll rewrite the code used to collect a list of member-joining dates using this reader macro:

```
(map #(% :member-since) users)                          ← Same result!
;=> ("2009-04-16" "2009-02-01" "2009-03-30")
```

That's much shorter! The `#(% :member-since)` is equivalent to the anonymous function used in the previous version. Let's examine this form in more detail.

The `#()`, with the body of the anonymous function appearing within the parentheses, creates an anonymous function. The `%` symbol represents a single argument. If the function needs to accept more than one argument, then `%1`, `%2`, ... can be used. The body can contain pretty much any code, except for nested anonymous functions defined using another #() reader macro. You can also use %& for the "rest" arguments for a variadic function: the rest arguments are those beyond the highest explicitly mentioned % argument. An example will clarify:

```
(#(vector %&) 1 2 3 4 5)
;=> [(1 2 3 4 5)]
(#(vector % %&) 1 2 3 4 5)
;=> [1 (2 3 4 5)]
(#(vector %1 %2 %&) 1 2 3 4 5)
;=> [1 2 (3 4 5)]
(#(vector %1 %2 %&) 1 2)
;=> [1 2 nil]
```

You'll now see another way to write such functions—a way that will result in even shorter code.

3.3.6 *Keywords and symbols*

Keywords are identifiers that begin with a colon—examples are :mickey and :mouse. You learned about keywords and symbols in chapter 2. They're some of the most heavily used values in Clojure code, and they have one more property of interest. They're also functions, and their use as functions is quite common in idiomatic Clojure.

Keyword functions accept one or two arguments. The first argument is a map, and the keyword looks itself up in this map. For example, consider one of the user maps from earlier:

```
(def person {:username "zak"
             :balance 12.95
             :member-since "2009-02-01"})
```

To find out what username this corresponds to, you'd do the following:

```
(person :username)
;=> "zak"
```

But now that you know that keywords behave as functions, you could write the same thing as

```
(:username person)
;=> "zak"
```

This would also return the same "zak". Why would you want to do such a strange-looking thing? To understand this, consider the code you wrote earlier to collect a list of all dates when users signed up, from the previous example:

```
(map #(% :member-since) users)
;=> ("2009-04-16" "2009-02-01" "2009-03-30")
```

Although this is short and easy to read, you could now make this even clearer by using the keyword as a function:

```
(map :member-since users)
;=> ("2009-04-16" "2009-02-01" "2009-03-30")
```

This is much nicer! Indeed, it's the idiomatic way of working with maps and situations such as this one. We said earlier that keyword functions could accept a second optional parameter. This parameter is what gets returned if there's no value in the map associated with the keyword. As an example, consider the following two calls:

```
(:login person)
;=> nil
(:login person :not-found)
;=> :not-found
```

The first call returns `nil` because `person` doesn't have a value associated with `:login`. But if `nil` was a legitimate value for some key in the hash map, you wouldn't be able to tell if it returned that or if no association was found. To avoid such ambiguity, you'd use the second form shown here, which will return `:not-found`. This return value tells you clearly that there was nothing associated with the key `:login`.

SYMBOLS

Now let's talk about symbols. In Clojure, *symbols* are identifiers that represent some value. Examples are `users` and `total-cost`, which as you've seen represent the list of users and a function. A symbol is a *name as a value*. To use the analogy of a dictionary, the word in a dictionary entry is the *symbol* but the definition of the word is a *binding* of that word to a particular meaning. A word and its definition aren't the same—for example, a word could have multiple definitions, or it could have a different definition at a different time. The same principle applies to symbols: the symbol `user` is always the same as another symbol `user`, but they could point to (that is, *be bound to*) different values. For example, one could point to a var containing a function, but another one could be a local variable pointing to a user hash map.

   Normally when the Clojure runtime sees a symbol like `users`, it automatically evaluates it and uses the value that the symbol represents. But you may wish to use symbols as is. You may desire to use symbols themselves as values, for instance, as keys in a map (or indeed in some kind of symbolic computation). To do this, you'd quote the symbols. Everything else works exactly the same as in the case of keywords, including its behavior as a function. Here's an example of working with a hash map:

```
(def expense {'name "Snow Leopard" 'cost 29.95M})
;=> #'user/expense
(expense 'name)
;=> "Snow Leopard"
('name expense)
;=> "Snow Leopard"
('vendor expense)
;=> nil
('vendor expense :absent)
;=> :absent
```

You can see here that symbols behave similarly to keywords in this context. The optional parameter that works as the default return value works just like in the case of Clojure keywords.

Furthermore, as you saw earlier in this chapter and also in the previous one, it turns out that maps and vectors have another interesting property, which is that they're also functions. Hash maps are functions of their keys, so they return the value associated with the argument passed to them. Consider the example from earlier:

```
(person :username)
;=> "zak"
```

person is a hash map, and this form works because it's also a function. It returns "zak". Incidentally, hash maps also accept an optional second parameter, which is what is returned when a value associated with the key isn't found, for instance:

```
(person :login :not-found)
;=> :not-found
```

Vectors also behave the same way; they're functions of their indices. Consider the following example:

```
(def names ["kyle" "zak" "rob"])
;=> #'user/names
(names 1)
;=> "zak"
```

The call to names returns "zak", and this works because the vector names is a function. Note here that vector functions *don't* accept a second argument, and if an index that doesn't exist is specified, an exception is thrown:

```
(names 10)
IndexOutOfBoundsException    clojure.lang.PersistentVector.arrayFor
    (PersistentVector.java:107)
(names 10 :not-found)
ArityException Wrong number of args (2) passed to: PersistentVector
    clojure.lang.AFn.throwArity (AFn.java:429)
```

The fact that vectors and hash maps are functions is useful when code is designed with function composition in mind. Instead of writing wrapper functions, these data structures can themselves be passed around as functions. This results in cleaner, shorter code.

It's worth spending some time and experimenting with the various ideas explored in this section, because any nontrivial Clojure program will use most of these concepts. A large part of gaining proficiency with a language like Clojure is understanding and gaining proficiency with functional programming. Functional programming languages are great tools for designing things in a bottom-up way, because small functions can easily be combined into more complex ones. Each little function can be developed and tested incrementally, and this also greatly aids rapid prototyping. Having a lot of small, general functions that then combine to form solutions to the specific problems of the domain is also an important way to achieve flexibility.

Having seen how functions work, you're ready to tackle another important element in the design of Clojure programs: its scoping rules. In the next section, we'll explore scope. Scoping rules determine what's visible where, and understanding this is critical to writing and debugging Clojure programs.

3.4   Scope

Now that you've seen the basics of defining functions, we'll take a bit of a detour and show how scope works in Clojure. *Scope*, as it's generally known, is the enclosing context where names resolve to associated values. Clojure, broadly, has two kinds of scope: static (or lexical) scope and dynamic scope. Lexical scope is the kind that programming languages such as Java and Ruby offer. A *lexically scoped variable* is visible only inside the textual block that it's defined in (justifying the term *lexical*) and can be determined at compile time (justifying the term *static*).

Most programming languages offer only lexical scoping, and this is the most familiar kind of scope. The Lisp family has always also offered special variables that follow a different set of rules for dynamic scope. We'll examine both in this section. We'll first explore vars and how they can operate as special variables with dynamic scope. Then, we'll examine lexical scope and how to create new lexically scoped bindings.

3.4.1   Vars and binding

Vars in Clojure are, in some ways, similar to globals in other languages. Vars are defined at the top level of any namespace, using the def special form. Here's an example:

```
(def MAX-CONNECTIONS 10)
```

After this call, the MAX-CONNECTIONS var is available to other parts of the program. Remember, def always creates the var at the level of the enclosing namespace no matter where it's called. For instance, even if you call def from inside a function, it will create the var at the namespace level. For local variables, you'll need the let form, which you've seen previously and which we'll examine again shortly. The value of a var is determined by its *binding*. In this example, MAX-CONNECTION is bound to the number 10, and such an initial binding is called a *root binding*. A var can be defined without any initial binding at all, in the following form:

```
(def RABBITMQ-CONNECTION)
```

Here, RABBITMQ-CONNECTION is said to be unbound. If another part of the code tries to use its value, an exception will be thrown saying that the var is unbound. To set a value for an unbound var, or to change the value bound to a var, Clojure provides the binding form. Unfortunately, as defined previously, calling binding will throw an exception complaining that you can't dynamically bind a non-dynamic var. To rebind vars, they need to be dynamic, which is done using the following metadata declaration:

```
(def ^:dynamic RABBITMQ-CONNECTION)
(binding [RABBITMQ-CONNECTION (new-connection)]
    (
      ;; do something here with RABBITMQ-CONNECTION
    ))
```

The general structure of the binding form is that it begins with the symbol `binding`, followed by a vector of an even number of expressions. The first of every pair in the vector is a var, and it gets bound to the value of the expression specified by the second element of the pair. Binding forms can be nested, which allows new bindings to be created within each other. You'll see a running example in a moment when we discuss the implications of `^:dynamic`.

By the way, if you do try to rebind a var that wasn't declared dynamic, you'll see this exception:

```
java.lang.IllegalStateException:
Can't dynamically bind non-dynamic var: user/RABBITMQ-CONNECTION
```

This should tip you off that you need to use the `^:dynamic` metadata on the var in question.

As you saw earlier in this chapter, the `defn` macro expands to a `def` form, implying that functions defined using `defn` are stored in vars. Functions can thus be redefined using a `binding` form as well. This is useful for things like implementing aspect-oriented programming or stubbing out behavior for unit tests.

SPECIAL VARIABLES

There's one thing to note about vars: when declared with the `^:dynamic` metadata, they become dynamically scoped. To understand what this means, again consider the following var:

```
(def ^:dynamic *db-host* "localhost")
```

If you now call a function like `expense-report`, which internally uses `*db-host*` to connect to a database, you'll see numbers retrieved from the local database. For now, test this with a function that prints the binding to the console:

```
(defn expense-report [start-date end-date]
  (println *db-host*)) ;; can do real work
```

Now, once you've tested things to your satisfaction, you can have the same code connect to the production database by setting up an appropriate binding:

```
(binding [*db-host* "production"]
    (expense-report "2010-01-01" "2010-01-07"))
```

This will run the same code as defined in the `expense-report` function but will connect to a production database. You can prove that this happens by running the previous code; you'd see `"production"` printed to the console.

Note here that you managed to change what the `expense-report` function does, without changing the parameters passed to it (the function connects to a database specified by the binding of the `*db-host*` var). This is called *action at a distance*, and it must be done with caution. The reason is that it can be similar to programming with global variables that can change out from underneath you. But used with caution, it can be a convenient way to alter the behavior of a function.

Such vars that need to be bound appropriately before use are called *special* variables. A naming convention is used to make this intent clearer: these var names begin and end with an asterisk. In fact, if you have warnings turned on, and you name a var with asterisks and don't declare it dynamic, Clojure will warn you of possible trouble.

DYNAMIC SCOPE

You've seen how vars in general (and special variables in specific) can be bound to different values. We'll now explore the earlier statement that vars aren't governed by lexical scoping rules. We'll implement a simple form of aspect-oriented programming, specifically a way to add a log statement to functions when they're called. You'll see that in Clojure this ends up being quite straightforward, thanks to dynamic scope.

Scope determines which names are visible at certain points in the code and which names shadow which other ones. Lexical scope rules are simple to understand; you can tell the visibility of all lexically scoped variables by looking at the program text (hence the term *lexical*). Ruby and Java are lexically scoped.

Dynamic scope doesn't depend on the lexical structure of code; instead, the value of a var depends on the execution path taken by the program. If a function rebinds a var using a `binding` form, then the value of the var is changed for all code that executes within that binding form, including other functions that may be called. This works in a nested manner, too. If a function were to then use another binding form later on in the call stack, then from that point on all code would see this second value of the var. When the second binding form completes (execution exits), the previous binding takes over again, for all code that executes from that point onward. Look at the contrived example in the following listing.

Listing 3.4   Dynamic scope in action

```
(def ^:dynamic *eval-me* 10)
(defn print-the-var [label]
  (println label *eval-me*))
(print-the-var "A:")
(binding [*eval-me* 20] ;; the first binding
  (print-the-var "B:")
  (binding [*eval-me* 30] ;; the second binding
    (print-the-var "C:"))
  (print-the-var "D:"))
(print-the-var "E:")
```

Running this code will print the following:

```
A: 10
B: 20
C: 30
D: 20
E: 10
```

Let's walk through the code. First, you create a var called *eval-me* with a root binding of 10. The `print-the-var` function causes the A: 10 to be printed. The first binding form changes the binding to 20, causes the following B: 20 to be printed. Then the second binding kicks in, causing the C: 30. Now, as the second binding form exits, the previous binding of 20 gets restored, causing the D: 20 to be printed. When the first binding exits after that, the root binding is restored, causing the E: 10 to be printed.

We'll contrast this behavior with the let form in the next section. In the meantime, you'll implement a kind of aspect-oriented logging functionality for function calls. Consider the following code.

Listing 3.5 A higher-order function for aspect-oriented logging

```
(defn ^:dynamic twice [x]
  (println "original function")
  (* 2 x))

(defn call-twice [y]
  (twice y))

(defn with-log [function-to-call log-statement]
  (fn [& args]
    (println log-statement)
    (apply function-to-call args)))

(call-twice 10)

(binding [twice (with-log twice "Calling the twice function")]
  (call-twice 20))

(call-twice 30)
```

If you run this, the output will be

```
original function
20
Calling the twice function
original function
40
original function
60
```

with-log is a higher-order function that accepts another function and a log statement. It returns a new function, which when called prints the log statement to the console and then calls the original function with any arguments passed in. Note the action at a distance behavior modification of the twice function. It doesn't even know that calls to it are now being logged to the console, and, indeed, it doesn't need to. Any code that uses twice also can stay oblivious to this behavior modification, and as call-twice shows, everything works. Note that when the binding form exits, the original definition of twice is restored. In this way, only certain sections of code (to be more specific, certain call chains) can be modified using the binding form. We'll use this concept of action at a distance in the mocking and stubbing framework in chapter 10 on unit testing with Clojure.

We'll now examine one more property of bindings.

THREAD-LOCAL STATE

As we mentioned in chapter 1, Clojure has language-level semantics for safe concurrency. It supports writing lock-free multithreaded programs. Clojure provides several ways to manage state between concurrently running parts of your programs, and vars is one of them. We'll say a lot more about concurrency and Clojure's support for lock-free concurrency in chapter 6. Meanwhile, we'll look at the dynamic scope property of vars with respect to thread-local storage.

A var's root binding is visible to all threads, unless a binding form overrides it in a particular thread. If a thread does override the root binding via a call to the `binding` macro, that binding isn't visible to any other thread. Again, a thread can create nested bindings, and these bindings exist until the thread exits execution. You'll see more interaction between `binding` and threads in chapter 6.

LAZINESS AND SPECIAL VARIABLES

We mentioned Clojure's lazy sequences in chapter 1 and talked about how functions like `map` are lazy. This laziness can be a source of frustration when interplay with dynamic vars isn't clearly understood. Consider the following code:

```
(def ^:dynamic *factor* 10)
(defn multiply [x]
  (* x *factor*))
```

This simple function accepts a parameter and multiplies it by the value of `*factor*`, which is determined by its current binding. You'll collect a few multiplied numbers using the following:

```
(map multiply [1 2 3 4 5])
```

This returns a list containing five elements: (10 20 30 40 50). Now, you'll use a binding call to set `*factor*` to 20, and repeat the `map` call:

```
(binding [*factor* 20]
  (map multiply [1 2 3 4 5]))
```

Strangely, this also returns (10 20 30 40 50), despite the fact that you clearly set the binding of `*factor*` to 20. What explains this?

The answer is that a call to `map` returns a lazy sequence and this sequence isn't realized until it's needed. Whenever that happens (in this case, as the REPL tries to print it), the execution no longer occurs inside the binding form, and so `*factor*` reverts to its root binding of 10. This is why you get the same answer as in the previous case. To solve this, you need to force the realization of the lazy sequence from within the binding form:

```
(binding [*factor* 20]
  (doall (map multiply [1 2 3 4 5])))
```

This returns the expected (20 40 60 80 100). This shows the need to be cautious when mixing special variables with lazy forms. `doall` is a Clojure function that forces realization of lazy sequences, and it's invaluable in such situations. Of course, sometimes you don't want to realize an entire sequence, particularly if it's large, so you need to be careful about this. Typically, the solution is to reestablish the bindings of the variable you care about locally within the function that's generating the elements of the sequence.

In this section, we looked at dynamic scope and the associated `binding`. Next, we'll take another look at the `let` form you saw earlier. Because they look so similar, we'll also explore the difference between the `let` and `binding` forms.

3.4.2 *The let form revisited*

We briefly explored the `let` form in chapter 2, where you used it to create local variables. Let's quickly look at another example of using it:

```
(let [x 10
      y 20]
  (println "x, y:" x "," y))
```

Here, x and y are locally bound values. Locals such as these are local because the lexical block of code they're created in limits their visibility and extent (the time during which they exist). When execution leaves the local block, they're no longer visible and may get garbage collected.

Clojure allows functions to be defined locally, inside a lexically scoped `let` form. Here's an example:

```
(defn upcased-names [names]
  (let [up-case (fn [name] (.toUpperCase name))]
    (map up-case names)))
;=> #'user/upcased-names
(upcased-names ["foo" "bar" "baz"])
;=> ("FOO" "BAR" "BAZ")
```

Here, upcased-names is a function that accepts a list of names and returns a list of the same names, all in uppercase characters. up-case is a locally defined function that accepts a single string and returns an upcased version of it. The .toUpperCase function (with a prefixed dot) is Clojure's way of calling the toUpperCase member function on a Java object (in this case a string). You'll learn about Java interop in chapter 5.

Now, let's examine the difference between the structurally similar `let` and `binding` forms. To do this, you'll first reexamine the behavior of binding via the use of `*factor*`, as follows:

```
(def ^:dynamic *factor* 10)
(binding [*factor* 20]
  (println *factor*)
  (doall (map multiply [1 2 3 4 5])))
```

This prints 20 and then returns (20 40 60 80 100), as expected. Now, try the same thing with a `let` form:

```
(let [*factor* 20]
  (println *factor*)
  (doall (map multiply [1 2 3 4 5])))
```

This prints 20 as expected but returns (10 20 30 40 50). This is because, although the let sets *factor* to 20 inside the let body, it has no effect on the dynamic scope of the *factor* var. Only the binding form can affect the dynamic scope of vars.

Now that you know how the let form works and what it can be used for, let's look at a useful feature of Clojure that's possible thanks to two things: lexical scope and the let form.

3.4.3   Lexical closures

Let's begin our exploration of what a lexical closure is by understanding what a free variable is. A variable is said to be free inside a given form if there's no binding occurrence of that variable in the lexical scope of that form. Consider the following example:

```
(defn create-scaler [scale]
  (fn [x]
    (* x scale)))
```

In this example, within the anonymous function being returned, scale doesn't appear in any kind of binding occurrence—specifically, it's neither a function parameter nor created in a let form. Within the anonymous function, therefore, scale is a free variable. Only lexically scoped variables can be free, and the return value of the form in which they appear depends on their value at closure creation time. Forms that enclose over free variables (such as the anonymous function shown previously) are called *closures*. Closures are an extremely powerful feature of languages such as Clojure—in fact, even the name *Clojure* is a play on the word.

How do you use a closure? Consider the following code:

```
(def percent-scaler (create-scaler 100))
```

Here, we're binding the percent-scaler var to the function object that gets returned by the create-scaler call. This anonymous function object closes over the scale parameter and now lives on inside the percent-scaler closure. You can see this when you make a call to the percent-scaler function:

```
(percent-scaler 0.59)
;=> 59.0
```

This trivial example shows how closures are easy to create and use. A closure is an important construct in Clojure (it's no coincidence that the name of the language sounds like the word!). It can be used for information hiding (encapsulation) because nothing from outside the closure can touch the closed-over variables. Because Clojure data structures are immutable (reducing the need to make things private), macros, closures, and multimethods allow for powerful paradigms in which to create programs. It makes traditional object-oriented ideas (a la Java or C++) feel rather confining. You'll learn about multimethods in chapter 4 and more about macros in chapter 7. We'll also look at closures a lot more in chapter 8, which takes a deeper look at functional programming concepts.

Now that you understand several basic structural aspects of writing Clojure code, we'll address an organizational construct of Clojure: the namespace. Understanding how to use namespaces will aid you in writing larger programs that need to be broken into pieces for the sake of modularity and manageability.

3.5 Namespaces

When a program becomes larger than a few functions, computer languages allow the programmer to break it up into parts. An example of this facility is the package system in Java. Clojure provides the concept of namespaces for the same purpose. Programs can be broken up into parts, each being a logical collection of code—functions, vars, and the like.

Another reason why namespaces are useful is to avoid name collisions in different parts of programs. Imagine that you were writing a program that dealt with students, tests, and scores. If you were to then use an external unit-testing library that also used the word *test*, Clojure might complain about redefinition! Such problems can be handled by writing code in its own namespace.

3.5.1 ns macro

There's a core var in Clojure called *ns*. This var is bound to the currently active namespace. Thus, you can influence what namespace the following code goes under by setting an appropriate value for this var. The ns macro does just this—it sets the current namespace to whatever you specify. Here's the general syntax of the ns macro:

```
(ns name & references)
```

The name, as mentioned previously, is the name of the namespace being made current. If it doesn't already exist, it gets created. The references that follow the name are optional and can be one or more of the following: use, require, import, load, or gen-class. You'll see some of these in action in this section and then again in chapter 5, which covers Java intcrop. First, let's look at an example of defining a namespace:

```
(ns org.currylogic.damages.calculators)
(defn highest-expense-during [start-date end-date]
 ;; (logic to find the answer)
)
```

highest-expense-during is now a function that lives in the namespace with the name of org.currylogic.damages.calculators. To use it, code outside this namespace would need to make a call (directly or indirectly) to use, require, or import (if the library is compiled into a JAR) or they can call it with its fully qualified name, which is org.currylogic.damages.calculators/highest-expense-during. We'll explore these now through examples.

Public versus private functions

Before moving on to the next section, let's take a quick look at private functions versus public functions. In Clojure, all functions belong to a namespace. The defn macro creates public functions, and these can be called from any namespace. To create private functions, Clojure provides the defn- macro, which works exactly the same, but such functions can only be called from within the namespace they're defined in. defn- is itself just a shorthand for adding the metadata {:private true} to the var.

USE, REQUIRE

Imagine that you're writing an HTTP service that responds to queries about a user's expenses. Further imagine that you're going to deal with both XML and JSON. To handle XML, you can use the Clojure-provided XML functions that live in the clojure.xml namespace.

As far as handling JSON is concerned, ideally you wouldn't have to write code to handle the format. It turns out that the Clojure ecosystem already has a great library for this purpose called clojure.data.json.

Listing 3.6 shows what the code looks like now that you've selected the two libraries you need. Remember, to get it to work, you'll need to add the dependency to the Lein configuration in project.clj by adding [org.clojure/data.json "0.2.1"] to the :dependencies list. (See appendix A for more information on setting up your Leiningen project and adding dependencies.) You'll also need to restart the REPL for the classpath to include the new dependency.

Listing 3.6   Using external libraries by calling use

```
(ns org.currylogic.damages.http.expenses)
(use 'clojure.data.json)
(use 'clojure.xml)

(declare load-totals)

(defn import-transactions-xml-from-bank [url]
  (let [xml-document (parse url)]
    ;; more code here
))

(defn totals-by-day [start-date end-date]
  (let [expenses-by-day (load-totals start-date end-date)]
    (json-str expenses-by-day)))
```

Here, parse and json-str are functions that come from the clojure.xml and clojure.data.json libraries. The reason they're available is that you called use on their namespaces. use takes all public functions from the namespace and includes them in the current namespace. The result is as though those functions were written in the current namespace. Although this is easy—and sometimes desirable—it often makes the code a little less understandable in terms of seeing where such functions are defined. require solves this problem, as shown in the following listing.

Listing 3.7 Using external libraries by calling `require`

```
(ns org.currylogic.damages.http.expenses)
(require '(clojure.data [json :as json-lib]))
(require '(clojure [xml :as xml-core]))

(declare load-totals)

(defn import-transactions-xml-from-bank [url]
  (let [xml-document (xml-core/parse url)]
    ;; more code here
))

(defn totals-by-day [start-date end-date]
  (let [expenses-by-day (load-totals start-date end-date)]
    (json-lib/json-str expenses-by-day)))
```

require makes functions available to the current namespace, as use does, but doesn't include them the same way. They must be referred to using the full namespace name or the aliased namespace using the as clause, as shown in listing 3.7. This improves readability by making it clear where a function is actually coming from.

Finally, although these ways of using require (and use) work just fine, the idiomatic way is shown in the next listing.

Listing 3.8 Using external libraries by calling `require`

```
(ns org.currylogic.damages.http.expenses
  (:require [clojure.data.json :as json-lib]
            [clojure.xml :as xml-core]))

(declare load-totals)

(defn import-transactions-xml-from-bank [url]
  (let [xml-document (xml-core/parse url)]
    ;; more code here
))

(defn totals-by-day [start-date end-date]
  (let [expenses-by-day (load-totals start-date end-date)]
    (json-lib/json-str expenses-by-day)))
```

Notice how the require clauses are tucked into the namespace declaration. Similar approaches can be used with :use and :import. In general, prefer require, because it avoids the aliasing problems that can occur with use. For instance, if a library you use suddenly were to introduce a function named the same as one in your namespace, it would break your code. The use of require avoids this problem while also making it abundantly clear where each required function comes from.

Before moving on, let's look at an aid for when you're working with namespaces at the REPL.

RELOAD AND RELOAD-ALL

As described in chapter 1, typical programming workflow in Clojure involves building up functions in an incremental fashion. As functions are written or edited, the namespaces that they belong to often need to be reloaded in the REPL. You can do this by using the following:

```
(use 'org.currylogic.damages.http.expenses :reload)
(require '(org.currylogic.damages.http [expenses :as exp]) :reload)
```

`:reload` can be replaced with `:reload-all` to reload all libraries that are used either directly or indirectly by the specified library. By the way, these functions are useful during development time, particularly when working with the REPL. When the program is deployed to run, the namespaces are all loaded during compile time, which happens only once.

Before wrapping up this section on namespaces, we'll explore some options that Clojure provides to work with them programmatically.

3.5.2 *Working with namespaces*

Apart from the convenience offered by namespaces in helping keep code modular (and guarding from name collisions), Clojure namespaces can be accessed programmatically. In this section, we'll review a few useful functions to do this.

CREATE-NS AND IN-NS

`create-ns` is a function that accepts a symbol and creates a namespace named by it if it doesn't already exist. `in-ns` is a function that accepts a single symbol as an argument and switches the current namespace to the one named by it. If it doesn't exist, it's created.

ALL-NS AND FIND-NS

The no-argument function `all-ns` returns a list of all namespaces currently loaded. The `find-ns` function accepts a single symbol as an argument (no wildcards) and checks to see if it names a namespace. If so, it returns `true`, else `nil`.

NS-INTERNS AND NS-PUBLICS

`ns-interns` is a function that accepts a single argument, a symbol that names a namespace, and returns a map containing symbols to var mappings from the specified namespace. `ns-publics` is similar to `ns-interns` but instead of returning a map that contains information about all vars in the namespace, it returns only the public ones.

NS-RESOLVE AND RESOLVE

`ns-resolve` is a function that accepts two arguments: a symbol naming a namespace and another symbol. If the second argument can be resolved to either a var or a Java class in the specified namespace, the var or class is returned. If it can't be resolved, the function returns `nil`. `resolve` is a convenience function that accepts a single symbol as its argument and tries to resolve it (such as `ns-resolve`) in the current namespace.

NS-UNMAP AND REMOVE-NS

`ns-unmap` accepts a symbol naming a namespace and another symbol. The mapping for the specified symbol is removed from the specified namespace. `remove-ns` accepts a symbol naming a namespace and removes it entirely. This doesn't work for the `clojure.core` namespace.

These are some of the functions provided by Clojure to programmatically work with namespaces. They're useful in controlling the environment in which certain code executes. An example of this will appear in chapter 11, on domain-specific languages.

So far, you've seen a lot of the basics of Clojure and should now be in a position to read and write programs of reasonable complexity. In the next section, you'll see a feature that isn't found in languages such as Java and Ruby, namely, destructuring.

3.6 Destructuring

Several programming languages provide a feature called pattern matching, which is a form of function overloading based on structural patterns of arguments (as opposed to their number or types). Clojure has a somewhat less general form of pattern matching called *destructuring*. In Clojure, destructuring lets programmers bind names to only those parts of certain data structures that they care about. To see how this works, look at the following code, which doesn't use destructuring:

```
(defn describe-salary [person]
  (let [first  (:first-name person)
        last   (:last-name  person)
        annual (:salary      person)]
    (println first last "earns" annual)))
```

Here, the `let` form doesn't do much useful work—it sets up local names for parts of the incoming `person` sequence. By using Clojure's destructuring capabilities, such code clutter can be eliminated:

```
(defn describe-salary-2 [{first  :first-name
                          last   :last-name
                          annual :salary}]
  (println first last "earns" annual))
```

Here, the incoming sequence (in this case a map) is destructured, and useful parts of it are bound to names within the function's parameter-binding form. In fact, extracting values of certain keys from inside maps is so common that Clojure provides an even more convenient way of doing this. You'll see that and more ways to destructure maps in section 3.6.2, "Map bindings," but before that let's examine destructuring vectors.

3.6.1 Vector bindings

Vector destructuring supports any data structure that implements the `nth` function, including vectors, lists, seqs, arrays, and strings. This form of destructuring consists of a vector of names, each of which is assigned to the respective elements of the expression, looked up via the `nth` function. An example will make this clear:

```
(defn print-amounts [[amount-1 amount-2]]
  (println "amounts are:" amount-1 "and" amount-2))
(print-amounts [10.95 31.45])
amounts are: 10.95 and 31.45
```

This implementation of print-amounts is short and clear: you can read the parameter list and see that the single argument will be broken into two parts named amount-1 and amount-2. The alternative is to use a let form inside the function body to set up amount-1 and amount-2 by binding them to the first and last values of the incoming vector.

There are several options when it comes to using vector bindings. Imagine that the function print-amounts takes a vector that could contain two or more amounts (instead of only two in this contrived example). The following shows how you could deal with that situation.

USING & AND :AS

Consider the following example of destructuring:

```
(defn print-amounts-multiple [[amount-1 amount-2 & remaining]]
  (println "Amounts are:" amount-1 "," amount-2 "and" remaining))
```

If you make the following call

```
(print-amounts-multiple [10.95 31.45 22.36 2.95])
```

Clojure will print the following:

```
Amounts are: 10.95 , 31.45 and (22.36 2.95)
```

As shown here, the name following the & symbol gets bound to a sequence containing all the remaining elements from the sequence being destructured.

Another useful option is the :as keyword. Here's another example:

```
(defn print-all-amounts [[amount-1 amount-2 & remaining :as all]]
  (println "Amounts are:" amount-1 "," amount-2 "and" remaining)
  (println "Also, all the amounts are:" all))
```

When you call this function as follows

```
(print-all-amounts [10.95 31.45 22.36 2.95])
```

it results in the following being printed to the console:

```
Amounts are: 10.95 , 31.45 and (22.36 2.95)
Also, all the amounts are: [10.95 31.45 22.36 2.95]
```

Notice that all, which was introduced via the :as destructuring option, was bound to the complete argument that was passed in.

Destructuring vectors makes it easy to deal with the data inside them. What's more, Clojure allows nesting of vectors in destructuring bindings.

NESTED VECTORS

Suppose you had a vector of vectors. Each inner vector was a pair of data—the first being a category of expense and the second the amount. If you wanted to print the category of the first expense amount, you could do the following:

```
(defn print-first-category [[[category amount] & _ ]]
  (println "First category was:" category)
  (println "First amount was:" amount))
```

Running this with an example, such as

```
(def expenses [[:books 49.95] [:coffee 4.95] [:caltrain 2.25]])
(print-first-category expenses)
```

results in Clojure printing the following:

```
First category was: :books
First amount was: 49.95
```

Note that in the argument list of print-first-category, & is used to ignore the remaining elements of the vector that you don't care about. One thing to remember is that destructuring can take place in any binding form, including function parameter lists and let forms. Another thing to remember is that vector destructuring works for any data type that supports the nth and nthnext functions. On a practical level, for instance, if you were to implement the ISeq interface and create your own sequence data type, you'd be able to natively use not only all of Clojure's core functions but also such destructuring.

Before closing out this section on destructuring, let's look at another useful form of destructuring binds—the one that uses maps.

3.6.2 *Map bindings*

You saw how convenient it is to destructure vectors into relevant pieces and bind only those instead of the whole vector. Clojure supports similar destructuring of maps. To be specific, Clojure supports destructuring of any associative data structure, which includes maps, strings, vectors, and arrays. Maps, as you know, can have any key, whereas strings, vectors, and arrays have integer keys. The destructuring binding form looks similar to ones you saw earlier; it's a map of key-expression pairs, where each key name is bound to the value of the respective initialization expression.

Take a look at the example from earlier in the chapter:

```
(defn describe-salary-2 [{first  :first-name
                          last   :last-name
                          annual :salary}]
   (println first last "earns" annual))
```

As noted earlier, first, last, and annual get bound to the respective values from the map passed to describe-salary-2. Now suppose that you also want to bind a bonus percentage, which may or may not exist. Clojure provides a convenient option in map-destructuring bindings to handle such optional values, using the :or keyword:

```
(defn describe-salary-3 [{first  :first-name
                          last   :last-name
                          annual :salary
                          bonus  :bonus-percentage
                          :or {bonus 5}}]
  (println first last "earns" annual "with a" bonus "percent bonus"))
```

When called with arguments that contain all keys that are being destructured, it works similarly to the previous case:

```
(def a-user {:first-name       "pascal"
             :last-name        "dylan"
             :salary           85000
             :bonus-percentage 20})
(describe-salary-3 a-user)
```

This prints the following to the console:

```
pascal dylan earns 85000 with a 20 percent bonus
```

Here's how it works if you call the function with an argument that doesn't contain a bonus:

```
(def another-user {:first-name "basic"
                   :last-name  "groovy"
                   :salary     70000})
(describe-salary-3 another-user)
```

This binds bonus to the default value specified via the :or option. The output is

```
basic groovy earns 70000 with a 5 percent bonus
```

Finally, similar to the case of vectors, map bindings can use the :as option to bind the complete hash map to a name. Here's an example:

```
(defn describe-person [{first  :first-name
                        last   :last-name
                        bonus  :bonus-percentage
                        :or {bonus 5}
                        :as p}]
  (println "Info about" first last "is:" p)
  (println "Bonus is:" bonus "percent"))
```

An example of using this function is

```
(def third-user {:first-name "lambda"
                 :last-name  "curry"
                 :salary     95000})
(describe-person third-user)
```

This causes the following to be echoed on the console:

```
Info about lambda curry is: {:first-name lambda,
                             :last-name curry,
                             :salary 95000}
Bonus is: 5 percent
```

This is all quite convenient and results in short, readable code. Clojure provides a couple of options that make it even more easy to destructure maps: the :keys, :strs, and :syms keywords. Here's how to use :keys by writing a small function to greet your users:

```
(defn greet-user [{:keys [first-name last-name]}]
   (println "Welcome," first-name last-name))
```

When you run this, first-name and last-name get bound to values of :first-name and :last-name from inside the argument map. You can try it:

```
(def roger {:first-name "roger" :last-name "mann" :salary 65000})
(greet-user roger)
```

The output looks like this:

```
Welcome, roger mann
```

If your keys were strings or symbols (instead of keywords as in these examples), you'd use :strs or :syms. Incidentally, we'll use map destructuring in chapter 7 to add keyword arguments to the Clojure language.

We covered various ways that Clojure supports destructuring large, complex data structures into their components. This is a useful feature because it results in code that's shorter and clearer. It improves the self-documentation nature of well-written code, because the destructuring binding tells the reader exactly what parts of the incoming data structure are going to be used in the code that follows.

3.7 Reader literals

In programming languages, a literal is the source code representation of a fixed value. For instance, the string "clojure" is a literal value, as is the number 42. Although most languages have data literal support for strings and numbers, a few go further. For instance, many have literal support for vectors and maps, expressed as something like [1 2 3 4] and {:a 1 :b 2}.

Some programming languages support many more varieties of literals, but almost no language lets you, the programmer, add more. Clojure lets you do this to a degree, through its reader literals.

You've seen reader macros already. Reader literals are a way to let the reader construct a specific data type for you, as defined by your data reader functions. For instance, imagine that you were using UUIDs in your program. The easiest way to construct them is via the java.util.UUID/randomUUID method:

```
(java.util.UUID/randomUUID)
;=> #uuid "197805ed-7aa2-4ff8-ae66-b94a838df2a8"
```

Imagine now in a test you want to control what UUIDs are generated. Here's a function that accepts the first eight characters of a UUID and cans the rest:

```
(ns clj-in-act.ch3.reader
  (:import java.util.UUID))
```

```
(defn guid [four-letters-four-digits]
  (java.util.UUID/fromString
    (str four-letters-four-digits "-1000-413f-8a7a-f11c6a9c4036")))
```

Now, instead of struggling with random UUIDs over which you have no naming control, you can create (or re-create) known UUIDs at will:

```
(use 'clj-in-act.ch3.reader)
;=> nil
(guid "abcd1234")
;=> #uuid "abcd1234-1000-413f-8a7a-f11c6a9c4036"
```

You can imagine such known values for universally unique identifiers (UUIDs) being very useful when writing tests that deal with UUIDs. But calling the guid function each time is quite noisy. It would be nice if you could clean that up. Enter Clojure's reader literals.

You'd create a file called data_readers.clj and put it in the root directory of the classpath. Because you're using Leiningen, this would be the src folder in your project directory. In it could be a map containing your reader literal syntax and the respective functions that handle them. For instance, the following would be the contents of data_readers.clj with just one entry:

```
{G clj-in-act.ch3.reader/guid}
```

Now, whenever you wanted a known UUID, you could just do this:

```
#G "abcd1234"
;=> #uuid "abcd1234-1000-413f-8a7a-f11c6a9c4036"
```

This makes for far cleaner code, especially when many UUIDs are being created. Please take notice of the # before the G to form #G. Note that although this shows how reader literals work, it's not okay to use unqualified syntax for your reader literals. In other words, G by itself is unqualified by any namespace, and so it could conflict with someone else's, were they to name theirs the same. For this reason, the following namespaced version is preferred:

```
{clj-in-act/G clj-in-act.ch3.reader/guid}
```

And you'd use it like this:

```
#clj-in-act/G "abcd1234"
;=> #uuid "abcd1234-1000-413f-8a7a-f11c6a9c4036"
```

By namespacing your reader literals, you can be sure that they won't ever collide with anyone else's. Reader literals should be used sparingly, but they make it particularly easy to work with data types, and they can enhance the readability of your code.

3.8 *Summary*

This was another long chapter! We explored a few important aspects of writing code in Clojure. We started off the chapter looking at metadata and exception handling. Then we looked at functions, which form the basis of the language, and you saw several ways to create and compose functions. We also examined scope—both lexical and dynamic—and how it works in Clojure. We then showed that once programs start getting large you can use namespaces to break up and organize them. Finally, we looked at the destructuring capabilities of Clojure—a feature that comes in handy when writing functions or `let` forms. We closed off the chapter by looking at Clojure's reader literals.

Between the previous chapter and this one, we covered most of the basic features of the language. You can write fairly nontrivial programs with what you've learned so far. The next few chapters focus on a few features that are unique to Clojure—things like Java interoperability, concurrency support, multimethods, the macro system, and more.

In the next chapter, you'll learn about multimethods. You'll see how inheritance-based polymorphism is an extremely limited way of achieving polymorphic behavior and how multimethods are an open-ended system to create your own version of polymorphism that could be specific to your problem domain. By combining ideas from the next chapter with those we explored in this one, such as higher-order functions, lexical closures, and destructuring, you can create some rather powerful abstractions.

Multimethod polymorphism 4

This chapter covers

- Polymorphism and its types
- Clojure multimethods for ad hoc polymorphism
- Using multi-argument dispatch
- Querying, modifying, and creating dispatch hierarchies

You should now know how to use Clojure's types and functions and even write some fairly advanced higher-order functions, but you may still be wondering how to build larger systems with functional programming. In this chapter, you'll learn how to use the most powerful and flexible tool Clojure has for creating and using abstractions in large programs: multimethods.

4.1 Polymorphism and its types

Polymorphism is the ability to use multiple types as though they were the same—that is, you can write the same code to operate on many different types. This kind of abstraction allows you to substitute different types or implementations without having to change all code that touches objects of those types. Polymorphism's ability to reduce the surface area between different parts of a program and easily substitute some parts for other parts is what makes some form of it essential in larger systems. In a certain sense polymorphism provides the ability to create your own abstractions.

There are multiple ways to achieve polymorphism, but three are common to many languages: *parametric, ad hoc,* and *subtype* polymorphism. We'll concentrate on what these look like in Clojure *without* multimethods but also glance at how other languages achieve the same kinds of polymorphism.

4.1.1 *Parametric polymorphism*

You've actually already come in contact with polymorphism in Clojure. As you saw in chapter 2, functions such as get, conj, assoc, map, into, reduce, and so on accept many different types in their arguments but always do the correct thing. Clojure collections are also polymorphic because they can hold items of any type. This kind of polymorphism is called *parametric polymorphism* because such code mentions only *parameters* and not *types.* It's common in dynamically typed languages because such languages by their nature don't often mention types explicitly. But it's also present in some statically typed programming languages, both object-oriented languages such as Java and C# (where it's called *generics*) and functional programming (OO) languages such as ML and Haskell.

This kind of polymorphism is usually invisible in Clojure: you just use the built-in function and collection types, and the Clojure runtime works out what should happen or throws an exception (or often returns nil) if the type doesn't work with that function. Underneath the covers are Java classes and interfaces checking types and implementing the polymorphism. It's possible in Clojure to create new types that work with Clojure built-in functions such as conj using a mix of Java interop and user-defined Clojure types: we'll demonstrate this technique in chapter 9.

But in Clojure if you want to create your *own* parametrically polymorphic functions, you need to look to other kinds of polymorphism to implement them. This seems like a curious statement: How can you implement one type of polymorphism using another? How can a piece of code represent two kinds of polymorphism simultaneously? Polymorphism is often a matter of perspective: from the perspective of the *calling* code (the code using your functions and types), your code can appear parametrically polymorphic—that's often precisely the goal. But internally, hidden from the caller, your code may use a form of polymorphism that's explicit about types. That's where the other two forms of polymorphism come in.

4.1.2 *Ad hoc polymorphism*

Ad hoc polymorphism is simply enumerating each possible type a function can use and writing an implementation for each one. You can recognize this pattern in Clojure easily: some function is called on the argument to produce a dispatch value, and cond, case, or condp selects an implementation with a matching dispatch value to produce a

result. Here's an example polymorphic function that simply returns a string naming
its argument's type:

```
(defn ad-hoc-type-namer [thing]
  (condp = (type thing)
    java.lang.String                "string"
    clojure.lang.PersistentVector "vector"))
;=> #'user/ad-hoc-type-namer
(ad-hoc-type-namer "I'm a string")
;=> "string"
(ad-hoc-type-namer [])
;=> "vector"
(ad-hoc-type-namer {})
IllegalArgumentException No matching clause: class
clojure.lang.PersistentArrayMap  user/ad-hoc-type-namer (NO_SOURCE_FILE:2)
```

Call `type` on `thing` argument
to return type of thing

Dispatch for implementation of
function appropriate to type; in this
case, type-specific implementation
is simply string `"string"`

If there's a type this function
doesn't know how to handle,
it throws exception.

Ad hoc polymorphism as "function overloading"

Other languages often call ad hoc polymorphism *function overloading* and have some
special syntax to support this type of polymorphism. For example, in Java you can
repeat the method but annotate the argument's types differently; the Java virtual
machine (JVM) will then perform the dispatch to the right method invisibly at compile
time. Here's a short example equivalent to the `ad-hoc-type-namer` Clojure function:

```java
public class TypeNamer extends Object {
    // ...
    public String typeName(String thing) { return "string"; }
    public String typeName(PersistentVector thing) {
        return "vector";
    }
}
```

Notice that this example of ad hoc polymorphism doesn't allow calling code to "train"
the `ad-hoc-type-namer` function to understand new types—you can't add new clauses
to the `condp` expression without rewriting the function. This property is called *closed
dispatch* because the list of available implementations (that is, to which you can dispatch) can't be changed from the outside. But you can implement *open dispatch* by
keeping the implementations *outside* your type-naming function:

```
(def type-namer-implementations
  {java.lang.String                (fn [thing] "string")
   clojure.lang.PersistentVector (fn [thing] "vector")})
;=> #'user/type-namer-implementations
(defn open-ad-hoc-type-namer [thing]
  (let [dispatch-value (type thing)]
    (if-let [implementation
              (get type-namer-implementations dispatch-value)]
      (implementation thing)
```

Pull implementations
out into a separate
redef-able map

Use a dispatch value as key
to implementation map

If find
implementation
for dispatch
value, use it
and return
result

Otherwise throw an exception just like before

```
          (throw (IllegalArgumentException.
                     (str "No implementation found for " dispatch-value)))))))
;=> #'user/open-ad-hoc-type-namer
(open-ad-hoc-type-namer "I'm a string")
;=> "string"
(open-ad-hoc-type-namer [])
;=> "vector"
(open-ad-hoc-type-namer {})
IllegalArgumentException No implementation found for class
clojure.lang.PersistentArrayMap  user/open-ad-hoc-type-namer
(NO_SOURCE_FILE:5)
(def type-namer-implementations
  (assoc type-namer-implementations
    clojure.lang.PersistentArrayMap (fn [thing] "map")))
;=> #'user/type-namer-implementations
(open-ad-hoc-type-namer {})
;=> "map"
```

Normal cases from before still work.

But it still doesn't understand maps.

So redefine implementation map, adding a case for `PersistentArrayMap`.

`open-ad-hoc-type-namer` **now understands maps.**

Ad hoc polymorphism is simple and easy to understand, but it's done from the perspective of the implementations that *use* a type, not from the perspective of the types being used. The next form of polymorphism is more from the type's perspective.

4.1.3 *Subtype polymorphism*

So far we've been concentrating on the *functions* that are polymorphic, but the *types* can also be polymorphic. *Subtype polymorphism* is a kind of polymorphism where one type says it can be substituted for another so that any function that can use one type can safely use the other. Stated more simply, one type says it's "a kind of" another type, and code that understands more general kinds of things will automatically work correctly with more specific things of the same general kind.

Subtype polymorphism is the dominant kind of polymorphism in OO languages and it's expressed as class or interface hierarchies. For example, if a Person class inherits from (or extends) an Animal class, then any method that works with Animal objects should automatically work with Person objects too. Some dynamic OO languages also allow a form of subtype polymorphism (called *structural subtyping*) that doesn't use an explicit hierarchy or inheritance. Instead methods are designed to work with any objects that have the necessary structure, such as properties or methods with the correct names. Python, Ruby, and JavaScript all allow this form of subtyping, which they call *duck typing*.

Clojure can use Java classes and interfaces through its Java interop features and Clojure's built-in types participate in Java interfaces and class hierarchies. For example, remember in a footnote in chapter 2 we briefly mentioned that Clojure map literals may be array-map when they're small but become hash-map when they get larger? In Java there's an abstract class that they share, as you can see in the following example:

```
(defn map-type-namer [thing]
  (condp = (type thing)
```

First attempt with ad hoc polymorphism checks each type explicitly.

```
      clojure.lang.PersistentArrayMap "map"
      clojure.lang.PersistentHashMap  "map"))
;=> #'user/map-type-namer
(map-type-namer (hash-map))
;=> "map"
(map-type-namer (array-map))
;=> "map"
(map-type-namer (sorted-map))
IllegalArgumentException No matching clause: class
clojure.lang.PersistentTreeMap  com.gentest.ConcreteClojureClass/map-type-
namer (NO_SOURCE_FILE:2)
(defn subtyping-map-type-namer [thing]
  (cond
    (instance? clojure.lang.APersistentMap thing)    "map"
    :else (throw (IllegalArgumentException.
                  (str "No implementation found for ") (type thing)))))
;=> #'user/subtyping-map-type-namer
(subtyping-map-type-namer (hash-map))
;=> "map"
(subtyping-map-type-namer (array-map))
;=> "map"
(subtyping-map-type-namer (sorted-map))
;=> "map"
```

◁┐ **Notice duplicate
   implementation**

◁┘ **There was a
   case missed.**

◁┐ **Second attempt
   using subtype
   polymorphism**

◁┘ **Function now works
   for anything maplike.**

Use `instance?` to query Java's class
hierarchy; `APersistent-Map` is Java
superclass of all maplike things in Clojure

By writing code that knows how to use `APersistentMap`, you know it works with any subtype using your single implementation; it even works for types that don't exist yet as long as they'll extend `APersistentMap`.

Clojure also offers some ways to create subtypes of your own using multimethod hierarchies (which we'll look at later in this chapter) or protocols (which we'll discuss in chapter 9), but beyond this Clojure offers no rigid notion of subtyping. The reason is that subtyping, while powerful because it allows you to write fewer implementations of functions, can also be restraining if applied too broadly because there's often no one, single, universally applicable arrangement of types. For example, if you're writing geometry code, it may be simpler for some functions to see a circle as a special case of an ellipse but for others to view an ellipse as a special case of a circle. You may also have a single thing belong to multiple, nonoverlapping type hierarchies at the same time: a person is a kind of material body to a physicist but a kind of animal to a biologist. More importantly, Clojure is focused on data and values, not types: the programming-language type used to contain some information (such as a map, list, or vector) is independent of the problem-domain type (such as animal, vegetable, or mineral), and it's the latter that should be the focus. But this means your own code, and not your programming language, will need to distinguish somehow between maps that represent animals and maps that represent minerals or to know that an animal can be represented with either a list form or a map form.

Multimethods provide features to express both ad hoc and subtype polymorphism and even to express multiple different kinds of subtype polymorphism at the same time. Let's leave polymorphic theory behind us now and look more concretely at how multimethods can help you write polymorphic code.

4.2 Polymorphism using multimethods

For the rest of the chapter we're going to focus exclusively on how to use multimethods to write polymorphic code, specifically to meet the needs of a hypothetical expense-tracking service you're building.

4.2.1 Life without multimethods

Consider the situation where the expense-tracking service you've written has become popular. You've started an affiliate program where you pay referrers if they get users to sign up for your service. Different affiliates have different fees. Let's begin with the case where you have two affiliates: mint.com and google.com.

You'd like to create a function that calculates the fee you pay to the affiliate. For the sake of illustration, let's decide you'll pay your affiliates a percentage of the annual salary the user makes. You'll pay Google 0.01%, Mint 0.03%, and everyone else 0.02%. You'll write this without polymorphism first (you'll accept percentage values as straight numbers and you'll translate them by multiplying by 0.01 within the function):

```
(def example-user {:login "rob" :referrer "mint.com" :salary 100000})
;=> #'user/example-user
(defn fee-amount [percentage user]
  (with-precision 16 :rounding HALF_EVEN          ◁─┐  Using BigDecimal
    (* 0.01M percentage (:salary user))))            because dealing
;=> #'user/fee-amount                                with money
(defn affiliate-fee [user]
  (case (:referrer user)
    "google.com" (fee-amount 0.01M user)
    "mint.com"   (fee-amount 0.03M user)
    (fee-amount 0.02M user)))
;=> #'user/affiliate-fee
(affiliate-fee example-user)
;=> 30.0000M
```

You should be able to recognize `affiliate-fee` as an example of closed dispatch, ad hoc polymorphism, which uses `:referrer` as a dispatch function. It also has a default implementation to use if no match is found.

The biggest problem with the `affiliate-fee` function is the closed dispatch: you can't add new affiliates without rewriting `affiliate-fee`. Now let's look at how you'd solve this problem with multimethods.

4.2.2 Ad hoc polymorphism using multimethods

Before you implement the same functionality using multimethods, let's take a moment to understand their syntax. Multimethods use a pair of macros: `defmulti` defines a multimethod and how to produce a dispatch value with which to find an implementation. The `defmethod` macro defines an implementation for a specific dispatch value. In other words, `defmulti` acts as the first clause of a case expression, and each `defmethod` acts as a single test-and-result pair of a `case` expression. This is what `affiliate-fee` looks like as a multimethod:

```
(defmulti affiliate-fee (fn [user] (:referrer user)))    ← Like (defn affiliate-
;=> #'user/affiliate-fee                                      fee-dispatch [user]
(defmethod affiliate-fee "mint.com" [user]           ←        (:referrer user))
  (fee-amount 0.03M user))
;=> #<MultiFn clojure.lang.MultiFn@8b3cf12>          Like a clause of case: (case
(defmethod affiliate-fee "google.com" [user]         (affiliate-fee-dispatch
  (fee-amount 0.01M user))                            user) "mint.com" (fee-
;=> #<MultiFn clojure.lang.MultiFn@8b3cf12>           amount 0.03M user))
(defmethod affiliate-fee :default [user]
  (fee-amount 0.02M user))                           Default case; multimethods use
;=> #<MultiFn clojure.lang.MultiFn@8b3cf12>          :default as a dispatch value when
(affiliate-fee example-user)                         no other defmethod matches.
;=> 30.0000M
```

Notice `defmethod` doesn't return a var

DEFMULTI
Multimethods are declared using the `defmulti` macro. Here's a simplified general form of this macro:

```
(defmulti name docstring? attr-map? dispatch-fn & options)
```

`name` is the name of the multimethod used to invoke it and to add implementations using `defmethod`. `docstring?` and `attr-map?` are optional documentation and metadata arguments—the same as in `defn`. The required `dispatch-fn` function is a regular Clojure function that accepts the same arguments that are passed in when the multimethod is called. The return value of `dispatch-fn` is the dispatch value used to select an implementation. The `options` are key-value pairs to provide optional specifications. There are only two options: `:default`, to select a new default dispatch value, and `:hierarchy`, to use a custom dispatch value hierarchy. Here's an example with a custom default:

```
(defmulti affiliate-fee :referrer :default "*")      defmulti returning
;=> nil                                              nil means it wasn't
(ns-unmap 'user 'affiliate-fee)                      redefined; see sidebar.
;=> nil
(defmulti affiliate-fee :referrer :default "*")      Dispatch function
;=> #'user/affiliate-fee                             :referrer, option
(defmethod affiliate-fee "*" [user]                  :default "*"
    (fee-amount 0.02M user))
;=> #<MultiFn clojure.lang.MultiFn@7eafa7a7>         Now default case
(affiliate-fee example-user)
;=> 20.0000M                                         Default case; "mint.com"
                                                     case is gone because of
                                                     redefined affiliate-fee.
```

A few notes before we continue. First, notice that you can use a plain keyword `:referrer` as a dispatch function: this is a common idiom where the argument to the `defmethod` is always a map and you want to dispatch by the value of one of its keys. Second, because you had to redefine the `defmulti`, all the existing `defmethods` were lost: see the following sidebar for more discussion of the issues surrounding redefining a `defmulti`. We'll talk about the `:hierarchy` option later: it's used for subtype polymorphism.

Redefining a defmulti

A big gotcha in Clojure is that the `defmulti` macro uses `defonce` to define the var that holds the multimethod. This means that if you try to change a multimethod's dispatch function or options, your reasserted `defmulti` will have no effect and you'll continue to use the old multimethod. This rarely happens in normal running code but can cause considerable hair pulling at the read-evaluate-print loop (REPL) where exploratory change and revision is common.

A redefined `defmulti` will return `nil` instead of a var like `#'user/mymulti`. If you notice the `nil` (or if you don't but your multimethod feels like it's not accepting your changes), use `(ns-unmap 'namespace 'defmultiname)` before reasserting the `defmulti` form as demonstrated in the previous code example.

Another related gotcha is that a `redef-ed` multimethod will lose all of its `defmethod` implementations. This is because multimethods are a rare example of mutation in Clojure: each `defmethod` is actually mutating the original object created by `defmulti` by adding new items to its dispatch table. (This is why `defmulti` uses `defonce` in the first place: so mutations to its dispatch table aren't lost by accidental redefinition.) By creating a new multimethod all the old methods were cleared out. You can see and manipulate this dispatch table using `methods` and `remove-method`, which we'll discuss shortly.

DEFMETHOD

Implementations of a multimethod declared with `defmulti` are added with the `defmethod` macro, which looks like a normal (docstring-less) `defn` except with a dispatch value between the name and the arguments:

```
(defmethod multifn dispatch-value & fn-tail)
```

This creates a concrete implementation for a previously defined multimethod. The `multifn` identifier should match the `name` in the previous call to `defmulti`. The `dispatch-value` will be compared with the return value of the `dispatch-fn` from earlier to determine which method will execute. The `fn-tail` is the body of the implementation and accepts anything you'd put inside a `(fn …)` form, including argument destructuring. Normally this is just an argument vector followed by a function body, but multiple arities are okay, too:

```
(defmethod my-multi :default [arg] "body")
(defmethod my-many-arity-multi :default
  ([] "no arguments"))
```

```
([x] "one argument")
([x & etc] "many arguments"))
```

defmethod will create a normal function from its function body and mutate the original defmulti object to add this function to its dispatch map under the dispatch-value key. You can inspect the dispatch map of a multimethod using the functions get-method and methods. get-methods takes a multimethod and a dispatch value and returns an implementation function for that value using the same dispatch logic as calling the multimethod directly. methods just returns the entire dispatch map for a multimethod. Let's see an example using the affiliate-fee multimethod from earlier:

**Get implementation
for dispatch value**

**First add back methods
lost after redef**

```
(defmethod affiliate-fee "mint.com" [user]
  (fee-amount 0.03M user))
;=> #<MultiFn clojure.lang.MultiFn@7eafa7a7>
(defmethod affiliate-fee "google.com" [user]
  (fee-amount 0.01M user))
;=> #<MultiFn clojure.lang.MultiFn@7eafa7a7>
(methods affiliate-fee)
;=> {"mint.com" #<user$eval8117$fn__8118 user$eval8117$fn__8118@36e433f1>,
    "*" #<user$eval6380$fn__6381 user$eval6380$fn__6381@2ebfd12f>,
    "google.com" #<user$eval8123$fn__8124 user$eval8123$fn__8124@2ad71f9f>}
(get-method affiliate-fee "mint.com")
;=> #<user$eval8117$fn__8118 user$eval8117$fn__8118@36e433f1>
(get (methods affiliate-fee) "example.org")
;=> nil
(get-method affiliate-fee "example.org")
;=> #<user$eval6380$fn__6381 user$eval6380$fn__6381@2ebfd12f>
((get-method affiliate-fee "mint.com") example-user)
;=> 30.0000M
```

**Get full dispatch map
for multimethod**

**get-method
isn't just get:
it understands
dispatch logic.**

**Entries in dispatch map
are normal functions.**

**The "*"
implementation**

You can also remove multimethod implementations using remove-method and remove-all-methods. remove-method removes the implementation for a dispatch value. Note that unlike get-method, the dispatch value to remove must be an exact match. Finally, remove-all-methods removes all implementations of a multimethod.

We've covered the basics of multimethods for ad hoc polymorphism using a single dispatch value to select a matching implementation. Now you're going to see how multimethods can consider multiple dispatch values to select an implementation.

4.2.3 *Multiple dispatch*

Imagine your expense-tracking service is even more successful than before and the affiliate program is working great. So great, in fact, that you'd like to pay more profitable users a higher fee. This would be a win-win situation for the affiliate network and your service. Here are a few more example users with a `:rating` key to indicate the user's profit rating:

```
(def user-1 {:login "rob"     :referrer "mint.com"   :salary 100000
             :rating :rating/bronze})
(def user-2 {:login "gordon"  :referrer "mint.com"   :salary 80000
             :rating :rating/silver})
(def user-3 {:login "kyle"    :referrer "google.com" :salary 90000
             :rating :rating/gold})
(def user-4 {:login "celeste" :referrer "yahoo.com"  :salary 70000
             :rating :rating/platinum})
```

Now let's consider the business rules shown in table 4.1.

Table 4.1 Affiliate fee business rules

Affiliate	Profit rating	Fee (% of salary)
mint.com	Bronze	0.03
mint.com	Silver	0.04
mint.com	Gold/platinum	0.05
google.com	Gold/platinum	0.03

From the rules it's clear that there are two values based on which fee percentage is calculated: the referrer and the profit rating. In a sense, the combination of these two values is the affiliate fee type. Because you'd like to dispatch on this virtual type, comprising two values, you'll create a function that computes the pair:

```
(defn fee-category [user]
  [(:referrer user) (:rating user)])
;=> #'user/fee-category
(map fee-category [user-1 user-2 user-3 user-4])
;=> (["mint.com"   :rating/bronze]
     ["mint.com"   :rating/silver]
     ["google.com" :rating/gold]
     ["yahoo.com"  :rating/platinum])
```

You'll use `fee-category` as your dispatch function for another multimethod, `profit-based-affiliate-fee`:

```
(defmulti profit-based-affiliate-fee fee-category)
(defmethod profit-based-affiliate-fee ["mint.com" :rating/bronze]
  [user] (fee-amount 0.03M user))
(defmethod profit-based-affiliate-fee ["mint.com" :rating/silver]
  [user] (fee-amount 0.04M user))
(defmethod profit-based-affiliate-fee ["mint.com" :rating/gold]
  [user] (fee-amount 0.05M user))
(defmethod profit-based-affiliate-fee ["mint.com" :rating/platinum]
  [user] (fee-amount 0.05M user))
(defmethod profit-based-affiliate-fee ["google.com" :rating/gold]
  [user] (fee-amount 0.03M user))
```

Multimethod uses `fee-category` function to create dispatch values.

```
(defmethod profit-based-affiliate-fee ["google.com" :rating/platinum]
  [user] (fee-amount 0.03M user))
(defmethod profit-based-affiliate-fee :default
  [user] (fee-amount 0.02M user))
```

Even with multiple dispatch, default value is always a single value, not [:default :default].

This reads a lot like the table with business rules, and adding new rules is still quite easy and doesn't involve modifying existing code. But how does this code work in practice?

```
(map profit-based-affiliate-fee [user-1 user-2 user-3 user-4])
;=> (30.0000M
     32.0000M
     27.0000M
     14.0000M)
```

mint.com bronze gets 0.03% of $100,000.

mint.com silver gets 0.04% of $80,000.

yahoo.com platinum gets default 0.02% of $70,000.

google.com gold gets 0.04% of $90,000.

All the business rules in table 4.1 are applied and the default fee is used if there's no affiliate program with the user's combination of referrer and rating. But notice that you did have to duplicate some code: the business rules treat gold and platinum profit ratings the same, but you still had to write a separate method (with the same implementation) for each. Duplicate defmethods that differ only by dispatch value are a strong hint that those dispatch values are the same kind of thing. This isn't something ad hoc polymorphism can help you with, but subtype polymorphism is great for removing redundant implementations. Fortunately, multimethods can make use of subtype polymorphism, as you'll see in the next section.

4.2.4 *Subtype polymorphism using multimethods*

Your profit-rating infrastructure is in place, but you still have some duplicated code you'd like to get rid of: namely, your implementations for the gold and platinum ratings of mint.com and google.com are the same. When you point this out to the business folks, they elaborate that the ratings are actually in a hierarchy: bronze and silver are basic-level and gold and platinum are premier-level profit ratings. In other words, bronze and silver are both "kinds of" basic profit ratings, and gold and platinum are "kinds of" premier profit ratings, as illustrated in figure 4.1.

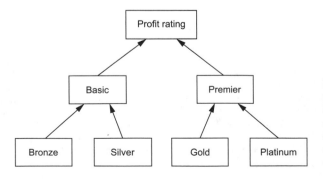

Figure 4.1 The hierarchy of profit rating levels as explained by the business folks. You can use this external-facing classification to simplify your code by defining a dispatch hierarchy reflecting this structure.

This talk of "kinds" is a big hint that you're dealing with subtype polymorphism here. Multimethods enable you to build and query your own hierarchies of types (represented by namespaced keywords) using a family of functions: derive, underive, isa?, parents, ancestors, and descendants.

BUILDING AND QUERYING TYPE HIERARCHIES

The derive function is used to establish a "kind of" or subtype relationship between two types. Multimethods represent types as keywords or Java classes.

The ordinary form of derive takes two arguments: a keyword representing a type and another keyword representing the parent. (You can remember this argument order by thinking "derive x from y," "x is a kind of y," or "x is a child of y.") In the two-argument form, derive will mutate a global hierarchy to establish the type relationship. Because you're mutating a *global* hierarchy, derive *requires* that your keywords have a namespace to reduce the chance of name collisions. (This requirement is relaxed for independent hierarchies, as explained later.) Here's an example implementing the hierarchy described in figure 4.1:

```
(derive :rating/bronze :rating/basic)     ◁─┤ nil return value is a hint
;=> nil                                        that mutation is occurring.
(derive :rating/silver :rating/basic)     ◁─┐
(derive :rating/gold :rating/premier)        │ Other nils omitted
(derive :rating/platinum :rating/premier)    │ for brevity.
(derive :rating/basic :rating/ANY)        ◁─┐
(derive :rating/premier :rating/ANY)         │ Use :rating/ANY as
                                             │ root type for all ratings
```

If you make a mistake or simply want to change the hierarchy, you can use the underive function to remove type relationships: it takes the same arguments as derive.

Now that you've created your hierarchy, how do you see it? The most important function is isa?: this is the function multimethods use internally to determine what method to select for a dispatch value. You can also use parents, ancestors, and descendants to inspect the hierarchy more directly. Here's an example using the hierarchy you just made:

```
(isa? :rating/gold :rating/premier)       isa? understands transitive
;=> true                                  relationships, too.
(isa? :rating/gold :rating/ANY)       ◁─┐
;=> true                                 Types are always
(isa? :rating/ANY :rating/premier)       kinds of themselves.
;=> false
(isa? :rating/gold :rating/gold)      ◁─┐ parents returns a set (not a single item)
;=> true                                 because it's legal to have multiple parents.
(parents :rating/premier)             ◁─┐
;=> #{:rating/ANY}                       ancestors returns parents
(ancestors :rating/gold)                 and their parents, etc.
;=> #{:rating/ANY :rating/premier}    ◁─┐
(descendants :rating/ANY)                descendants returns children
                                      ◁─┤ and their children, etc.
;=> #{:rating/basic :rating/bronze :rating/gold :rating/premier :rating/
     silver :rating/platinum}
```

Multimethod interop with Java hierarchies

Multimethods understand Java class and interface hierarchies for the purposes of dispatch, and all the functions described here (`isa?`, `parents`, and so on) work with Java types. But you can't use `derive` to modify the Java class hierarchy! But what you can still do is group Java types under some non-Java parent type, for example (`derive java.lang.String ::stringy-things`).

Even though `isa?` works with Java types, you should use the much faster `instance?` instead if you don't need to consider the multimethod hierarchy.

Now you can use this hierarchy in a simple example multimethod that returns an appropriate greeting depending on a user's profit rating:

```
(defmulti greet-user :rating)
;=> #'user/greet-user
(defmethod greet-user :rating/basic [user]
  (str "Hello " (:login user) \.))
;=> #<MultiFn clojure.lang.MultiFn@d81fe85>
(defmethod greet-user :rating/premier [user]
  (str "Welcome, " (:login user) ", valued affiliate member!"))
;=> #<MultiFn clojure.lang.MultiFn@d81fe85>
(map greet-user [user-1 user-2 user-3 user-4])
;=> ("Hello rob." "Hello gordon." "Welcome, kyle, valued affiliate member!"
    "Welcome, celeste, valued affiliate member!")
```

Notice that even though you supplied only two method implementations, the multimethod was able to correctly handle all four profit ratings by considering the subtype relationships you defined using `derive`. Can this help you remove some duplicate code from the `profit-based-affiliate-fee` methods? Yes!

SUBTYPES AND MULTIPLE-DISPATCH

Multimethods let you combine multiple-dispatch and type hierarchies. If you return a vector from your dispatch function, the multimethod will consider each item in the vector separately with `isa?` when trying to find a matching implementation. So you can finally clean up your `profit-based-affiliate-fee` code to remove those annoying duplicates:

First remove duplicate methods

```
(remove-method profit-based-affiliate-fee ["mint.com" :rating/gold])
;=> #<MultiFn clojure.lang.MultiFn@5d98c6f3>
(remove-method profit-based-affiliate-fee ["mint.com" :rating/platinum])
;=> #<MultiFn clojure.lang.MultiFn@5d98c6f3>
(remove-method profit-based-affiliate-fee ["google.com" :rating/gold])
;=> #<MultiFn clojure.lang.MultiFn@5d98c6f3>
(remove-method profit-based-affiliate-fee ["google.com" :rating/platinum])
;=> #<MultiFn clojure.lang.MultiFn@5d98c6f3>
(defmethod profit-based-affiliate-fee ["mint.com" :rating/premier]
  [user] (fee-amount 0.05M user))
;=> #<MultiFn clojure.lang.MultiFn@5d98c6f3>
```

Now add two methods matching `:rating/premier` to replace previous four

```
(defmethod profit-based-affiliate-fee ["google.com" :rating/premier]
  [user] (fee-amount 0.03M user))
;=> #<MultiFn clojure.lang.MultiFn@5d98c6f3>
(map profit-based-affiliate-fee [user-1 user-2 user-3 user-4])
;=> (30.0000M 32.0000M 27.0000M 14.0000M)
```

> **Check if you get same results**

> **You do!**

Not only have you removed some duplicate code, but you've also captured more precisely the intention of the business rules and protected the code against future changes to the profit-rating levels. So subtype polymorphism allowed you to reduce code duplication by sharing implementations (something it's especially good at), but it also introduces some complexity that you'll learn to manage in the next section.

Multiple-dispatch and :default

A subtlety of the `:default` case is that it's used only when an *entire* dispatch fails; it's not substituted for *individual* values of a multiple-dispatch vector. The reason is that `(isa? x :default)` is never true for any x (except `:default` itself), so you can't specify a dispatch value like `["mint.com" :default]` and expect it to match when no other more-specific rating matches. Instead, you must explicitly link the value to some base type, as you did with `:rating/ANY`, and use it as your fallback case in multiple dispatch.

This also means that you can't specify a default case for the `:referrer` slot (for example, `"mint.com"`) because you're using strings. You need to call `(derive "mint.com" :referrer/ANY)` to create a default case but derive only works with keywords, symbols, and classes, not strings. A workaround is either to create a keyword dynamically in the dispatch function (for example, `(keyword "site" (:referrer user)))` and match on that instead or to have the `:default` implementation invoke `(get-method profit-based-affiliate-fee [:site/ANY (:rating user)])` to force a specific dispatch value and call the matching method it returns.

RESOLVING METHOD AMBIGUITIES

There's a downside to using subtyping with multiple dispatch: it introduces the possibility of ambiguity. This is best demonstrated by an example. Suppose your expense-tracking service has gotten so popular that it has expanded to become a massive multiplayer online role-playing game. You still have your users and profit ratings, but now you want users to be able to size up other users before going into battle. Here's a first draft of the size-up multimethod, which takes two users—an observer and an observed—and returns a description of the observer for the observed:

```
(defmulti size-up (fn [observer observed]
  [(:rating observer) (:rating observed)]))
;=> #'user/size-up
(defmethod size-up [:rating/platinum :rating/ANY] [_ observed]
  (str (:login observed) " seems scrawny."))
;=> #<MultiFn clojure.lang.MultiFn@50e0a48d>
```

> **Everyone should look scrawny to platinum users.**

But what
happens if
a platinum
user looks
at another
platinum
user?

```
(defmethod size-up [:rating/ANY :rating/platinum] [_ observed]
  (str (:login observed) " shimmers with an unearthly light."))
;=> #<MultiFn clojure.lang.MultiFn@50e0a48d>
(size-up {:rating :rating/platinum} user-4)
IllegalArgumentException Multiple methods in multimethod 'size-up' match
dispatch value: [:rating/platinum :rating/platinum] -> [:rating/ANY :rating/
platinum] and [:rating/platinum :rating/ANY], and neither is preferred
clojure.lang.MultiFn.findAndCacheBestMethod (MultiFn.java:182)
```

**Platinum users should look
imposing to everyone.**

The problem here is that the type system, combined with multiple dispatch, introduces an ambiguity about which method implementation should be used: Do platinum users look scrawny to other platinum users, or do they shimmer with an unearthly light like themselves?

Suppose you decide that platinum users should shimmer to other platinum users, not look scrawny. There are a few ways you could remove the ambiguity. First, you could avoid the use of :rating/ANY in the scrawny defmethod and instead enumerate every rating that isn't platinum. But this means you've duplicated code again: you need a defmethod for at least :rating/basic and :rating/gold, and they both will have the same body. Further, you need to remember to add more cases if more profit ratings are added in the future. A second possibility is to add an explicit [:rating/platinum :rating/platinum] method, but this also means you'll need to duplicate the "shimmers" code.

Clojure offers a third possibility: you can explicitly prefer one implementation over another using the prefer-method function. This function takes the multimethod and a pair of dispatch values and instructs the multimethod to prefer the first dispatch value over the second when there's an ambiguity between the two. Here's an example:

Now
Celeste
shimmers!

```
(prefer-method size-up [:rating/ANY :rating/platinum]
  [:rating/platinum :rating/ANY])
;=> #<MultiFn clojure.lang.MultiFn@50e0a48d>
(size-up {:rating :rating/platinum} user-4)
;=> "celeste shimmers with an unearthly light."
(prefers size-up)
;=> {[:rating/ANY :rating/platinum] #{[:rating/platinum :rating/ANY]}}
```

**When size-up can't
decide between these
two dispatch values,
prefer first one.**

**prefers shows all of a
multimethod's preferences.**

Using prefer-method you're able both to avoid duplicate code and to future-proof it against modifications to the rating hierarchy.

You've now learned all there is to know about multimethods except for one last rarely used feature, which we'll examine next.

USER-DEFINED HIERARCHIES

All the multimethods we've defined and the hierarchies you've derived so far have been inspecting and mutating a single, program-wide global hierarchy. In most cases this is fine, but Clojure's multimethods also allow you to create your own blank hierarchy and use it explicitly instead of using the invisible global hierarchy. Most of the macros and functions we've introduced in this chapter also accept an optional hierarchy argument, which you can create with the `make-hierarchy` function. Here's a whirlwind tour of its use:

```
(def myhier (make-hierarchy))
;=> #'user/myhier
myhier
;=> {:parents {}, :descendants {}, :ancestors {}}
(derive myhier :a :letter)
;=> {:parents {:a #{:letter}}, :ancestors {:a #{:letter}},
     :descendants {:letter #{:a}}}
myhier
;=> {:parents {}, :descendants {}, :ancestors {}}
(def myhier (-> myhier
                (derive :a :letter)
                (derive :b :letter)
                (derive :c :letter)))
;=> #'user/myhier
(isa? myhier :a :letter)
;=> true
(parents myhier :a)
;=> #{:letter}
(defmulti letter? identity :hierarchy #'myhier)
;=> #'user/letter?
(defmethod letter? :letter [_] true)
;=> #<MultiFn clojure.lang.MultiFn@17c26ef7>
(letter? :d)
IllegalArgumentException No method in multimethod 'letter?' for dispatch
value: :d  clojure.lang.MultiFn.getFn (MultiFn.java:160)
(def myhier (derive myhier :d :letter))
;=> #'user/myhier
(letter? :d)
;=> true
```

Hierarchies are just ordinary maps.

Three-arg `derive` doesn't return `nil`.

Unlike two-arg `derive` it doesn't mutate.

Need to redef to "mutate" hierarchy

Notice keywords without namespaces

`isa?` can also take a hierarchy ...

... as can `parents`, `ancestors`, `descendants`, and `underive`

`defmulti` has a `:hierarchy` option that takes a var.

Taking a var allows mutation.

There are a few important differences between this code with an explicit hierarchy and the code you've been writing up until now using the global hierarchy. First, you call `make-hierarchy` to create a new (empty) hierarchy. A hierarchy is really just a map with three familiar-looking keys—it's not anything special. Second, `derive` and `underive` have three-argument forms that accept a hierarchy, but these don't return `nil` like their two-argument forms. Instead, they return a *new* hierarchy map and don't mutate the existing map. Third, notice that the three-argument form of `derive` doesn't require namespaced keywords; because the hierarchy is empty and isolated there isn't as much concern about type name collisions as there is in the global namespace. Fourth, a multimethod is created to use a custom hierarchy by calling `defmulti` with the `:hierarchy` keyword option. You must pass the hierarchy as a *var*, not a plain map. It would be impossible to change the type hierarchy later if you were to pass a plain (immutable) map. Instead you pass a var containing the hierarchy map, and the multimethod `derefs` it every time it needs to call `isa?`. This is demonstrated in the previous code by adding the `:d` type to the hierarchy after defining the method: note that the change is seen by `letter?`.

Why would you ever want to create your own hierarchy? There are two primary reasons. The first is hierarchy isolation: if you use an independent hierarchy, you're never in danger of someone's code accidentally changing your type relationships while manipulating the global hierarchy. In fact, it's even possible to make your type hierarchy completely nonextensible simply by making it private to your library and inaccessible to other namespaces (for example, by using `^:private` or a closure). This allows other code to add their own *methods* but not their own *types*, which may occasionally be desirable. Because hierarchies are isolated, `derive`'s three-argument form also relaxes the requirement that your types have a namespace, so you can name your types bare keywords like `:letter`. Note, however, that your own hierarchies are *not* isolated from the *Java* type hierarchy! `(isa? (make-hierarchy) java.lang.String java.lang.Object)` still returns `true`!

The second reason you might want your own hierarchy is if multiple methods share the same *types* but dispatch according to different (possibly contradictory) *type hierarchies*. A classic example is circles and ellipses: an `area` function may be able to say that a `:circle` is a kind of `:ellipse` and use the same formula ($2\pi wh$) to calculate the area for both, but a `stretch` function may need to make the opposite assumption and implement ellipse-stretching as a special case of circle-stretching.[1] Separate multimethod hierarchies are used very rarely in Clojure, but they're available if you need them.

4.3 Summary

We began this chapter by defining polymorphism as the ability to use multiple types as though they were the same—to substitute one type for another without changing code. We then distinguished three different kinds of polymorphism: parametric, ad hoc, and subtype. Parametric polymorphism is where the types aren't mentioned at all; ad hoc is where multiple implementations name types explicitly but provide a parametric interface; subtype is where types are placed in a hierarchy so they can share implementations transparently.

We then introduced multimethods in the context of ad hoc polymorphism and showed how they enable explicit mapping of types to implementations (via a dispatch function and value) but are still extensible with new types from the outside (called *open dispatch*). We then showed how you could dispatch with multiple different values at the same time (called *multiple dispatch*).

We then discussed how multimethods have subtype polymorphism features as well because they allow you to build your own type hierarchies with `derive` that are

---

[1] The discussion of whether a circle is an ellipse or vice versa is so classic in subtype polymorphism and object-oriented programming that it has its own name: the circle–ellipse problem; see http://en.wikipedia.org/wiki/Circle-ellipse_problem.

matched with `isa?`. You were able to combine subtype polymorphism with multiple dispatch to eliminate duplicated code. But this introduced the possibility of dispatch values with ambiguous method implementations, but you were able to resolve these ambiguities using `prefer-method`. Finally, you saw that it's possible for each multimethod to have its own independent type hierarchy.

This chapter covered an interesting feature of Clojure, and using it in the right situation will make your programs richer. The next chapter will focus on another great capability of Clojure: seamless interoperability with Java code.

5

Exploring Clojure and Java interop

This chapter covers

- Introducing Clojure's Java interop functionality
- Calling Java from Clojure
- Compiling Clojure down to bytecode
- Calling Clojure from Java

Java is the new COBOL. This pronouncement has been made year after year for a few years now, but it hasn't quite come to pass. Java was originally designed in the early 1990s, was officially released in the mid-1990s, and went on to become one of the most significant technologies of its time. Today, the Java stack is one of the most popular in the industry. It isn't going away anytime soon.

With the sheer amount of Java code in production (and more being written every day), no modern programming language can hope to succeed without being able to interoperate with it. Rich Hickey chose well when he picked the Java virtual machine (JVM) to host the Clojure language. Not only does Clojure benefit from the state-of-the-art technology (raw performance, HotSpot, just-in-time compilation, adaptive optimization, garbage collection, and more), but it also makes the goal of seamless Java interoperability easier to achieve. The result is that Java interop with Clojure is both elegant and easy to use. We'll explore this facility in this chapter.

We'll start out by demonstrating how to use Java classes from Clojure code. Clojure provides a lot of convenient macros that make the resulting code simple and clean. After that, we'll show how Clojure code can be converted into Java bytecode via the compilation facility provided by Clojure. Before wrapping up this chapter, we'll take a brief look at how Clojure code can be called from Java programs.

This chapter talks about several macros that are provided by the Clojure language. You've seen a few macros already, even though we haven't examined them in detail yet. For now, you can think of these as features of the language itself. Once you learn how to write your own macros in chapter 7, you'll be able to appreciate the elegance of the macros from this chapter even more. In any case, by the end of this chapter, you'll have mastered another extremely powerful feature of Clojure— that of being able to use the extensive set of Java libraries out there from within your Clojure programs.

5.1   Calling Java from Clojure

The availability of a good set of standard libraries can make or break a programming language. This is why Clojure has such a great advantage; being hosted on the JVM means that programs have instant access to literally thousands of libraries and frameworks. It's a bit like having the privilege of living most of your programming life in the advanced environment of Clojure but being able to cherry-pick any Java library to use when you need to.

You can do pretty much everything you need to do in Java from within Clojure. We'll explore the most common tasks you might need to do in the following sections, including the following:

- Creating new instances of Java classes
- Accessing methods and fields of Java objects
- Implementing interfaces and extending classes
- Compiling Clojure code

So let's begin our exploration of Clojure's Java interop features by learning how to use external Java classes in your programs.

5.1.1   Importing Java classes into Clojure

Writing large programs in any language quickly reaches a point where code needs to be organized into logical units. This is a simple way of managing complexity, because it breaks things down into more understandable chunks of code. In Clojure, the basic unit of code organization is namespaces, which we explored in chapter 3. We also showed how to `require` and `use` namespaces. In Java, the analogous unit of code organization is called the *package*. The `import` macro is used to import complete packages or specific classes from inside packages into Java programs that need them. In keeping with that, Clojure also provides the import function. Here's the general form:

```
(import & import-symbols-or-lists)
```

As you can tell, import takes a variable number of arguments. Each argument can be either

- A sequence, where the first part of the list is a Java package name, followed by the names of those classes from inside that package that you want to import
- A symbol naming the Java package-qualified class name

Here's an example:

```
(import 'java.util.Date 'java.text.SimpleDateFormat)
```

This makes the Date and SimpleDateFormat classes available to the rest of the code in the namespace. Notice the quote (') reader macro to instruct the runtime not to evaluate the symbol. Similarly, the following imports the Date and Set classes, both from the java.util package:

```
(import '[java.util Date Set])
```

The recommended way to import Java classes into a namespace is to use the :import option in the namespace declaration:

```
(ns com.clojureinaction.book
  (:import (java.util Set Date)))
```

Typically, when you're playing at the read-evaluate-print loop (REPL), you can use the import form directly, and when you're ready to write the code in your actual source files, you can convert them to the namespace form just shown. Once classes have been imported, they can be used easily in the rest of the code.

5.1.2 Creating instances

Here you'll create a new instance of a Java class. Consider the following code:

```
(import '(java.text SimpleDateFormat))
(def sdf (new SimpleDateFormat "yyyy-MM-dd"))
```

After the call to def, the sdf var has a root binding that's a new instance of the class SimpleDateFormat. The new special form works similarly to the new keyword in Java: it accepts a class name and arguments that can be applied to a matching constructor.

Clojure also has an alternative to using the new form via its support of a special notation for symbols containing a dot (.). If the first symbol in a list ends with a dot, that symbol is assumed to be a class name, and the call is assumed to be to a constructor of that class. The remaining symbols are assumed to be arguments to the matching constructor. This form gets converted into the equivalent new form.

Here's the previous example again, rewritten to use this macro syntax:

```
(def sdf (SimpleDateFormat. "yyyy-MM-dd"))
```

Note the dot at the end of `SimpleDateFormat.`.

Now that you know how to create new Java objects, let's examine accessing their members.

5.1.3 *Accessing methods and fields*

In Java, member access refers to accessing methods and fields of objects. Doing this from within Clojure is easy because Clojure provides another convenient dot macro to do this. Consider the following code:

```
(defn date-from-date-string [date-string]
  (let [sdf (SimpleDateFormat. "yyyy-MM-dd")]
    (.parse sdf date-string)))
```

You first create a `SimpleDateFormat` object as you did earlier. To call the `parse` method on that object, you use the dot form by prefixing a dot to the symbol `parse`. The first operand in that form is the object of the `parse` method you're calling. The remaining operands are arguments to the `parse` instance method.

STATIC METHODS
Calling static methods on classes is slightly different but just as easy:

```
(Long/parseLong "12321")
```

Here, `parseLong` is a static method on the class `Long`, which accepts a string containing a long number. This example returns `12321` as an instance of `java.lang.Long`. Note that you don't have to import the `java.lang.Long` class. This is because all `java.lang.*` classes are already loaded by the Clojure runtime. Calling a static method in general has the following form:

```
(Classname/staticMethod args*)
```

The first element of this list is a class name and static method combination like `Long/parseLong`, whereas the remaining elements in the list are arguments to that method.

STATIC FIELDS
Accessing static fields is similar to calling static methods. Here's an example: Let's say you want to do work with Java dates. In this example, you'll access the static fields `JANUARY` and `FEBRUARY` from the `Calendar` class:

```
(import '(java.util Calendar))
;=> java.util.Calendar
Calendar/JANUARY
;=> 0
Calendar/FEBRUARY
;=> 1
```

These two examples access the static fields JANUARY and FEBRUARY from the Calendar class.

You've now seen how easy it is to access regular methods as well as static ones and also to get at static fields from within Java objects and classes. Next, let's look at the dot special form provided by Clojure to make Java access easier.

5.1.4 *Macros and the dot special form*

In Clojure, all underlying Java access is done via the dot special form. The macro forms we just discussed get converted into forms using this dot special form. The Clojure documentation says that the dot special form can be read as "in the scope of." This means that the member access happens in the scope of the value of the first symbol.

Let's examine how it works. Consider the following pair of general forms:

```
(. ClassnameSymbol methodSymbol args*)
(. ClassnameSymbol (methodSymbol args*))
```

These forms allow static methods to be called on classes specified as the first argument. Here's an example of using them:

```
(. System getenv "PATH")
(. System (getenv "PATH"))
```

Both these forms return the system path as a string. The second form uses parentheses to enclose the name of the method being called. This is convenient when such a call is being made inside other macros. Typically in code, if you use the dot special form directly, the first form is preferred, but inside macros or while generating code, the second form is okay. Having said that, idiomatic code uses the form described in the previous section.

Now let's look at another example that's similar but operates on instances of Java classes (objects) as opposed to classes. Here are the general forms:

```
(. instanceExpr methodSymbol args*)
(. instanceExpr (methodSymbol args*))
```

Say you want to write a function that will return a number randomly picked between 0 and 10. The following example illustrates both these forms:

```
(import '(java.util Random))
;=> java.util.Random
(def rnd (Random.))
;=> #'user/rnd
(. rnd nextInt 10)
;=> 4
(. rnd (nextInt 10))
;=> 3
```

The second form, with the extra parentheses, is useful when this kind of call is made inside other macros. Also as pointed out in the previous section, when using the dot special form in this way, the first option is preferred. The forms described in the previous section are the idiomatic way to access members of Java objects.

Finally, consider the following two general forms:

```
(. ClassnameSymbol memberSymbol)
(. instanceExpr memberSymbol)
```

These access public fields from either a class or an instance of a class. Here's an example of accessing a static field from the `Calendar` class that you saw earlier, rewritten using the dot special form:

```
(. Calendar DECEMBER)
```

Now that you've seen how the dot special form works, it's worth repeating that it's idiomatic to use the regular forms as described in the previous section. The dot special form is usually reserved for use within macros. We'll now look at another couple of convenience macros, the dot-dot macro (two dots) and `doto`.

.. (DOT-DOT)

Java code tends to be verbose. It isn't only the syntax; the mutable state, its idea of object orientation, and the lack of higher-order functions all contribute to its verbosity. One common pattern is a sequence of dot method calls that need to be chained together, each operating on the result of the previous one. The `..` (dot-dot) macro helps with this.

Consider the following code snippet:

```
(import '(java.util Calendar TimeZone))
;=> java.util.TimeZone
(. (. (Calendar/getInstance) (getTimeZone)) (getDisplayName))
;=> "Pacific Standard Time"
```

May vary on your system

But writing that code is a bit unwieldy—where the dots and the brackets go can get confusing. Imagine if you had another method call to make! You can simplify this by using the form without the extra parentheses as described earlier, to make it a little cleaner:

```
(. (. (Calendar/getInstance) getTimeZone) getDisplayName)
```

This is better, but not by much. This is where the dot-dot form comes in. It's a convenient macro that chains together method calls. The previous code can be rewritten using this macro as follows:

```
(.. (Calendar/getInstance) (getTimeZone) (getDisplayName))
```

This can be simplified (without the extra parentheses, because you're passing no arguments to either the `getTimeZone` or `getDisplayName` methods) to the following:

```
(.. (Calendar/getInstance) getTimeZone getDisplayName)
```

If you were using method signatures that accepted arguments, you'd do so as follows:

```
(.. (Calendar/getInstance)
  getTimeZone
  (getDisplayName true TimeZone/SHORT))
```

This might return something like "PDT", again depending on where you are. Note that the code reads better, too, because the sequence of method calls is clearer. Having examined this convenience macro, let's look at another way to write clearer code in such situations.

DOTO

The doto macro helps you write code where multiple methods are called on the same Java object. Consider this contrived function that starts with the current time and works out the most recent midnight using the set method of java.util.Calendar objects:

```
(import '(java.util Calendar))
(defn the-past-midnight-1 []
  (let [calendar-obj (Calendar/getInstance)]
    (.set calendar-obj Calendar/AM_PM Calendar/AM)
    (.set calendar-obj Calendar/HOUR 0)
    (.set calendar-obj Calendar/MINUTE 0)
    (.set calendar-obj Calendar/SECOND 0)
    (.set calendar-obj Calendar/MILLISECOND 0)
    (.getTime calendar-obj)))
```

As you can see, there's tedious repetition of the symbol calendar-obj in this code. The doto macro eliminates this sort of duplication. Here's an example:

```
(defn the-past-midnight-2 []
  (let [calendar-obj (Calendar/getInstance)]
    (doto calendar-obj
      (.set Calendar/AM_PM Calendar/AM)
      (.set Calendar/HOUR 0)
      (.set Calendar/MINUTE 0)
      (.set Calendar/SECOND 0)
      (.set Calendar/MILLISECOND 0))
    (.getTime calendar-obj)))
```

In general, it accepts a symbol followed by a body of forms. The symbol is spliced into the form without the doto. This kind of macro used to eliminate duplication is quite common in Clojure code.

5.1.5   *Helpful Clojure macros for working with Java*

Before wrapping up this section, let's look at a couple of macros that make life easier when dealing with Java code. We'll first talk about memfn, which is a convenient way to convert Java instance methods into Clojure functions. We'll then cover bean, a super-convenient way to convert a Java bean object into a Clojure map.

MEMFN

Let's say you wanted to collect the byte arrays that compose a few strings. Here's how you might do it:

```
(map (fn [x] (.getBytes x)) ["amit" "rob" "kyle"])
```

This can be simplified using the reader macro for anonymous functions:

```
(map #(.getBytes %) ["amit" "rob" "kyle"])
```

Creating this anonymous function is necessary because an instance method like getBytes can't be used as a regular higher-order Clojure function. The reason is that when the code is read, Clojure (and Java) doesn't know which method with the name getBytes you mean—it could be from any class that defines a method with this name or even a method that takes a different number or type of arguments. (Remember, in Java String.getBytes(), String.getBytes(Charset charset), and String.getBytes(String string) are all different methods!) To disambiguate getBytes to the no-argument method of java.lang.String, Clojure needs to see an object instance at runtime or know what Java class it will be at compile time using type hints.

But there's a convenient macro called memfn (which stands for member-as-function) that makes it easy to convert an instance member call into a Clojure function. The previous use of the higher-order function map is a typical example of such use. Here's an example of using memfn:

```
(memfn getBytes)
```

Clojure will determine the method to call at runtime using Java reflection on the instance it sees. But if you include a type hint, Clojure will avoid using runtime reflection and emit the call to the correct method directly at compile time for increased performance. Here's an example using reflection:

```
(memfn ^String getBytes)
```

Using it in the context of map, for instance, looks like this:

```
(map (memfn getBytes) ["amit" "rob" "kyle"])
```

memfn also works with member functions that accept more than one argument. Consider the following call to the subSequence member function on a String object:

```
(.subSequence "Clojure" 2 5)
;=> "oju"
```

The equivalent form with optional type hints is

```
((memfn ^String subSequence ^Long start ^Long end) "Clojure" 2 5)
;=> "oju"
```

The Clojure function returned by the call to (memfn subSequence start end) can be used as a regular function in all the usual constructs. Now we'll look at bean, another function that's quite useful when working with Java code.

BEAN

bean is a convenient function that's useful when dealing with Java code, especially JavaBeans, which are classes that conform to a simple standard involving exposing their data via getter and setter methods. Instead of having to deal with calling the getters via the macros described previously (which can get tedious rather quickly if you're dealing with large objects), you could use the Clojure-provided bean function to convert the object into a hash map. Consider the following examples:

```
(bean (Calendar/getInstance))
```

This returns a Clojure map that contains all its bean properties. Being a Clojure data structure, it's immutable. It looks like the following:

```
{:timeInMillis 1257466522295,
 :minimalDaysInFirstWeek 1,
 :lenient true,
 :firstDayOfWeek 1,
 :class java.util.GregorianCalendar
;; other properties
}
```

This map is a lot easier to work with when compared to calling getters on the original object. Next we'll look at Clojure's mechanism for dealing with arrays.

> **Number of parentheses**
>
> People often talk about the sheer number of parentheses that Clojure uses. Despite the advantages this syntax offers, first-time Clojure programmers can find the code a bit hard to read.
>
> This is why it's somewhat amusing to note that when compared to Java code, Clojure code often has fewer parentheses, all used and placed in a consistent and regular manner. It's true that the placement of the parentheses is different, but it's a point worth noticing.

ARRAYS

A Java array is a container object that holds values of the same type. It's a random-access data structure that uses integers as its keys. Although not used as often as other container classes from the standard Java library, it's rather common in Java programs. Clojure has native support for dealing with Java arrays. Consider the following snippet:

```
(def tokens (.split "clojure.in.action" "\\."))
```

tokens is a Java array of String objects.

Let's now look at a few of the functions that Clojure provides that help in working with Java arrays:

- (alength tokens)—alength returns the size of the array, which in this case returns 3.
- (aget tokens 2)—aget returns the element of the array at the index specified, which in this case returns the string "action".
- (aset tokens 2 "actionable")—This mutates the tokens array so that the last token is now actionable.

It's worth remembering at this point that unlike any of Clojure's core data structures, Java arrays are mutable—as are most objects in Java. You'll see in chapter 6 how mutability can cause problems in multithreaded programs, and you'll also learn about Clojure's approach to dealing with concurrency.

Clojure provides several other functions that allow sequences to be converted into Java arrays (to-array, to array 2d, and into-array) and one that allows arbitrary new Java arrays to be created (make-array). There are also array-specific versions of the previously seen map and reduce functions, called amap and areduce.

All these functions make working with Java arrays easy. Having said that, because arrays need special handling and are a bit unwieldy compared to regular sequences, you should limit their use to situations where they're absolutely needed.

We've covered quite a few aspects of Clojure's support for interoperating with the world of Java code. We're nearly finished; the last thing we'll discuss is how to implement Java interfaces and extend Java classes from within Clojure code. By the end of the next section, you'll have a mostly complete Java interop toolkit under your belt.

5.1.6 *Implementing interfaces and extending classes*

When working with Java libraries and frameworks, it's often necessary to define new classes that implement certain interfaces or extend certain classes. It would be a shame if any of that required writing Java code. Luckily, Clojure has a macro called proxy that allows you to do this from within Clojure code.

MOUSEADAPTER

Consider, for instance, the good-old MouseAdapter. This is a class you might use while creating a GUI program using Java. It's an adapter class that implements several event listener interfaces with default (do-nothing) implementations. This class is useful when creating GUI programs with the Abstract Windowing Toolkit (AWT) library. Let's explore the following method on this class:

```
void mousePressed(MouseEvent e)
```

Here's a simple example of creating an implementation of the MouseAdapter class:

```
(import 'java.awt.event.MouseAdapter)
(proxy [MouseAdapter] []
  (mousePressed [event]
    (println "Hey!")))
```

The general form of the proxy macro is

```
(proxy [class-and-interfaces] [args] fs+)
```

This shows that the proxy form accepts a vector of Java classes and interfaces, followed by a vector of arguments (possibly empty) that will be passed to the superclass constructor, followed by any methods being defined. In the previous example, the Mouse-Adapter interface is specified, and the method mousePressed is implemented.

REIFY

There's another way to implement Java interfaces, and that's using the reify macro. We'll study this macro in more detail in chapter 9, but here's a simplified version of its interface:

```
(reify specs*)
```

Here, specs consist of an interface name, followed by zero or more method bodies. For instance, here's an example of creating an instance of Java's FileFilter interface:

```
(reify java.io.FileFilter
  (accept [this f]
    (.isDirectory f)))
```

You can have any number of interface and method body definitions within a call to reify. Again, reify does a lot more, and you'll see it in action again soon.

This section was quite dense and filled with a lot of detail! You should now be in a position to use any kind of Java library in your Clojure programs. This is a great feature of the Clojure language and is quite critical to writing real-world programs.

Now that you understand Clojure's support for Java interoperability, you'll generate some static Java classes from Clojure code.

5.2   *Compiling Clojure code to Java bytecode*

As you saw in chapter 1, Clojure doesn't have an interpreter. Code is evaluated one s-expression at a time. During that process, if something needs to be compiled, the Clojure runtime does so. Ultimately, because Clojure is hosted on the JVM, everything is converted to Java bytecode before execution, and the programmer doesn't have to worry about when and how this happens.

Clojure provides a mechanism to do this compilation ahead of time (AOT). AOT compilation has its advantages. Packaging the code lets you deliver it as class files (and without including the source code) for use by other Java applications, and it speeds up the program's startup time. In this section, we'll examine how to AOT compile Clojure code.

5.2.1   *Example: A tale of two calculators*

Let's examine some code that implements a couple of financial calculators that you might use to manage investments in stocks and bonds. We'll lay out the code in a

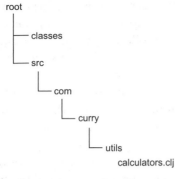

Figure 5.1 **Typical organization of a Clojure project. The src directory contains the source code, organized in a similar way to Java packages.**

directory structure for easy organization—one that's somewhat idiomatic in the Clojure world. Figure 5.1 shows this organization.

Note that calculators.clj is located in the src/com/curry/utils directory and is the file that contains the namespace of our current interest. Here are the contents:

```
(ns com.curry.utils.calculators
  (:gen-class))
(defn present-value [data]
  (println "calculating present value..."))
```

The :gen-class directive used in the namespace declaration is used to generate a named class for this namespace when compiled. You can compile this code from a REPL that has both classes and src directories on the classpath. The compile function is used to do this, and it accepts the namespace to be compiled:

```
(compile 'com.curry.utils.calculators)
```

If successful, this function returns the name of the namespace that was compiled. Let's now examine what the output of this compilation process is, what class files are generated, and where they're located.

GENERATED CLASSES

As noted, the compile function compiles the specified namespace. In this case, it generates class files for the com.curry.utils.calculators namespace. Three class files that get generated here are calculators_init.class, calculators.class, and calculators$present_value__xx.class, and they're located in the classes/com/curry/utils directory.

Generated classes using Leiningen
The paths of generated classes described here are the defaults for the raw Clojure REPL. If you're using Clojure through Leiningen as we suggest in appendix A, then your generated classes will have the same paths but be under the target/ directory instead of the root. For example, instead of being under classes/com/curry/utils (raw Clojure REPL), generated classes will be under target/classes/com/curry/utils. This difference is governed by the *compile-path* dynamic var explained shortly.

A class file is created for each Clojure function. In this case, the `present-value` function causes the calculators$present_value__xx.class file to be created, the name of which will vary each time the namespace is recompiled (because it's a generated name). A class file is also generated for each `gen-class`, and in this case this corresponds to the calculators.class file.

Finally, the class files that have the __init in their names contain a loader class, and one such file is generated for every Clojure source file. Typically, this loader class doesn't need to be referenced directly, because `use`, `require`, and `load` all figure out which file to use when they're called.

`:gen-class` has a lot of options that allow control over various aspects of the generated code. These are explored in section 5.2.2. Now that we've covered the basics of compilation, you'll try to compile a namespace that's spread across files.

ADDITIONAL FILES

Here you'll add a couple more calculators to the `calculators` namespace. You'll create two more files to do this, one for each new calculator function. The resulting file structure is shown in figure 5.2.

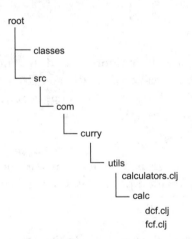

Figure 5.2 Adding two new files, dcf.clj and fcf.clj, in a subdirectory of utils that have code for the same `com.curry.utils.calculators` namespace.

The contents of dcf.clj are

```
(in-ns 'com.curry.utils.calculators)
(defn discounted-cash-flow [data]
  (println "calculating discounted cash flow..."))
```

And the contents of fcf.clj are

```
(in-ns 'com.curry.utils.calculators)
(defn free-cash-flow [data]
  (println "calculating free cash flow..."))
```

Note that they both use in-ns to ensure that these files all belong to the same namespace. calculators.clj is modified as follows:

```
(ns com.curry.utils.calculators
  (:gen-class))
(load "calc/fcf")
(load "calc/dcf")
(defn present-value [data]
  (println "calculating present value..."))
```

Note the use of load using relative paths, because the fcf.clj and dcf.clj files are inside the calc subdirectory of utils. Calling compile, as you did before, results in new class files being generated in the classes directory. Two files, namely dcf__init.class and fcf__init.class, are generated in the classes/com/curry/utils/calc directory. New files are also created for the new functions, namely discounted-cash-flow and free-cash-flow, in the classes/com/curry/utils directory.

COMPILE-PATH

In case you're curious as to why the generated code is being output to the classes directory, it's because it's the default value of the global var *compile-path*. It's easy to change this by calling set! to alter the value of the var or to call compile inside a binding form with *compile-path* bound to something appropriate. The thing to remember is that the directory must exist, and it should be on the classpath.

5.2.2 *Creating Java classes and interfaces using gen-class and gen-interface*

Clojure also has a standalone utility for generating Java classes and interfaces in the gen-class and gen-interface macros. (gen-interface works in a similar fashion to gen-class but has fewer options because it's limited to defining an interface.) When code containing these calls is compiled, it generates bytecode for the specified classes or interfaces and writes them into class files, as you saw earlier.

In this section, you'll see an example of how gen-class works. Consider the following listing, which is a contrived example of an abstract Java class that we'll use to illustrate gen-class.

Listing 5.1 An abstract Java class that will be used to illustrate gen-class

```
package com.gentest;
public abstract class AbstractJavaClass {
    public AbstractJavaClass(String a, String b) {
        System.out.println("Constructor: a, b");
    }
    public AbstractJavaClass(String a) {
        System.out.println("Constructor: a");
    }
    public abstract String getCurrentStatus();
```

```
    public String getSecret() {
        return "The Secret";
    }
}
```

Once `AbstractJavaClass` is compiled with `javac AbtractJavaClass.java`, the
AbstractJavaClass.class file needs to be on Clojure's classpath and in a subdirectory
that matches the package specification. For example, if target/classes/ is in the classpath, this class file needs to be at target/classes/com/gentest/AbstractJavaClass.class.
After ensuring that the Clojure runtime can see the class, you can use `gen-class` as
shown in this next listing.

Listing 5.2   `gen-class` generates a Java class to reference `AbstractJavaClass`

```
(ns com.gentest.gen-clojure
  (:import (com.gentest AbstractJavaClass))
  (:gen-class
    :name com.gentest.ConcreteClojureClass
    :extends com.gentest.AbstractJavaClass
    :constructors {[String] [String]
                   [String String] [String String]}
    :implements [Runnable]
    :init initialize
    :state localState
    :methods [[stateValue [] String]]))
(defn -initialize
  ([s1]
    (println "Init value:" s1)
    [[s1 "default"] (ref s1)])
  ([s1 s2]
    (println "Init values:"  s1 "," s2)
    [[s1 s2] (ref s2)]))
(defn -getCurrentStatus [this]
  "getCurrentStatus from - com.gentest.ConcreteClojureClass")
(defn -stateValue [this]
  @(.localState this))
(defn -run [this]
  (println "In run!")
  (println "I'm a" (class this))
  (dosync (ref-set (.localState this) "GO")))
(defn -main []
  (let [g (new com.gentest.ConcreteClojureClass "READY")]
    (println (.getCurrentStatus g))
    (println (.getSecret g))
    (println (.stateValue g)))
  (let [g (new com.gentest.ConcreteClojureClass "READY" "SET")]
    (println (.stateValue g))
    (.start (Thread. g))
    (Thread/sleep 1000)
    (println (.stateValue  g))))
```

Now, let's go over the code in listing 5.2 to understand what's going on. The call to
ns should be familiar by now. It uses `:import` to pull in `AbstractJavaClass` from

listing 5.1. This was why it needs to be on the classpath. The next option, `:gen-class`, is our primary interest. It can take several options, some of which are used in this example and some aren't. Table 5.1 describes the options used in listing 5.2.

Table 5.1 `gen-class` options used in listing 5.2

Option	Description
`:name`	The name of the class that will be generated when this namespace is compiled.
`:extends`	The fully qualified name of the superclass.
`:constructors`	Explicit specification of constructors via a map where each key is a vector of types that specifies a constructor signature. Values are similar vectors that identify the signature of a superclass constructor.
`:implements`	A vector of Java interfaces that the class implements.
`:init`	The name of a function that will be called with the arguments to the constructor. Must return a vector of two elements, the first being a vector of arguments to the superclass's constructor, and the second an object to contain the current instance's state (usually an atom).
`:methods`	Specifies the signatures of additional methods of the generated class. This is not needed for public methods defined in inherited interfaces or superclasses: `gen-class` will declare those automatically.

Functions such as `-initialize`, `-getCurrentStatus`, and `-run` implement or override interface or superclass methods. The reason they're prefixed with a dash (`-`) is so that they can be identified via convention. The prefix can be changed using the `:prefix` option (see table 5.2). Now that you understand what each option in the example does, you're ready to run it.

RUNNING THE EXAMPLE

Run (`compile 'com.gentest.gen-clojure`) from a REPL to create the Concrete-ClojureClass.class file like you did in the previous example. The classpath needs to have clojure.jar on it as well as the locations of AbstractJavaClass.class and ConcreteClojure-Class.class. The following command assumes the `CLASSPATH` environment variable has been set up appropriately. The command to test the generated class is

```
java com.gentest.ConcreteClojureClass
```

This outputs the following to the console:

```
Init value: READY
Constructor: a
getCurrentStatus from - com.gentest.ConcreteClojureClass
The Secret
READY
Init values: READY , SET
Constructor: a, b
SET
```

```
In run!
I'm a com.gentest.ConcreteClojureClass
GO
```

As the code shows, you've used both constructor signatures to create instances of the generated class. You've also called a superclass method getSecret and the overridden method getCurrentStatus. Finally, you've run the second instance as a thread and checked the mutating state localState, which changed from "SET" to "GO".

Table 5.2 shows the other options available to gen-class.

Table 5.2 More gen-class options

Option	Description
:post-init	Specifies a function by name that's called with the newly created instance as the first argument and each time an instance is created, after all constructors have run. Its return value is ignored.
:main	Specifies whether a main method should be generated so this class can be run as an application entry point from the command line. Defaults to true.
:factory	Specifies the name of the factory function(s) that will have the same signature as the constructors. A public final instance of the class will also be created. An :init function will also be needed to supply the initial state.
:exposes	Exposes protected fields inherited from the superclass. The value is a map where the keys are the name of the protected field and the values are maps specifying the names of the getters and setters. The format is :exposes {protected-field-name {:get name :set name}, ...}
:exposes-methods	Exposes overridden methods from the superclass via the specified name. The format of this option is :exposes-methods {super-method-name exposed-name, ...}
:prefix	Defaults to the dash (-). When methods like getCurrentStatus are called, they will be looked up by prefixing this value (for example, -getCurrentStatus).
:impl-ns	The name of the namespace in which to find method implementations. Defaults to the current namespace but can be specified here if the methods being implemented or overridden are in a different namespace.
:load-impl-ns	Whether the generated Java class will load its Clojure implementations when it's initialized. Defaults to true; can be turned to false if you need to load either the Clojure or the generated Java classes separately. (This is a specialized setting you're unlikely to need.)

This is quite an exhaustive set of options, and it lets the programmer influence nearly every aspect of the generated code.

LEININGEN AND JAVA PROJECTS
The Java and Clojure code you used to create the ConcreteClojureClass class is an example of a mixed Clojure and Java project. Leiningen makes managing such projects

much easier. You can instead create a project.clj like in listing 5.3 instead of invoking java, javac, and Clojure's `compile` function manually. With Leiningen all you need to do is place your source files in the right directories and execute `lein run` from the command line: this command will automatically compile AbstractJavaClass.java and the gen-classed `ConcreteClojureClass` in gen-clojure.clj and run the `main` method of `ConcreteClojureClass`.

Leiningen can alleviate much of the confusion and tedium out of managing Clojure projects, especially when the project mixes Java and Clojure code. Appendix A has more information on how to install Leiningen if you haven't been using it already.

Listing 5.3   Leiningen project file for `ConcreteClojureClass`

```
(defproject gentest "0.1.0"
  :dependencies [[org.clojure/clojure "1.6.0"]]

  ; Place our "AbstractJavaClass.java" and "gen-clojure.clj" files under
  ; the src/com/gentest directory.
  :source-paths ["src"]
  :java-source-paths ["src"]

  ; :aot is a list of clojure namespaces to compile.
  :aot [com.gentest.gen-clojure]

  ; This is the java class "lein run" should execute.
  :main com.gentest.ConcreteClojureClass)
```

Now that you've seen how to compile and generate Java code from the Clojure source, we're ready to move on. You're now going to see how to go the other way: to call Clojure functions from Java programs. This will allow you to write appropriate parts of your application in Clojure using all the facilities provided by the language and then use it from other Java code.

5.3   Calling Clojure from Java

One of the great things about most languages hosted on the JVM is that they can be embedded into other Java programs. This is useful when you need to script the larger system. Let's review how to call Clojure functions from Java code.

Consider the following Clojure function, defined in the `clj.script.examples` namespace:

```
(ns clj.script.examples)
(defn print-report [user-name]
  (println "Report for:" user-name)
  10)
```

If this Clojure code is in a file named clojure_script.clj, you can now call the `print-report` function from a Java method, as shown in the following code:

```
import clojure.lang.RT;
import clojure.lang.Var;
```

```
public class Driver {
    public static void main(String[] args) throws Exception {
        RT.loadResourceScript("clojure_script.clj");
        Var report = RT.var("clj.script.examples", "print-report");
        Integer result = (Integer) report.invoke("Siva");
        System.out.println("Result: " + result);
    }
}
```

You'll need to import `clojure.lang.RT` and `clojure.lang.Var` for this code to work. Here, RT is the class that represents the Clojure runtime. You initialize it by calling the static method `loadResourceScript` on the RT class. It accepts the name of the Clojure script file and loads the code defined within. The RT class also has a var static method, which accepts a namespace name along with a var name (both as strings). It looks up a var as specified and returns a var object, which can then be invoked using the `invoke` method. The `invoke` method can accept an arbitrary number of arguments.

As you can see, the basics of calling Clojure from Java are quite straightforward. This is by design; Clojure was created to embrace the JVM, and does so in a seamless, user-friendly manner.

5.4   Summary

This chapter explored Clojure's excellent support for interoperability with Java. This is an important feature, because it gives programmers instant access to thousands of libraries and frameworks. As you'll see in later parts of the book, this is a huge advantage when it comes to building real-world systems in Clojure. You can write your application-specific code in Clojure and use well-tested, production-quality Java libraries for infrastructure-related requirements—for example, accessing HBase (an open source implementation of Google's BigTable) and using RabbitMQ (an extremely fast messaging system).

This availability of a large number of battle-tested libraries and frameworks makes a huge difference to a language such as Clojure. Apart from making all this functionality available to use from Clojure, the Java interop also makes it possible to write code that coexists with and leverages existing investments in Java systems. This allows Clojure to be brought into environments and organizations in an incremental fashion. Lastly, the elegance of the interop makes it easy to use Java code from within Clojure. All these factors contribute to making Clojure's embrace of the Java platform a huge plus when considering the adoption of the language. In fact, once you're familiar with all the convenient features that Clojure provides for creating and using Java classes and objects, you might decide it's easier to work with Java code from Clojure than from Java itself!

In the next chapter we'll look at Clojure's features for handling state and concurrency.

State and the concurrent world

This chapter covers

- The problems with mutable state
- Clojure's approach to state
- Refs, agents, atoms, and vars
- Futures and promises

State—you're doing it wrong.

—Rich Hickey[1]

The preceding quote is from a presentation by Rich Hickey in which he discusses Clojure's approach to concurrency and state. He means that most languages use an approach to modeling state that doesn't work very well. To be precise, it used to work when computers were less powerful and ran programs in a single-threaded fashion, but in today's world of increasingly multicore and multi-CPU computers, the model has broken down. This is evidenced by the difficulty of writing bug-free multithreaded code in typical object-oriented (OO) languages like Java and C++.

---

[1] From a presentation at the Boston Lisp meeting, 2012, http://www.youtube.com/watch?v=7mbcYxHO 0nM&t=00h21m04s.

Still, programmers continue to make the attempt, because today's demands on software *require* that it take advantage of all available CPU cores. As software requirements grow in complexity, parallelism is becoming an implicit requirement.

This chapter is about concurrent programs and the problems they face in dealing with state. We'll first examine what these problems are and then look at the traditional solutions. We'll then look at Clojure's approach to dealing with these issues and show that when trying to solve difficult problems, it's sometimes worth starting with a fresh slate.

6.1 *The problem with state*

State is the current set of values associated with things in a program. For example, a payroll program might deal with employee objects. Each employee object represents the state of the employee, and every program usually has a lot of such state. There's no problem with state, per se, or even with mutating state. The real world is full of perceived changes: people change, plans change, the weather changes, and the balance in a bank account changes. The problem occurs when concurrent (multithreaded) programs share this sort of state among different threads and then attempt to make updates to it. When the illusion of single-threaded execution breaks down, the code encounters all manner of inconsistent data. In this section, we'll look at a solution to this problem. But before we do, let's recap the issues faced by concurrent programs operating on shared data.

6.1.1 *Common problems with shared state*

Most problems with multithreaded programs happen because changes to shared data aren't correctly protected. For the purposes of this chapter, we'll summarize the issues as follows.

LOST OR BURIED UPDATES

Lost updates occur when two threads update the same data one after the other. The update made by the first thread is lost because the second one overwrites it. A classic example is two threads incrementing a counter, the current value of which is 10. Because execution of threads is interleaved, both threads can do a read on the counter and think the value is 10, and then both increment it to 11. The problem is that the final value should have been 12, and the update done by one of the threads was lost.

DIRTY AND UNREPEATABLE READS

A dirty read happens when a thread reads data that another thread is in the process of updating. Before the one thread could completely update the data, the other thread has read inconsistent (dirty) data. Similarly, an unrepeatable read happens when a thread reads a particular data set, but because other threads are updating it, the thread can never do another read that results in it seeing the same data again.

PHANTOM READS

A phantom read happens when a thread reads data that's been deleted (or more data is added). The reading thread is said to have performed a phantom read because it has summarily read data that no longer exists.

Brian Goetz's book *Java Concurrency in Practice* (Addison-Wesley Professional, 2006) does an incredible job of throwing light on these issues. The book uses Java to illustrate examples, so it isn't directly useful, but it's still highly recommended.

6.1.2 Traditional solution

The most obvious solution to these problems is to impose a level of control on those parts of the code that deal with such mutable, shared data. This is done using locks, which are constructs that control the execution of sections of code, ensuring that only a single thread runs a lock-protected section of code at a time. When using locks, a thread can execute a destructive method (one that mutates data) that's protected with a lock only if it's able to first obtain an associated lock. If a thread tries to execute such code while some other thread holds the lock, it blocks until the lock becomes available again. The blocking thread is allowed to resume execution only after it obtains the lock at a later time.

This approach might seem reasonable, but it gets complicated the moment more than one piece of mutable data needs a coordinated change. When this happens, each thread that needs to make the change must obtain multiple locks, leading to more contention and resulting in concurrency problems. It's difficult to ensure correctness of multithreaded programs that have to deal with multiple mutating data structures. Further, finding and fixing bugs in such programs is difficult thanks to the inherently nondeterministic nature of multithreaded programs.

Still, programs of significant complexity have been written using locks. It takes a lot more time and money to ensure things work as expected and a larger maintenance budget to ensure things continue to work properly while changes are being made to the program. It makes you wonder if there isn't a better approach to solving this problem.

This chapter is about such an approach. Before we get into the meat of the solution, we'll examine a couple of things. First, we'll look at the general disadvantages of using locks in multithreaded programs. Then, we'll take a quick overview of the new issues that arise from the presence of locking.

DISADVANTAGES OF LOCKING

The most obvious disadvantage of locking is that code is less multithreaded than it was before the introduction of locks. When one thread obtains and holds a lock, no other thread can execute that code, causing other threads to wait. This can be wasteful, and it reduces throughput of multithreaded applications.

Further, locks are an excessive solution. Consider the case where a thread only wants to read some piece of mutable data. To ensure that no other thread makes changes while it's doing its work, the reader thread must lock all concerned mutable data. This causes not only writers to block but other readers too. This is unnecessarily wasteful.

Lastly, another disadvantage of locking is that you, the programmer, must *remember* to lock, and lock the right things, and in the right order. If someone introduces a bug that involves a forgotten lock, it can be difficult to track down and fix. There are no automatic mechanisms to flag this situation and no compile-time or runtime warnings associated with such situations, other than the fact that the program behaves in an unexpected manner! The knowledge of what to lock and in what order to lock things (so that the locks can be released in the reverse order) can't be expressed within program code—typically, it's recorded in technical documentation. Everyone in the software industry knows how well documentation works.

Unfortunately, these aren't the only disadvantages of using locking; it causes new problems too. We'll examine some of them now.

NEW PROBLEMS WITH LOCKING

When a single thread needs to change more than one piece of mutable data, it needs to obtain locks for all of them. This is the only way for a lock-based solution to ensure coordinated changes to multiple items. The fact that threads need to obtain locks to do their work causes contention for these locks. This contention results in a few issues that are typically categorized as shown in table 6.1.

Table 6.1   Issues that arise from the use of locks

Issue	Description
Deadlock	This is the case where two or more threads wait for the other to release locks that they need. This cyclic dependency results in all concerned threads being unable to proceed.
Starvation	This happens when a thread isn't allocated enough resources to do its job, causing it to starve and never complete.
Livelock	This is a special case of starvation, and it happens when two threads continue executing (that is, changing their states) but make no progress toward their final goal. Imagine two people meeting in a hallway and each trying to pass the other. If they both wait for the other to move, it results in a deadlock. If they both keep moving toward the other, they still end up blocking each other from passing. This situation results in a livelock, because they're both doing work and changing states but are still unable to proceed.
Race condition	This is a general situation where the interleaving of execution of threads causes an undesired computational result. Such bugs are difficult to debug because race conditions happen in relatively rare scenarios.

With all these disadvantages and issues that accompany the use of locks, you must wonder if there isn't a better solution to the problem of concurrency and state. We'll explore this in the next section, beginning with a fresh look at modeling state itself.

6.2 *Separating identities and values*

Now that we've explored the landscape of some of the common problems of concurrent programs and shared state, including the popular solution of locks, we're ready to examine an alternative point of view. Let's begin by reexamining a construct offered by most popular programming languages to deal with state—that of objects. OO languages like Java, C++, Ruby, and Python offer the notion of classes that contain state and related operations. The idea is to provide the means to encapsulate things to separate responsibility among various abstractions, allowing for cleaner design. This is a noble goal and is probably even achieved once in a while. But most languages have a flaw in this philosophy that causes problems when these same programs need to run as multithreaded applications. And most programs eventually do need multithreading, either because requirements change or to take advantage of multicore CPUs.

The flaw is that these languages conflate the idea of what Rich Hickey calls identity with that of state. Consider a person's favorite set of movies. As a child, this person's set might contain films made by Disney and Pixar. As a grownup, the person's set might contain other movies, such as ones directed by Tim Burton or Robert Zemeckis. The entity represented by favorite-movies changes over time. Or does it?

In reality, there are two different sets of movies. At one point (earlier), favorite-movies referred to the set containing children's movies; at another point (later), it referred to a different set that contained other movies. What changes over time, therefore, isn't the set itself but which set the entity favorite-movies refers to. Further, at any given point, a set of movies itself doesn't change. The timeline demands different sets containing different movies over time, even if some movies appear in more than one set.

To summarize, it's important to realize that we're talking about two distinct concepts. The first is that of an identity—someone's favorite movies. It's the subject of all the action in the associated program. The second is the sequence of values that this identity assumes over the course of the program. These two ideas give us an interesting definition of state—the value of an identity at a particular point time. This separation is shown in figure 6.1.

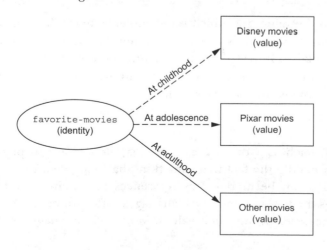

Figure 6.1 **It's important to recognize the separation between** *what* **we're talking about (say, favorite movies, which is an identity) and the** *values* **of that identity. The identity itself never changes, but it refers to different values over time.**

This idea of state is different from what traditional implementations of OO languages provide out of the box. For example, in a language like Java or Ruby, the minute a class is defined with stateful fields and destructive methods (those that change a part of the object), concurrency issues begin to creep into the world and can lead to many of the problems discussed earlier. This approach to state might have worked a few years ago when everything was single threaded, but it doesn't work anymore.

Now that you understand some of the terms involved, let's further examine the idea of using a series of immutable values to model the state of an identity.

6.2.1 *Immutable values*

An immutable object is one that can't change once it has been created. To simulate change, you'd have to create a whole new object and replace the old one. In the light of our discussion so far, this means that when the identity of favorite-movies is being modeled, it should be defined as a reference to an immutable object (a set, in this case). Over time, the reference would point to different (also immutable) sets. This ought to apply to objects of any kind, not only sets. Several programming languages already offer this mechanism in some of their data types, for instance, numbers and strings. As an example, consider the following assignment:

```
x = 101
```

Most languages treat the number 101 as an immutable value. Languages provide no constructs to do the following, for instance:

```
x.setUnitsDigit(3)
x.setTensDigit(2)
```

No one expects this to work, and no one expects this to be a way to transform 101 into 123. Instead, you might do the following:

```
x = 101 + 22
```

At this point, x points to the value 123, which is a completely new value and is also immutable. Some languages extend this behavior to other data types. For instance, Java strings are also immutable. In programs, the identity represented by x refers to different (immutable) numbers over time. This is similar to the concept of favorite-movies referring to different immutable sets over time.

6.2.2 *Objects and time*

As you've seen, objects (such as x or favorite-movies) don't have to physically change for programs to handle the fact that something has happened to them. As discussed previously, they can be modeled as references that point to different objects over time. This is the flaw that most OO languages suffer from: they conflate identities (x or favorite-movies) and their values. Most such languages make no distinction between an identity such as `favorite-movies` and the memory location where the data relating to that identity is stored. A variable `kyle`, for example, might directly point to the memory location containing the data for an instance of the `Person` class.

In typical OO languages, when a destructive method (or procedure) executes, it directly alters the contents of the memory where the instance is stored. Note that this doesn't happen when the same language deals with primitives, such as numbers or strings. The reason no one seems to notice this difference in behavior is that most languages have conditioned programmers to think that composite objects are different from primitives such as strings and numbers. But this isn't how things need to be, and there *is* another way. Instead of letting programs have direct access to memory locations via pointers such as `favorite-movies` and allowing them to change the content of that memory location, programs should have only a special reference to immutable objects. The only thing they should be allowed to change is this special reference itself, by making it point to a completely different, suitably constructed object that's also immutable. This concept is illustrated in figure 6.2.

This should be the default behavior of all data types, not only select ones like numbers or strings. Custom classes defined by a programmer should also work this way.

Now that we've talked about this new approach to objects and mutation over time, let's see why this might be useful and what might be special about such references to immutable objects.

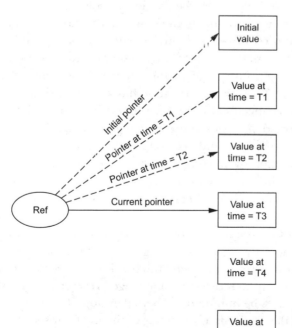

Figure 6.2 A reference that points to completely different immutable values over time

6.2.3 *Immutability and concurrency*

It's worth remembering that the troubles with concurrency happen only when multiple threads attempt to update the *same* shared data. In the first part of this chapter, we reviewed the common problems that arise when shared data is mutated incorrectly in a multithreaded scenario. The problems with mutation can be classified into two general types:

- Losing updates (or updating inconsistent data)
- Reading inconsistent data

If all data is immutable, then we eliminate the second issue. If a thread reads something, it's guaranteed to never change while it's being used. The concerned thread can go about its business, doing whatever it needs to with the data—calculating things, displaying information, or using it as input to other things. In the context of the example concerning favorite movies, a thread might read someone's favorite set of movies at a given point and use it in a report about popular movies. Meanwhile, a second thread might update a person's favorite movies. In this scenario, because the sets are immutable, the second thread would create a new set of movies, leaving the first thread with valid and consistent (and merely stale) data.

We've glossed over some of the technicalities involved in ensuring that this works, and we'll explore Clojure's approach in much greater depth in the following sections. In particular, threads should be able to perform repeated reads correctly, even if another thread updated some or all of the data. Assuming things do work this way, the read problem in a multithreaded situation can be considered solved. It leaves only the issue of when two or more threads try to update the same data at the same time.

Solving this second problem requires some form of supervision by the language runtime and is where the special nature of references comes into play. Because no identity has direct access to the contents of various memory locations (which in turn contain the data objects), the language runtime has a chance of doing something to help supervise writes. Specifically, because identities are modeled using special references, as mentioned previously, the language can provide constructs that allow supervised changes to these indirect references. These constructs can have concurrency semantics, thereby making it possible for multiple threads to update shared data correctly. The semantics can ensure more than safe writes; they can signal errors when writes fail or enforce certain other constraints when a write is to be made.

This isn't possible in most other popular languages today, because they allow direct access to (and mutation of) memory locations. A language that satisfies two requirements can hope to solve the concurrency problem: the first is that identities not point directly to memory locations but do so indirectly via managed references, and the second is that data objects themselves be immutable. The separation of identity and state is the key. You'll see Clojure's flavor of this approach over the next few sections.

6.3 Clojure's way

As you saw in the previous section, there's an alternative when it comes to modeling identities and their state. Instead of letting an identity be a simple reference (direct access to a memory location and its contents), it can be a managed reference that points to an immutable value. Over the course of the program, this reference can be made to point to other immutable values as required by the program logic. If state is modeled this way, then the programming language facilities that allow a managed reference to point to different things can support concurrency semantics—they can check for modified data, enforce validity, enforce that other programming constructs be used (such as transactions), and so forth. This is exactly the Clojure way.

Clojure provides managed references to state, as described previously. It provides four different kinds of managed references, each suitable in different situations. It also provides language-level constructs that help in changing what these references point to. Further, to coordinate changes to more than one reference, Clojure exposes an interesting take on a software transactional memory (STM) system. We'll examine each of these in detail right after we talk about performance.

6.3.1 Immutability and performance

For any language to work this way (managed references, immutable objects), an important requirement must be met—that of performance. Working with this model of state and mutation needs to be as fast as the old way of in-place mutation. Traditional solutions to this issue have been unsatisfactory, but Clojure solves it in an elegant way.

IMMUTABILITY BY COPYING

Let's again consider the example concerning movies and multiple threads. Imagine that the first thread is dealing with Rob's set of favorite movies when he was a child. If a second thread were to update his favorites to a new set, the data seen by the first thread should still be valid. One way to achieve this is to make a copy of the object being updated so that readers still have valid (if old) data while the writer updates it to the new object.

The problem with this approach is that naïvely copying something over in this manner is extremely inefficient. Often, the speed of such a copy operation grows linearly with the size of the objects being copied. If every write involved such an expensive operation, it would be impossible to use in a production environment. Therefore, given that an approach involving blind copying of data isn't viable, the alternative must involve sharing the data structures in question. Specifically, the new and updated objects must in some way point to the old values while making additional changes required to perform updates.

To make the performance requirements clearer, such an implementation must have approximately the same performance characteristics as the old mutable implementation. For example, a hash table must behave in a constant time (or near enough) manner. This performance guarantee must be satisfied, in addition to satisfying the previous constraint that the older version still be usable. This would allow other threads that had read the data prior to the update to continue with their job. In summary, the requirements are that the immutable structures do the following:

- Leave the old version of itself in a usable state when it mutates
- Satisfy the same performance characteristics as the mutable versions of themselves

You'll now see how Clojure satisfies these requirements.

PERSISTENT DATA STRUCTURES

The common use of the term *persistence* in computer science refers to persisting data into a nonvolatile storage system, such as a database. But there's another way that term is used, one that's quite common in the functional programming space. A persistent data structure is one that preserves the previous version of itself when it's modified. Older versions of such data structures persist after updates. Such data structures are inherently immutable, because update operations yield new values every time.

All of the core data structures offered by Clojure are persistent. These include maps, vectors, lists, and sets. These persistent data structures also perform extremely well because instead of using copying, they share structure when an update needs to be done. Specifically, they maintain nearly all the performance guarantees that are made by such data structures, and their performance is on par with or extremely close to that of similar data structures that are provided by the Java language.

With this implementation, Clojure has the means to provide the managed reference model for mutating state. We'll examine this in the next section.

6.3.2 *Managed references*

Given Clojure's efficient implementation of persistent data structures, the approach of modeling state through managed references becomes viable. Clojure has four distinct offerings in this area, each useful in certain scenarios. Table 6.2 gives an overview of the options available, and we'll discuss each of these types in this order in the following sections.

Table 6.2 Clojure provides four different types of managed references.

Managed reference type	Useful for
ref	Shared, synchronous, coordinated changes
agent	Shared, asynchronous, uncoordinated changes
atom	Shared, synchronous, uncoordinated changes
var	Isolated changes

Clojure provides a managed reference for the different situations that arise when writing programs that use multiple threads. This ranges from the case that needs to isolate any change to within the thread making it, to the case when threads need to coordinate changes that involve multiple shared data structures. In the next few sections, we'll examine each one in turn.

In the first section of this chapter, we examined the problems faced by multi-threaded programs when shared data is involved. These problems are typically handled using locks, and we also examined the problems associated with locks.

Managed references and language-level support for concurrency semantics offer an alternative to locks. In the next section, we'll examine the first of Clojure's managed references—the ref—and show how the language provides lock-free concurrency support.

6.4   Refs

Clojure provides a special construct in ref (short for reference) to create a managed reference that allows for synchronous and coordinated changes to mutable data. A ref holds a value that can be changed in a synchronous and coordinated manner. As an example, let's consider an expense-tracking domain.

6.4.1   Creating refs

First, you'll want to create a ref to hold all the users of your imaginary system. The following is an example of this, and the ref is initialized with an empty map:

```
(def all-users (ref {}))
```

At this point, `all-users` is a ref that points to the initial value of an empty map. You can check this by dereferencing it using the `deref` function, which returns the current value from within the ref:

```
(deref all-users)
;=> {}
```

Clojure also provides a convenient reader macro to dereference such a managed reference: the @ character. The following works the same way as calling `deref`:

```
@all-users
;=> {}
```

By the way, if you just ask for the value of the `all-users` ref, here's what you might see:

```
all-users
;=> #<Ref@227e9896: {}>
```

This is the ref itself, so you always have to remember to dereference it when you want the underlying value. Now that you know how to create and read back a ref, you're ready to see how you can go about changing what it points to.

6.4.2   Mutating refs

Now, you'll write a function that adds a new user to your existing set. Clojure's refs can be changed using the `ref-set`, `alter`, or `commute` functions.

REF-SET

ref-set is the most basic of these functions; it accepts a ref and a new value and replaces the old value with the new. Try the following to see it in action:

```
(ref-set all-users {})
IllegalStateException No transaction running
clojure.lang.LockingTransaction.getEx (LockingTransaction.java:208)
```

Because refs are meant for situations where multiple threads need to coordinate their changes, the Clojure runtime demands that mutating a ref be done inside an STM transaction. An STM transaction is analogous to a database transaction but for changes to in-memory data structures. We'll say more about Clojure's STM system in the following section; for now, you'll start an STM transaction using a built-in macro called dosync.

You can check that this works by trying your previous call to ref-set but this time inside the scope of a dosync:

```
(dosync
  (ref-set all-users {}))
;=> {}
```

That works as expected, and you can use ref-set like this to reset your list of users. dosync is required for any function that mutates a ref, including the other two mentioned earlier, alter and commute.

ALTER

Typically, a ref is mutated by taking its current value, applying a function to it, and storing the new value back into it. This read-process-write operation is a common scenario, and Clojure provides the alter function that can do this as an atomic operation. The general form of this function is

```
(alter ref function & args)
```

The first and second arguments to alter are the ref that's to be mutated and the function that will be applied to get the new value of the ref. When the function is called, the first argument will be the current value of the ref, and the remaining arguments will be the ones specified in the call to alter (args).

Before examining the commute function, let's get back to the intention of writing a function to add a new user to your list of existing users. First, here's a function to create a new user:

```
(defn new-user [id login monthly-budget]
  {:id id
   :login login
   :monthly-budget monthly-budget
   :total-expenses 0})
```

This uses a Clojure map to represent a user—a common pattern used where traditional objects are needed. We've deliberately kept the representation simple; in real life your users would probably be a lot more, well, real. Next, here's the add-user function:

```
(defn add-new-user [login budget-amount]
  (dosync
    (let [current-number (count @all-users)
          user (new-user (inc current-number) login budget-amount)]
      (alter all-users assoc login user))))
```

Note the use of dosync. As mentioned previously, it starts an STM transaction, which allows you to use alter. In the preceding code snippet, alter is passed the all-users ref, which is the one being mutated. The function you pass it is assoc, which takes a map, a key, and a value as parameters. It returns a new map with that value associated with the supplied key. In this case, your newly created user gets associated with the login name. Note that while the first argument to alter is the all-users ref itself, assoc will receive the current value of the ref all-users.

Further note that the code includes the entire let form inside the transaction started by dosync. The alternative would have been to call only alter inside the dosync. Clojure wouldn't have complained because dereferencing a ref (@all-users) doesn't need to happen inside a transaction. You do this to ensure that you see a consistent set of users. You want to avoid the buried update problem where two threads read the count and one thread commits a new user (increasing the real count), causing the other thread to commit a new user with a duplicate ID. Here's the functionality in action:

```
(add-new-user "amit" 1000000)
;=> {"amit" {:id 2, :login "amit", :monthly-budget 1000000, :total-expenses 0}}
```

Notice that alter returns the final state of the ref. If you now call it again, you'll see the following:

```
(add-new-user "deepthi" 2000000)
;=> {"deepthi" {:id 3, :login "deepthi", :monthly-budget 2000000,
                :total-expenses 0},
     "amit" {:id 2, :login "amit", :monthly-budget 1000000,
             :total-expenses 0}}
```

As you can see, the ref is mutating as expected. One final note: except for the :id value it doesn't matter in what order you add users in the previous example. If two threads were both trying to add a user to your system, you wouldn't care in what order they're added. Such an operation is said to be commutative, and Clojure has optimized support for commutes.

COMMUTE

When two threads try to mutate a ref using either ref-set or alter, and one of them succeeds (causing the other to fail), the second transaction starts over with the latest value of the ref in question. This ensures that a transaction doesn't commit with inconsistent values. The effect of this mechanism is that a transaction may be tried multiple times.

For those situations where it doesn't matter what the most recent value of a ref is (only that it's consistent and recent), Clojure provides the `commute` function. The name derives from the commutative property of functions, and you might remember this from your high school math classes. A function is commutative if it doesn't matter in which order the arguments are applied. For example, addition is commutative, whereas subtraction isn't:

```
a + b = b + a
a - b != b - a
```

The `commute` function is useful where the order of the function application isn't important. For instance, imagine that a number was being incremented inside a transaction. If two threads were to go at it in parallel, at the end of the two transactions, it wouldn't matter which thread had committed first. The result would be that the number was incremented twice.

When the `alter` function is applied, it checks to see if the value of the ref has changed because of another committed transaction. This causes the current transaction to fail and for it to be retried. The `commute` function doesn't behave this way; instead, execution proceeds forward and all calls to `commute` are handled at the end of the transaction. The general form of `commute` is similar to `alter`:

```
(commute ref function & args)
```

As explained earlier, the function passed to `commute` should be commutative. Similar to `alter`, the `commute` function also performs the read-apply-write operation on one atomic swoop.

You've now seen the three ways in which a ref can be mutated. In showing these, we've mentioned STM transactions quite a bit. In the next section, you'll learn a little more about Clojure's implementation of the STM system.

6.4.3 *Software transactional memory*

A common solution to the problems of shared data and multithreading is the (careful) use of locks. But this approach suffers from several problems, as we already discussed. These issues make using locks messy and error prone while also making code based on locks infamously difficult to debug.

STM is a concurrency control mechanism that works in a fashion similar to database transactions. Instead of controlling access to data stored on disks, inside tables and rows, STMs control access to shared memory. Using an STM system offers many advantages to multithreaded programs, the most obvious being that it's a lock-free solution. You can think of it as getting all the benefits of using locks but without any of the problems. You also gain increased concurrency because this is an optimistic approach compared with the inherently pessimistic approach of locking.

In this section, you'll get a high-level overview of what STM is and how it works.

STM TRANSACTIONS

Lock-based solutions prevent more than one thread from executing a protected part of the code. Only the thread that acquired the right set of locks is allowed to execute code that has been demarcated for use with those locks. All other threads that want to execute that same code block it until the first thread completes and relinquishes those locks.

An STM system takes a nearly opposite approach. First, code that needs to mutate data is put inside a transaction. In the case of Clojure, this means using the dosync macro. Once this is done, the language runtime takes an optimistic approach in letting threads execute the transaction. Any number of threads are allowed to begin the transaction. Changes made to refs within the transaction are isolated, and only the threads that made the changes can see the changed values.

The first thread that completely executes the block of code comprising the transaction is allowed to commit the changed values. Once a thread commits, when any other thread attempts to commit, that transaction is aborted and the changes are rolled back.

The commit performed when a transaction is successful is atomic in nature. This means that even if a transaction makes changes to multiple refs, as far as the outside world is concerned, they all appear to happen at the same instant (when the transaction commits). STM systems can also choose to retry failed transactions, and many do so until the transaction succeeds. Clojure also supports this automatic retrying of failed transactions, up to an internal limit.

Now that you know how transactions work at a high level, let's recap an important set of properties that the STM system exhibits.

ATOMIC, CONSISTENT, ISOLATED

The Clojure STM system has ACI properties (atomicity, consistency, isolation). It doesn't support durability because it isn't a persistent system and is based on volatile, in-memory data. To be specific, if a transaction mutates several refs, the changes become visible to the outside world at one instant. Either all the changes happen, or, if the transaction fails, the changes are rolled back and no change happens. This is how the system supports atomicity.

When refs are mutated inside a transaction, the changed data is called *in-transaction* values. This is because they're visible only to the thread that made the changes inside the transaction. In this manner, transactions isolate the changes within themselves (until they commit).

If any of the refs are changed during the course of a transaction, the entire transaction is retried. In this manner, the STM system supports consistency. For extra protection, Clojure's refs (and also agents and atoms) accept validator functions when created. These functions are used to check the consistency of the data when changes are made to it. If the validator function fails, the transaction is rolled back.

Before moving onto the other types of managed references in Clojure, we'll make one final point about the STM.

MVCC

Clojure's STM system implements multiversion concurrency control (MVCC). This is the type of concurrency supported by several database systems such as Oracle and PostgreSQL. In an MVCC system, each contender (threads in the case of Clojure) is given a snapshot of the mutable world when it starts its transaction.

Any changes made to the snapshot are invisible to other contenders until the changes are committed at the end of a successful transaction. But thanks to the snapshot model, readers never block writers (or other readers), increasing the inherent concurrency that the system can support. In fact, writers never block readers either, thanks to the same isolation. Contrast this with the old locking model where both readers and writers block while one thread does its job.

Having seen the way managed references work in Clojure and also how the associated mechanism of the STM works, you can write multithreaded programs that need to coordinate changes to shared data. In the next section, we'll examine a method to mutate data in an uncoordinated way.

6.5 Agents

Clojure provides a special construct called an *agent* that allows for asynchronous and independent changes to shared mutable data. For instance, you may want to time the CPU while it executes some code of interest. In this section, you'll see how to create, mutate, and read agents. The agent function allows the creation of agents, which hold values that can be changed using special functions. Clojure provides two functions, send and send-off, that result in mutating the value of an agent. Both accept the agent that needs to be updated, along with a function that will be used to compute the new value. The application of the function happens at a later time, on a separate thread. By corollary, an agent is also useful to run a task (function) on a different thread, with the return value of the function becoming the new value of the agent. The functions sent to agents are called *actions*.

6.5.1 Creating agents

Creating an agent is similar to creating a ref. As mentioned, the agent function allows you to create an agent:

```
(def total-cpu-time (agent 0))
```

Dereferencing an agent to get at its current value is similar to using a ref:

```
(deref total-cpu-time)
;=> 0
```

Clojure also supports the @ reader macro to dereference agents, so the following is equivalent to calling deref:

```
@total-cpu-time
;=> 0
```

Having created an agent, let's see how you can mutate it.

6.5.2 *Mutating agents*

As described in the preceding paragraphs, agents are useful when changes to a particular state need to be made in an asynchronous fashion. The changes are made by sending an action (a regular Clojure function) to the agent, which runs on a separate thread at a later time. There are two flavors of this—send and send-off—and we'll examine them both.

SEND

The general form of the send function is as follows:

```
(send the-agent the-function & more-args)
```

As an example, consider adding a few hundred milliseconds to the total-cpu-time agent you created earlier:

```
(send total-cpu-time + 700)
```

The addition operator in Clojure is implemented as a function, no different from regular functions. The action function sent to an agent should accept one or more parameters. When it runs, the first parameter it's supplied is the current value of the agent, and the remaining parameters are the ones passed via send.

In this example, the + function is sent to the total-cpu-time agent, and it uses the current value of the agent (which is 0) as the first argument and 700 as the second argument. At some point in the future, although it isn't noticeable in the example because it happens almost immediately, the + function executes and the new value of total-cpu-time will be set as the value of the agent. You can check the current value of the agent by dereferencing it:

```
(deref total-cpu-time)
;=> 700
```

If the action takes a long time to run, it may be a while before dereferencing the agent shows the new value. Dereferencing the agent before the agent runs will continue to return the old value. The call to send itself is nonblocking, and it returns immediately.

Actions sent to agents using send are executed on a fixed thread pool maintained by Clojure. If you send lots of actions to agents (more than the number of free threads in this pool), they get queued and will run in the order in which they were sent. Only one action runs on a particular agent at a time. This thread pool doesn't grow in size, no matter how many actions are queued up. This is depicted in figure 6.3. This is why you should use send for actions that are CPU intensive and don't block, because blocking actions will use up the thread pool. For blocking actions, Clojure provides another function—send-off—and we'll look at that now.

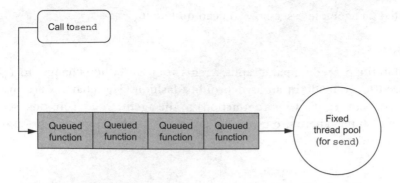

Figure 6.3   The thread pool used for the `send` function is fixed based on the number of cores available. If all the threads are busy, then functions get queued.

SEND-OFF

The function `send-off` can handle potential blocking actions. The general form of the `send-off` function is exactly the same as for `send`:

```
(send-off the-agent the-function & more-args)
```

The semantics of what happens when `send-off` is called are the same as that of `send`, the only difference being that it uses a different thread pool from the one used by `send`, and this thread pool can grow in size to accommodate more actions sent using `send-off`. Again, only one action runs on a particular agent at a time.

We'll now look at a few convenient constructs provided by Clojure that are useful when programming using agents.

6.5.3   *Working with agents*

This section will examine a few functions that come in handy when working with agents. First, a common scenario when using agents to do work asynchronously is that several actions are sent (using either `send` or `send-off`), and then one waits until they all complete. Clojure provides two functions that help in this situation: `await` and `await-for`.

Next, we'll look at ways to test agents for errors. After all, you can send any function to an agent, which means you can send any arbitrary code to the agent thread pools. If your code throws an error, there needs to be a way to examine what went wrong.

And finally, another common use case is that a notification is desired when an action sent to an agent completes successfully. This is where watchers come in. You'll see how the value of an agent can be kept consistent by validating it with some business rules each time an attempt is made to change it.

AWAIT AND AWAIT-FOR

`await` is a function that's useful when execution must stop and wait for actions that were previously dispatched to certain agents to be completed. The general form is

```
(await & the-agents)
```

As an example, let's say you had agents named `agent-one`, `agent-two`, and `agent-three`. Let's also say you sent several actions to these three agents, either from your own thread, other threads, or from another agent. At some point, you could cause the current thread to block until all actions sent to your three agents completed, by doing the following:

```
(await agent-one agent-two agent-three)
```

`await` blocks indefinitely, so if any of the actions didn't return successfully, the current thread wouldn't be able to proceed. To avoid this, Clojure also provides the `await-for` function. The general form looks similar to that of `await`, but it accepts a maximum timeout in milliseconds:

```
(await-for timeout-in-millis & the-agents)
```

Using `await-for` is safer in the sense that the max wait time can be controlled. If the timeout does occur, `await-for` returns `nil`. Here's an example:

```
(await-for 1000 agent-one agent-two agent-three)
```

This will abort the blocking state of the thread if the timer expires before the actions have completed. It's common to check if the actions succeeded or not by testing the agents for any errors after using `await-for`.

AGENT ERRORS

When an action doesn't complete successfully (it throws an exception), the agent knows about it. If you try to dereference an agent that's in such an error state, it will return the previous successful result. Take a look:

```
(def bad-agent (agent 10))
```

This sets up an agent with an initial value of `10`. You'll now send it an action that will cause an error, leaving the agent in an error state:

```
(send bad-agent / 0)
;=> #<Agent@125b9ec1 FAILED: 10>
```

Notice the agent is in the FAILED state, with an unchanged value of `10` (caused by the intentional divide-by-zero error). You can now try to dereference `bad-agent`:

```
(deref bad-agent)
;=> 10
```

Further, if you now try to send it another action, even if it might have succeeded, the agent will complain about its error state, for instance:

```
(send bad-agent / 2)
ArithmeticException Divide by zero  clojure.lang.Numbers.divide
(Numbers.java:156)
```

You can always programmatically discern what the error is by using the `agent-error` function:

```
(agent-error bad-agent)
;=> #<ArithmeticException java.lang.ArithmeticException: Divide by zero>
```

`agent-error` returns the exception thrown during the agent thread's execution. The error object returned is an instance of the particular exception class corresponding to the error that happened and can be queried using Java methods, for example:

```
(let [e (agent-error bad-agent)
      st (.getStackTrace e)]
  (println (.getMessage e))
    (println (clojure.string/join "\n" st)))
```

As mentioned, if an agent has an error, you can't send it any more actions. If you do, Clojure throws the same exception, informing you of the current error. To make the agent usable again, Clojure provides the `clear-agent-errors` function:

```
(clear-agent-errors bad-agent)
```

The agent is now ready to accept more actions.

VALIDATIONS

You've seen how to create new agents. You can create them with more options as well. Here's the complete general form of the `agent` function that creates new agents:

```
(agent initial-state & options)
```

The options allowed are

```
:meta metadata-map
:validator validator-fn
```

If the `:meta` option is used, then the map supplied with it will become the metadata of the agent. If the `:validator` option is used, it should be accompanied by either `nil` or a function that accepts one argument. The `validator-fn` is passed the intended new state of the agent, and it can apply any business rules to allow or disallow the change to occur. If the validator function returns `false` or throws an exception, then the state of the agent isn't mutated.

You've now seen how agents can be used in Clojure. Before moving on to the next kind of managed reference, you'll see how agents can also be used to cause side effects from inside STM transactions.

6.5.4 *Side effects in STM transactions*

We said earlier that Clojure's STM system automatically retries failed transactions. After the first transaction commits, all other transactions that had started concurrently will abort when they, in turn, try to commit. Aborted transactions are then started over. This implies that code inside a dosync block can potentially execute multiple times before succeeding, and for this reason, such code shouldn't contain side effects. If you do, you can expect the side effect to also occur multiple times. There's no way to alter this behavior, so you have to be careful that you don't do this.

As an example, if there was a call to println inside a transaction, and the transaction was tried several times, the println will be executed multiple times. This behavior would probably not be desirable.

There are times when a transaction does need to generate a side effect. It could be logging or anything else, such as writing to a database or sending a message on a queue. Agents can be used to facilitate such intended side effects. Consider the following pseudo-code:

```
(dosync
  (send agent-one log-message args-one)
  (send-off agent-two send-message-on-queue args-two)
  (alter a-ref ref-function)
    (some-pure-function args-three))
```

Clojure's STM system holds all actions that need to be sent to agents until transactions succeed. In the pseudo-code shown here, log-message and send-message-on-queue are actions that will be sent only when the transaction succeeds. This ensures that even if the transaction is tried multiple times, the side effect causing actions gets sent only once. This is the recommended way to produce side effects from within a transaction.

This section walked through the various aspects of using agents. You saw that agents allow asynchronous and independent changes to mutable data. The next kind of managed reference is called an atom, which allows for synchronous and independent changes to mutable data.

6.6 *Atoms*

Clojure provides a special construct in an atom that allows for synchronous and independent changes to mutable data. The difference between an atom and an agent is that updates to agents happen asynchronously at some point in the future, whereas atoms are updated synchronously (immediately). Atoms differ from refs in that changes to atoms are independent from each other and can't be coordinated, so they either all happen or none do.

6.6.1 *Creating atoms*

Creating an atom looks similar to creating either refs or agents:

```
(def total-rows (atom 0))
```

`total-rows` is an atom that starts out being initialized to zero. You could use it to hold the number of database rows inserted by a Clojure program as it restores data from a backup, for example. Reading the current value of the atom uses the same dereferencing mechanism used by refs and agents:

```
(deref total-rows)
;=> 0
```

Or it uses the @ reader macro:

```
@total-rows
;=> 0
```

Now that you've seen how to create atoms and read their values, let's address mutating them.

6.6.2 Mutating atoms

Clojure provides several ways to update the value of an atom. There's an important difference between atoms and refs, in that changes to one atom are independent of changes to other atoms. Therefore, there's no need to use transactions when attempting to update atoms.

RESET!

The `reset!` function doesn't use the existing value of the atom and simply sets the provided value as the new value of the atom. The general form of the function is

```
(reset! atom new-value)
```

This might remind you of the `ref-set` function, which also does the same job but for refs.

SWAP!

The `swap!` function has the following general form:

```
(swap! the-atom the-function & more-args)
```

You could pass `swap!` the addition function whenever you finish inserting a batch of rows:

```
(swap! total-rows + 100)
```

Here, in a synchronous manner, the + function is applied to the current value of `total-rows` (which is zero) and 100. The new value of `total-rows` becomes 100. If you were to use a mutation function that didn't complete before another thread changed the value of the atom, `swap!` would then retry the operation until it did succeed. For this reason, mutation functions should be free of side effects.

Clojure also provides a lower-level function called `compare-and-set!` that can be used to mutate the value of an atom. `swap!` internally uses `compare-and-set!`.

COMPARE-AND-SET!

Here's the general form of the `compare-and-set!` function:

```
(compare-and-set! the-atom old-value new-value)
```

This function atomically sets the value of the atom to the new value, if the current value of the atom is equal to the supplied old value. If the operation succeeds, it returns `true`; otherwise it returns `false`. A typical workflow of using this function is to dereference the atom in the beginning, do something with the value of the atom, and then use `compare-and-set!` to change the value to a new one. If another thread had changed the value in the meantime (after it had been dereferenced), then the mutation would fail.

The `swap!` function does that internally: it dereferences the value of the atom, applies the provided mutation function, and attempts to update the value of the atom using `compare-and-set!` by using the value that was previously dereferenced. If `compare-and-set!` returns `false` (the mutation failed because the atom was updated elsewhere), the `swap!` function reapplies the mutation function until it succeeds.

Atoms can be used whenever there's a need for some state but not for coordination with any other state. Using refs, agents, and atoms, all situations that demand mutation of shared data can be handled. Our last stop will be to study vars, because they're useful when state needs to be modified but not shared.

6.7 Vars

We introduced vars in chapter 3. In this section, we'll take a look at how vars can be used to manage state in an isolated (thread-local) manner.

6.7.1 Creating vars and root bindings

Vars can be thought of as pointers to mutable storage locations, which can be updated on a per-thread basis. When a var is created, it can be given an initial value, which is referred to as its root binding:

```
(def hbase-master "localhost")
```

In this example, `hbase-master` is a var that has a binding of `"localhost"`. Here, it acts as a constant. You could also use it as a special var, by declaring it as follows:

```
(def ^:dynamic *hbase-master* "localhost")
```

The starting and ending asterisks are conventions that denote that this var ought to be rebound before use. (If you name a var like this but without `^:dynamic`, Clojure will emit a warning.) In normal use dynamic vars are just like normal vars:

```
(def ^:dynamic *hbase-master* "localhost")
;=> #'user/*hbase-master*
(println "Hbase-master is:" *hbase-master*)
Hbase-master is: localhost
;=> nil
```

Also just like normal vars, if you attempt to use a dynamic var without a root binding you'll get a special Unbound object:[2]

```
(def ^:dynamic *rabbitmq-host*)
;=> #'user/*rabbitmq-host*
(println "RabbitMQ host is:" *rabbitmq-host*)
RabbitMQ host is: #<Unbound Unbound: #'user/*rabbitmq-host*>
;=> nil
(bound? #'*rabbitmq-host*)
;=> false
```

> You can test if a var is bound using the bound? function.

Now that you know how to make a dynamic var, we'll review how to rebind its value.

6.7.2 Var bindings

Whether a var has a root binding or not, when the binding form is used to update the var, that mutation is visible only to that thread. If there was no root binding, other threads would see no root binding; if there was a root binding, other threads would continue to see that value. Let's look at an example. You'll create a function that will fetch the number of rows in a Users table from different databases: test, development, and staging. Imagine that you define the database host using a var like so:

```
(def ^:dynamic *mysql-host*)
```

This var has no root binding, so it will need to be bound before use. You'll do that in a function that's meant to do a database query, but for the purposes of this example it will return some dummy data such as the length of the hostname. In the real world, you'd run the query against the database using something like a JDBC library:

```
(defn db-query [db]
  (binding [*mysql-host* db]
    (count *mysql-host*)))
```

Next, you'll create a list of the hosts you want to run your function against:

```
(def mysql-hosts ["test-mysql" "dev-mysql" "staging-mysql"])
```

Finally, you could run your query function against all the hosts:

```
(pmap db-query mysql-hosts)
;=> (10 9 13)
```

pmap works like map, but each time the supplied function is called on an element of the list, it's done so on a different available thread from an internally maintained thread pool. The call to binding sets up *mysql-host* to point to a different host, and the query function proceeds appropriately. Each execution of the db-query function sees a different value of *myql-host*, as expected.

---

[2] In earlier versions of Clojure, using an unbound var would throw an exception.

We've covered the four different options that Clojure offers when it comes to concurrency, state, and performing updates—refs, agents, atoms, and vars—and some different scenarios in which each would be useful. You'll eventually run into a situation where depending on your situation, one of these is a good fit, and you'll be grateful for Clojure's language-level support for lock-free concurrency.

6.8 State and its unified access model

This section is a quick recap of the constructs Clojure offers for managing state. We covered each of them over the past few sections, and it's now possible to make an observation. All of the constructs for managing state enjoy a unified access model that allows you to manage them similarly. This is true whether the managed reference is a ref, an agent, or an atom. Let's take another quick look at these functions.

6.8.1 Creating

Here are the functions that can create each type of managed reference:

```
(def a-ref (ref 0))
(def an-agent (agent 0))
(def an-atom (atom 0))
```

Notice how each accepts an initial value during creation.

6.8.2 Reading

All three kinds of references can be dereferenced the same way:

```
(deref a-ref) or @a-ref
(deref an-agent) or @an-agent
(deref an-atom) or @an-atom
```

This uniformity makes Clojure's references easier to use, because they work in such a similar manner. Let's also recap how their values can be changed.

6.8.3 Mutation

Changing a managed reference in Clojure always follows the same model: a function is applied to the current value, and the return value is set as the new value of the reference. Table 6.3 shows the functions that allow such mutation.

Table 6.3 Ways to mutate refs, agents, and atoms

Refs	Agents	Atoms
(ref-set ref new-value) (alter ref function & args) (commute ref function & args)	(send agent function & args) (send-off agent function & args)	(reset! atom new-value) (swap! atom function & args) (compare-and-set! atom old-value new-value)

While we're on the topic of mutation, it's worthwhile to note that Clojure provides a hook, which can be used to run arbitrary code when a reference changes state. This mechanism works for refs, agents, atoms, and vars.

6.8.4 *Transactions*

Finally, there's the question of which references need transactions and which don't. Because refs support coordinated changes, mutating them needs the protection of STM transactions: all such code needs to be inside the dosync macro. Agents and atoms don't need STM transactions. Functions used to calculate new values of refs or atoms must be free of side effects, because they could be retried several times.

6.8.5 *Watching for mutation*

Sometimes it's useful to add an event listener that gets notified when the value of a stateful construct changes. Clojure provides the add-watch function for this purpose.

ADD-WATCH

The add-watch function allows you to register a regular Clojure function as a "watcher" against any kind of reference. When the value of the reference changes, the watcher function is run.

The watcher must be a function of four arguments:

- A key to identify the watcher (the-key)
- The reference it's being registered against (the-ref)
- The old value of the reference (old-value)
- The new value of the reference (new-value)

The add-watch function itself accepts three arguments: the reference to watch, a key to identify the watch you're adding, and the watcher function. You can use the key argument to remove the watch later. Here it is in action:

```
(def adi (atom 0))
(defn on-change [the-key the-ref old-value new-value]
  (println "Hey, seeing change from" old-value "to" new-value))
(add-watch adi :adi-watcher on-change)
```

Now that it's all set up, you can test it. You'll check the current value of adi and then update it:

```
@adi
;=> 0
(swap! adi inc)
Hey, seeing change from 0 to 1
;=> 1
```

As mentioned before, this can be used for all of Clojure's special-managed references.

REMOVE-WATCH

It's also possible to remove a watch if it's no longer required. Clojure provides the `remove-watch` function to do this. Using it is simple: call `remove-watch` with the reference to stop watching and the key you used in the `add-watch` call. The following example removes the watch you added earlier:

```
(remove-watch adi :adi-watcher)
```

6.9 *Deciding which reference type to use*

We have now covered all four options Clojure gives you for managing state mutation. You may be a little dizzy with choices and unsure which to use for any given problem. Here's a guide to your decision making.

The most basic reference type is the var. It's only useful for *isolating* changes (either to a particular thread or a particular scope of code), not coordinating or sharing those changes. When you have an ordinarily global variable (such as a database connection or configuration map) but just need to change it to another value for a particular run of code, use a dynamic var with `binding` to rebind its value. But vars can't be written to by multiple parts of your code.

Atoms are one step more powerful than vars: they're the simplest way to manage a state change that must be written to and read by multiple threads. The vast majority of the time you'll be using atoms because you don't need anything more. But they have two drawbacks. First, multiple atoms cannot be changed together in an atomic and coordinated way. Second, changes to an atom must be free of side effects because its `swap!` function may be run multiple times. If you need coordination or side effects, you need to use one of the remaining two options.

Refs are atoms with coordination. Instead of using a giant atom, you can split up your state into multiple refs and read and write to several of them atomically inside a `dosync` transaction. If you have multiple pieces of shared state that must be updated together but rarely all of them in a single transaction, you can reduce the amount of contention in your application and increase concurrency. (This is similar to the tradeoff you'd make when deciding to use a single big lock or multiple smaller locks.) Refs add coordination to atoms, but like atoms all changes to them inside a transaction must be free of side effects because the transaction may be retried.

Agents are the only reference type that can tolerate side effects, but the cost for this ability is more complex management. Because side-effecting operations cannot be safely retried, agents have error states that must be checked and cleared if their operation fails. Additionally, the side-effecting action runs asynchronously: you must explicitly `send` a mutation function to run and wait a possibly indefinite amount of time for it to complete in another thread. But agents can be easily combined with refs inside `dosync` if you have a mostly pure mutation (using refs) with just a little bit of side effect that must be done only when the transaction is successful (using an agent).

We've completed our examination of Clojure's reference types. In the next section we'll look at another mechanism Clojure provides just to increase concurrency.

6.10   *Futures and promises*

A future is an object that represents the result of a function that will execute on a different thread. A promise is an object that represents a value that will be delivered to it at some point in the future. Clojure provides futures and promises as easy ways to increase concurrency in your program. But they aren't really for state management because unlike reference types they can only ever have one value. What distinguishes futures and promises from ordinary values is that their value may not yet be known.

We'll explore the use of futures first.

6.10.1   *Futures*

A future is a simple way to run code on a different thread, and it's useful for long-running computations or blocking calls that can benefit from multithreading. To understand how to use it, examine this contrived function that takes more than 5 seconds to run:

```
(defn long-calculation [num1 num2]
  (Thread/sleep 5000)
  (* num1 num2))
```

Now that you have this slow-running function, let's imagine you needed to run multiple such computations. The code might look like the following:

```
(defn long-run []
  (let [x (long-calculation 11 13)
        y (long-calculation 13 17)
        z (long-calculation 17 19)]
    (* x y z)))
```

If you run this in the read-evaluate-print loop (REPL) and use time to see how long this takes, you might see something like this:

```
(time (long-run))
"Elapsed time: 14998.165 msecs"
;=> 10207769
```

Now, you can see the long-run will benefit from being multithreaded. That's where futures come in. The general form of a future is

```
(future & body)
```

It returns an object that will invoke body on a separate thread.[3] The returned object can be dereferenced for the value of body. The deref asking for the value will block

---

[3] You may remember that vars can have different values in different threads and different dynamic scopes. The code run in a future or an agent will always see the vars as having the value of the context that created the future or sent to an agent at the moment future or send/send-off is called. Thus you can create a future or call send inside a binding and rest easy that the value of the binding will be the same inside the future or agent's thread.

until the result is available. The result of the computation is cached, so subsequent queries for the value are immediate. Now you'll write a faster version of the long-run function:

```
(defn fast-run []
  (let [x (future (long-calculation 11 13))
        y (future (long-calculation 13 17))
        z (future (long-calculation 17 19))]
    (* @x @y @z)))
```

future creates a thread that will run long calculation without blocking current thread.

Futures x, y, and z can potentially all run in parallel.

Each dereference here will block in order listed.

You need to test this using the time function as well. If none of the futures can run in parallel (such as on a single-core machine) this may still take 15 seconds, but if you have at least four cores on your machine you may find that the entire operation completes in 5 seconds:

```
(time (fast-run))
"Elapsed time: 5000.078 msecs"
;=> 10207769
```

As you can see, futures are a painless way to get things to run on a different thread. Here are a few future-related functions Clojure provides:

- future?—Checks to see if the object is a future, and returns true if it is.
- future-done?—Returns true if the computation represented by this future object is completed.
- future-cancel—Attempts to cancel this future. If it has already started executing, it doesn't do anything.
- future-cancelled?—Returns true if the future has been cancelled.

So you can use futures whenever you need something to run asynchronously on a different thread. As you've seen, Clojure makes this very straightforward. Let's cover promises next.

6.10.2 Promises

A promise is an object that represents a commitment that a value will be delivered to it. You create one using the no-argument promise function:

```
(def p (promise))
```

To ask for the promised value, you can dereference it:

```
(def value (deref p))
```

Or, as usual, you can use the reader macro version of dereferencing:

```
@p
```

WARNING   Don't dereference the preceding promise at the REPL; it will block and you'll have no way to unblock it!

The way the value delivery system works is via the use of the `deliver` function. The general form of this function is

```
(deliver promise value)
```

Typically, this function is called from a different thread, so it's a great way to communicate between threads. The `deref` function (or the reader macro version of it) will block the calling thread if no value has been delivered to it yet. The thread automatically unblocks when the value becomes available. Here's an example of delivering a value to a promise via a future:

```
(let [p (promise)]
  (future (Thread/sleep 5000)
          (deliver p :done))
  @p)
;=> :done
```

Promises always start out with no value, so `promise` is a no-argument function.

Run this future only for side effects (`deliver`); don't bind it to a variable.

Dereferencing promise will block 5 seconds, then return the `:done` value after promise receives it.

Together, futures and promises are ways to write concurrent programs that need to pass data between threads in a simple way. They're nice, complementary additions to the various other concurrency semantics you saw earlier in this chapter.

6.11 *Summary*

We've covered some fairly heavy material in this chapter! We began with a look at the new reality of an increasing number of cores inside CPUs and the need for increasingly multithreaded software. We then looked at some of the problems encountered when programs have more than one thread of execution, specifically when these threads need to make changes to shared data. We looked at the traditional way of solving these problems—using locks—and then briefly looked at the new problems that they introduce.

Finally, we looked at Clojure's approach to these issues. It has a different approach to state, one that involves immutability. Changes to state are modeled by carefully changing managed references so that they point to different immutable values over time. And because the Clojure runtime itself manages these references, it's able to offer the programmer a great deal of automated support in their use.

First, data that needs to change must use one of the four options that Clojure offers. This makes it explicit to anyone reading the code in the future. Next, it offers a STM system that helps in making coordinated changes to more than one piece of data. This is a huge win, because it's a lock-free solution to a hairy problem!

Clojure also offers agents and atoms, which allow independent changes to mutable data. These are different in that they're asynchronous and synchronous, respectively, and each is useful in different situations. Finally, Clojure offers vars that can be used where changes to data need to be isolated within threads. The great thing is that despite offering options that are quite different from each other, they have a uniform way of creating and accessing the data inside them.

   Clojure's approach to state and mutation is an important step forward in terms of the current status quo of dealing with state and multithreaded programming. As we discussed in section 6.2, most popular OO languages confuse identities and state, whereas Clojure keeps them distinct. This allows Clojure to provide language-level semantics that make concurrent software easier to write (and read and maintain) and more resilient to bugs that afflict lock-based solutions.

Evolving Clojure
through macros

7

This chapter covers

- A deep dive into macros
- Macro examples from within Clojure
- Writing your own macros

Macros are the most distinguishing feature of Clojure when compared to languages such as Java and Ruby. Macros make possible things that can only be dreamed of in other languages. The macro system is why Lisp is known as the programmable programming language, and this chapter will show you how you can grow your own language on top of Clojure. Macros are a useful ingredient in bottom-up programming, the approach where an application is written by first modeling low-level entities in a domain and then combining them to create complex ones. Understanding and using macros well is the key to becoming a master Clojure programmer.

If you talk to seasoned Lisp or Clojure programmers, you'll find that opinion about the use of macros varies a great deal. Some say that macros are almost too powerful and that they should be used with great caution. I've always thought that any feature of a programming language can be misused when it isn't fully understood. Further, the advantages of using macros far outweigh the perceived disadvantages. After all, the whole point of Clojure being homoiconic is to make the macro system possible.

This chapter discusses what macros are and how to use them. We'll begin with an example macro, which will help you explore Clojure's macro-writing facilities. Then, we'll dig into the Clojure source code to examine a few well-written macros. It's inspiring to learn that large parts of Clojure itself are written as macros and that you can use this facility in your own programs. Finally, you'll write a few macros of your own. We'll begin with explaining what a macro is and why a language might need a macro system.

7.1 Macro basics

To explain what a macro is, we'll take a step back and examine language runtimes again. Recall from chapter 1 that the Clojure runtime processes source code differently compared to most other languages. Specifically, there's a read phase followed by an evaluation phase. In the first phase, the Clojure reader converts a stream of characters (the source code) into Clojure data structures. These data structures are then evaluated to execute the program. The trick that makes macros possible is that Clojure offers a hook between the two phases, allowing the programmer to process the data structures representing the code before they're evaluated. Figure 7.1 illustrates these phases.

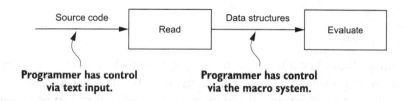

Figure 7.1   Phases of the Clojure runtime. This separation is what makes the macro system possible.

Code is converted into data structures and these data structures are then evaluated. Macros are functions that the programmer can write that act upon these data structures before they're evaluated. Macros allow code to be modified programmatically before evaluation, making it possible to create whole new kinds of abstractions. Macros operate at the syntactic level by operating on the code itself. Consequently, you can use them to add features to Clojure, the language. You'll see examples of this in this chapter.

7.1.1 Textual substitution

As an example, imagine that you had a ref called a-ref:

```
(def a-ref (ref 0))
```

Now, imagine that you wanted to change the value of a-ref to 1. You might do something like this:

```
(dosync
  (ref-set a-ref 1))
```

Remember that code is data, which means that this code snippet is just a list containing symbols and other lists—the first one being dosync, followed by a nested list where the symbols are ref-set, a-ref, and 1.

Even if your program used only the single ref shown here, the need to wrap every call to ref-set in a dosync would quickly become tedious. In the real world, you could use an atom, but using a ref is acceptable for the purposes of this example. You could write a macro called sync-set that wouldn't need a dosync when called and then would do what ref-set does.

You could implement this using a macro called sync-set that manipulates the code as data to insert the required dosync in the appropriate place. The following call would be transformed into the previous one:

```
(sync-set a-ref 1)
```

Now, you'll write the macro. Recall that new lists can be created using the list function and that things can be quoted using the ' macro character, for instance:

```
(defmacro sync-set [r v]
  (list 'dosync
    (list 'ref-set r v)))
```

A macro definition looks like a function definition. Internally, macros are functions, tagged as macros via metadata. The difference between functions and macros is that functions execute to return a value, whereas macros execute to return s-expressions that in turn are evaluated to return a value.

An important point to note is that macros operate well before evaluation time and have no notion of what values might be passed in as arguments later on. For instance, you couldn't dereference a-ref and output different kinds of s-expressions depending on the value, because during macro expansion time there's no ref, just the symbols r and v. Macros operate on symbols directly, and this is why they're useful for symbolic manipulation of code.

All this might seem a bit much to achieve the functionality provided by sync-set, because it would be trivial to write it as a function instead. In the real world, you'd indeed write it as a function. It does, of course, serve quite well to illustrate the mechanism of how macros work. Now you know what macros do: they transform or generate arbitrary s-expressions. We'll now look at something macros can do that functions can't.

7.1.2 The unless example

Since the book *The C Programming Language* came out, almost all programming language books have used the "Hello, world!" program as an introductory example.

There's a similar tradition when it comes to explaining macros, and it involves adding the `unless` control structure to the language. `unless` is kind of the opposite of the `if` form. Here's the general `if` form, as a reminder:

```
(if test then else)
```

If the `test` expression returns `true` (or a truthy value), the `then` expression is evaluated. The optional `else` expression will be evaluated if the `test` returns `false` (or a falsey value). Here's an example:

```
(defn exhibits-oddity? [x]
  (if (odd? x)
    (println "Very odd!")))
```

The Ruby programming language provides an `unless` form, which is also a conditional that can be used in similar functions. Clojure doesn't provide `unless`, but if it were there, it might work as follows:

```
(defn exhibits-oddity? [x]
  (unless (even? x)
    (println "Very odd, indeed!")))
```

Obviously, trying this won't work in Clojure because it will complain that it's unable to resolve the symbol `unless`. Your first attempt at fixing this error will involve writing a function.

THE UNLESS FUNCTION

Here's a function that implements `unless`:

```
(defn unless [test then]
  (if (not test)
    then))
```

After defining `unless` as shown here, the previous definition of `exhibits-oddity?` will work without a problem. It will even work correctly, as is evident if you test it at the read-evaluate-print loop (REPL) by calling it with an odd number like 11:

```
(exhibits-oddity? 11)
Very odd, indeed!
;=> nil
```

Trouble arises when it's tested with an even number, such as 10:

```
(exhibits-oddity? 10)
Very odd, indeed!
;=> nil
```

It appears that `exhibits-oddity?` declares all numbers as odd. The reason for this is that `unless` is a function, and all functions execute according to the following rules:

1 Evaluate all arguments passed to the function call form.
2 Evaluate the function using the values of the arguments.

Rule 1 causes the arguments to be evaluated. In the case of the `unless` function, those are the `test` and `then` expressions. This happens *before* execution of the `if` form even begins. Because all functions follow these rules, there's no way that you can use a function to implement your desired functionality for `unless`. No matter what you try, the arguments would be evaluated first.

You could cheat a little by insisting that your callers not pass in raw expressions such as `(println "Odd!")` but instead pass them in wrapped-in functions. Consider the following new definition of the `unless` function:

```
(defn unless [test then-thunk]
  (if (not test)
    (then-thunk)))
```

Here, `then-thunk` is a function that's evaluated only if the test condition isn't true. You can rewrite `exhibits-oddity?` as follows:

```
(defn exhibits-oddity? [x]
  (unless (even? x)
    #(println "Rather odd!")))
```

Recall that the `#()` reader macro characters create an anonymous function. This function now works as expected:

```
(exhibits-oddity? 11)
Rather odd!
;=> nil
(exhibits-oddity? 10)
;=> nil
```

This solution still isn't quite satisfactory. It forces callers to wrap the `then` expression inside a function. Using the `#()` reader macro involves just one extra character, but the language gives no warning if the caller forgets to use it. What you want is something that works similar to `if`, which is a special form built into Clojure. Now, you'll write a macro to solve this problem.

THE UNLESS MACRO

You know that the `if` form can be used to write the `unless` form, as long as you can avoid the evaluation of the `then` argument, unless it's needed. You tried the approach of delaying evaluation using the function wrapper in the previous section, but you can do a lot better with a macro. Consider the following definition:

```
(defmacro unless [test then]
  (list 'if (list 'not test)
    then))
```

This generates an s-expression of the form `(if (not test) then)` when the macro is expanded. You'll rewrite `exhibits-oddity?` using this macro:

```
(defn exhibits-oddity? [x]
  (unless (even? x)
    (println "Very odd, indeed!")))
```

This works as expected. The `unless` form is replaced by the new expression generated by the macro expansion. You can check this at the REPL using the `macroexpand` function:

```
(macroexpand
  '(unless (even? x) (println "Very odd, indeed!")))
;=> (if (not (even? x)) (println "Very odd, indeed!"))
```

⟵ **Note you quote argument**

Once this expanded form of `unless` replaces the `unless` form itself, it's in turn evaluated to produce the right result. This final definition of `unless` works as expected, and the callers don't need to know that there's anything special about it. In fact, as far as callers are concerned, `unless` could have been supplied by the Clojure language itself.

> **macroexpand, macroexpand-1, and macroexpand-all**
>
> `macroexpand-1` is a useful function when writing macros, because it can be used to check if the transformation of s-expressions is working correctly. `macroexpand-1` expands an s-expression by evaluating the macro named by the first symbol in the form. If the first symbol doesn't name a macro, the form is returned as is.
>
> `macroexpand` is a function that repeatedly calls `macroexpand-1` until the first symbol of the expanded form is no longer a macro. It can be used to test cases where macros expand to forms that in turn call macros.
>
> `macroexpand-all` is a utility function in the `clojure.walk` namespace. It's like `macroexpand`, except it will expand a form recursively until the entire form contains no macros at all. Often this is too much expansion, but sometimes when debugging a macro you need to see the fully expanded form to understand what code Clojure will finally execute.

If it isn't obvious already, you just added a feature to the Clojure language. That's neat! What's more, such macros are quite common. For instance, Clojure provides `when`, `when-not`, `cond`, `if-not`, and so on that are all constructs that allow conditional execution of code and are all implemented as macros. This is cool; after all, if macros are good enough to create parts of Clojure itself, then they're good enough for your programs.

The example in this section showed you the basics of creating a control-flow macro. But the way you generated s-expressions in the previous `unless` macro can become unwieldy quickly. Clojure provides a more convenient way to write macros that doesn't involve constructing lists using the `list` function. This approach involves generating code via templates.

7.1.3 Macro templates

Consider the `unless` macro again. Here it is, for convenience:

```
(defmacro unless [test then]
  (list 'if (list 'not test)
    then))
```

This is a tiny macro, and the s-expression it generates is quite simple. If you wanted to generate or transform a large, nested s-expression, the repeated calls to `list` would become quite tedious. It would also be hard to see the structure of the s-expression being generated because the repeated occurrence of the symbol `list` would be in the way of reading the structure easily. Clojure provides a way out through its backquote reader macro, which we'll explore now.

TEMPLATING USING THE BACKQUOTE (`` ` ``) MACRO

Anyone who has programmed a web application in the last few years knows what a templating system is. It allows HTML generation from a sort of blueprint. Some parts are fixed and some are to be filled in when the template is expanded. Examples are JSP (JavaServer Pages) and RHTML (Rails HTML) pages.

If generating HTML code can be made easier using templates, you can imagine the same thing would be true for generating Clojure code. This is why the macro system supports templates through the backquote (`` ` ``) reader macro. Here you see it in action by rewriting the `unless` macro from before:

```
(defmacro unless [test then]
  `(if (not ~test)
     ~then))
```

> **NOTE** When you redefine a macro, you have to reevaluate any functions that use it. If you don't, such functions will appear to use the old definition of the macro. This happens because macro expansion happens only once, and in the case of such function definitions, the expansions were from the older definition. Remember to reevaluate your functions when you change a macro used by any of them.

This new macro definition certainly looks much clearer! The exact form is immediately obvious, minus a few characters: the backquote and the unquote (~). The backquote starts the template. The template will be expanded into an s-expression and will be returned as the return value of the macro. Clojure calls the backquote the *syntax quote character*.

UNQUOTING

Symbols that appear inside the template are used as is when the template is expanded. In the JSP analogy, these might be fixed text that doesn't change each time the page is rendered. Things that do need to change—say, parameters passed to the macro—are unquoted using the ~ character. Unquoting is the opposite of quoting. Because the whole template is inside a backquote (a quote), the ~ is used to undo that quotation so that values can be passed through.

Imagine if you hadn't unquoted the `then` parameter in your macro definition:

```
(defmacro unless [test then]
  `(if (not ~test)
     then))
```

This would cause the symbol then to appear in the s-expression returned by this macro. That could cause Clojure to throw an error when the macro is used in a definition, complaining that it is unable to resolve the then symbol. You can see why this would happen by examining the output of the macro:

```
(macroexpand '(unless (even? x) (println "Very odd, indeed!")))
;=> (if (clojure.core/not (even? x)) user/then)
```

Based on this expansion, you can infer that if this macro were used, Clojure would complain that user/then is an unknown var: Clojure will automatically qualify symbols inside a syntax-quoted form with the namespace in which the form appears (in this case user). This is why you need to unquote anything that must be replaced with its value in the template. Next, we'll look at another form of unquoting.

SPLICING

You'll now try to use the unless macro to do more than one thing if the test condition is satisfied. Consider the following new definition of exhibits-oddity?:

```
(defn exhibits-oddity? [x]
  (unless (even? x)
    (println "Odd!")
    (println "Very odd!")))
```

This won't work, because unless accepts only two parameters, and you're attempting to pass it more arguments. You can overcome this using the do form that you learned about in chapter 2:

```
(defn exhibits-oddity? [x]
  (unless (even? x)
    (do
      (println "Odd!")
      (println "Very odd!"))))
```

This works but is a bother; you have to use the do form everywhere you want more than one thing in the then part of your unless form. To make things more convenient for the callers of your macro, you can include the do form in the expansion:

```
(defmacro unless [test & exprs]
  `(if (not ~test)
     (do ~exprs)))
```

Now the unless macro accepts multiple expressions that will be executed if the test condition fails, and they'll be enclosed inside a do form. You can try it with the latest exhibits-oddity? function:

```
(exhibits-oddity? 11)
Odd!
Very odd!
NullPointerException   user/exhibits-oddity? (NO_SOURCE_FILE:4)
```

Hmm, that's strange. It does print text from both calls but then aborts with an exception. The previously seen function `macroexpand-1` can help you debug this situation:

```
(macroexpand-1 '(unless (even? x)
                  (println "Odd!")
                  (println "Very odd!")))
;=> (if (clojure.core/not (even? x))
     (do ((println "Odd!") (println "Very odd!"))))
```

There's an extra pair of parentheses around the expressions you passed into the `unless` macro as `then`. The return value of `println` is `nil`, which causes the `then` clause to reduce to `(nil nil)`. The extra parentheses cause this expression to be interpreted as a function call, throwing the `NullPointerException` that you saw earlier.

The solution is to eliminate the extra pair of parentheses. But because `then` is passed in as the remaining arguments to `unless`, it's a list. This is where the unquote splice reader macro (`~@`) comes in.

UNQUOTE SPLICE READER MACRO (~@)

Instead of taking a list and unquoting it as is using the unquote (`~`), the unquote splicing macro splices the contents of the list into the container list. You'll rewrite the `unless` macro using it:

```
(defmacro unless [test & exprs]
  `(if (not ~test)
     (do ~@exprs)))
```

With this definition of `unless`, the `exhibits-oddity?` function works just fine. This use of `do` that wraps the returned expressions from a macro is quite common, and it's a convenience all the callers of your macros will appreciate.

One final aspect of writing macros that we'll consider before moving on is that of variable capture.

GENERATING NAMES

In most Lisps, writing macros can get tricky. Well, they can get tricky in Clojure too, but the language makes things easier than other Lisps. Consider the following (incorrect) example:

```
(defmacro def-logged-fn [fn-name args & body]
  `(defn ~fn-name ~args
     (let [now (System/currentTimeMillis)]
       (println "[" now "] Call to" (str (var ~fn-name)))
       ~@body)))
```

The idea behind this macro is to create a function that logs the fact that it was called. This can be useful for debugging code. Although Clojure allows the macro to be defined, using it throws an exception:

```
(def-logged-fn printname [name]
  (println "hi" name))
CompilerException java.lang.RuntimeException: Can't let qualified name: user/
now, compiling:(NO_SOURCE_PATH:1:1)
```

The problem is that the macro attempts to use a namespace-qualified name in the let binding, which is illegal. You can confirm this using macroexpand-1:

```
(macroexpand-1 '(def-logged-fn printname [name]
  (println "hi" name)))
;=> (clojure.core/defn printname [name]
      (clojure.core/let [user/now (java.lang.System/currentTimeMillis)]
        (clojure.core/println "[" user/now ":] Call to"
          (clojure.core/str (var printname)))
        (println "hi" name)))
```

The let form can't use qualified names like user/now, and that's what Clojure is complaining about. If Clojure didn't expand now into a namespace-qualified user/now (where user is the current namespace), then now might shadow another value with the same name. This situation is illustrated here, where daily-report is a function that might run a report for a given day (note that this won't work yet, because the current implementation of def-logged-fn isn't right yet):

```
(def-logged-fn daily-report [the-day]
 ;; code to generate a report here
)
```

Now, see what happens if you use the function in the following way:

```
(let [now "2009-10-22"]
  (daily-report now))
```

This doesn't work as expected, because the value of now that the daily-report function sees isn't "2009-10-22" but a number like 1259828075387. This is because the value set up in the previous let form is captured by the one in the let form generated by the macro. This behavior is known as *variable capture*, and it can happen in most Lisps.

To avoid this, Clojure expands the names into their fully qualified names, causing the exception you saw earlier. So how do you use the let form to introduce new names? This is where the reader macro # comes in. It generates unique names that won't conflict with others that might be used in the code that's passed into the macro. This facility is called auto-gensym, because it automatically generates a symbol that's unique enough to be used as a name for things. Here's the def-logged-fn that uses this facility:

```
(defmacro def-logged-fn [fn-name args & body]
  `(defn ~fn-name ~args
     (let [now# (System/currentTimeMillis)]
       (println "[" now# "] Call to" (str (var ~fn-name)))
       ~@body)))
```

It's that simple. The auto-gensym uses the specified prefix when generating a name. For example, now# might expand to now__14187__auto__. Clojure will replace all occurrences of each use of now# with the same generated symbol.

This new definition of def-logged-fn will create a function that logs calls to it correctly. You can redefine the previously defined printname function, and try calling it now:

```
(printname "deepthi")
[ 1259955655338 ] Call to #'user/printname
hi deepthi
;=> nil
```

Variable capture is a fact of life in all Lisps, and you need to avoid it when it's undesired. Clojure makes this easier than most Lisps through this auto-gensym facility and automatic namespace qualification of syntax-quoted symbols. In chapter 11, you'll see why you might *want* the effect of variable capture when we explore anaphoric macros.

We've covered a lot of macro basics so far. Before moving on, let's take a moment to summarize the reasons to use macros.

7.1.4 *Recap: Why macros?*

As you saw in the previous section, macros can be more powerful than functions because they can do things functions can't: delay (or even choose not to do) the execution of code, change the normal flow of execution, add syntactic forms, add brand-new abstractions to the language, or just make things convenient for callers. This chapter has examples of some of these uses. Macros can also move parts of computation from runtime to compile time, and you'll see examples of this in chapter 11.

In this section, we'll discuss the possibilities offered by a programming language that features a macro system.

CODE GENERATION

Generating or transforming code is a rather common way of dealing with certain aspects of writing programs. Most programmers use code generation, even if they aren't always cognizant of doing so. The most obvious example is the use of a compiler: it takes source code and generates some form of executable code, either machine language or bytecode for a virtual machine. Parts of compilers are themselves often generated from descriptions of the language grammar. XSLT transforms are often used to convert one kind of structured XML document to other types of documents.

There are many other examples. API documentation is often created via an automated process that extracts annotated comments from the source code. Database access layers often generate all the SQL they need from high-level descriptions of tables or the model classes themselves. User interface toolkits often have associated programs that can generate code to create GUI layouts. Web service frameworks can generate standards-compliant interfaces from descriptions. Web application frameworks usually include template-based systems that generate HTML code.

Sometimes programs are written to explicitly generate source code files to handle some kind of pattern in the main application under development. For instance, in a multitier Java system, you might generate code for JavaBean classes from some other set of domain classes. Such programs often manipulate strings of text to do their job.

This kind of metaprogramming is primitive, and languages such as Ruby improve on it by providing language-level facilities to define classes and methods at runtime. Clojure provides almost an ultimate form of metaprogramming by allowing the programmer to generate or manipulate code as data.

SYNTAX AND DSLs

We've already looked at how you can use macros to add syntactic forms to Clojure. When combined with bottom-up design and domain-specific abstractions, macros can transform the solution space into one or more domain-specific languages (DSLs) with which to code the application. We'll examine examples of such a design approach in later chapters of this book.

PLAIN CONVENIENCE

Macros can make life easy for the callers of your functions. Things like the implicit do form that you saw in the previous section are common additions to macros. In the next section, you'll see some examples of macros. This will give you an idea of how people use them and how you might use them in your own programs.

7.2   *Macros from within Clojure*

In this section, we'll look at some macros. Many come from the source code of the Clojure language itself; some are from elsewhere. These examples should give you a flavor of macro style and ideas about how to use macros in your own code.

Let's begin our journey with examples of macros from the Clojure language itself. As mentioned in the previous section, much of Clojure is implemented in Clojure itself, and a lot of that code is macros. This allows the core language to remain small; Clojure has only about a dozen special forms. This approach allows most other features of the language to be developed in Clojure itself. We'll examine a few macros now.

7.2.1   *comment*

The comment macro is a great one to start with because it's so simple. It literally does nothing; this is an example of ignoring code altogether, as opposed to changing the flow of execution or delaying it. This macro allows you to comment out parts of your program or to add comments to your code.

Here's the complete implementation:

```
(defmacro comment [& body])
```

The comment macro returns nil.

7.2.2   *declare*

Here's a macro that does a little bit more. The declare macro accepts one or more symbols to let Clojure know that there may be references to them in the code that follows. The macro goes through each argument and creates a var with that name. Typically, these vars are redefined at a later point in the program.

A slightly simplified version of how the `declare` macro is implemented follows:

```
(defmacro declare [& names]
  `(do
     ~@(map #(list 'def %) names)))
```

You can see how it works by using the `macroexpand` function:

```
(macroexpand '(declare add multiply subtract divide))
;=> (do
      (def add)
      (def multiply)
      (def subtract)
      (def divide))
```

The formatting isn't part of the macro expansion. It's just a simple way to get rid of duplication from having to define multiple vars. You couldn't accomplish this with a function, by the way, because `def` is a special form that accepts only a symbol. Inside of macros, all special forms become available because we're operating at the s-expression (or symbolic) level. This is an important advantage of macros.

7.2.3   defonce

We'll now look at a macro that evaluates conditional expressions. `defonce` is a macro that accepts the name of a var and an initialization expression. But if the var has already been initialized once (has a root binding), it won't be reinitialized. The implementation of this macro is straightforward, so we don't even need to use macro expansion to see what's going on:

```
(defmacro defonce [name expr]
  `(let [v# (def ~name)]
     (when-not (.hasRoot v#)
       (def ~name ~expr))))
```

Notice the unquoting going on here in the last line—it's what substitutes the name of the var in the `def` form, as well as the expression being passed in.

A `def` isn't normally evaluated more than once, so you may be wondering why `defonce` exists. When using an editor with an integrated REPL, it's common to reevaluate an entire namespace to refresh the REPL environment with updates from the editor: this means that any `def`s will be reevaluated, even if they take a long time to evaluate or contain a stateful resource such as a database connection. `defonce` is used to avoid this problem.

7.2.4   and

Let's now look at a slightly more complex example. In most languages and as well as other logical operators are implemented as special forms. In other words, they're built into the core of the language. In Clojure, and is just another macro:

```
(defmacro and
  ([] true)
  ([x] x)
```

```
([x & next]
  `(let [and# ~x]
     (if and# (and ~@next) and#))))
```

This is an elegant piece of code! When and is called with no arguments, it returns
true. When it's called with a single argument, the return value is the argument itself
(remember that anything other than nil or false is treated as true). When there are
multiple arguments, the macro evaluates the first argument. It then tests it with the if
form. If the value is logically true, the macro calls itself with the remaining arguments. The process then repeats. If the evaluation of any argument returns a logical
false, the if form returns that value as is.

You can use macroexpand to see what happens:

```
(macroexpand '(and (even? x) (> x 50) (< x 500)))
;=> (let* [and__4357__auto__ (even? x)]
      (if and__4357__auto__
        (clojure.core/and (> x 50) (< x 500))
        and__4357__auto__))
```

You may see something slightly different because the auto-gensym will create different names for the local symbols. Also, remember that macroexpand doesn't expand
macros contained in subexpressions. In reality, the macro will be completely expanded,
and the final expanded s-expression will replace the original call to and.

7.2.5 *time*

time is a rather handy macro, useful for quick checks on how slow or fast your code is
running. It accepts an expression, executes it, prints the time it took to execute, and
then returns the result of the evaluation. Here's an example:

```
(time (* 133) 13331))
"Elapsed time: 0.04 msecs"
;=> 18009761
```

Using the time macro isn't as sophisticated as using a profiler, for instance, but it can
be quite useful for quick benchmarks of your code. Here's how it's implemented:

```
(defmacro time [expr]
  `(let [start# (. System (nanoTime))
         ret# ~expr]
     (prn
       (str "Elapsed time: "
            (/ (double (- (. System (nanoTime)) start#)) 1000000.0)
            " msecs"))
     ret#))
```

As you can see, the macro starts a timer before evaluating the expression passed in.
The value of the expression is captured and returned after the timer is stopped and
the duration printed to the console.

These are just a few macros that can be found in Clojure's source code. As mentioned earlier, it's advantageous for a language to have a small core and have all other

features built on top of it using regular code. Clojure does this in an elegant fashion, and reading through the source code is a great way to learn the tricks of the trade. You'll now write some macros of your own.

7.3   *Writing your own macros*

So far, you've learned the basic theory of Clojure's macro system. You've also seen some macros that form part of the Clojure language. You'll now write a few of your own to see how you might use macros in your own programs.

To help you get started, we'll start with a simple macro called `infix`. Next, you'll write one called `randomly`, which will appear to add a new control structure to Clojure. Third, you'll write a macro called `defwebmethod`, which could be the beginning of a DSL for writing web applications. Building on the `defwebmethod` macro, you'll create `defnn`, a macro that will aid in creating functions that accept named arguments. And finally, you'll write the `assert-true` macro, which could be the beginning of a unit-testing framework for Clojure.

7.3.1   *infix*

In chapter 1, we talked about an `infix` macro, which would allow you to call mathematical operators using infix notation. Here's how you might implement it:

```
(defmacro infix [expr]
  (let [[left op right] expr]
    (list op left right)))
```

It's a trivial implementation: it just rearranges the function symbol and the arguments back into prefix notation. It's also a fairly naïve implementation because it supports only two terms and doesn't do any kind of error checking. Still, it's a fun little macro.

7.3.2   *randomly*

There are often situations where you want to randomly pick a path of execution. Such a requirement might arise, for instance, if you wanted to introduce some randomness into your code. The `randomly` macro accepts any number of s-expressions and picks one at random. Here's the implementation:

```
(defmacro randomly [& exprs]
  (let [len (count exprs)
        index (rand-int len)
        conditions (map #(list '= index %) (range len))]
    `(cond ~@(interleave conditions exprs))))
```

`rand-int` is a function that returns a random integer between zero and its argument. Here you pass the length of the incoming exprs to the `rand-int` function. Now test it:

```
(randomly (println "amit") (println "deepthi") (println "adi"))
adi
;=> nil
```

Try it one more time:

```
(randomly (println "amit") (println "deepthi") (println "adi"))
deepthi
;=> nil
```

And once more:

```
(randomly (println "amit") (println "deepthi") (println "adi"))
adi
;=> nil
```

The macro works as expected, evaluating only one of the three expressions. Obviously, given the randomization, your output will look different. Here's what the macro transforms the passed-in s-expressions into:

```
(macroexpand-1
  '(randomly (println "amit") (println "deepthi") (println "adi")))
;=> (clojure.core/cond
      (= 0 0) (println "amit")
      (= 0 1) (println "deepthi")
      (= 0 2) (println "adi"))
```

Again, given the randomization, your expansion may look different. Indeed, if you expand it several times, you'll see that the condition clauses in the cond form change.

Incidentally, there's an easier way to achieve the same effect. Consider the following implementation:

```
(defmacro randomly-2 [& exprs]
  (nth exprs (rand-int (count exprs))))
```

Try it at the REPL to confirm that it works. There's one unintended consequence of these macros: each selects an expression when it's expanded, not later when the code the macro expands to is run. This means that if the macro is expanded inside another macro—say, inside a function—it will always return the *same* random value. To fix this, you need a new call to rand-int every time the body is evaluated, not just once when the macro is expanded. Here's a possible fix:

```
(defmacro randomly-2 [& exprs]
  (let [c (count exprs)]
    `(case (rand-int ~c) ~@(interleave (range c) exprs))))
```

7.3.3 *defwebmethod*

You'll now write a macro that has nothing to do with changing the flow of execution of your code but is a convenience macro that makes life easier for those who use it. It will also appear to add a feature that's specific to building web applications to Clojure.

In essence, the web is made dynamic through programs that generate different HTML documents based on certain input parameters. You can use Clojure functions for this purpose, where each function might correspond to something the user requests. For instance, you could write a function that accepts a username and a date and returns a report of that day's expenses. The parameters of the request might be bundled in a hash map and given to each function as a `request` object. Each function could then query the `request` object for the parameters it needs, process the request as required, and then return appropriate HTML.

Here's what such a function might look like:

```
(defn login-user [request]
  (let [username (:username request)
        password (:password request)]
    (if (check-credentials username password)
      (str "Welcome back, " username ", " password " is correct!")
      (str "Login failed!"))))
```

Here, `check-credentials` might be a function that would look up authentication information from a database. For your purposes, let's define it as follows:

```
(defn check-credentials [username password]
  true)
```

Also, `login-user` would return real HTML as opposed to the strings you're returning. It should give a general idea about the structure of such functions, though. Now try it:

```
(def request {:username "amit" :password "123456"})
;=> #'user/request
(login-user request)
;=> "Welcome back, amit, 123456 is correct!"
```

The trouble with this is that every function like `login-user` must manually query values out of the `request` map. The example here needs two parameters—username and password—but you can certainly imagine functions that need many more. It would be quite tedious to have to pull them out from the `request` map each time. Consider the following macro:

```
(defmacro defwebmethod [name args & exprs]
  `(defn ~name [{:keys ~args}]
     ~@exprs))
```

You can now use this macro to define a new version of `login-user` as follows:

```
(defwebmethod login-user [username password]
  (if (check-credentials username password)
    (str "Welcome, " username ", " password " is still correct!")
    (str "Login failed!")))
```

You can try this version of the function on the REPL:

```
(login-user request)
;=> "Welcome, amit, 123456 is still correct!"
```

For programmers who don't know the internals of `defwebmethod`, it appears that it's literally a new language abstraction, designed specifically for web applications. Any names specified in the parameters list are automatically pulled out of the `request` map and set up with the correct value (the function defined still takes the same argument). You can specify the names of the function parameters in any order, which is a nice convenience.

You can imagine other domain-specific additions to Clojure written this way.

7.3.4 defnn

You used map destructuring in the previous example to create a function that broke apart an incoming map into constituent, named parts. Now, you're going to let named arguments be passed into a function in any order, for instance:

```
(defnn print-details [name salary start-date]
  (println "Name:" name)
  (println "Salary:" salary)
  (println "Started on:" start-date))
;=> #'user/print-details
```

And in using it, you'd be able to do something like this:

```
(print-details :start-date "10/22/2009" :name "Rob" :salary 1000000)
Name: Rob
Salary: 1000000
Started on: 10/22/2009
```

Notice how you can change the order of the arguments because they're named using keywords. If you didn't pass some of those arguments in, they'd default to `nil`. Here's the implementation:

```
(defmacro defnn [fname [& names] & body]
  (let [ks {:keys (vec names)}]
    `(defn ~fname [& {:as arg-map#}]
       (let [~ks arg-map#]
         ~@body))))
```

How does it work? You can check using `macroexpand`:

```
(def print-details
 (clojure.core/fn
  ([& {:as arg-map__2045__auto__}]
   (clojure.core/let [{:keys [name salary start-date]}
                      arg-map__2045__auto__]
    (println "Name:" name)
    (println "Salary:" salary)
    (println "Started on:" start-date)))))
```

Again, you're using map destructuring in a `let` form to tease apart named arguments and to set up names for the specified values. The `let` form also converts the pairs of keywords and values into a hash map. This is a limited form of named arguments, and it certainly doesn't do any error checks or allow for default values. Still, it can be built upon to add those features.

7.3.5   *assert-true*

For the last example, you'll write a macro that you can use to assert that an s-expression evaluates to true. Let's see how you might use it:

```
(assert-true (= (* 2 4) (/ 16 2)))
;=> true
(assert-true (< (* 2 4) (/ 18 2)))
;=> true
```

You might use assert-true in a set of unit tests. You might be tempted to have multiple such assertions in a single unit test, all verifying related functionality. The trouble with having several assertions in one unit test is that when something fails, it isn't immediately obvious what failed. Line numbers are useful, as are custom error messages that some unit-testing frameworks allow.

In your little macro, you'd like to see the code that failed. It might work as follows:

```
(assert-true (>= (* 2 4) (/ 18 2)))
;=> RuntimeException (* 2 4) is not >= 9
```

Using literal code like this is a natural fit for macros. Here's the macro:

```
(defmacro assert-true [test-expr]
  (let [[operator lhs rhs] test-expr]
    `(let [rhsv# ~rhs ret# ~test-expr]
       (if-not ret#
         (throw (RuntimeException.
                  (str '~lhs " is not " '~operator " " rhsv#)))
         true))))
```

It's a straightforward implementation. A binding form is used to tease apart test-expr into its constituent operator, lhs, and rhs parts. The generated code then uses these to do their thing, best understood by looking at a sample macro expansion:

```
(macroexpand-1 '(assert-true (>= (* 2 4) (/ 18 2))))
;=> (clojure.core/let [rhsv__11966__auto__ (/ 18 2)
                       ret__11967__auto__ (>= (* 2 4) (/ 18 2))]
      (clojure.core/if-not ret__11967__auto__
        (throw (java.lang.RuntimeException.
          (clojure.core/str (quote (* 2 4))
             " is not " (quote >=) " " rhsv__11966__auto__)))
        true))
```

As mentioned earlier, this macro is actually quite simple. Notice how '~lhs, for instance, expands to (quote (* 2 4)). This is desirable, because by quoting it, you're able to stop the form from being evaluated and replaced with its result. This makes it more useful when a failure occurs, because it's the actual code that the user passed into the assertion. Imagine how hard doing something like this would be in a language such as Java, C++, or even Ruby or Python.

You can improve it by adding some semantic error checking to handle situations where invalid expressions are passed. Consider the following definition:

```
(defmacro assert-true [test-expr]
  (if-not (= 3 (count test-expr))
    (throw (RuntimeException.
         "Argument must be of the form
             (operator test-expr expected-expr)")))
  (if-not (some #{(first test-expr)} '(< > <= >= = not=))
    (throw (RuntimeException.
       "operator must be one of < > <= >= = not=")))
  (let [[operator lhs rhs] test-expr]
    `(let [rhsv# ~rhs ret# ~test-expr]
       (if-not ret#
         (throw (RuntimeException.
           (str '~lhs " is not " '~operator " " rhsv#)))
         true))))
```

This works for the two situations where someone passes a malformed expression into the macro:

```
(assert-true (>= (* 2 4) (/ 18 2) (+ 2 5)))
;=> RuntimeException Argument must be of the form
                 (operator test-expr expected-expr)
```

It also checks for the case where someone tries to use an operator that isn't supported:

```
(assert-true (<> (* 2 4) (/ 16 2)))
;=> RuntimeException operator must be one of < > <= >= = not=
```

This example shows how macros can make it easy to perform domain specific semantic checking of not just values but of the code itself. In other languages, this might have required some serious parsing. Clojure's code-as-data approach pays off in this scenario.

7.4 *Summary*

We said in the beginning of this chapter that macros distinguish Clojure (and other Lisps) from most other programming languages. Macros allow the programmer to add new language features to Clojure. Indeed, you can build whole new layers of functionality on top of Clojure, which make it appear that an entire new language has been created. An example of this is Clojure's concurrency system: it isn't part of the language per se; it's implemented as a set of Java classes and associated Clojure functions and macros.

Macros truly blur the distinction between the language designer and the application programmer, allowing you to add to the language as you see fit. For instance, should you feel that Clojure lacks a construct that would allow you to express something, you don't have to wait for the next version of the language or wish you were using a different language. You can add that feature yourself. You'll see an example of this in the next chapter, where we'll show you how you can build an object system in Clojure using macros and higher-order functions.

More on functional programming

So far you've seen a lot of the Clojure programming language, and you've used it to write a good number of functions. Because it's a functional programming language, understanding and mastering the functional programming paradigm is key to being successful with it. In this chapter, we'll explore this topic some more.

Instead of approaching this from, say, a mathematical (or plain theoretical) standpoint, we'll review code to explore some of the main ideas. We'll start by implementing a few common higher-order functions that you often see used in functional programs. The idea is to help you become comfortable with recursion, lazy sequences, functional abstraction, and function reuse.

Next, we'll visit the land of partial application. This exposure will give you further insight into functional programming and what you can do with it. Although partial application doesn't find particularly widespread use in Clojure, sometimes it's the perfect fit for the job. Incidentally, you'll also see the alternatives to partial application later in the chapter.

The final stop will be to explore closures. The last section puts everything together to write a little object system that illustrates the ideas of OOP vis-à-vis functional programming. You may wonder why there's a section on OOP in a chapter on functional programming. Once you read through to the end of this chapter, you'll realize how functional programming can be thought of as a superset of OOP—and in fact transcends it.

8.1 Using higher-order functions

We talked about higher-order functions in chapter 3. A *higher-order function* is one that either accepts another function or returns a function. Higher-order functions allow the programmer to abstract out patterns of computation that would otherwise result in duplicated code. In this section, we'll look at a few examples of higher-order functions that can greatly simplify many things you'll come across. You've seen several of these functions before, in other forms, and we'll point these out as you implement them.

Overall, this section will give you a sense of how higher-order functions can be used to implement a variety of solutions in Clojure; indeed, how it's an integral part of doing so.

8.1.1 Collecting results of functions

Let's begin our look at higher-order functions by considering the idea of a function named `square-all` that accepts a list of numbers and returns a list of the squares of each element. You may need such a sequence in a graphics program or in some other math computation:

```
(defn square [x]
  (* x x))
(defn square-all [numbers]
  (if (empty? numbers)
    nil                                    ⟵  Idiomatic
    (cons (square (first numbers))            equivalent to
          (square-all (rest numbers)))))))    empty list
```

A quick note about returning `nil` in the empty case: you could also return an empty list, but in Clojure it's idiomatic to return `nil` instead because it's falsey (unlike an empty list, which is truthy) and all `seq`-related functions treat `nil` like an empty list anyway (for example, `conj`-ing onto `nil` returns a list).

Notice that the `cons` function is used to build a new sequence. It accepts a single element, and another sequence, and returns a new one with that element inserted in the first position. Here, the first element is the square of the first number, and the body is the sequence of the squares of the remaining numbers. This works as expected, and you can test this at the read-evaluate-print loop (REPL) as follows:

```
(square-all [1 2 3 4 5 6])
;=> (1 4 9 16 25 36)
```

Now let's look at another function, cube-all, which also accepts a list of numbers but returns a list of cubes of each element:

```
(defn cube [x]
    (* x x x))
(defn cube-all [numbers]
  (if (empty? numbers)
    ()
    (cons (cube (first numbers))
          (cube-all (rest numbers)))))
```

Again, this is easy to test:

```
(cube-all [1 2 3 4 5 6])
;=> (1 8 27 64 125 216)
```

They both work as expected. The trouble is that there's a significant amount of duplication in the definitions of square-all and cube-all. You can easily see this commonality by considering the fact that both functions are applying a function to each input element and are collecting the results before returning the list of collected values.

You've already seen that such functions can be captured as higher-order functions in languages such as Clojure:

```
(defn do-to-all [f numbers]
  (if (empty? numbers)
    ()
    (cons (f (first numbers))
          (do-to-all f (rest numbers)))))
```

With this, you can perform the same operations easily:

```
(do-to-all square [1 2 3 4 5 6])
;=> (1 4 9 16 25 36)
(do-to-all cube [1 2 3 4 5 6])
;=> (1 8 27 64 125 216)
```

You can imagine that the do-to-all implementation is similar to that of the map function that's included in Clojure's core library. You've seen this function earlier in the book. The map function is an abstraction that allows you to apply any function across sequences of arguments and collect results into another sequence. This implementation is quite limited when compared with the core map function, and it also suffers from a rather fatal flaw: it will blow the call stack if a long enough list of elements is passed in. Here's what it will look like:

```
(do-to-all square (range 11000))
StackOverflowError   clojure.lang.Numbers$LongOps.multiply (Numbers.java:459)
```

This is because every item results in another recursive call to `do-to-all`, thus adding another stack frame until you eventually run out. Consider the following revised implementation:

```
(defn do-to-all [f numbers]
  (lazy-seq
    (if (empty? numbers)
      ()
      (cons (f (first numbers))
            (do-to-all f (rest numbers))))))
```

Now, because this return is a lazy sequence, it no longer attempts to recursively compute all the elements to return. The `lazy-seq` macro takes a body of code that returns a sequence (or `nil`) and returns an object that's "seqable"—that is, it behaves like a sequence. But it invokes the body only once and on demand (lazily) and returns cached results thereafter. The function now works as expected:

```
(take 10 (drop 10000 (do-to-all square (range 11000))))
;=> (100000000 100020001 100040004 100060009 100080016 100100025 100120036
     100140049 100160064 100180081)
```

This is similar to the `map` function that comes with Clojure (although the Clojure version does a lot more). Here's what that might look like:

```
(take 10 (drop 10000 (do-to-all square (range 11000))))
;=> (100000000 100020001 100040004 100060009 100080016 100100025 100120036
     100140049 100160064 100180081)
```

Notice all that was done here was to replace `do-to-all` with `map`. The map function is an extremely useful higher-order function, and as you've seen over the last few chapters, it sees heavy use.

Let's now look at another important operation, which can be implemented using a different higher-order function.

8.1.2 Reducing lists of things

It's often useful to take a list of things and compute a value based on all of them. An example might be totaling a list of numbers or finding the largest number. You'll implement the total first:

```
(defn total-of [numbers]
  (loop [nums numbers sum 0]
    (if (empty? nums)
      sum
      (recur (rest nums) (+ sum (first nums))))))
```

This works as expected, as you can see in the following test at the REPL:

```
(total-of [5 7 9 3 4 1 2 8])
;=> 39
```

Now you'll write a function to return the greatest from a list of numbers. First, write a simple function that returns the greater of two numbers:

```
(defn larger-of [x y]
  (if (> x y) x y))
```

This is a simple enough function, but now you can use it to search for the largest number in a series of numbers:

```
(defn largest-of [numbers]
  (loop [l numbers candidate (first numbers)]
    (if (empty? l)
      candidate
      (recur (rest l) (larger-of candidate (first l))))))
```

You need to see if this works:

```
(largest-of [5 7 9 3 4 1 2 8])
;=> 9
(largest-of [])
;=> nil
```

It's working, but there's clearly some duplication in total-of and largest-of. Specifically, the only difference between them is that one adds an element to an accumulator, whereas the other compares an element with a candidate for the result. Next, you'll extract the commonality into a function:

```
(defn compute-across [func elements value]
  (if (empty? elements)
    value
    (recur func (rest elements) (func value (first elements)))))
```

Now you can easily use compute-across to implement total-of and largest-of:

```
(defn total-of [numbers]
  (compute-across + numbers 0))
(defn largest-of [numbers]
  (compute-across larger-of numbers (first numbers)))
```

To ensure that things still work as expected, you can test these two functions at the REPL again:

```
(total-of [5 7 9 3 4 1 2 8])
;=> 39
(largest-of [5 7 9 3 4 1 2 8])
;=> 9
```

compute-across is generic enough that it can operate on any sequence. For instance, here's a function that collects all numbers greater than some specified threshold:

```
(defn all-greater-than [threshold numbers]
  (compute-across #(if (> %2 threshold) (conj %1 %2) %1) numbers []))
```

Before getting into how this works, you need to check if it works:

```
(all-greater-than 5 [5 7 9 3 4 1 2 8])
;=> [7 9 8]
```

It works as expected. The implementation is simple: you've already seen how compute-across works. The initial value (which behaves as an accumulator) is an empty vector. You need to conjoin numbers to this when it's greater than the threshold. The anonymous function does this.

The compute-across function is similar to something you've already seen: the reduce function that's part of Clojure's core functions. Here's all-greater-than rewritten using the built-in reduce:

```
(defn all-greater-than [threshold numbers]
  (reduce #(if (> %2 threshold) (conj %1 %2) %1) [] numbers))
```

And here it is in action:

```
(all-greater-than 5 [5 7 9 3 4 1 2 8])
;=> [7 9 8]
```

Both the compute-across and reduce functions allow you to process sequences of data and compute a final result. Let's now look at another related example of using compute-across.

8.1.3   Filtering lists of things

You wrote a function in the previous section that allows you to collect all numbers greater than a particular threshold. Now you'll write another one that collects those numbers that are less than a threshold:

```
(defn all-lesser-than [threshold numbers]
  (compute-across #(if (< %2 threshold) (conj %1 %2) %1) numbers []))
```

Here's the new function in action:

```
(all-lesser-than 5 [5 7 9 3 4 1 2 8])
;=> [3 4 1 2]
```

Notice how easy it is, now that you have your convenient little compute-across function (or the equivalent reduce). Also, notice that there's duplication in the all-greater-than and all-lesser-than functions. The only difference between them is in the criteria used in selecting which elements should be returned.

Now you need to extract the common part into a higher-order `select-if` function:

```
(defn select-if [pred elements]
  (compute-across #(if (pred %2) (conj %1 %2) %1) elements []))
```

You can now use this to select all sorts of elements from a larger sequence. For instance, here's an example of selecting all odd numbers from a vector:

```
(select-if odd? [5 7 9 3 4 1 2 8])
;=> [5 7 9 3 1]
```

To reimplement the previously defined `all-lesser-than` function, you could write it in the following manner:

```
(defn all-lesser-than [threshold numbers]
  (select-if #(< % threshold) numbers))
```

This implementation is far more readable, because it expresses the intent with simplicity and clarity. The `select-if` function is another useful, low-level function that you can use with any sequence. In fact, Clojure comes with such a function, one that you've seen before: `filter`. Here, for instance, is the same selection of odd numbers you just saw:

```
(filter odd?  [5 7 9 3 4 1 2 8])
;=> (5 7 9 3 1)
```

Note that although `filter` returns a lazy sequence here, and the `select-if` function returned a vector, as long as your program expects a sequence, either function will work.

Over the last few pages, you've created the functions `do-to-all`, `compute-across`, and `select-if`, which implement the essence of the built-in `map`, `reduce`, and `filter` functions. The reason for this was two-fold: to demonstrate common use cases of higher-order functions and to show that the basic form of these functions is rather simple to implement. The `select-if` isn't lazy, for instance, but with all the knowledge you've gained so far, you can implement one that is. With this background in place, let's explore a few other topics of interest of functional programs.

8.2   *Partial application*

In the last section you wrote several higher-order functions that accepted a function as one argument and applied it to other arguments. Now we're going to look at another kind of higher-order function—those that create and return new functions. This is a crucial aspect of functional programming, and in this section you'll write functions that return new functions of less arity than the ones they accept as an argument. You'll do this by "partially applying" the function. (Don't worry; the meaning of this will become clear shortly.)

8.2.1 Adapting functions

Let's imagine that you have a function that accepts a tax percentage (such as 8.0 or 9.75) and a retail price and returns the total price with tax using a threading macro:

```
(defn price-with-tax [tax-rate amount]
  (->> (/ tax-rate 100)
       (+ 1)
       (* amount)))
```

Now you can find out what something truly costs, because you can calculate its price including the sales tax, as follows:

```
(price-with-tax 9.5M 100)
;=> 109.500M
```

Notice that you use the BigDecimal type for money (specified by the M suffix): using floating-point numbers for financial applications is asking for rounding errors! If you had a list of prices that you wanted to convert into a list of tax-inclusive prices, you could write the following function:

```
(defn with-california-taxes [prices]
  (map #(price-with-tax 9.25M %) prices))
```

And you could then batch-calculate pricing with taxes:

```
(def prices [100 200 300 400 500])
;=> #'user/prices
(with-california-taxes prices)
;=> (109.2500M 218.5000M 327.7500M 437.0000M 546.2500M)
```

Notice that in the definition of with-california-taxes, there's an anonymous function that accepted a single argument (a price) and applied price-with-tax to 9.25 and the price. Creating this anonymous function is convenient; otherwise, you might have had to define a separate function that you may never have used anywhere else, such as this:

```
(defn price-with-ca-tax [price]
  (price-with-tax 9.25M price))
```

And if you had to handle New York, it would look like this:

```
(defn price-with-ny-tax [price]
  (price-with-tax 8.0M price))
```

If you had to handle any more, the duplication would certainly get to you. Luckily, a functional language such as Clojure can make short work of it:

```
(defn price-calculator-for-tax [state-tax]
  (fn [price]
    (price-with-tax state-tax price)))
```

This function accepts a tax rate, presumably for a given state, and then returns a new function that accepts a single argument. When this new function is called with a price, it returns the result of applying `price-with-tax` to the originally supplied tax rate and the price. In this manner, the newly defined (and returned) function behaves like a closure around the supplied tax rate. Now that you have this higher-level function, you can remove the duplication you saw earlier by defining state-specific functions as follows:

```
(def price-with-ca-tax (price-calculator-for-tax 9.25M))
(def price-with-ny-tax (price-calculator-for-tax 8.0M))
```

Figure 8.1 shows how this works.

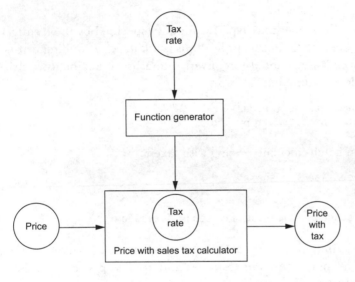

Figure 8.1 The `tax-rate` initially passed into the `price-calculator-for-tax` function is captured by the resulting function (such as `price-with-ca-tax`). It's then able to use that value when it's called with a price, to return the correct price with the tax applied to it.

Notice again that you're creating new vars (and that you're directly using `def` here, not `defn`) that are bound to the anonymous functions returned by the `price-calculator-for-tax` function.

These new functions accept a single argument and are perfect for functions such as `with-california-taxes` that accept a list of prices, and call `map` across them. A single-argument function serves well in such a case, and you can use any of the previous functions for this purpose. This is a simple case where you started out with a function of a certain arity (in this case, `price-with-tax` accepts two arguments), and you needed a new function that accepted a lesser number of arguments (in this case, a single-argument function that could map across a sequence of prices).

This approach of taking a function of n arguments and creating a new function of k arguments (where $n > k$) is a form of adaptation (you may be familiar with the adapter pattern from OOP literature). You don't need special ceremony to do this in functional languages, thanks to first-class functions. Let's see how Clojure makes this easy.

PARTIAL APPLICATION

Let's say you have a function of n arguments and you need to fix $(n - k)$ arguments to create a new function of k arguments. Here's a function to illustrate this:

```
(defn of-n-args [a b c d e]
  (str a b c d e ))
```

Now, to fix, say, the first three arguments to 1, 2, and 3, you could do the following:

```
(defn of-k-args [d e]
  (of-n-args 1 2 3 d e))
```

You need to ensure that this function works as expected:

```
(of-k-args \a \b)
;=> "123ab"
```

Okay, so that works. If you needed to create a function that fixed, say, two or four arguments, you'd have to write similar code again. As you can imagine, if you had to do this a lot, it would get rather repetitive and tedious.

You could improve things by writing a function that generalizes the idea, such as

```
(defn partially-applied [of-n-args & n-minus-k-args]
  (fn [& k-args]
    (apply of-n-args (concat n-minus-k-args k-args))))
```

Now, you could create any number of functions that fixed a particular set of arguments of a particular function, for example:

```
(def of-2-args (partially-applied of-n-args \a \b \c))
;=> #'user/of-2-args
(def of-3-args (partially-applied of-n-args \a \b))
;=> #'user/of-3-args
```

And you can see if these work as expected:

```
(of-2-args 4 5)
;=> "abc45"
(of-3-args 3 4 5)
;=> "ab345"
```

The new function is called `partially-applied` because it returns a function that's a partially applied version of the function you passed into it. For example, `of-3-args` is a partially applied version of `of-n-args`. This is such a common technique in functional programming that Clojure comes with a function that does this, and it's called `partial`.

It's used the same way:

```
(def of-2-args (partial of-n-args \a \b \c))
;=> #'user/of-2-args
(def of-3-args (partial of-n-args \a \b))
;=> #'user/of-3-args
```

And here it is in action:

```
(of-2-args 4 5)
;=> "abc45"
(of-3-args 3 4 5)
;=> "ab345"
```

You now understand what it means to partially apply a function. Partial application is an abstraction that comes out of having higher-order functions. Although the examples showed this technique where you needed to adapt a function of a given arity to a function of a lower arity, there are other uses as well. You'll see one such use in the next section.

8.2.2   Defining functions

In this section, we'll use the technique of partial application to define new functions. Recall the select-if function from the previous section:

```
(defn select-if [pred elements]
  (compute-across #(if (pred %2) (conj %1 %2) %1) elements []))
```

Note that the compute-across function is passed an empty vector as the last argument. Here, you'll write a modified version of select-if called select-into-if, which will accept an initial container:

```
(defn select-into-if [container pred elements]
  (compute-across #(if (pred %2) (conj %1 %2) %1) elements container))
```

Again, as you saw in the previous section, if you had a list of numbers such as

```
(def numbers [4 9 5 7 6 3 8])
```

then you could use the new function as follows:

```
(select-into-if [] #(< % 7) numbers)
;=> [4 5 6 3]
```

Similarly, you could also pass in an empty list instead of an empty vector, as shown here:

```
(select-into-if () #(< % 7) numbers)
;=> (3 6 5 4)
```

Note that depending on whether you want to filter results up or down (in the same order as the elements appear or in the reverse), you can use either the empty vector as your container or the empty list. This ordering may be useful when you have a situation where the order matters, and you either want to preserve it or perhaps reverse it. Now you'll further abstract this idea of filtering results up or down as follows:

```
(def select-up (partial select-into-if []))
```

This is a new function using `partial`. You fixed the first argument of the select-into-if function to the empty vector. Similarly, you could define the concept of selecting down a sequence of elements as follows:

```
(def select-down (partial select-into-if ()))
```

It's time to test these two functions to ensure that they work:

```
(select-up  #(< % 9)  [5 3 9 6 8])
;=> [5 3 6 8]
(select-down  #(< % 9)  [5 3 9 6 8])
;=> (8 6 3 5)
```

Obviously, there are specific implications that arise from using a vector versus a list, and depending on the situation, these may be a convenient way to filter elements of a sequence.

As you've seen, partial application of functions can be a useful tool. This section showed two situations where this technique might come in handy. The first is to adapt functions to a suitable arity by fixing one or more arguments of a given function. The second is to define functions by partially applying a more general function to get specific functions that have one or more arguments fixed.

There's a more general principle at work here, a principle that makes partial function application possible: lexical closures.

8.3   Closures

In this section, we're going to explore the lexical closure, which is a central concept of functional programming. How central it is can be seen from the fact that the name *Clojure* itself is a play on the term *closure*. We'll begin by reviewing what closures are and what they close over. Then we'll look at a couple of closure use cases in functional programming. Specifically, we'll look at how closures can be used to delay computation and how they can be used as objects (in the OO sense of the word). At the end, we'll create a little OO layer for Clojure to demonstrate that Clojure (and Lisps in general) go beyond traditional ideas of OOP.

8.3.1   Free variables and closures

Before we jump into what closures are, let's look at the concept of free variables. A free variable is one that's neither an argument nor a local variable. For instance, take a look at adder in this code:

```
(defn adder [num1 num2]
  (let [x (+ num1 num2)]
    (fn [y]
      (+ x y))))
```

x is a free variable: its value will come from outside scope of function that uses it.

Here, num1 and num2 are arguments of the adder function and so they aren't free variables. The let form creates a lexically scoped block of code, and within that block, num1 and num2 are free variables. Further, the let form creates a locally named value called x. Therefore, within the let block, x isn't a free variable. Finally, an anonymous function is created that accepts an argument called y. Within this anonymous function, y isn't a free variable, but x is (because it's neither an argument nor a local variable within the function block).

Now that you understand what a free variable is, let's examine this function a little more. Consider the following code:

```
(def add-5 (adder 2 3))
;=> #'user/add-5
```

add-5 is a var that's bound to the return value of the call to adder, which is the anonymous function returned by the adder function. The function object contains within it a reference to x, which exists for only as long as the let block inside adder lives. Consider that the following works as expected:

```
(add-5 10)
;=> 15
```

Given the fact that the life of a locally named value such as x lasts only until the enclosing lexical block lasts, how can add-5 do its work? You might imagine that the x referenced inside add-5 ceased to be the moment add-5 was created.

The reason this works, though, is that the anonymous function returned by adder is a closure, in this case closing over the free variable x. The extent (life) of such closed-over free variables is that of the closure itself. This is why add-5 is able to use the value of x, and it adds 10 to 5 to return 15 in the example.

In summary, a free variable will have the value that variable has in its enclosing scope at the moment that its own scope is created. Now let's look at what closures can do for your Clojure programs.

8.3.2 *Delayed computation and closures*

One aspect of closures is that they can be executed at any time, any number of times, or not at all. This property of delayed execution can be useful. Consider the following code:

```
(let [x 1
      y 0]
  (/ x y))
ArithmeticException Divide by zero   clojure.lang.Numbers.divide
(Numbers.java:156)
```

You know what this code will do: it will promptly throw a nice divide-by-zero exception. Let's wrap the code with a try-catch block so as to control the situation programmatically:

```
(let [x 1
      y 0]
     (try
       (/ x y)
       (catch Exception e (println (.getMessage e)))))
Divide by zero
;=> nil
```

This pattern is common enough that you might want to extract it out into a higher-order control structure:

```
(defn try-catch [the-try the-catch]
  (try
    (the-try)
    (catch Exception e (the-catch e))))
```

Now that you have this, you could write

```
(let [x 1
      y 0]
  (try-catch #(/ x y)
             #(println (.getMessage %))))
```

Notice here that you're passing in an anonymous function that closes around x and y. You could have written a macro to do this same thing, but this shows that you don't need macros for something like this, even though the macro solution would be nicer (syntactically more convenient to use, resulting in code that's easier to read).

When we compared macros to functions, we noted that Clojure evaluates function arguments in an eager manner. This behavior is one of the reasons why macros have an advantage, in that macros don't evaluate arguments, allowing us as programmers to be in control. Here, the try-catch function achieves the same intended effect by accepting functions that will be evaluated later. To be specific, although your anonymous functions are created immediately (when you passed them in as arguments), they're only *evaluated* later (within the try-catch block). Further, because the free variables x and y were enclosed within a closure correctly, the try-catch function was able to work correctly.

You can imagine creating other control structures in a similar manner. In the next section, you'll see another interesting aspect of closures.

8.3.3 *Closures and objects*

In this section, we're going to examine another benefit of the closure. As you've seen over the past few paragraphs, a closure captures the bindings of any free variables visible at the point of creation. These bindings are then hidden from view to the rest of the world, making the closure a candidate for private data. (Data hiding is somewhat of an overrated concept, especially in a language such as Clojure. You'll see more on this in the next section.)

For the moment, let's continue exploring the captured bindings inside closures. Imagine that you needed to handle users' login information and email addresses in your application. Consider the following function:

```
(defn new-user [login password email]
  (fn [a]
    (case a
      :login login
      :password password
      :email email
      nil)))
```

There's nothing particularly new here; you saw such code in the previous section. Here it is in action:

```
(def arjun (new-user "arjun" "secret" "arjun@zololabs.com"))
;=> #'user/arjun
(arjun :login)
;=> "arjun"
(arjun :password)
;=> "secret"
(arjun :email)
;=> "arjun@zololabs.com"
(arjun :name)
;=> nil
```

First, a new function object is created by calling the new-user function with "arjun", "secret", and "arjun@currylogic.com" as arguments. Then, you were able to query it for the login, password, and email address. arjun appears to behave something like a map, or at least a data object of some kind. You can query the internal state of the object using the keywords :login, :password, and :email, as shown previously.

It's also worth noting that this is the only way to access the internals of arjun. This is a form of message passing: the keywords are messages that you're sending to a receiver object, which in this case is the function object arjun. You can implement fewer of these should you choose to. For instance, you might deem the password to be a hidden detail. The modified function might look as follows:

```
(defn new-user [login password email]
  (fn [a]
    (case a
      :login login
      :email email
      :password-hash (hash password)      Inner function can
      nil)))                              access password.
;=> #'user/new-user
(def arjun (new-user "arjun" "secret" "arjun@zololabs.com"))
;=> #'user/arjun
(arjun :password)          Doesn't ever return
;=> nil                    password to callers
(arjun :password-hash)           Enables information hiding; can use password
;=> 1614358358                   without letting anyone else see it
```

Although the new-user function and the returned inner function can see password, anyone using the returned inner function can only see the hash of the password. Using a closure, you were able to hide information from callers of a function that's still visible to the function itself. Having come this far, we'll take a short break to compare functions such as arjun with objects from other languages.

DATA OR FUNCTION?

Already the line between what's clearly a function and what might be construed to be data in languages such as Java and Ruby should have started to blur. Is arjun a function or is it a kind of data object? It certainly behaves similarly to a hash map, where you can query the value associated with a particular key. In this case, you wrote code to expose only those keys that you considered public information, while hiding the private pieces. Because arjun is a closure, the free variables (the arguments passed to new-user) are captured inside it and hang around until the closure itself is alive. Technically, although arjun is a function, semantically it looks and behaves like data.

Although data objects such as hash maps are fairly static (in that they do little more than hold information), traditional objects also have behavior associated with them. Let's blur the line some more by adding behavior to your user objects. Here you'll add a way to see if a given password is the correct one. Consider this code:

```
(defn new-user [login password email]
  (fn [a & args]
    (case a
      :login login
      :email email
      :authenticate (= password (first args)))))
```

Now try it out:

```
(def adi (new-user "adi" "secret" "adi@currylogic.com"))
;=> #'user/adi
(adi :authenticate "blah")
;=> false
(adi :authenticate "secret")
;=> true
```

Your little closure-based users can now authenticate themselves when asked to do so. As mentioned earlier, this form of message passing resembles calling methods on objects in languages such as Java and Ruby. The format for doing so could be written like so:

```
(object message-name & arguments)
```

Objects in OOP are usually defined as entities that have state, behavior, and equality. Most languages also allow them to be defined in a manner that allows inheritance of functionality. So far, we've handled state (information such as login, password, and email) and behavior (such as :authenticate). Equality depends on the domain of use of these objects, but you could conceivably create a generic form of equality testing based on, say, a hash function. In the next section, we'll consolidate the ideas we talked about in this section and add inheritance and a nicer syntax to define such objects.

8.3.4   An object system for Clojure

In the previous section, you created a function named new-user that behaves as a sort of factory for new user objects. You could call new-user using the data elements that a user comprises (login, password, and email address), and you'd get a new user object. You could then query it for certain data or have it perform certain behaviors. You made this possible by implementing a simple message passing scheme, with messages such as :login and :authenticate.

In this section, we'll generalize the idea of creating objects that have certain data and behavior into what traditional OO languages call classes. First, you'll allow a simple class hierarchy, and you'll let objects refer to themselves by providing a special symbol, traditionally named this. Finally, you'll wrap this functionality in a syntactic skin to make it appear more familiar.

DEFINING CLASSES

We'll start simple. You'll create the ability to define classes that have no state or behavior. You'll lay the foundations of your object system starting with the ability to define a class that's empty. For instance, you'd like to be able to say

```
(defclass Person)
```

This would define a class that would behave as a blueprint for future instances of people. You could then ask for the name of such a class:

```
(Person :name)
;=> "Person"
```

That would return the string "Person", which is the name of the class you're defining. Once you implement this, you can start adding more functionality to your little object system. Consider the following implementation:

```
(defn new-class [class-name]
  (fn [command & args]
    (case command
      :name (name class-name))))
(defmacro defclass [class-name]
  `(def ~class-name (new-class '~class-name)))
```

So your little Person class is a function that closes over the class-name, passed in along with a call to defclass. Again, remember that the notation '~class-name quotes the value of the `class-name` argument, so that it's passed in as the argument to `new-class` as a symbol itself.

Your classes support a single message right now, which is `:name`. When passed `:name`, the `Person` function returns the string `"Person"`. Try the following at the REPL now:

```
(defclass Person)
;=> #'user/Person
(Person :name)
;=> "Person"
```

Further, because you're simply working with vars and functions, the following also works:

```
(def some-class Person)
;=> #'user/some-class
(some-class :name)
;=> "Person"
```

This is to show that the name of the class isn't associated with the var (in this case `Person`) but with the class object itself. Now that you can define classes, we'll make it so you can instantiate them.

CREATING INSTANCES

Because your classes are closures, you can also implement instantiated classes as closures. You'll create this with a function called `new-object` that will accept the class that you'd like to instantiate. Here's the implementation:

```
(defn new-object [klass]
  (fn [command & args]
    (case command
      :class klass)))
```

Here it is in action:

```
(def cindy (new-object Person))
```

As you can tell, the only message you can send this new object is one that queries its class. You can say

```
(new-object Person)
;=> #<user$new_object$fn__2259 user$new_object$fn__2259@1f106fec>
```

That isn't terribly informative, because it's returning the class as the function object. You can instead further ask its name:

```
((cindy :class) :name)
;=> "Person"
```

You could add this functionality as a convenience message that an instantiated object itself could handle:

```
(defn new-object [klass]
  (fn [command & args]
    (case command
      :class klass
      :class-name (klass :name))))
```

You can test this now, but you'll need to create the object again, because you redefined the class. Here it is:

```
(def cindy (new-object Person))
;=> #'user/cindy
(cindy :class-name)
;=> "Person"
```

Finally, you're going to be instantiating classes a lot, so you can add a more convenient way to do so. You'd like something like a new operator that's common to several languages such as Java and Ruby. Luckily, you've already set up your class as a function that can handle incoming messages, so you'll add to the vocabulary with a :new message. Here's the new implementation of new-class:

```
(defn new-class [class-name]
  (fn klass [command & args]
    (case command
      :name (name class-name)
      :new (new-object klass))))
```

Notice that new-object accepts a class, and you need to refer to the class object from within it. You were able to do this by giving the anonymous function a name (klass) and then refer to it by that name in the :new clause. With this, creating new objects is easier and more familiar (remember to evaluate the definition of Person again):

```
(defclass Person)
;=> #'user/Person
(def nancy (Person :new))
;=> #'user/nancy
(nancy :class-name)
;=> "Person"
```

So here you are: you're able to define new classes as well as instantiate them.

Our next stop will be to allow your objects to maintain state.

OBJECTS AND STATE

In chapter 6 we explored Clojure's support for managing state. In this section, you'll use one of those available mechanisms to allow objects in your object system to also become stateful. You'll use a ref so that your objects will be able to participate in coordinated transactions. You'll also expand the vocabulary of messages that your objects can understand by supporting :set! and :get. They'll allow you to set and fetch values from your objects, respectively.

Consider the following updated definition of the new-object function:

```
(defn new-object [klass]
  (let [state (ref {})]
    (fn [command & args]
      (case command
        :class klass
        :class-name (klass :name)
        :set! (let [[k v] args]
                (dosync (alter state assoc k v))
                nil)
        :get (let [[key] args]
               (@state key))))))
```

So now the messages that you can pass to your objects include :class, :class-name, :set!, and :get. Let's see your new stateful objects in action:

```
(def nancy (Person :new))
;=> #'user/nancy
(nancy :get :name)
;=> "Nancy Warhol"
```

You can also update your objects using the same :set! message, as follows:

```
(nancy :set! :name "Nancy Drew")
;=> nil
(nancy :get :name)
;=> "Nancy Drew"
```

You're coming along in the journey to create a simple object system. You now have the infrastructure to define classes, instantiate them, and manage state. Our next stop will be to add support for method definitions.

DEFINING METHODS

So far, we've dealt with the state side of objects. In this section, we'll start working on behavior by adding support for method definitions.

In keeping with languages such as Java and C++, you'd like to support a syntax that lists the methods along with the class definition, like so:

```
(defclass Person
  (method age []
    (* 2 10))
  (method greet [visitor]
    (str "Hello there, " visitor)))
```

You've started with simple methods. The age method, for instance, doesn't take any arguments and returns the result of a simple computation. Similarly, the greet method accepts a single argument and returns a simple computation involving it.

Now that the expected syntax is laid out, you can go about the implementation. First, you'll work on defclass, to make the previous notation valid. Consider the following function, which operates on a single method definition s-expression:

```
(defn method-spec [sexpr]
  (let [name (keyword (second sexpr))
    body (next sexpr)]
    [name (conj body 'fn)]))
```

This creates a vector containing the name of the method definition (as a keyword) and another s-expression, which can later be evaluated to create an anonymous function. Here's an example:

```
(method-spec '(method age [] (* 2 10)))
;=> [:age (fn age [] (* 2 10))]
```

Because you're going to specify more than one method inside the class definition, you'll need to call method-spec for each of them. The following method-specs function will accept the complete specification of your class, pick out the method definitions by filtering on the first symbol (it should be method), and then call method-spec on each:

```
(defn method-specs [sexprs]
  (->> sexprs
       (filter #(= 'method (first %)))
       (mapcat method-spec)
       (apply hash-map)))
```

The easiest way to see what's going on is to examine a sample output:

```
(method-specs '((method age [] (* 2 10))
                (method greet [visitor] (str "Hello there, " visitor))))
;=> {:age (fn age [] (* 2 10)),
     :greet (fn greet [visitor] (str "Hello there, " visitor))}
```

You now have a literal map that can be evaluated to return one containing keywords as keys for each method definition and an associated anonymous function. This map could then be passed to the new-class function for later use. Here's the associated revision of new-class:

```
(defn new-class [class-name methods]
  (fn klass [command & args]
    (case command
      :name (name class-name)
      :new (new-object klass))))
```

Now that all the supporting pieces are in place, you can make the final change to def-class, which will allow you to accept method definitions:

```
(defmacro defclass [class-name & specs]
  (let [fns (or (method-specs specs) {})]
    `(def ~class-name (new-class '~class-name ~fns))))
```

Now, your desired syntax from before will work:

```
(defclass Person
  (method age [] (* 2 10))
  (method greet [visitor] (str "Hello there, " visitor)))
;=> #'user/Person
```

So you've successfully made it possible to specify methods along with the class definitions. Note that the definition of new-class doesn't yet do anything with methods. Now, all you have to do is extend your objects so that you can invoke these methods.

INVOKING METHODS

To be able to invoke a method on one of your objects, such as nancy, you'll need some way to look up the definition from the associated class. You'll need to be able to query the class of a given object for a particular method. Let's add the :method message to your classes, which would accept the name of the method you're looking for. Consider the following revision to the new-class function:

```
(defn new-class [class-name methods]
  (fn klass [command & args]
    (case command
      :name (name class-name)
      :new (new-object klass)
      :method (let [[method-name] args]
                (find-method method-name methods)))))
```

We haven't defined find-method yet, so this code isn't quite ready to be compiled. To find a method from your previously created map of methods, you can do a simple hash map lookup. Therefore, the implementation of find-method is simple:

```
(defn find-method [method-name instance-methods]
  (instance-methods method-name))
```

With this addition, you can look up a method in a class, using the same keyword notation you've been using for all your other messages. Here's an example:

```
(Person :method :age)
;=> #<user$age user$age@42443032>
```

Now that you can get a handle on the function object that represents a method, you're ready to call it. Indeed, you can call the previous function on the REPL, and it will do what you laid out in the class definition:

```
((Person :method :age))
;=> 20
```

That works, but it's far from pretty. You should be able to support the same familiar interface of calling methods on objects that they belong to. Let's expand the capability of the message-passing system you've built so far to handle such methods also. Here's an updated version of new-object that does this:

```
(defn new-object [klass]
  (let [state (ref {})]
    (fn [command & args]
      (case command
        :class klass
        :class-name (klass :name)
        :set! (let [[k v] args]
                (dosync (alter state assoc k v))
                nil)
        :get (let [[key] args]
               (@state key))
        (if-let [method (klass :method command)]
          (apply method args)
          (throw (RuntimeException.
                   (str "Unable to respond to " command)))))))))
```

What's added here is a default clause to case. If the message passed in isn't one of :class, :class-name, :set!, or :get, then you assume it's a method call on the object. You ask the class for the function by passing along the received command as the method name, and if you get back a function, you execute it. Here it is in action:

```
(def shelly (Person :new))
;=> #'user/shelly
(shelly :age)
;=> 20
(shelly :greet "Nancy")
;=> "Hello there, Nancy"
```

Remember, for this to work, the definition of Person would need to be reevaluated after these changes.

Once you're satisfied that your implementation does what you want so far, you'll be ready to move on to enabling objects to refer to themselves.

REFERRING TO THIS

So far, the method definitions have been simple. But there's often a need for methods within a class definition to call each other. Most programming languages that support this feature do so via a special keyword (usually named this or self), which refers to the object itself. Here you'll support the same functionality by providing a special name, which is also called this.

Once you've finished, you'd like to be able to say the following:

```
(defclass Person
  (method age [] (* 2 10))
  (method about [diff]
    (str "I was born about " (+ diff (this :age)) " years ago")))
```

Notice how the about method calls the age method via the this construct. To implement this, you'll first create a var named this, so that the class definitions continue to work (without complaining about unresolved symbols):

```
(declare ^:dynamic this)
```

This var will need a binding when any method executes so that its bound value refers to the object itself. A simple binding form will do, as long as you have something to bind to. You'll employ the same trick you did when you named the anonymous class function klass earlier, by naming the anonymous object function thiz. Here's the updated code for the new-object function:

```
(defn new-object [klass]
  (let [state (ref {})]
    (fn thiz [command & args]
      (case command
        :class klass
        :class-name (klass :name)
        :set! (let [[k v] args]
                (dosync (alter state assoc k v))
                nil)
        :get (let [[key] args] (@state key))
        (let [method (klass :method command)]
          (if-not method
            (throw (RuntimeException.
              (str "Unable to respond to " command))))
          (binding [this thiz]
            (apply method args)))))))
```

And that's all there is to it. Remember to evaluate the new, revised definition of new-object (and Person), and then you can confirm that it works on the REPL:

```
(def shelly (Person :new))
;=> #'user/shelly
(shelly :about 2)
;=> "I was born about 22 years ago"
```

You've added almost all the features you wanted to when we started this section. The last thing you'll add is the ability of a class to inherit from another.

CLASS INHERITANCE

You're about to add a final feature to your little object system. Traditional OOP languages such as Java and Ruby allow modeling of objects using inheritance so that problems can be decomposed into hierarchies of functionality. The lower in a hierarchy you go, the more specific you get. For instance, Animal might be a parent class of Dog. In this section, you'll add the ability to do that.

The first thing you'll do is allow the class definition to specify the parent class. Imagine that your syntax will look like this, with a choice of the word extends to signify the hierarchy:

```
(defclass Woman
  (extends Person)
  (method greet [v] (str "Hello, " v))
  (method age [] (* 2 9)))
```

Here, the new Woman class inherits from a previously defined Person class. The term extends is used to signify this relationship, as is common to other OO languages.

Now that you have your notation, you need to implement it. The first step is to write a function that can extract the parent class information from the class definition. Before you can do so, you have to decide what to do if a parent class isn't provided.

Again, you'll look at other languages for the answer. Your class hierarchies will all be singly rooted, and the top-level class (highest parent class) will be OBJECT. We'll define this shortly. For now, you're ready to write parent-class-spec, the function that will parse the specification of the parent class from a given class definition:

```
(defn parent-class-spec [sexprs]
  (let [extends-spec (filter #(= 'extends (first %)) sexprs)
        extends (first extends-spec)]
    (if (empty? extends)
      'OBJECT
      (last extends))))
```

To confirm that this works, try it at the REPL. You'll pass it the specification part of a class definition:

```
(parent-class-spec '((extends Person)
                     (method age [] (* 2 9))))
;=> Person
```

Now that you have the parent class, you'll pass it to the new-class function. You don't want to pass a symbol as the parent class but rather the var named by that symbol. For instance, the value returned by the call to parent-class-spec is a Clojure symbol. If you have a symbol, you can find the var named by the symbol using the var special form:

```
(var map)
;=> #'clojure.core/map
```

There's a reader macro for the var special form, #' (the hash followed by a tick). With this information in hand, you can make the needed modification to defclass:

```
(defmacro defclass [class-name & specs]
  (let [parent-class (parent-class-spec specs)
        fns (or (method-specs specs) {})]
    `(def ~class-name (new-class '~class-name #'~parent-class ~fns))))
```

Note that you're now passing an extra parameter (the parent class) to the `new-class` function, so you'll have to change that to accommodate it:

```
(defn new-class [class-name parent methods]
  (fn klass [command & args]
    (case command
      :name (name class-name)
      :parent parent
      :new (new-object klass)
      :method (let [[method-name] args]
                (find-method method-name methods)))))
```

There's one more thing to handle before you can use your new `defclass`. You're look-ing up the parent class using the var special form, so you'll need `OBJECT` to resolve to something. It's now time to define it:

```
(def OBJECT (new-class :OBJECT nil {}))
```

With these changes, the definition of the `Woman` class from earlier in this section should work. Check this on the REPL as follows:

```
(defclass Person
     (method age [] (* 2 10))
     (method about [diff]
       (str "I was born about " (+ diff (this :age)) " years ago")))
;=> #'user/Person
```

This is your parent class; now you'll inherit from it to create the `Woman` class:

```
(defclass Woman
     (extends Person)
     (method greet [v] (str "Hello, " v))
     (method age [] (* 2 9)))
;=> #'user/Woman
```

You've only half-finished the job you started out to do. Although you can specify the parent class in your calls to `defclass`, method calls on your objects won't work right with respect to parent classes.

The following illustrates the problem:

```
(def donna (Woman :new))
;=> #'user/donna
(donna :greet "Shelly")
;=> "Hello, Shelly"
(donna :age)
;=> 18
(donna :about 3)
RuntimeException Unable to respond to :about  user/new-object/thiz--2733
(NO_SOURCE_PATH:1:1)
```

To fix this last error, you'll have to improve the method lookup to find the method in the parent class. Indeed, you'll have to search up the hierarchy of classes (parent of the parent of the parent …) until you hit OBJECT. You'll implement this new method lookup by modifying the find-method function as follows:

```
(defn find-method [method-name klass]
  (or ((klass :methods) method-name)
      (if-not (= #'OBJECT klass)
        (find-method method-name (klass :parent)))))
```

For this to work, you'll need to have the classes handle another message, namely :methods. Also, the classes will use this new version of find-method to perform a method lookup. Here's the updated code:

```
(defn new-class [class-name parent methods]
  (fn klass [command & args]
    (case command
      :name (name class-name)
      :parent parent
      :new (new-object klass)
      :methods methods
      :method (let [[[method-name] args]
                (find-method method-name klass)))))
```

With this final change, your object system will work as planned. Figure 8.2 shows the conceptual model of the class system you've built.

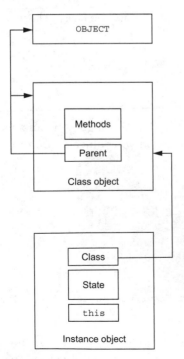

Figure 8.2   **The minimal object system you've built implements a major portion of features that are supported by most common OO systems. Everything ultimately derives from a common entity called** OBJECT. **Instances look up the class they derive from and look up methods there. Methods can also be looked up in the chain of hierarchy.**

Here's the call to the `:about` method that wasn't working a few paragraphs back:

```
(donna :about 3)
;=> "I was born about 21 years ago"
```

Again, remember to reevaluate everything after the last change, including the definitions of `Person`, `Woman`, and `donna` itself. Notice that the `:about` method is being called from the parent class `Person`. Further notice that the body of the `:about` method calls `:age` on the `this` reference, which is defined in both `Person` and `Woman`. Your object system correctly calls the one on `donna`, because you overrode the definition in the `Woman` class.

You've completed what you set out to do. You've written a simple object system that does most of what other languages provide. You can define classes, inherit from others, create instances, and call methods that follow the inheritance hierarchy. Objects can even refer to themselves using the `this` keyword. The following listing shows the complete code.

Listing 8.1   A simple object system for Clojure

```clojure
(declare ^:dynamic this)
(declare find-method)
(defn new-object [klass]
  (let [state (ref {})]
    (fn thiz [command & args]
      (case command
        :class klass
        :class-name (klass :name)
        :set! (let [[k v] args]
                (dosync (alter state assoc k v))
                nil)
        :get (let [[key] args]
               (@state key))
        (let [method (klass :method command)]
          (if-not method
            (throw (RuntimeException.
                     (str "Unable to respond to " command))))
          (binding [this thiz]
            (apply method args)))))))
(defn new-class [class-name parent methods]
  (fn klass [command & args]
    (case command
      :name (name class-name)
      :parent parent
      :new (new-object klass)
      :methods methods
      :method (let [[method-name] args]
                (find-method method-name klass)))))
(def OBJECT (new-class :OBJECT nil {}))
(defn find-method [method-name klass]
  (or ((klass :methods) method-name)
      (if-not (= #'OBJECT klass)
        (find-method method-name (klass :parent)))))
```

```
(defn method-spec [sexpr]
  (let [name (keyword (second sexpr))
    body (next sexpr)]
    [name (conj body 'fn)]))
(defn method-specs [sexprs]
  (->> sexprs
      (filter #(= 'method (first %)))
      (mapcat method-spec)
      (apply hash-map)))
(defn parent-class-spec [sexprs]
  (let [extends-spec (filter #(= 'extends (first %)) sexprs)
        extends (first extends-spec)]
    (if (empty? extends)
      'OBJECT
      (last extends))))
(defmacro defclass [class-name & specs]
  (let [parent-class (parent-class-spec specs)
        fns (or (method-specs specs) {})]
    `(def ~class-name (new-class '~class-name  #'~parent-class ~fns))))
```

So that's it, clocking in at a little over 50 lines of code. We haven't added several features that are provided by more robust object systems, but you can certainly do so. For instance, this function doesn't perform a lot of error checking. You should extend this code to add syntactic checks to see if the made-up syntax is being used correctly, for instance.

The key to this implementation is the lexical closure. It's up to you to take a stand on the old debate: Are objects a poor man's closures, or is it the other way around? More than anything else, though, it's important to remember this: although this example showed some of the power of functional programming (and that traditional OOP features aren't particularly special), in most cases, such artificial constructs are unnecessary in languages such as Clojure. We'll talk about why this is next.

DATA ABSTRACTION

We mentioned that constructs such as the object system aren't particularly useful in a language such as Clojure. There are two reasons for this.

The first relates to abstraction. Despite popular belief, you don't need objects to create data abstraction. There's a real alternative in Clojure in its core data structures: each implementation of the sequence abstraction (the hash map, the vector, and so on) is a suitable candidate to represent data in an application. Given that these are immutable and therefore thread safe, there's no strict need for procedural abstractions that wrap their mutation. Further, when you need to make a *new* abstraction of your own that existing types might want to participate in, you can use Clojure's protocol feature introduced in the next chapter.

The second reason is a bit more subjective. Alan Perlis once said that it's better to have 100 functions that operate on a single data structure instead of 10 functions that operate on 10 data structures.[1] Having a common data structure (in Clojure's case,

---

[1] "Epigrams on Programming," *SIGPLAN Notices* 17(9), September 1982. Archived at http://goo.gl/6PtaEm.

the sequence abstraction) allows for more code reuse, because code that works on sequences can be used no matter what specific data it contains. An example is the large sequence library, which works no matter what the specific implementation is.

Using the let-over-lambda technique shown previously has its value, as you saw in the earlier part of the chapter. But creating an object system like the one created in the second half raises a barrier of inoperability with other libraries that don't know about it. In conclusion, although the object system serves to illustrate the use of closures and some traditional OOP concepts, using the built-in core data structures is a much better choice in your own programs.

FINAL NOTES

It's worth recalling that the implementation of this little object system was done using functions. Fewer than half of the total lines of code were for manipulating the functions, and the rest were to make the syntax look a certain way. The macro `defclass` and the supporting functions (`parent-class-spec`, `method-specs`, and `method-spec`) account for over half the code. This syntactic layer sports an arbitrarily chosen syntax. The semantics of the object system wouldn't change if you decided to use a different syntax. The syntax isn't important (in this case certainly, and also in general); instead, it's the underlying mechanisms and features that make a piece of code useful. Having said that, a nice syntax certainly helps! The first reason is that it makes for convenient, intuitive use. The second is that you can write error checkers that analyze the code as data and give meaningful errors that are easier to understand and correct. You could certainly do more at the syntactic level to make this library easier to use.

Similarly, there are many features that you could add at a semantic level. For instance, there's no reason for a class hierarchy to be static. Instead of it being cast in stone when `defclass` is called, you could add messages that support modifying the hierarchy at runtime. As an example, your classes could respond to `:set-class!` and `:set-parent!`. Adding such features might be an interesting exercise for a spare afternoon.

8.4   *Summary*

This chapter was about functional programming, the understanding of which is crucial to programming in Clojure. If you're coming from an imperative background, this transition can take some effort. But the results are sweet, because functional code is more expressive, more reusable, and usually shorter.

We started out by having you create your own implementations of `map`, `reduce`, and `filter`—the workhorses of functional programming languages. Thinking recursively and in terms of lazy sequences is another important skill that will have a big impact on your Clojure programs.

We then looked at the technique of using partial function application to create specialized functions. To understand how partial application works, we explored lexical closures, another fundamental tool in the functional programmer's tool belt.

Once we presented a basic explanation of them, you gathered everything from this chapter (and from the ones so far!) to create your own little object system. This exercise was meant to demonstrate the power of closures and to also shed light on the fact that functional programming transcends traditional OOP.

Next we'll look at Clojure's protocols, which allow you to add function implementations specific to a particular object type.

Protocols, records, and types

This chapter covers

- An overview of the expression problem
- A custom solution to the expression problem
- Clojure's solution to the expression problem
- Working with types and records: `deftype`, `defrecord`, and `reify`

Abstraction is an important tenet of software development because it results in code that's more maintainable and extensible. Clojure itself is built on abstractions. For instance, most things in Clojure are coded to interfaces rather than being concrete implementations. This allows for reuse of code that expects those interfaces and allows for the seamless addition of more implementations to the mix.

Sooner or later, during your time on most projects, you'll run into an abstraction-oriented issue known as the *expression problem*. It has to do with how to cleanly extend or use existing code—either something you wrote yourself or, more important, something you don't own. In this chapter, we'll explore the expression problem in some depth, as well as Clojure's approach to handling it (protocols). Then, we'll come up with a solution. Finally, we'll explore the Clojure solution in more depth by looking at protocols, data types, and the `reify` macro.

217

9.1 The expression problem

Let's imagine that you've been writing an application to manage employee expenses, one that will eventually replace an existing Java application that does a similar job. Naturally, you're writing it in Clojure. If you find yourself needing to take two or more classes or sets of classes (or any other abstractions) and make them work together in a seamless way, you're likely experiencing what's known as the expression problem. This is a situation that comes up quite often. Whatever solution you come up with to do this, it's likely you'll need to support further extensibility, perhaps to support even more operations or data types.

There are two sides to solving the expression problem—namely, data types and the operations on them. We'll start by looking at the operations side of the situation and follow up by looking at a couple ways to define data types. But before we dive into that, let's take a moment to set up the example scenario.

9.1.1 Setting up the example scenario

There are two parts to this example: new code written in Clojure and legacy code written in Java. Both will have to coexist in the same program, so the functions you write need to operate on both native Clojure and native Java types seamlessly. First, you'll write code using only the Clojure features you've learned so far; then we'll take a look at the legacy Java code.

CREATING A BASE

Here's a portion of the expense namespace, with a function to create a simple map containing expense information:

```
(ns clj-in-act.ch9.expense
  (:import [java.text SimpleDateFormat]))
(defn new-expense [date-string dollars cents category merchant-name]
  {:date (.parse (SimpleDateFormat. "yyyy-MM-dd") date-string)
   :amount-dollars dollars
   :amount-cents cents
   :category category
   :merchant-name merchant-name})
```

As you've seen several times already, using a map is straightforward and is often the idiomatic way in Clojure to hold data of any kind. Now, for the purposes of illustration, here's a function called total-cents that computes the expense amount in cents:

```
(defn total-cents [e]
  (-> (:amount-dollars e)
      (* 100)
      (+ (:amount-cents e))))
```

Nothing in this function ought to be unfamiliar, including the threading macro, which you saw in chapter 2.

ADDING SOME FUNCTIONS

You'll also add a function to calculate the total amount, given a list of expenses, and possibly a criteria function by which to select expenses from a list:

```
(defn total-amount
  ([expenses-list]
    (total-amount (constantly true) expenses-list))
  ([pred expenses-list]
    (->> expenses-list
        (filter pred)
        (map total-cents)
        (apply +))))
```

Then you'll add a couple functions to help you create the predicate functions that can be used with `total-amount`, specifically to select a particular category of expenses:

```
(defn is-category? [e some-category]
  (= (:category e) some-category))
(defn category-is [category]
  #(is-category? % category))
```

The second function is syntactic sugar to help create single-argument predicates so your code reads easier. Let's see how it looks by having you write some code that tests these functions. Consider a new namespace, such as `expense-test`, which you'll start by creating a few sample expenses to play with:

```
(ns clj-in-act.ch9.expense-test
  (:require [clj-in-act.ch9.expense :refer :all]
          [clojure.test :refer :all]))
(def clj-expenses [(new-expense "2009-8-20" 21 95 "books" "amazon.com")
                   (new-expense "2009-8-21" 72 43 "food" "mollie-stones")
                   (new-expense "2009-8-22" 315 71 "car-rental" "avis")
                   (new-expense "2009-8-23" 15 68 "books" "borders")])
```

TESTING THE CODE

Here's a test that uses this data set to compute the total amounts:

```
(deftest test-clj-expenses-total
  (is (= 42577 (total-amount clj-expenses)))
  (is (=  3763 (total-amount (category-is "books") clj-expenses))))
```

> ## Clojure unit tests
>
> This chapter may make it seem like you've been thrown into the deep end of the pool with regard to writing unit tests in Clojure. Rest assured that the next chapter will go into a lot of detail around this developer activity. You'll need to know some basics to get through these pages.

(continued)

You're going to use the `clojure.test` library to write the tests. You start by `require`-ing (or use-ing) the `clojure.test` namespace and using the `deftest` macro to write tests. You run tests by calling the `run-tests` function, passing in symbols of your test namespaces. In this example, you'd evaluate

```
(run-tests 'clj-in-act.ch9.expense-test)
```

This would output the results of your test run, and you can see if your tests passed.

If you run these tests, you'll see that they pass. So now you have some basic code that shows the intent of the application. You can imagine a lot more functionality that helps an organization track expenses, but you've written sufficient code to demonstrate the issues you set out to face, so let's move on.

THE JAVA WORLD

It's now time to face a kind of reality you often face when working on application rewrites: business reasons might compel you to deal with the old codebase alongside the new one. For the purposes of this example, it means that you're going to have to deal with instances of the Java-based `Expense` class. You could imagine such a class being similar to the one shown in the following listing.

Listing 9.1 Skeleton Java class implementing the concept of the expense item

```java
package com.curry.expenses;
import java.util.Calendar;
import java.text.SimpleDateFormat;
import java.text.ParseException;
public class Expense {
    private Calendar date;
    private int amountDollars;
    private int amountCents;
    private String merchantName;
    private String category;
    public Expense(String dateString, int amountDollars, int amountCents,
            String category, String merchantName) throws ParseException {
        this.date = Calendar.getInstance();
        this.date.setTime(new SimpleDateFormat(
                        "yyyy-MM-dd").parse(dateString));
        this.amountDollars = amountDollars;
        this.amountCents = amountCents;
        this.merchantName = merchantName;
        this.category = category;
    }
    public Calendar getDate() {
        return date;
    }
    public int getAmountDollars() {
        return amountDollars;
    }
```

```
    public int getAmountCents() {
        return amountCents;
    }
    public String getMerchantName() {
        return merchantName;
    }
    public String getCategory() {
        return category;
    }
    public int amountInCents() {
        return this.amountDollars*100 + this.amountCents;
    }
}
```

To begin working with this class, you'll write a sanity test to ensure everything is in order. Consider the following:

```
(def java-expenses [(Expense. "2009-8-24" 44 95 "books" "amazon.com")
                    (Expense. "2009-8-25" 29 11 "gas" "shell")])
(deftest test-java-expenses-total
  (let [total-cents (map #(.amountInCents %) java-expenses)]
    (is (= 7406 (apply + total-cents)))))
```

Getting JAR files onto the classpath

Once you compile the `Expense` class and create a JAR file, you'll need to make sure that it's included in the Clojure classpath. With Lein version 2.x, the easiest way to do this is to create a local Maven repository, deploy your JAR file into there, and then refer to the dependency in your project.clj file.

There's a convenient Lein plugin called `lein-localrepo` that makes this much easier. It's an open source contribution to the Clojure ecosystem, and it's available on GitHub at https://github.com/kumarshantanu/lein-localrepo.

It's recommended because it makes adding local JAR files to your project a breeze. Just follow the instructions at the GitHub web address.

You'll need to import your `Expense` class into the test namespace for this to work. Once you do, you'll see that running this test will result in it passing. Now that you're able to access the Java class, you need to tackle the situation where you have both kinds of expenses together. For instance, you have to deal with a list of Clojure expense maps constructed via the new-expense function, as well as instances of the com.curry.expenses.Expense class.

You'll capture this requirement in another test. Consider the following:

```
(def mixed-expenses (concat clj-expenses java-expenses))
(deftest test-mixed-expenses-total
  (is (= 49983 (total-amount mixed-expenses)))
  (is (= 8258 (total-amount (category-is "books") mixed-expenses))))
```

Now this test won't pass. Indeed, the first assertion will print a long exception stack trace, because `total-amount` (and the underlying `total-cents` and `is-category?`) function only knows how to deal with Clojure map versions of expenses. To fix this, you're going to have to deal with a design issue.

9.1.2 *A closer look at the expression problem and some potential solutions*

Philip Wadler is an ACM fellow and a computer science professor at the University of Edinburgh. He has made several important contributions to the field of functional programming, including the theory behind the Haskell programming language. He also coined the term *expression problem*:

> The Expression Problem is a new name for an old problem. The goal is to define a data-type by cases, where one can add new cases to the data-type and new functions over the data-type, without recompiling existing code, and while retaining static type safety (e.g., no casts).[1]

How can you add functionality to the code (your data type) so it plays well with code (data types) written by someone else (or any other code that you have no control over)? The last test you wrote to handle the case of mixed expenses has forced you to face the expression problem. Specifically, you need the `total-amount` function to accept and work with an entirely new data type that has its own set of operations (functions) defined for it. You'd also like the `category-is` function to create functions that can operate on this new data type, even though the new data type has no notion of such a category selector function right now.

The expression problem is common in our industry. There are several approaches to handle the issue, and we'll briefly look at a few.

WRAPPERS

Because you have no control over the new data type (the `Expense` class), you could create a new wrapper class around it with the right methods that you can call from your program.

The trouble with this approach is that it increases incidental complexity because you've added a new class to your system. You've confused the identity: is an object that wraps an instance of `Expense` identical to it? How should code written elsewhere treat this new wrapper class if it's passed in? Such an identity crisis is an example of the kind of nonlocal trouble that can arise when an instance of the wrapper is passed to unsuspecting code elsewhere in the system. You'd also have to create a wrapper class each time a new data type such as this comes along, leading to an explosion of such wrappers.

---

[1] Philip Wadler, The Expression Problem, November 12, 1998, http://homepages.inf.ed.ac.uk/wadler/papers/expression/expression.txt.

When all is said and done, languages such as Java often have no other choice than to go this route.

MONKEY PATCHING

Once classes have been written and compiled in Java, they can't be modified (without manipulating bytecode). This is in contrast with languages such as Ruby, which are more dynamic and support open classes—classes that can be changed by anyone using the class, without directly editing the source code of that class. This is called *monkey patching*. Often, the syntax looks the same as writing the class the first time around, and any new methods defined (or redefined) become part of the original class.

The problem with this approach is that it's a dangerous one, almost even more so than the wrapper approach. Because all changes to a class happen in a global manner (the class itself being the namespace), it has the potential for collisions. If you open a class and monkey patch it with a new method named `total-cents`, and someone else comes along and does the same, they will overwrite your patch. Such a collision can cause insidious problems, because the cause isn't immediately obvious.

IF-THEN-ELSE

Finally, there's the approach of not using any well-structured tactic at all and checking for types inline with the code as needed. Client code such as the `total-amount` function will need to do different things depending on whether it was passed a Clojure map or an instance of the Java `Expense` class, using good-old if-then-else constructs.

This quickly gets complex, depending on how many data types need to be handled. Moreover, if support for a new data type needs to be added at a later point, it isn't possible without modifying the code in all the places where this type checking is done. The incidental complexity of this approach is too great given that the solution is both rigid and inelegant.

What's needed is an approach that doesn't suffer from these problems. The Clojure programming language has the feature for this, and you saw it earlier in chapter 4. We're talking about multimethods, and in the next section, you'll write an implementation that works as desired.

9.1.3 Clojure's multimethods solution

Multimethods allow you to decouple data types and operations on the data types in an elegant manner. We demonstrated this in chapter 4, where you used multimethods to handle a situation that would have required the visitor pattern in a language such as Java. In this section, you'll use multimethods to get the latest test to pass without modifying the Java code for the `Expense` class and without creating wrappers or monkey patches.

Let's refresh your memory by looking at the test that won't pass right now:

```
(deftest test-mixed-expenses-total
  (is (= 49983 (total-amount mixed-expenses)))
  (is (= 8258 (total-amount (category-is "books") mixed-expenses)))))
```

As noted before, the trouble is that the `total-amount`, `is-category?`, and `total-cents` functions only know how to work with Clojure maps. Your first step, then, will be to address this issue by changing the implementation of the `total-cents` and `is-category?` functions. You won't touch `total-amount`, because it's an example of client code (perhaps written by someone using the expense library). You can assume that you don't control it and, indeed, that it's a requirement of solving the expression problem, and you can't change the alien data type or the client code.

Consider the following code, which is a replacement of the `total-cents` function:

```
(defmulti total-cents class)
(defmethod total-cents clojure.lang.IPersistentMap [e]
  (-> (:amount-dollars e)
      (* 100)
      (+ (:amount-cents e))))
```

Similarly, the following code will serve as the replacement of the `is-category?` function:

```
(defmulti is-category? (fn [e category] (class e)))
(defmethod is-category? clojure.lang.IPersistentMap [e some-category]
  (= (:category e) some-category))
```

You haven't changed a lot of code; the bodies of the functions are the same as before. All you did was convert the functions to multimethods and redefine the old functions as methods, focusing on the fact that the expense object will be an instance of `clojure.lang.IPersistentMap` (which all Clojure maps are). Refer to chapter 4 to get a refresher on how this works with respect to dispatch functions and dispatch values.

At this point, if you run the tests, the old tests should still pass. Also, the new test will still fail because you haven't written any code to deal with the Java `Expense` class. You'll do that now, starting with the `total-cents` function:

```
(defmethod total-cents com.curry.expenses.Expense [e]
  (.amountInCents e))
```

And similarly, here's the `is-category?` function:

```
(defmethod is-category? com.curry.expenses.Expense [e some-category]
  (= (.getCategory e) some-category))
```

With this, the new test will pass. Note, once again, that you didn't change the Java `Expense` class in any way: you didn't write a wrapper class for it, and you didn't change the calling code (the `total-amount` function). You also kept all the code in your own namespace, allowing others to create their own functions named `total-cents` and `is-category?` without the fear of collisions.

Using multimethods has allowed you to solve this problem of handling new data types in an easy and elegant manner. You're even set up to deal with more data types now, for example, if you need to ever deal with a third-party expense library.

There are a couple of downsides to this approach, though. The first is that even though multimethods allow you to dispatch via arbitrary functions, you're using only the class of the first argument, which is either the Clojure map containing expense information or the Java Expense class. You don't need the full power of multimethods here, and it would be nice if you didn't have to explicitly write the dispatch functions the way you did previously.

The second issue is that even though the two multimethods you wrote are related to the task of computing totals, it isn't obvious in the code. If someone were to read this code later, the fact that the two belong together wouldn't jump out at them. This is even more apparent when you have several multimethods that should ideally show some kind of logical grouping. We'll solve these issues next.

9.2   Examining the operations side of the expression problem

In this section, we'll solve the two issues mentioned in the previous section. First, you don't need the conceptual or syntactic complexity of full multimethods when you only want to dispatch on the class of the first argument. Second, you want to group related multimethods together so they read better.

We'll call the solution to this *modus operandi*, which is a Latin phrase that means "method of operating." The name reflects our intention here, which is to describe a set of operating procedures for something.

9.2.1   def-modus-operandi

Let's start with the code you'd like to be able to write.

```
(def-modus-operandi ExpenseCalculations
  (total-cents [e])
  (is-category? [e category]))
```

What you're saying here is that you're defining a modus operandi called Expense-Calculations that will consist of two methods, namely total-cents and is-category?. You won't specify the dispatch function as you did before, because you always want it to be the class of the first argument of each method. In this case, both methods will dispatch based on the class of the expense object, be it a Clojure map or the Java Expense class or any other data type you end up supporting.

Now, let's look at implementing it. As you can imagine, def-modus-operandi is a macro. Here's the code along with a couple of associated helper functions to make the code easier to read:

```
(defn dispatch-fn-for [method-args]
  `(fn ~method-args (class ~(first method-args))))
(defn expand-spec [[method-name method-args]]
  `(defmulti ~method-name ~(dispatch-fn-for method-args)))
(defmacro def-modus-operandi [mo-name & specs]
  `(do
     ~@(map expand-spec specs)))
```

So all you're doing is generating code that creates multimethods. Here's what the expanded version looks like:

```
(do
  (clojure.core/defmulti total-cents (clojure.core/fn [e]
                                        (clojure.core/class e)))
  (clojure.core/defmulti is-category? (clojure.core/fn [e category]
                                         (clojure.core/class e))))
```

Notice that the expanded form of is-category? is the same as when you wrote it by hand earlier. The expansion for total-cents is slightly different, only because you can generate the same dispatch function no matter how many arguments the function takes.

   Now that you have a way to specify the methods in your modus operandi, you need a way to detail it for the types you'd like to support. We'll do that next.

9.2.2 *detail-modus-operandi*

After defining the *what* of a modus operandi, you need to define the *how.* You'll create a new macro called detail-modus-operandi that you'll use in the following manner:

```
(detail-modus-operandi ExpenseCalculations
  clojure.lang.IPersistentMap
  (total-cents [e]
    (-> (:amount-dollars e)
        (* 100)
        (+ (:amount-cents e))))
  (is-category? [e some-category]
    (= (:category e) some-category)))
```

Most of the code should be familiar to you, because it's nearly identical to the code from the previous section. Because all the methods are being defined for the same dispatch value, you've made it so that you have to specify it only once. Here's the implementation of the macro, along with an associated helper function:

```
(defn expand-method [data-type [name & body]]
  `(defmethod ~name ~data-type ~@body))
(defmacro detail-modus-operandi [mo-name data-type & fns]
  `(do
     ~@(map #(expand-method data-type %) fns)))
```

The expansion of this call to detail-modus-operandi is as follows:

```
(do
  (clojure.core/defmethod total-cents clojure.lang.IPersistentMap [e]
    (-> (:amount-dollars e)
        (* 100)
        (+ (:amount-cents e))))
  (clojure.core/defmethod is-category?
    clojure.lang.IPersistentMap [e some-category]
   (= (:category e) some-category)))
```

So you've done what you set out to do. You have a new abstraction that sits atop multi-methods that behave like subtype polymorphism. The methods dispatch on the type of the first argument.

Notice that even though you specified the name of your modus operandi here (called `ExpenseCalculations`), you haven't used it for anything. You can make your modus operandi more useful if you use the named objects to track such things as what it contains and who implements it. Let's do that next.

9.2.3 *Tracking your modus operandi*

So far, you've allowed declarations of a modus operandi that's a set of related multi-methods that dispatches on the type of the first argument. In this section, you'll collect some meta-information about these methods that you can use to programmatically query things about the modus operandi.

DURING DEF-MODUS-OPERANDI

The first thing you'll do is define a var with the name of the modus operandi. Doing that by itself is easy enough: you add a call to `def` in the `def-modus-operandi` macro. The question is what should the var be bound to? A simple option is to create a map containing information about the modus operandi. Try that approach:

```
(defmacro def-modus-operandi [mo-name & specs]
  `(do
     (def ~mo-name ~(mo-methods-registration specs))
     ~@(map expand-spec specs)))
```

You've delegated to a helper function called `mo-methods-registration`, so implement that next:

```
(defn mo-method-info [[name args]]
  {(keyword name) {:args `(quote ~args)}})
(defn mo-methods-registration [specs]
  (apply merge (map mo-method-info specs)))
```

You're collecting the name and arguments of each method into a map. This map, with all the information about the methods being specified as part of the modus operandi, will become the root binding of a var by the same name as the modus operandi. You can try it. First, you'll redefine the modus operandi:

```
(def-modus-operandi ExpenseCalculations
  (total-cents [e])
  (is-category? [e category]))
;=> #'user/is-category?
```

Next, see what the `ExpenseCalculations` var is bound to:

```
ExpenseCalculations
;=> {:is-category? {:args [e category]}, :total-cents {:args [e]}}
```

So you have the basic information. Next, you'll collect some more information every time `detail-modus-operandi` is called.

DURING DETAIL-MODUS-OPERANDI

To collect information of the implementer of a modus operandi, you'll first need to pass the modus operandi into the `expand-method` function:

```
(defmacro detail-modus-operandi [mo-name data-type & fns]
  `(do
     ~@(map #(expand-method mo-name data-type %) fns)))
```

Now that the `expand-method` knows which modus operandi it's going to create a method for, you can collect information about it:

```
(defn expand-method [mo-name data-type [method-name & body]]
  `(do
     (alter-var-root (var ~mo-name) update-in
              [(keyword '~method-name) :implementors] conj ~data-type)
     (defmethod ~method-name ~data-type ~@body)))
```

To better understand this addition to the `expand-method` function, let's talk about the data you're collecting. Recall that the modus operandi var is bound to a map that contains a key for each method. The value for each such key is another map. The only key in the inner map so far is `:args`, and to collect the data types of the implementors to this map, you'll introduce another key called `:implementors`. So here you're going to `conj` the data type onto the list of implementors (if any) each time a method of a modus operandi is implemented.

Finally, let's look at the function `alter-var-root`. Here's the doc string:

```
(doc alter-var-root)
-----------------------
clojure.core/alter-var-root
([v f & args])
  Atomically alters the root binding of var v by applying f to its
  current value plus any args
```

So you're passing it the var for the modus operandi and the function `update-in`. The arguments to `update-in` are a sequence of keys that locates a nested value and a function that will be applied to the existing value along with any other arguments. In this case, `update-in` is passed the function `conj` along with the data type you'd like recorded.

Phew, that's a lot of work for a single line of code! The following listing shows the complete implementation of modus operandi in a single namespace.

Listing 9.2   **Implementing modus operandi on top of multimethods**

```
(ns clj-in-act.ch9.modus-operandi)
(defn dispatch-fn-for [method-args]
  `(fn ~method-args (class ~(first method-args))))
```

```
(defn expand-spec [[method-name method-args]]
  `(defmulti ~method-name ~(dispatch-fn-for method-args)))
(defn mo-method-info [[name args]]
  {(keyword name) {:args `(quote ~args)}})
(defn mo-methods-registration [specs]
  (apply merge (map mo-method-info specs)))
(defmacro def-modus-operandi [mo-name & specs]
  `(do
     (def ~mo-name ~(mo-methods-registration specs))
     ~@(map expand-spec specs)))
(defn expand-method [mo-name data-type [method-name & body]]
  `(do
     (alter-var-root (var ~mo-name) update-in [(keyword '~method-name)
     :implementors] conj ~data-type)
     (defmethod ~method-name ~data-type ~@body)))
(defmacro detail-modus-operandi [mo-name data-type & fns]
  `(do
     ~@(map #(expand-method mo-name data-type %) fns)))
```

Let's look at it in action. First, make a call to `detail-modus-operandi`:

```
(detail-modus-operandi ExpenseCalculations
  clojure.lang.IPersistentMap
  (total-cents [e]
    (-> (:amount-dollars e)
        (* 100)
        (+ (:amount-cents e))))
  (is-category? [e some-category]
    (= (:category e) some-category)))
;=> #<MultiFn clojure.lang.MultiFn@4aad8dbc>
```

Now look at the `ExpenseCalculations` var:

```
ExpenseCalculations
;=> {:is-category? {:implementors (clojure.lang.IPersistentMap),
                    :args [e category]},
     :total-cents {:implementors (clojure.lang.IPersistentMap),
                   :args [e]}}
```

As you can see, you've added the new `:implementors` key to the inner maps, and they have a value that's a sequence of the implementors so far. Now implement the modus operandi for the Java `Expense` class:

```
(detail-modus-operandi ExpenseCalculations
  com.curry.expenses.Expense
  (total-cents [e]
    (.amountInCents e))
  (is-category? [e some-category]
    (= (.getCategory e) some-category)))
;=> #<MultiFn clojure.lang.MultiFn@4aad8dbc>
```

You can now see what the `ExpenseCalculations` var is bound to:

```
ExpenseCalculations
;=> {:is-category? {:implementors (com.curry.expenses.Expense
                                   clojure.lang.IPersistentMap),
                    :args [e category]},
     :total-cents {:implementors (com.curry.expenses.Expense
                                  clojure.lang.IPersistentMap),
                   :args [e]}}
```

And there you have it: you're collecting a sequence of all implementing classes inside the map bound to the `modus-operandi` var. You should now ensure that everything still works with the original code. Figure 9.1 shows a conceptual view of the process of defining a modus operandi and then detailing it. Listing 9.3 shows the complete code for the expense namespace.

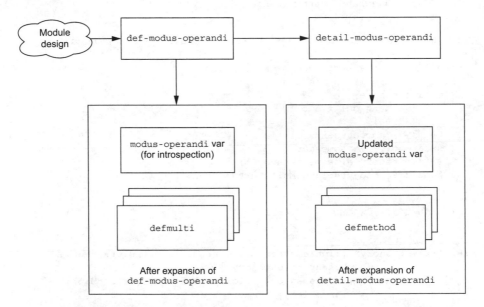

Figure 9.1 Calling `def-modus-operandi` creates a var that will hold information about the modus operandi that can later be used to introspect it. The macro itself makes as many calls to `defmulti` as needed. The `detail-modus-operandi` macro is the other side of the modus operandi concept: it fills out the implementation details by expanding to as many `defmethod` calls as specified. It also updates the `modus-operandi` var to reflect the implementor information.

Listing 9.3   The `expense` namespace using the modus operandi multimethod syntax

```
(ns clj-in-act.ch9.expense-modus-operandi
  (:require [clj-in-act.ch9.modus-operandi :refer :all])
  (:import [java.text SimpleDateFormat]
           [java.util Calendar]))
```

```
(defn new-expense [date-string dollars cents category merchant-name]
  (let [calendar-date (Calendar/getInstance)]
    (.setTime calendar-date
          (.parse (SimpleDateFormat. "yyyy-MM-dd") date-string))
    {:date calendar-date
     :amount-dollars dollars
     :amount-cents cents
     :category category
     :merchant-name merchant-name}))
(def-modus-operandi ExpenseCalculations
  (total-cents [e])
  (is-category? [e category]))
(detail-modus-operandi ExpenseCalculations
  clojure.lang.IPersistentMap
  (total-cents [e]
    (-> (:amount-dollars e)
        (* 100)
        (+ (:amount-cents c))))
  (is-category? [e some-category]
    (= (:category e) some-category)))
(detail-modus-operandi ExpenseCalculations
  com.curry.expenses.Expense
  (total-cents [e]
    (.amountInCents e))
  (is-category? [e some-category]
    (= (.getCategory e) some-category)))
(defn category-is [category]
  #(is-category? % category))
(defn total-amount
  ([expenses-list]
    (total-amount (constantly true) expenses-list))
  ([pred expenses-list]
    (->> expenses-list
         (filter pred)
         (map total-cents)
         (apply +))))
```

Similarly, the following listing shows the tests you've written so far, all in one place. You'll run the tests next.

Listing 9.4   Testing the implementation of modus operandi calculating expense totals

```
(ns clj-in-act.ch9.expense-test
  (:import [com.curry.expenses Expense])
  (:require [clj-in-act.ch9.expense-modus-operandi :refer :all]
            [clojure.test :refer :all]))
(def clj-expenses [(new-expense "2009-8-20" 21 95 "books" "amazon.com")
                   (new-expense "2009-8-21" 72 43 "food" "mollie-stones")
                   (new-expense "2009-8-22" 315 71 "car-rental" "avis")
                   (new-expense "2009-8-23" 15 68 "books" "borders")])
(deftest test-clj-expenses-total
  (is (= 42577 (total-amount clj-expenses)))
  (is (=  3763 (total-amount (category-is "books") clj-expenses))))
```

```
(def java-expenses [(Expense. "2009-8-24" 44 95 "books" "amazon.com")
                    (Expense. "2009-8-25" 29 11 "gas" "shell")])
(deftest test-java-expenses-total
  (let [total-cents (map #(.amountInCents %) java-expenses)]
    (is (= 7406 (apply + total-cents)))))
(def mixed-expenses (concat clj-expenses java-expenses))
(deftest test-mixed-expenses-total
  (is (= 49983 (total-amount mixed-expenses)))
  (is (= 8258 (total-amount (category-is "books") mixed-expenses))))
```

These tests now all pass:

```
(use 'clojure.test) (run-tests 'clj-in-act.ch9.expense-test)
Testing clj-in-act.ch9.expense-test
Ran 3 tests containing 5 assertions.
0 failures, 0 errors.
;=> {:type :summary, :test 3, :pass 5, :fail 0, :error 0}
```

Finally, before wrapping up this section, you'll write a couple of functions that will make it easy to query data about your modus operandi, like ExpenseCalculations.

QUERYING MODUS OPERANDI

The first function you'll write discerns what data types implement a particular modus operandi. Consider this code:

```
(defn implementors [modus-operandi method]
  (get-in modus-operandi [method :implementors]))
```

And this allows you to do things like this:

```
(implementors ExpenseCalculations :is-category?)
;=> (com.curry.expenses.Expense clojure.lang.IPersistentMap)
```

Now you'll write another function that when given a class of a particular data type can tell you if it implements a particular method of a modus operandi. Here's the code:

```
(defn implements? [implementor modus-operandi method]
  (some #{implementor} (implementors modus-operandi method)))
```

Now test it at the REPL:

```
(implements? com.curry.expenses.Expense ExpenseCalculations :is-category?)
;=> com.curry.expenses.Expense
```

Note that implements? returns the class itself, which is truthy. Here's a negative scenario:

```
(implements? java.util.Date ExpenseCalculations :is-category?)
;=> nil
```

Now that you have a function such as `implements?`, you can also write a broader function to see if a class implements a modus operandi completely:

```
(defn full-implementor? [implementor modus-operandi]
  (->> (keys modus-operandi)
       (map #(implements? implementor modus-operandi %))
       (not-any? nil?)))
```

Here it is in action:

```
(full-implementor? com.curry.expenses.Expense ExpenseCalculations)
;=> true
```

To test the negative side, you'll partially implement the modus operandi:

```
(detail-modus-operandi ExpenseCalculations
    java.util.Date
    (total-cents [e]
       (rand-int 1000)))
;=> #<MultiFn clojure.lang.MultiFn@746ac18c>
```

And now you can test what you were after:

```
(full-implementor? java.util.Date ExpenseCalculations)
;=> false
```

You can implement other functions such as these, because the value bound to the `modus-operandi` var is a regular map that can be inspected like any other. Next, let's examine the downsides to the modus operandi approach to the expression problem.

9.2.4   *Error handling and trouble spots in this solution*

In this section, you took multimethods and wrote a little DSL on top of them that allows you to write simpler, clearer code when you want to dispatch on the class of the first argument. You were also able to group related multimethods together via this new syntax, and this allowed the code to be self-documenting by communicating that certain multimethods are related to each other.

What we haven't touched on at all is error handling. For instance, if you `eval` the same `detail-modus-operandi` calls multiple times, the data-collection functions would add the class to your modus operandi metadata map multiple times. It's an easy fix, but this isn't the most robust code in the world, because it was written to demonstrate the abstraction.

There are other trouble spots as well. For instance, because you built this on top of multimethods, and multimethods support hierarchies (and Java inheritance hierarchies by default), the `implements?` and related functions won't give accurate answers as they stand now.

Further, because this is such a bare-bones implementation, many other features might be desirable in a more production-ready version. The other downside is that there's a small performance hit when using multimethods because they have to call the dispatch function and then match the dispatch value against available multimethods. After all, this approach is syntactic sugar on top of multimethods.

In the next section, you'll see Clojure's version of the solution.

9.3   *Examining the data types side of the expression problem with protocols*

You've already seen what the expression problem is and a variety of ways to solve it. Clojure's multimethods are perfectly suited to writing code that allows independent extension of the supported data types and operations. You also created an abstraction called modus operandi that supports the most common use of multimethods: single dispatch (the first argument) based on the type (or class).

Clojure's multimethods are more expressive than Java's object methods but much slower because Java is optimized for single dispatch on type, not arbitrary multiple dispatch. In most cases the performance difference is negligible and the increased expressiveness of code more than makes up for it. But as Clojure matures and moves more of its implementation into Clojure itself, there needs to be a way to support its abstraction and data-definition facilities without this performance hit. Protocols and data types are that solution, and they also offer a high-performance solution to a commonly encountered subset of the expression problem by using Java's extremely fast single dispatch on type.

In this section, we'll examine what protocols and data types are and how they can be used. Keep in mind your design of modus operandi as you work through this.

9.3.1   *defprotocol and extend-protocol*

The term *protocol* means the way something is done, often predefined and followed by all participating parties. Clojure protocols are analogous to your modus operandi, and `defprotocol` is to protocols what `def-modus-operandi` is to modi operandi. Similarly, `extend-protocol` is to protocols what `detail-modus-operandi` is to modi operandi.

Listing 9.3 showed the implementation of the expense calculation, and the next listing shows the same logic implemented using Clojure protocols.

> **Listing 9.5   expense namespace using a Clojure protocol**

```
(ns clj-in-act.ch9.expense-protocol
  (:import [java.text SimpleDateFormat]
           [java.util Calendar]))
(defn new-expense [date-string dollars cents category merchant-name]
  (let [calendar-date (Calendar/getInstance)]
    (.setTime calendar-date (.parse (SimpleDateFormat. "yyyy-MM-dd")
                                                       date-string))

    {:date calendar-date
     :amount-dollars dollars
```

```
      :amount-cents cents
      :category category
      :merchant-name merchant-name}))
(defprotocol ExpenseCalculations
  (total-cents [e])
  (is-category? [e category]))
(extend-protocol ExpenseCalculations
  clojure.lang.IPersistentMap
  (total-cents [e]
    (-> (:amount-dollars e)
        (* 100)
        (+ (:amount-cents e))))
  (is-category? [e some-category]
    (= (:category e) some-category)))
(extend-protocol ExpenseCalculations
  com.curry.expenses.Expense
  (total-cents [e]
    (.amountInCents e))
  (is-category? [e some-category]
    (= (.getCategory e) some-category)))
(defn category-is [category]
  #(is-category? % category))
(defn total-amount
  ([expenses-list]
    (total-amount (constantly true) expenses-list))
  ([pred expenses-list]
    (->> expenses-list
        (filter pred)
        (map total-cents)
        (apply +))))
```

The only things that are different from the implementation based on your modus operandi are that the dependence on the `clj-in-act.ch9.modus-operandi` namespace is removed and the calls to `def-modus-operandi` and `detail-modus-operandi` are replaced with calls to `defprotocol` and `extend-protocol`. At a conceptual level, the code in listing 9.5 should make sense. We'll get into the specifics now.

DEFINING NEW PROTOCOLS

As you might have guessed, new protocols are defined using the `defprotocol` macro. It defines a set of named methods, along with their signatures. Here's the official syntax:

```
(defprotocol AProtocolName
  "A doc string for AProtocol abstraction"      ◁─┐   Optional doc string
  (bar [this a b] "bar docs")
  (baz [this a] [this a b] [this a b c] "baz docs"))   Method signatures
```

The protocol as well as the methods that form it can accept doc strings. A call to `defprotocol` results in a bunch of vars being created: one for the protocol itself and one for each polymorphic function (or method) that's a part of the protocol. These functions dispatch on the type of the first argument (and therefore must have at least one argument), and by convention, the first argument is called this. So from listing 9.5, the following snippet defines a protocol named ExpenseCalculations:

```
(defprotocol ExpenseCalculations
  (total-cents [e])
  (is-category? [e category]))
```

You're defining a set of related methods (total-cents and is-category?) that can be implemented any number of times by any data type. A call to defprotocol also generates an underlying Java interface. So, because the previous code exists in the namespace clj-in-act.ch9.expense-protocol, it will result in a Java interface called chapter_protocols.expense_protocol.ExpenseCalculations. The methods in this interface will be the ones specified in the definition of the protocol, total _cents and is_category_QMARK. The reference to QMARK is thanks to the translated name of a Clojure function (one that ends with a question mark) into Java.[2] The fact that defprotocol generates a Java interface also means that if some other Java code wants to participate in a protocol, it can implement the generated interface and proceed as usual.

Now that you've defined a protocol, any data type can participate in it.

PARTICIPATING IN PROTOCOLS

Having defined a protocol, let's see how you can use it. As an example, consider the call to extend-protocol, also from listing 9.5:

```
(extend-protocol ExpenseCalculations
  com.curry.expenses.Expense
  (total-cents [e]
    (.amountInCents e))
  (is-category? [e some-category]
    (= (.getCategory e) some-category)))
```

This means that the com.curry.expenses.Expense data type will participate in the ExpenseCalculations protocol, and when either total-cents or is-category? is called with an instance of this class as the first argument, it will be correctly dispatched to the previous implementation.

You can also specify more than one participant at a time; you can define the implementations of the protocol methods for more than a single data type. Here's an example:

```
(extend-protocol ExpenseCalculations
  clojure.lang.IPersistentMap
  (total-cents [e]
    (-> (:amount-dollars e)
        (* 100)
        (+ (:amount-cents e))))
```

---

[2] This translation from Clojure names to legal Java names is called *munging*. Normally, munging is transparently handled by Clojure, and you don't need to know about it, but it's important to keep in mind for two reasons: Clojure imports understand only Java names, and the filenames for your namespaces should use munged names.

```
(is-category? [e some-category]
  (= (:category e) some-category))
com.curry.expenses.Expense
(total-cents [e]
  (.amountInCents e))
(is-category? [e some-category]
  (= (.getCategory e) some-category)))
```

We'll now look at another way to specify how data types can participate in protocols.

EXTEND-TYPE MACRO

`extend-protocol` is a helper macro, defined on top of another convenient macro named `extend-type`. It's sort of the other way of specifying a participant of a protocol, in that it focuses on the data type. Here's an example of `extend-type` in use:

```
(extend-type com.curry.expenses.Expense
  ExpenseCalculations
  (total-cents [e]
    (.amountInCents e))
  (is-category? [e some-category]
    (= (.getCategory e) some-category)))
```

Again, because a single data type can participate in multiple protocols, `extend-type` lets you specify any number of protocols. Although `extend-protocol` and `extend-type` make it quite easy to use protocols, they both ultimately resolve to calls to the `extend` function.

EXTEND FUNCTION

The `extend` function lives in Clojure's core namespace, and it's the one that does the work of registering protocol participants and associating the methods with the right data types. Here's an example of the `extend` function in action:

```
(extend com.curry.expenses.Expense
  ExpenseCalculations {
    :total-cents (fn [e]
                    (.amountInCents e))
    :is-category? (fn [e some-category]
                    (= (.getCategory e) some-category))})
```

This might look similar to the code you generated in the implementation of your modus operandi. For each protocol and data type pair, `extend` accepts a map that describes participation of that data type in the protocol. The keys of the map are keyword versions of the names of the methods, and the values are the function bodies that contain the implementation for each. The `extend` function is the most flexible in terms of building an implementation of a protocol.

Figure 9.2 shows the conceptual flow of defining and using protocols.

We've covered protocols and how they're defined and used. We'll say another couple of things about them before moving on to the remaining topics of this chapter.

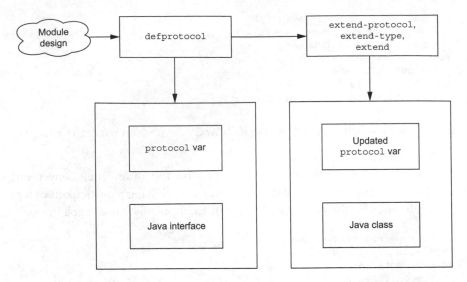

Figure 9.2 Calling `defprotocol` performs an analogous operation where a var is created to hold information about the protocol and its implementors. The underlying implementation will also result in a Java interface that pertains to the protocol being defined. Calls to `extend`, `extend-type`, and `extend-protocol` will update the var with implementor details and generate Java classes that implement the protocol.

PROTOCOLS AND NIL

You've seen that protocol methods are dispatched based on the class of the first argument. A natural question arises: What will happen if the first argument to a protocol method is `nil`? What is the class of `nil`?

```
(class nil)
;=> nil
```

If you call a protocol method, say `total-cents` from the expense example with `nil`, you'll get an error complaining that no implementation was found. Luckily, protocols can be extended on `nil`:

```
(extend-protocol ExpenseCalculations nil
  (total-cents [e] 0))
```

After this, calling `total-cents` with `nil` will return 0. Similarly, you can implement the `is-category?` function to return something appropriate for `nil`, perhaps `false`. Our last stop in this section will be to explore a few functions that help you reflect on defined protocols.

REFLECTING ON PROTOCOLS

Sometimes it's useful to programmatically reflect on specific protocols and their extenders. When you wrote your modus operandi, you also wrote some helper functions that let you reflect on `implements?`, `implementors`, and `full-implementor`. Clojure protocols also have functions that work in a similar fashion:

```
(extends? ExpenseCalculations com.curry.expenses.Expense)
;=> true
(extends? ExpenseCalculations clojure.lang.IPersistentMap)
;=> true
(extends? ExpenseCalculations java.util.Date)
;=> false
```

Needless to say, the function `extends?` can be used to check if a particular data type participates in a given protocol. The next function that's useful around such querying is `extenders`:

```
(extenders ExpenseCalculations)
;=> (nil com.curry.expenses.Expense clojure.lang.IPersistentMap)
```

Again, the `extenders` function lists all the data types that participate in a particular protocol. The final function of interest is called `satisfies?` and it works like this:

```
(satisfies? ExpenseCalculations (com.curry.expenses.Expense. "10-10-2010" 20
    95 "books" "amzn"))
;=> true
(satisfies? ExpenseCalculations (new-expense "10-10-2010" 20 95 "books"
    "amzn"))
;=> true
(satisfies? ExpenseCalculations (java.util.Random.))
;=> false
```

Note that the `satisfies?` function works on instances of extenders, not extender data types themselves. You'll find this function even more useful once you've seen the `reify` macro in action, which we'll explore in the next section.

We've now covered all the topics about protocols that we set out to cover. The next section is about the other side of this picture; we'll review a couple of ways to define data types.

9.3.2 Defining data types with deftype, defrecord, and reify

We started this chapter by considering the expression problem, and as you might recall, there are two sides to it, namely, data types and the operations on them. So far, we've been looking primarily at the operations side of the situation; in this section we'll look at a couple ways to define data types.

The mechanisms we're going to talk about create underlying classes on the host platform (namely Java today, but it could be others tomorrow). This means that they share the same performance as the native version of such data types, as well as the same polymorphic capabilities supported by the host. We'll first look at `defrecord`, followed by `deftype`. We'll close the section with a look at `reify`.

DEFRECORD

Let's start with an example of using `defrecord`:

```
(defrecord NewExpense [date amount-dollars amount-cents category
                       merchant-name])
```

The `defrecord` macro call defines a named class (in this case `chapter_protocols`
`.expense_record.NewExpense`) that has the specified set of fields, a class constructor,
and two constructor functions (in this case `->NewExpense` and `map->NewExpense`).
Because this is a proper class on the host environment, the type of class is fully specified and known, allowing for a high-performance dispatch of fields and methods. Similarly, it has a named constructor, similar to other Java classes. Here's how you'd create
an instance of the `NewExpense` data type:

**Printer shows this is
a class instance ...**

**Must use munged Java
classpath: underscores
instead of hyphens**

**Java
constructor
on class**

```
(import 'chapter_protocols.expense_record.NewExpense)
;=> chapter_protocols.expense_record.NewExpense
(NewExpense. "2010-04-01" 29 95 "gift" "1-800-flowers")
;=> #chapter_protocols.expense_record.NewExpense{:date "2010-04-01",
                                     :amount-dollars 29,
                                     :amount-cents 95,
                                     :category "gift",
                                     :merchant-name "1-800-flowers"}
```

**... but it's
more
idiomatic
to use
constructor
functions
that are in
namespace.**

```
(require '[clj-in-act.ch9.expense-record :as er])
;=> nil
(er/->NewExpense "2010-04-01" 29 95 "gift" "1-800-flowers")
;=> #chapter_protocols.expense_record.NewExpense{:date "2010-04-01",
    :amount-dollars 29, :amount-cents 95, :category "gift",
    :merchant-name "1-800-flowers"}
(er/map->NewExpense {:date "2010-04-01", :merchant-name "1-800-flowers",
    :message "April fools!"})
;=> #chapter_protocols.expense_record.NewExpense{:date "2010-04-01",
    :amount-dollars nil, :amount-cents nil, :category nil,
    :merchant-name "1-800-flowers", :message "April fools!"}
```

**map->RECORDNAME
constructor accepts
a single map.**

**->RECORDNAME
constructor accepts
positional parameters.**

Notice a few things about creating a record instance. `defrecord` creates a real Java class,
which is why you need to use `import` and a classpath (with Clojure-to-Java name munging) to access the record and Java instance-creation interop to construct it directly. If
you hadn't used `import`, you'd have gotten a `ClassNotFoundException` when you
tried to invoke the constructor. But `defrecord` also creates Clojure constructor functions in the same namespace: this is the more common and idiomatic way to create
instances of records from Clojure. The two constructors created are `->RECORDNAME`
(where `RECORDNAME` is the name of the record), which accepts positional parameters

identical to those of the Java constructor, and `map->RECORDNAME`, which accepts a map. Keys in the map that match record field names become record fields; fields with no matching keys in the map will get the value `nil`; any extra keys will be added to the record in a spillover map.

Now that you've come this far, go ahead and change the implementation of the expense namespace to use this. The following listing shows the new implementation.

Listing 9.6 expense namespace using a Clojure protocol and `defrecord`

```
(ns clj-in-act.ch9.expense-record
  (:import [java.text SimpleDateFormat]
           [java.util Calendar]))
(defrecord NewExpense [date amount-dollars amount-cents
                       category merchant-name])
(defn new-expense [date-string dollars cents category merchant-name]
  (let [calendar-date (Calendar/getInstance)]
    (.setTime calendar-date (.parse (SimpleDateFormat. "yyyy-MM-dd")
                                    date-string))
    (->NewExpense calendar-date dollars cents category merchant-name)))
(defprotocol ExpenseCalculations
  (total-cents [e])
  (is-category? [e category]))
(extend-type NewExpense
  ExpenseCalculations
  (total-cents [e]
    (-> (:amount-dollars e)
        (* 100)
        (+ (:amount-cents e))))
  (is-category? [e some-category]
    (= (:category e) some-category)))
(extend com.curry.expenses.Expense
  ExpenseCalculations {
    :total-cents (fn [e] (.amountInCents e))
    :is-category? (fn [e some-category] (= (.getCategory e)
                                           some-category))})
(extend-protocol ExpenseCalculations nil
  (total-cents [e] 0))
(defn category-is [category]
  #(is-category? % category))
(defn total-amount
  ([expenses-list]
    (total-amount (constantly true) expenses-list))
  ([pred expenses-list]
    (->> expenses-list
         (filter pred)
         (map total-cents)
         (apply +))))
```

Notice the call to `extend-type` and how you use the name of the newly defined record `NewExpense` instead of the previously used, more generic `IPersistentMap`. This shows that records can participate fully in protocols and indeed can participate in as many as needed. By the way, for completeness, it's worth modifying the `test` namespace to depend on the new `clj-in-act.ch9.expense-record` namespace and checking to see if all tests pass. They should.

Notice how you can access the fields of the `NewExpense` instances using keywords. This is because `defrecord` creates a class that already implements several interfaces, including `IPersistentMap`, `IKeywordLookup`, and `ILookup`. In this manner, they work in the same way as regular Clojure maps, including with respect to destructuring, metadata, and the use of functions such as `assoc` and `dissoc`. A useful point to note is that records are extensible in that they can accept values for keys that weren't originally specified as part of the `defrecord` call. The only penalty to this is that such keys have the same performance as Clojure maps. Records also implement the `hashCode` and `equals` methods, to support value-based equality out of the box. A final note is that the field specification supports type hints. By the way, it's worth noting here that records aren't functions, and so they can't be used as functions when looking up values. For instance, you can look up a key inside a Clojure map by using the map as a function and the key as a parameter, but you can't do this with records. Here's an example to illustrate records' maplike features:

```
(defrecord Foo [a b])
;=> user.Foo
(def foo (->Foo 1 2))
;=> #'user/foo
(assoc foo :extra-key 3)
;=> #user.Foo{:a 1, :b 2, :extra-key 3}
(dissoc (assoc foo :extra-key 3) :extra-key)
;=> #user.Foo{:a 1, :b 2}
(dissoc foo :a)
;=> {:b 2}
(foo :a)
ClassCastException user.Foo cannot be cast to clojure.lang.IFn  user/eval2640
(NO_SOURCE_FILE:1)
```

> If you assoc onto a record, you always get a new record with key added.

> Dissoc a nonfield key, and you still get a record.

> If you dissoc a field key, you get an ordinary map.

> Records aren't callable like maps.

Listing 9.6 shows how records can participate in protocols. There's nearly no change to the code from the previous implementation in listing 9.5, but records have more direct support for protocols. They can supply the implementations of protocols inline with their definition. The following listing shows this version.

Listing 9.7 expense namespace with `defrecord` and inline protocol

```
(ns clj-in-act.ch9.expense-record-2
  (:import [java.text SimpleDateFormat]
           [java.util Calendar]))
(defprotocol ExpenseCalculations
  (total-cents [e])
  (is-category? [e category]))
(defrecord NewExpense [date amount-dollars amount-cents
                                    category merchant-name]

  ExpenseCalculations
  (total-cents [this]
```

```
        (-> amount-dollars
           (* 100)
           (+ amount-cents)))
   (is-category? [this some-category]
     (= category some-category)))
(defn new-expense [date-string dollars cents category merchant-name]
  (let [calendar-date (Calendar/getInstance)]
    (.setTime calendar-date (.parse (SimpleDateFormat. "yyyy-MM-dd")
                                                      date-string))
    (->NewExpense calendar-date dollars cents category merchant-name)))
(extend com.curry.expenses.Expense
  ExpenseCalculations {
    :total-cents (fn [e] (.amountInCents e))
    :is-category? (fn [e some-category] (= (.getCategory e)
                                          some-category))})
(extend-protocol ExpenseCalculations nil
  (total-cents [e] 0))
(defn category-is [category]
  #(is-category? % category))
(defn total-amount
  ([expenses-list]
     (total-amount (constantly true) expenses-list))
  ([pred expenses-list]
     (->> expenses-list
         (filter pred)
         (map total-cents)
         (apply +))))
```

The main change is in the following snippet:

```
(defrecord NewExpense [date amount-dollars amount-cents category
                        merchant-name]
  ExpenseCalculations
  (total-cents [this]
    (-> amount-dollars
       (* 100)
       (+ amount-cents)))
  (is-category? [this some-category]
    (= category some-category)))
```

Notice that the field names are followed with the protocol name that you want to implement. The protocol name is followed by the implementations of the protocol methods. You can similarly follow that with more protocol specifications (the protocol name followed by the implementation).

JAVA SUPPORT

What's more, this isn't restricted to protocols; you can also specify and implement Java interfaces. The code would look similar to the previous protocol specification: you'd specify the interface name followed by the implementation of the interface methods. Instead of a protocol or an interface, you can also specify Object to override methods from the Object class. Recall that the first parameter of all protocol methods is the implementor instance itself, so you must pass the conventionally named this parameter as before. This means that there will be one more parameter for each interface or object method when compared to the corresponding definition. Finally, if the method implementation needs to call `recur`, the `this` parameter shouldn't be passed, because it will be passed automatically.

With this discussion, we've covered records. They can be used in all places where maps might have been used because they're faster and also support protocols. Note that the implementation of protocol methods didn't result in closures, and when this functionality is needed, you can use the `reify` macro. You'll see that shortly, but our next stop is the `deftype` macro.

DEFTYPE

When you use `defrecord`, you get a whole bunch of functionality for free. You get maplike behavior of using keywords to look up stuff, you get value-based equality behavior, you get metadata support, and you get serialization. This is usually exactly what you need when developing application domain data types, such as the `expense` data type from the previous few sections.

But there are times when you don't need any of this; indeed, at times you want to specify your own implementations for some of these interfaces. It's for these times that Clojure also provides the `deftype` macro:

```
(deftype Mytype [a b])
```

This generates an underlying Java class that looks like the following:

```
public final class Mytype {
    public final Object a;
    public final Object b;
    public Mytype(Object obj, Object obj1) {
        a = obj;
        b = obj1;
    }
}
```

As you can see, the fundamental difference between `defrecord` and `deftype` is that the latter produces a bare-metal class that you can do whatever you want with. The most common use case of `deftype` is to build infrastructure abstractions. Examples of such an abstraction might be a special collection to hold your domain-specific objects or a custom transaction manager. When you do need such a data type, with the performance characteristics of the native host, you can use `deftype`. In most other cases, `defrecord` should suffice.

We're nearly finished! In the previous section, we briefly mentioned closures. In the next section, we'll show how to create anonymous data types and instances of them using the `reify` macro.

REIFY

Reification means to bring something into being or to turn something into a concrete form. The `reify` macro takes a protocol, which by itself is an abstract set of methods, and creates a concrete instance of an anonymous data type that implements that protocol or interface. It does so with the full power of Clojure's lexical closures. For example, you might implement the new-expense function as follows:

```
(defn new-expense [date-string dollars cents category merchant-name]
  (let [calendar-date (Calendar/getInstance)]
    (.setTime calendar-date
              (.parse (SimpleDateFormat. "yyyy-MM-dd") date-string))
    (reify ExpenseCalculations
      (total-cents [this]
        (-> dollars
          (* 100)
          (+ cents)))
      (is-category? [this some-category]
        (= category some-category)))))
```

In a pattern that's similar to one you've seen before, reify accepts one or more protocols or interfaces and their implementations. In this example, reify was passed the ExpenseCalculations protocol along with the implementations of the total-cents and is-category? methods. The object returned by reify is a closure; in the case of new-expense, the lexically bound closure includes the parameters passed to new-expense, along with the names created in the let form.

You've now learned enough about protocols and data types to use them in your own programs. To round off this chapter, we'll make a few observations about protocols and compare them to multimethods.

9.4   Summary

Protocols were originally introduced to satisfy the need for low-level implementation techniques that would be fast enough to implement the language itself in, a la Clojure in Clojure. They also serve to solve 90% of the expression problem cases, where class-based single dispatch is acceptable. In this way, they're less powerful than multimethods.

Even with that, protocols have several advantages. Similar to multimethods, they don't tie polymorphism to inheritance. They allow grouping of related methods into a conceptual unit, which makes for clearer, self-documenting code. Because protocols generate interfaces from the underlying host, they're able to provide performance that's on par with the host itself. Similar to multimethods, they're an open way of solving the expression problem. This means that new data types and operations can be added while making minimum changes to existing code. Similarly, openness is maintained with respect to who is allowed to participate in protocols. Any number of data types can implement a single protocol, and a data type can implement any number of protocols. Finally, because protocols belong to the namespace they're defined in, there's no danger of name collisions if someone defines a protocol with the same name that you chose.

As a parting note, it's worth mentioning that even before the introduction of defrecord, using maps to store information was the idiomatic way to implement things.

Hiding information behind nongeneric interfaces (such as getters/setters or even more custom methods) makes such information less reusable by code that wasn't designed to access such an API. Maps provide far more generic manipulability, and records take that one step further by making it perform as fast as the host platform can make it.

When coupled with protocols, your Clojure code will be built on abstractions. This will ensure that it's more flexible and easier to maintain, as well as being easy for other people to work with. In this manner, protocols realize a huge benefit even beyond solving the most common case of the expression problem.

In the next chapter you'll learn how to use Clojure's built-in testing library and how to write Clojure using a test-driven method of development.

Test-driven development and more

10

This chapter covers

- An introduction to unit testing Clojure
- Writing test-driven Clojure code
- Mocking and stubbing code in Clojure
- Improving test organization

Test-driven development (TDD) has become something of the norm on most software development projects. It's easy to understand why, because TDD has several advantages. It allows the programmer to look at code being developed from the point of view of a consumer, which results in a more useful design when compared with a library that might be designed in relative isolation. Further, because code developed using TDD must be testable (by definition), the resulting design is often better in terms of lower coupling as well. Finally, the suite of tests that results from the process is a good way to ensure that functionality doesn't regress in the face of enhancements and bug fixes.

Clojure has excellent support for unit testing. Further, because Clojure is a Lisp, it's also extremely well suited for rapid application development. The read-evaluate-print loop (REPL) supports this by offering a means to develop code in an incremental manner. In this chapter, as you learn about TDD, you'll use the REPL for quick experiments and such. As you'll discover, this combination of TDD and the REPL makes for a productive development environment. The specific unit-testing library we'll explore is called `clojure.test`, and it comes as a standard part of the Clojure distribution. Finally, we'll look into mocking and stubbing needs that you might run into, and you'll write code to handle such situations.

10.1   Getting started with TDD: Manipulating dates in strings

In this section, you'll develop some code in a test-first manner. The first example is a set of functions that help with strings that represent dates. Specifically, you'll write functions to increment and decrement such date strings. Such operations are often needed in many applications, so this functionality may prove useful as a utility. Although this example is simple, it illustrates the technique of writing unit tests and then getting them to pass, while also using the REPL to make the process quicker.

In TDD, you begin by writing a test. Obviously, because no code exists to support the test, it will fail. Making that failing test pass becomes the immediate goal, and this process repeats. So the first thing you'll need is a test, which you'll start writing next.

In this simple example, the test you'll write is for a function that can accept a string containing a date in a particular format, and you'll check to see if you can access its components.

10.1.1 First assertion

In this initial version of the test, you'll check that the day portion is correct. Consider the following code (remember to put it in a file called date_operations_spec.clj in a folder named clj_in_act/ch10 within your source directory):

```
(ns clj-in-act.ch10.date-operations-spec
  (:require [clojure.test :refer :all]
            [clj-in-act.ch10.date-operations :refer :all]))
(deftest test-simple-data-parsing
  (let [d (date "2009-01-22")]
    (is (= (day-from d) 22))))
```

You're using the `clojure.test` unit-testing library for Clojure, which began life as an independent project and was later included as part of the distribution. There are other open source unit-testing libraries for Clojure (such as Midje (https://github.com/marick/Midje), expectations (http://jayfields.com/expectations/), and others), but for most purposes, the basic `clojure.test` is sufficient. The first evidence that you're looking at a unit test is the use of the `deftest` macro. Here's the general form of this macro:

```
(deftest [name & body])
```

It looks somewhat like a function definition, without any parameters. The body here represents the code that will run when the unit test is executed. The `clojure.test` library provides a couple of assertion macros, the first being is, which was used in the previous example. You'll see the use of the other macro in the following paragraphs.

Meanwhile, let's return to the test. If you try to evaluate the test code at the REPL, Clojure will complain that it can't find the `clj-in-act.ch10.date-operations` namespace. The error might look something like the following:

```
FileNotFoundException Could not locate clj_in_act/ch10/date_operations
__init.class or clj_in_act/ch10/date_operations.clj on classpath:
clojure.lang.RT.load (RT.java:443)
```

To move past this error, create a new namespace in an appropriately located file. This namespace has no code in it, so your test code still won't evaluate, but the error will be different. It will complain that it's unable to find the definition of a function named date:

```
CompilerException java.lang.RuntimeException: No such var: clj-in-
act.ch10.date-operations/date, compiling:(NO_SOURCE_PATH:1:1)
```

Getting past this error is easy; define a date function in your new `date-operations` namespace. To begin with, it doesn't even have to return anything. The same goes for the day-from function:

```
(ns clj-in-act.ch10.date-operations)
(defn date [date-string])
(defn day-from [d])
```

This will cause your test to evaluate successfully, leaving it ready to be run. You can also do this from the REPL, like so:

```
(use 'clojure.test)
;=> nil
(run-tests 'clj-in-act.ch10.date-operations-spec)
Testing clj-in-act.ch10.date-operations-spec
FAIL in (test-simple-data-parsing) (NO_SOURCE_FILE:1)
expected: (= (day-from d) 22)
  actual: (not (= nil 22))
Ran 1 tests containing 1 assertions.
1 failures, 0 errors.
;=> {:type :summary, :test 1, :pass 0, :fail 1, :error 0}
```

Now you're set. You have a failing test that you can work on, and once you have it passing, you'll have the basics of what you want. To get this test to pass, you'll write some real code in the `clj-in-act.ch10.date-operations` namespace. One way to implement this functionality is to use classes from the JDK standard library (there are other options as well, such as the excellent Joda Time library available as open source). You'll stick with the standard library, specifically with the GregorianCalendar and the

SimpleDateFormat classes. You can use these to convert strings into dates. You can experiment with them on the REPL:

```
(import '(java.text SimpleDateFormat))
;=> java.text.SimpleDateFormat
(def f (SimpleDateFormat. "yyyy-MM-dd"))
;=> #'user/f
(.parse f "2010-08-15")
;=> #inst "2010-08-15T05:00:00.000-00:00"
```

So you know SimpleDateFormat will work, and now you can check out the Gregorian-Calendar:

```
(import '(java.util GregorianCalendar))
;=> java.util.GregorianCalendar
(def gc (GregorianCalendar.))
;=> #'user/gc
```

Now that you have an instance of GregorianCalendar in hand, you can set the time by parsing a date string and then calling setTime:

```
(def d (.parse f "2010-08-15"))
;=> #'user/d
(.setTime gc d)
;=> nil
```

Because setTime returns nil, you're going to have to explicitly pass back the Gregorian-Calendar object. Once you've performed this experiment, you can write the code, which ends up looking like this:

```
(ns clj-in-act.ch10.date-operations
  (:import (java.text SimpleDateFormat)
           (java.util Calendar GregorianCalendar)))
(defn date [date-string]
  (let [f (SimpleDateFormat. "yyyy-MM-dd")
        d (.parse f date-string)]
    (doto (GregorianCalendar.)
      (.setTime d))))
;=> #'clj-in-act.ch10.date-operations/date
(date "2010-08-15")
;=> #inst "2010-08-15T00:00:00.000-05:00"
```

Also, you have to figure out the implementation of day-from. A look at the API documentation for GregorianCalendar reveals that the get method is what you need. You can try it at the REPL:

```
(import '(java.util Calendar))
;=> java.util.Calendar
(.get gc Calendar/DAY_OF_MONTH)
;=> 15
```

Again, you're all set. The day-from function can be

```
(defn day-from [d]
  (.get d Calendar/DAY_OF_MONTH))
```

The test should pass now. Remember that for the REPL to see the new definitions of the code in the date-operations namespace, you may need to reload it (using the :reload option). Here's the output:

```
(run-tests 'clj-in-act.ch10.date-operations-spec)
Testing clj-in-act.ch10.date-operations-spec
Ran 1 tests containing 1 assertions.
0 failures, 0 errors.
;=> {:type :summary, :test 1, :pass 1, :fail 0, :error 0}
```

Now that you can create date objects (represented by instances of GregorianCalendar) and can access the day from these objects, you can implement accessors for month and year. Again, you'll begin with writing a test.

10.1.2 *month-from and year-from*

The test for getting the month and year is similar to what you wrote before. You can include these assertions in the previous test:

```
(deftest test-simple-data-parsing
  (let [d (date "2009-01-22")]
    (is (= (month-from d) 1))
    (is (= (day-from d) 22))
    (is (= (year-from d) 2009))))
```

This won't evaluate until you at least define the month-from and year-from functions. You'll skip over the empty functions and write the implementation as

```
(defn month-from [d]
  (inc (.get d Calendar/MONTH)))
(defn year-from [d]
  (.get d Calendar/YEAR))
```

With this code in place, the test should pass:

```
(run-tests 'clj-in-act.ch10.date-operations-spec)
Testing clj-in-act.ch10.date-operations-spec
Ran 1 tests containing 3 assertions.
0 failures, 0 errors.
;=> {:type :summary, :test 1, :pass 3, :fail 0, :error 0}
```

Again, you're ready to add more features to your little library. You'll add an as-string function that can convert your date objects into the string format.

10.1.3 *as-string*

The test for this function is quite straightforward, because it's the same format you began with:

```
(deftest test-as-string
  (let [d (date "2009-01-22")]
    (is (= (as-string d) "2009-01-22"))))
```

Because you have functions to get the day, month, and year from a given date object, it's trivial to write a function that constructs a string containing words separated by dashes. Here's the implementation, which will compile and run after you include clojure.string in the namespace via a require clause:

```
(require '[clojure.string :as str])
(defn as-string [date]
  (let [y (year-from date)
        m (month-from date)
        d (day-from date)]
    (str/join "-" [y m d])))
```

You can confirm that this works by running it at the REPL:

```
(def d (clj-in-act.ch10.date-operations/date "2010-12-25"))
;=> #'user/d
(as-string d)
;=> "2010-12-25"
```

So that works, which means your test should pass. Running the test now gives the following output:

```
(run-tests 'clj-in-act.ch10.date-operations-spec)
Testing clj-in-act.ch10.date-operations-spec
FAIL in (test-as-string) (NO_SOURCE_FILE:1)
expected: (= (as-string d) "2009-01-22")
  actual: (not (= "2009-1-22" "2009-01-22"))
Ran 2 tests containing 4 assertions.
1 failures, 0 errors.
;=> {:type :summary, :test 2, :pass 3, :fail 1, :error 0}
```

The test failed! The problem is that instead of returning "2009-01-22", your as-string function returns "2009-1-22", because the various parts of the date are returned as numbers without leading zeroes even when they consist of only a single digit. You'll either have to change your test (which is fine, depending on the problem at hand) or pad such numbers to get your test to pass. For this example, you'll do the latter:

```
(defn pad [n]
  (if (< n 10) (str "0" n) (str n)))
(defn as-string [date]
  (let [y (year-from date)
        m (pad (month-from date))
        d (pad (day-from date))]
    (str/join "-" [y m d])))
```

Running the test now should show a better response:

```
(run-tests 'clj-in-act.ch10.date-operations-spec)
Testing clj-in-act.ch10.date-operations-spec
Ran 2 tests containing 4 assertions.
0 failures, 0 errors.
;=> {:type :summary, :test 2, :pass 4, :fail 0, :error 0}
```

So, you now have the ability to create date objects from strings, get at parts of the dates, and also convert the date objects into strings. You can either continue to add features or take a breather to refactor your code a little.

10.1.4 *Incrementing and decrementing*

Because you're just getting started, we'll postpone refactoring until after adding one more feature: adding functionality to advance and turn back dates. You'll start with addition, and then you'll write a test:

```
(deftest test-incrementing-date
  (let [d (date "2009-10-31")
        n-day (increment-day d)]
    (is (= (as-string n-day) "2009-11-01"))))
```

This test will fail, citing the inability to find the definition of `increment-day`. You can implement this function using the `add` method on the `GregorianCalendar` class, which you can check on the REPL:

```
(def d (date "2009-10-31"))
;=> #'user/d
(.add d Calendar/DAY_OF_MONTH 1)
;=> nil
(as-string d)
;=> "2009-11-01"
```

So that works quite nicely, and you can convert this into a function, as follows:

```
(defn increment-day [d]
  (doto d
    (.add Calendar/DAY_OF_MONTH 1)))
```

Now, you can add a couple more assertions to ensure you can add not only days but also months and years. The modified test looks like this:

```
(deftest test-incrementing-date
  (let [d (date "2009-10-31")
        n-day (increment-day d)
        n-month (increment-month d)
        n-year (increment-year d)]
    (is (= (as-string n-day) "2009-11-01"))
    (is (= (as-string n-month) "2009-11-30"))
    (is (= (as-string n-year) "2010-10-31"))))
```

The code to satisfy this test is simple, now that you already have `increment-day`:

```
(defn increment-month [d]
  (doto d
    (.add Calendar/MONTH 1)))
(defn increment-year [d]
  (doto d
    (.add Calendar/YEAR 1)))
```

Running this results in the following output:

```
(run-tests 'clj-in-act.ch10.date-operations-spec)
Testing clj-in-act.ch10.date-operations-spec
FAIL in (test-incrementing-date) (NO_SOURCE_FILE:1)
expected: (= (as-string n-day) "2009-11-01")
  actual: (not (= "2010-12-01" "2009-11-01"))
FAIL in (test-incrementing-date) (NO_SOURCE_FILE:1)
expected: (= (as-string n-month) "2009-11-30")
  actual: (not (= "2010-12-01" "2009-11-30"))
FAIL in (test-incrementing-date) (NO_SOURCE_FILE:1)
expected: (= (as-string n-year) "2010-10-31")
  actual: (not (= "2010-12-01" "2010-10-31"))
Ran 4 tests containing 8 assertions.
3 failures, 0 errors.
;=> {:type :summary, :test 4, :pass 5, :fail 3, :error 0}
```

All the tests failed! Even the one that was passing earlier (incrementing the date by a day) is now failing. Looking closely, all three failures are because the incremented date seems to be `"2010-12-01"`. It appears that `"2009-10-31"` was incremented first by a day, then by a month, and then by a year! You've been bitten by the most-Java-objects-are-not-immutable problem. Because `d` is a mutable object, and you're calling `increment-day`, `increment-month`, and `increment-year` on it, you're accumulating the mutations, resulting in a final date of `"2010-12-01"`. (As a side note, this also illustrates how easy it is to get used to Clojure's immutability and then to expect everything to behave like Clojure's core data structures. Within a few days of using Clojure, you'll begin to wonder why you ever thought mutable objects were a good idea!)

To address this problem, you'll return a new date from each mutator function. The `clone` method in Java does this, and you can use it in your new definitions:

```
(defn increment-day [d]
  (doto (.clone d)
    (.add Calendar/DAY_OF_MONTH 1)))
(defn increment-month [d]
  (doto (.clone d)
    (.add Calendar/MONTH 1)))
(defn increment-year [d]
  (doto (.clone d)
    (.add Calendar/YEAR 1)))
```

With this change, all the tests pass, allowing us to now tackle decrementing. Again, you'll start with a test:

```
(deftest test-decrementing-date
  (let [d (date "2009-11-01")
        n-day (decrement-day d)
        n-month (decrement-month d)
        n-year (decrement-year d)]
    (is (= (as-string n-day) "2009-10-31"))
    (is (= (as-string n-month) "2009-10-01"))
    (is (= (as-string n-year) "2008-11-01"))))
```

To get this test to pass, you can go with the same structure of functions that did the incrementing. The code might look like the following:

```
(defn decrement-day [d]
  (doto (.clone d)
    (.add Calendar/DAY_OF_MONTH -1)))
(defn decrement-month [d]
  (doto (.clone d)
    (.add Calendar/MONTH -1)))
(defn decrement-year [d]
  (doto (.clone d)
    (.add Calendar/YEAR -1)))
```

Each function calls an appropriate Java method, and this passes all the tests. You now have code that works and a library that can accept date strings and return dates as strings. It can also increment and decrement dates by days, months, and years. But the code isn't quite optimal, so you're now going to improve it.

10.1.5 *Refactor mercilessly*

Extreme programming (XP) is an Agile methodology that espouses several specific guidelines. One of them is to "refactor mercilessly." It means that you should continuously strive to make code (and design) simpler by removing clutter and needless complexity. An important part of achieving such simplicity is to remove duplication. You'll do that with the code you've written so far.

Before you start, it's pertinent to make an observation. There's one major requirement to any sort of refactoring: for it to be safe, there needs to be a set of tests that can verify that nothing broke because of the refactoring. This is another benefit of writing tests (and TDD in general). The tests from the previous section will serve this purpose.

You'll begin refactoring by addressing the duplication in the increment/decrement functions. Here's a rewrite of those functions:

```
(defn date-operator [operation field]
  (fn [d]
    (doto (.clone d)
      (.add field (operation 1)))))
(def increment-day (date-operator + Calendar/DAY_OF_MONTH))
(def increment-month (date-operator + Calendar/MONTH))
```

```
(def increment-year (date-operator + Calendar/YEAR))
(def decrement-day (date-operator - Calendar/DAY_OF_MONTH))
(def decrement-month (date-operator - Calendar/MONTH))
(def decrement-year (date-operator - Calendar/YEAR))
```

After replacing all six of the old functions with this code, the tests still pass. You've removed the duplication from the previous implementation and also made the code more declarative: the job of each of the six functions is clearer with this style. The benefit may seem small in this example, but for more complex code, it can be a major boost in readability, understandability, and maintainability. This refactored version can be further reduced via some clever use of convention, but it may be overkill for this particular task. As it stands, you've reduced the number of lines from 18 to 10, showing that the old implementation was a good 80% larger than this new one.

Imagine a similar refactoring being applied to the month-from, day-from, and year-from functions. What might that look like?

This section showed how to use the built-in Clojure unit-testing library called clojure.test. As you saw through the course of building the example, using the REPL is a critical element to writing Clojure code. You can use the REPL to quickly check how things work and then write code once you understand the APIs. It's great for such short experiments and allows for incrementally building up code for larger, more complex functions. When a unit-testing library is used alongside the REPL, the combination can result in an ultrafast development cycle while keeping quality high. In the next section, you'll see how you can write a simple mocking and stubbing library to make your unit testing even more effective.

10.2 *Improving tests through mocking and stubbing*

Unit testing is testing at a unit level, which in the case of Clojure is the function. Functions are often composed of other functions, and there are times when testing such upper-level functions that it's useful to mock out calls to certain underlying functions. *Mocking* functions is a useful technique (often used during unit testing) where a particular function is replaced with one that doesn't do anything. This allows you to focus only on those parts of the code where the unit test is being targeted.

At other times, it's useful to *stub* the calling of a function, so instead of doing what it's implemented to do, the stubbed function returns canned data.

You'll see examples of both of these in this section. You'll also write a simple library to handle mocking and stubbing functions in this manner. Clojure, being the dynamic functional language that it is, makes this extremely easy to do.

10.2.1 *Example: Expense finders*

In this example, you'll write a few functions to load certain expense records from a data store and then filter them based on some criteria (such as greater than a particular amount). You might do this as part of an expense report builder, for instance.

Because you're dealing with money, you'll also throw in a requirement that your functions must log to an audit log.

Also, the focus of this section isn't the TDD that you saw in the previous section. This section will focus on the need to stub calls to certain functions. The following listing shows the code you're trying to test.

```clojure
(ns clj-in-act.ch10.expense-finders
  (:require [clojure.string :as str]))
(defn log-call [id & args]
  (println "Audit - called" id "with:" (str/join ", " args))
  ;;do logging to some audit data-store
)
(defn fetch-all-expenses [username start-date end-date]
  (log-call "fetch-all" username start-date end-date)
  ;find in data-store, return list of expense maps
)
(defn expenses-greater-than [expenses threshold]
  (log-call "expenses-greater-than" threshold)
  (filter #(> (:amount %) threshold) expenses))
(defn fetch-expenses-greater-than [username start-date end-date threshold]
  (let [all (fetch-all-expenses username start-date end-date)]
    (expenses-greater-than all threshold)))
```

Here again, expense records are represented as Clojure maps. The `log-call` function presumably logs calls to some kind of an audit database. The two `fetch` functions both depend on loading expenses from some sort of a data store. To write a test for, say, the `fetch-expenses-greater-than` function, you'll need to populate the data store to ensure it's loaded from the test via the `fetch-all-expenses` call. In case any test alters the data, you must clean it up so subsequent runs of the tests also work.

This is a lot of trouble. Moreover, it couples your tests to the data store and the data in it. Presumably, as part of a real-world application, you'd test the persistence of data to and from the data store elsewhere, so having to deal with hitting the data store in this test is a distraction and plain unnecessary. It would be nice if you could stub the call and return canned data. You'll implement this stubbing functionality next. Further, you'll look at dealing with another distraction, the `log-call` function, in the following section.

10.2.2 Stubbing

In your test for `fetch-expenses-greater-than`, it would be nice if you could do the following:

```clojure
(let [filtered (fetch-expenses-greater-than "" "" "" 15.0)]
  (is (= (count filtered) 2))
  (is (= (:amount (first filtered)) 20.0))
  (is (= (:amount (last filtered)) 30.0)))
```

You're passing blank strings to `fetch-expenses-greater-than` because you don't care what the values are (you could have passed anything). Inside the body of `fetch-expenses-greater-than`, they're used only as arguments to `fetch-all-expenses`, and you want to stub the call to this latter function (the one parameter that you do pass correctly is the last one, with a value of `15.0`). What you'd also like is for the stubbed call to return canned data, which you might define as follows:

```
(def all-expenses [{:amount 10.0 :date "2010-02-28"}
                    {:amount 20.0 :date "2010-02-25"}
                    {:amount 30.0 :date "2010-02-21"}])
```

So, the question is how do you express the requirement for these two things: the call to `fetch-all-expenses` is faked out (stubbed), and it returns `all-expenses`?

STUBBING MACRO

To make the process of stubbing functions feel as natural as possible, you'll create a new construct for your tests and give it the original name `stubbing`. After you have it all implemented, you'll be able to say something like this:

```
(deftest test-fetch-expenses-greater-than
  (stubbing [fetch-all-expenses all-expenses]
    (let [filtered (fetch-expenses-greater-than "" "" "" 15.0)]
      (is (= (count filtered) 2))
      (is (= (:amount (first filtered)) 20.0))
      (is (= (:amount (last filtered)) 30.0)))))
```

The general form of the stubbing macro is as follows:

```
(stubbing [function-name1 stubbed-return-value1
           function-name2 stubbed-return-value2 …]
  code-body)
```

This reads a little like the `let` and `binding` forms, and whenever you add such constructs to your code, it makes sense to make them look and feel like one of the built-in features of Clojure to keep things easy for others to understand. Now let's see how you might implement it.

IMPLEMENTING STUBBING

Clojure makes implementing this quite easy. Because it's a functional language, you can easily create a dummy function on the fly, one that accepts an arbitrary number of parameters and returns whatever you specify. Next, because function definitions are held in vars, you can then use the binding form to set them to your newly constructed stub functions. Here's the implementation:

```
(ns clj-in-act.ch10.stubbing)
(defmacro stubbing [stub-forms & body]
  (let [stub-pairs (partition 2 stub-forms)
        returns (map last stub-pairs)
        stub-fns (map #(list 'constantly %) returns)
        real-fns (map first stub-pairs)]
```

```
`(with-redefs [~@(interleave real-fns stub-fns)]
   ~@body)))
```

Considering that many languages have large, complex libraries for stubbing functions and methods, this code is almost disappointingly short!

Before we look at a sample expansion of this macro, let's look at an example of two functions, `calc-x` and `calc-y`, being called from some client code:

```
(defn calc-x [x1 x2]
  (* x1 x2))
(defn calc-y [y1 y2]
  (/ y2 y1))
(defn some-client []
  (println (calc-x 2 3) (calc-y 3 4)))
```

Let's see how `some-client` behaves under normal conditions:

```
(some-client)
6 4/3
;=> nil
```

And here's how it behaves using the new stubbing macro:

```
(stubbing [calc-x 1
           calc-y 2]
  (some-client))
1 2
;=> nil
```

So now that we've confirmed that this works as expected, let's look at how it does so:

```
(macroexpand-1' (stubbing [calc-x 1 calc-y 2]
       (some-client)))
;=> (clojure.core/with-redefs [calc-x (constantly 1)
                               calc-y (constantly 2)]
       (some-client))
```

The `constantly` function does the job well, but to make things easier for you later on, you'll introduce a function called `stub-fn`. It's a simple higher-order function that accepts a value and returns a function that returns that value no matter what arguments it's called with. Hence, it's equivalent to `constantly`. The rewritten code is shown here:

```
(defn stub-fn [return-value]
  (fn [& args]
    return-value))
(defmacro stubbing [stub-forms & body]
  (let [stub-pairs (partition 2 stub-forms)
        returns (map last stub-pairs)
        stub-fns (map #(list `stub-fn %) returns)
        real-fns (map first stub-pairs)]
    `(with-redefs [~@(interleave real-fns stub-fns)]
       ~@body)))
```

> Backtick quote on `stub-fn` is so expanded symbol is namespace qualified

This extra layer of indirection will allow you to introduce another desirable feature into this little library (if you can even call it that!)—*mocking*, the focus of the next section.

10.2.3 Mocking

Let's begin by going back to what you were doing when you started the stubbing journey. You wrote a test for `fetch-expenses-greater-than`, a function that calls `expenses-greater-than`. This function does two things: it logs to the audit log, and then it filters out the expenses based on the threshold parameter. You should be unit testing this lower-level function as well, so let's look at the following test:

```
(ns clj-in-act.ch10.expense-finders-spec
  (:require [clj-in-act.ch10.expense-finders :refer :all]
            [clojure.test :refer :all]))
(deftest test-filter-greater-than
  (let [fetched [{:amount 10.0 :date "2010-02-28"}
                 {:amount 20.0 :date "2010-02-25"}
                 {:amount 30.0 :date "2010-02-21"}]
        filtered (expenses-greater-than fetched 15.0)]
    (is (= (count filtered) 2))
    (is (= (:amount (first filtered)) 20.0))
    (is (= (:amount (last filtered)) 30.0))))
```

Running the test gives the following output:

```
(run-tests 'clj-in-act.ch10.expense-finders-spec)
Testing clj-in-act.ch10.expense-finders-spec
Audit - called expenses-greater-than with: 15.0
Ran 1 tests containing 3 assertions.
0 failures, 0 errors.
;=> {:type :summary, :test 1, :pass 3, :fail 0, :error 0}
```

It works, and the test passes. The trouble is that the `audit` function also runs as part of the test, as can be seen from the text `Audit - called expenses-greater-than with: 15.0` that was printed by the `log-call` function. In the present case, all it does is print some text, but in the real world, it could do something useful—perhaps write to a database or send a message on a queue.

Ultimately, it causes the tests to be dependent on an external system such as a database server or a message bus. It makes the tests less isolated, and it detracts from the unit test itself, which is trying to check whether the filtering works correctly.

One solution is to not test at this level at all but to write an even lower-level function that tests only the filtering. But you'd like to test at least at the level that clients of the code will work at, so you need a different solution. One approach is to add code to the `log-call` function so that it doesn't do anything when running in test mode. But that adds unnecessary code to functions that will run in production, and it also clutters the code. In more complex cases, it will add noise that will detract from easily understanding what the function does.

Luckily, you can easily fix this problem in Clojure by writing a simple mocking library.

10.2.4 *Mocks versus stubs*

A *mock* is similar to a stub because the original function doesn't get called when a function is mocked out. A stub returns a canned value that was set up when the stub was set up. A mock records the fact that it was called, with a specific set of arguments. Later on, the developer can programmatically verify if the mocked function was called, how many times it was called, and with what arguments.

CREATING MOCKS WITH STUBS

Now that you have a separate function called `stub-fn`, you can modify this to add mocking capabilities. You'll begin by creating an `atom` called `mock-calls` that will hold information about the various mocked functions that were called:

```
(def mock-calls (atom {}))
```

Now, you'll modify `stub-fn` to use this atom:

```
(defn stub-fn [the-function return-value]
  (swap! mock-calls assoc the-function [])
  (fn [& args]
    (swap! mock-calls update-in [the-function] conj args)
    return-value))
```

When `stub-fn` is called, an empty vector is stored in the atom against the function being stubbed. Later, when the stub is called, it records the call in the atom (as shown in chapter 6) along with the arguments it was called with. It then returns the `return-value` it was created with, thereby working as before in that respect.

Now that you've changed the way `stub-fn` works, you have to also slightly refactor the stubbing macro for it to stay compatible:

```
(defmacro stubbing [stub-forms & body]
  (let [stub-pairs (partition 2 stub-forms)
        real-fns (map first stub-pairs)
        returns (map last stub-pairs)
        stub-fns (map #(list `stub-fn %1 %2) real-fns returns)]
    `(with-redefs [~@(interleave real-fns stub-fns)]
       ~@body)))
```

Okay, now you've laid the basic foundation on which to implement the mocking features. Because a mock is similar to a stub, you can use `stub-fn` to create a new one. You don't care about a return value, so you'll use `nil`:

```
(defn mock-fn [the-function]
  (stub-fn the-function nil))
```

Now for some syntactic sugar. You'll create a new macro called `mocking`, which will behave similar to `stubbing`, except that it will accept any number of functions that need to be mocked:

```
(defmacro mocking [fn-names & body]
  (let [mocks (map #(list `mock-fn (keyword %)) fn-names)]
    `(with-redefs [~@(interleave fn-names mocks)]
       ~@body)))
```

Now that you have the basics ready, you can rewrite your test:

```
(deftest test-filter-greater-than
  (mocking [log-call]
    (let [filtered (expenses-greater-than all-expenses 15.0)]
      (is (= (count filtered) 2))
      (is (= (:amount (first filtered)) 20.0))
      (is (= (:amount (last filtered)) 30.0)))))
```

all-expenses
defined in
section 10.2.2

When you run this test, it won't execute the `log-call` function, and the test is now independent of the whole audit-logging component. As noted earlier, the difference between `mocking` and `stubbing` so far is that you don't need to provide a return value when using `mocking`.

Although you don't want the `log-call` function to run as is, it may be important to verify that the code under test calls a function by that name. Perhaps such calls are part of some security protocol in the overall application. It's quite easy for you to verify this, because you're recording all calls to your mocked functions in the `mock-calls` atom.

VERIFYING MOCKED CALLS

The first construct that you'll provide to verify mocked function use will confirm the number of times they were called. Here it is:

```
(defmacro verify-call-times-for [fn-name number]
  `(is (= ~number (count (@mock-calls ~(keyword fn-name))))))
```

This makes it easy to see if a mocked function was called a specific number of times. Another way to verify the mocked calls would be to ensure they were called with specific arguments. Because you're recording that information as well, it's quite easy to provide verification functions to do this:

```
(defmacro verify-first-call-args-for [fn-name & args]
  `(is (= '~args (first (@mock-calls ~(keyword fn-name))))))
```

Finally, because a mocked function may be called multiple times by the code under test, here's a macro to verify any of those calls:

```
(defmacro verify-nth-call-args-for [n fn-name & args]
  `(is (= '~args (nth (@mock-calls ~(keyword fn-name)) (dec ~n)))))
```

Let's look at these verification mechanisms in action:

```
(deftest test-filter-greater-than
  (mocking [log-call]
    (let [filtered (expenses-greater-than all-expenses 15.0)]
      (is (= (count filtered) 2))
      (is (= (:amount (first filtered)) 20.0))
      (is (= (:amount (last filtered)) 30.0)))
    (verify-call-times-for log-call 1)
    (verify-first-call-args-for log-call "expenses-greater-than" 15.0)
    (verify-nth-call-args-for 1 log-call "expenses-greater-than" 15.0)))
```

What you now have going is a way to mock any function so that it doesn't get called with its regular implementation. Instead, a dummy function is called that returns `nil` and lets the developer also verify that the calls were made and with particular arguments. This makes testing code with various types of dependencies on external resource much easier. The syntax is also not so onerous, making the tests easy to write and read.

You can now also refactor `verify-first-call-args-for` in terms of `verify-nth-call-args-for` as follows:

```
(defmacro verify-first-call-args-for [fn-name & args]
  `(verify-nth-call-args-for 1 ~fn-name ~@args))
```

So that's the bulk of it! Listing 10.2 shows the complete `mocking` and `stubbing` macro implementation. It allows functions to be dynamically mocked out or stubbed, depending on the requirement. It also provides a simple syntactic layer in the form of the `mocking` and `stubbing` macros, as shown previously.

Listing 10.2 Simple stubbing and mocking macro functionality for Clojure tests

```
(ns clj-in-act.ch10.mock-stub
  (:use clojure.test))
(def mock-calls (atom {}))
(defn stub-fn [the-function return-value]
  (swap! mock-calls assoc the-function [])
  (fn [& args]
    (swap! mock-calls update-in [the-function] conj args)
    return-value))
(defn mock-fn [the-function]
  (stub-fn the-function nil))
(defmacro verify-call-times-for [fn-name number]
  `(is (= ~number (count (@mock-calls ~(keyword fn-name))))))
(defmacro verify-nth-call-args-for [n fn-name & args]
  `(is (= '~args (nth (@mock-calls ~(keyword fn-name)) (dec ~n)))))
(defmacro verify-first-call-args-for [fn-name & args]
  `(verify-nth-call-args-for 1 ~fn-name ~@args))
(defmacro mocking [fn-names & body]
  (let [mocks (map #(list `mock-fn (keyword %)) fn-names)]
    `(with-redefs [~@(interleave fn-names mocks)]
       ~@body)))
```

```
(defmacro stubbing [stub-forms & body]
  (let [stub-pairs (partition 2 stub-forms)
        real-fns (map first stub-pairs)
        returns (map last stub-pairs)
        stub-fns (map #(list `stub-fn %1 %2) real-fns returns)]
    `(with-redefs [~@(interleave real-fns stub-fns)]
       ~@body)))
```

That's not a lot of code: under 30 lines. But it's sufficient for your purposes and indeed as a basis to add more complex functionality. We'll now look at a couple more things before closing this section.

10.2.5 *Managing stubbing and mocking state*

As the tests are set up and run, you build up state for things like canned return values and metrics around what was called with what arguments. In this section, we'll look at managing this state.

CLEARING RECORDED CALLS

After a test run such as the previous one, the `mock-calls` atom contains all the recorded calls to mocked functions. The verification macros you create work against this to ensure that your mocks were called the way you expected. When all is said and done, though, the data that remains is useless. You can add a function to clear out the recorded calls:

```
(defn clear-calls []
  (reset! mock-calls {}))
```

In case you wondered why running the same test multiple times doesn't cause an accumulation in the `mock-calls` atom, it's because the call to `stub-fn` resets the entry for that function. Further, this global state will cause problems if you happen to run tests in parallel, because the recording will no longer correspond to a single piece of code under test. The atom will, instead, contain a mishmash of all calls to various mocks from all the tests. This isn't what's intended, so you can fix this by making the state local.

REMOVING GLOBAL STATE

By removing the global `mock-calls` atom, you'll be able to improve the ability of tests that use mocking to run in parallel. The first thing you'll do is make the global binding for `mock-calls` dynamic:

```
(def ^:dynamic *mock-calls*)
```
◁— **"Earmuffs" (surrounding asterisks) mark dynamic vars by convention.**

Next, for things to continue to work as they did, you have to reestablish the binding at some point. You'll create a new construct called `defmocktest`, which will be used instead of `deftest`. Its only job is to create a binding for mock calls before delegating back to good-old `deftest`:

```
(defmacro defmocktest [test-name & body]
  `(deftest ~test-name
     (binding [*mock-calls* (atom {})]
       (do ~@body))))
```

After this, your previously defined tests would need to be redefined using `defmocktest`:

```
(defmocktest test-fetch-expenses-greater-than
  (stubbing [fetch-all-expenses all-expenses]
    (let [filtered (fetch-expenses-greater-than "" "" "" 15.0)]
      (is (= (count filtered) 2))
      (is (= (:amount (first filtered)) 20.0))
      (is (= (:amount (last filtered)) 30.0)))))
```

And here's the other one:

```
(defmocktest test-filter-greater-than
  (mocking [log-call]
    (let [filtered (expenses-greater-than all-expenses 15.0)]
      (is (= (count filtered) 2))
      (is (= (:amount (first filtered)) 20.0))
      (is (= (:amount (last filtered)) 30.0)))
    (verify-call-times-for log-call 1)
    (verify-first-call-args-for log-call "expenses-greater-than" 15.0)))
```

The trade-off is that you have to include the calls to your verify macros inside the scope of the call to `defmocktest`. This is because the mock calls are recorded inside the atom bound by the binding created by the `defmocktest` macro, and outside such scope there's nothing bound to `*mock-calls*`.

You've completed what you set out to do: you started by exploring the `clojure.test` library and then added functionality to allow simple stubbing and mocking of functions. Our final stop will be to look at another couple of features of `clojure.test`.

10.3 *Organizing tests*

A couple other constructs that are part of the `clojure.test` unit-testing library are worth knowing about. They help with organizing asserts inside the body of a test function. Although it's usually better to keep the number of asserts in each test to the lowest possible number, sometimes it's logical to add asserts to existing tests rather than add new tests.

When a test does have several assertions, it often becomes more difficult to understand and maintain. When an assertion fails, it isn't always clear what the specific failure is and what specific functionality is breaking. In this section, we'll look at two macros that can help you manage assertions: the `testing` macro and the `are` macro.

The `testing` macro documents groups of test assertions. The `are` macro does two things: it removes duplication when several assertions using `is` are used with minor variations, and it groups such assertions together. We'll look at an example of the `testing` macro in action first.

10.3.1   *The testing macro*

Let's revisit the `test-filter-greater-than` test from the previous section. There are two distinct sets of things you're checking for here: first that the filtering itself works and second that the call to `log-call` happens correctly. You'll use the `testing` macro to group these according to those goals:

```
(defmocktest test-filter-greater-than
  (mocking [log-call]
    (let [filtered (expenses-greater-than all-expenses 15.0)]
      (testing "the filtering itself works as expected"
        (is (= (count filtered) 2))
        (is (= (:amount (first filtered)) 20.0))
        (is (= (:amount (last filtered)) 30.0))))
    (testing "Auditing via log-call works correctly"
      (verify-call-times-for log-call 1)
      (verify-first-call-args-for log-call "expenses-greater-than" 15.0))))
```

This code deliberately changed the number of times you expect `log-call` to be called to 2, so you can see how things look when this test fails:

```
(test-filter-greater-than)
FAIL in (test-filter-greater-than) (NO_SOURCE_FILE:1)
Auditing via log-call works correctly
expected: (clojure.core/= 2 (clojure.core/count ((clojure.core/deref
clj-in-act.ch10.mock-stub2/*mock-calls*) :log-call)))
  actual: (not (clojure.core/= 2 1))
```

As you can see, now when anything within a group of assertions fails, the `testing` string is printed along with the failure. It gives immediate feedback about what the problem is, and it also makes reading and understanding the test much easier.

Now let's look at the `are` macro.

10.3.2   *The are macro*

We'll now look at the `are` macro, which is an additional construct to group assertions with and one that also helps remove unnecessary duplication. Imagine that you had to create a function to uppercase a given string:

```
(deftest test-to-upcase
  (is (= "RATHORE" (to-upper "rathore")))
  (is (= "1" (to-upper 1)))
  (is (= "AMIT" (to-upper "amit"))))
```

Here's a function that will satisfy this test:

```
(defn to-upper [s]
  (.toUpperCase (str s)))
```

You can remove the duplication in this test by using the `are` macro:

```
(deftest test-to-upcase
  (are [l u] (= u (to-upper l))
  "RATHORE" "rathore"
  "1"       "1"
  "AMIT"    "amit"))
```

Using the `are` macro combines several forms into a single form. When any of them fail, the failure is reported as a single failure. This is why it should be used to group related assertions, not as a means to remove duplication.

10.4 Summary

In this chapter, we looked at test-driven development in Clojure. As you saw, TDD in a language such as Clojure can work as well as it does in other dynamic languages. In fact, when combined with the REPL, it gets an additional boost of productivity. The typical process is this: you write a failing unit test and follow that up with trying out various implementation ideas at the REPL. When it becomes clear what approach to take, you test various implementations quickly at the REPL. Finally, you copy the code over to the test files and add additional assertions and tests.

You then wrote some simple code to stub functions, and then you added functionality to mock functions and verify the calls made to them. Clojure made it extremely easy—and the complete code for this clocked in at fewer than 30 lines. Although it probably didn't satisfy every requirement from a stubbing and mocking library, it served your purposes well and it can be used as the basis for something more complex. It certainly showed how easily you can implement seemingly complex things in Clojure.

Overall, this chapter demonstrated that using the REPL and test-driven development significantly amplifies the natural productivity boost that comes from using a modern and functional Lisp.

In this chapter, you created new "syntax" using macros to simplify and clarify mocking and stubbing in your testing code. In the next and final chapter, you'll learn more advanced macro techniques and how to use them to construct your own domain-specific languages.

More macros and DSLs

11

This chapter covers

- Anaphoric macros
- Shifting computation to compile time
- Macro-generating macros
- Designing, writing, and optimizing domain-specific languages in Clojure

---

This final chapter is about what many consider the most powerful feature of Clojure. John McCarthy, the inventor of the Lisp programming language, once said that Lisp is a local maximum in the space of programming languages.[1] Clojure macros make it possible to do arbitrary code transformations of Clojure code, using Clojure itself. No programming language outside the Lisp family can do this in such a simple way. This is possible because code is data.

You've seen a lot of macros in the course of this book, including in chapter 7, which served as an introduction to the topic. In this section, you're going to see a lot more but with two new points of focus: the advanced uses of macros and the

---

[1] History of Lisp (paper presented at the first History of Programming Languages conference, June 1–3, 1978), http://www-formal.stanford.edu/jmc/history/lisp/lisp.html.

268

conscious design of a simple domain-specific language. Mastering these topics will let you design elegant abstractions for even the most demanding of problem domains.

11.1 A quick review of macros

You've already used macros quite a bit, but as a refresher here you'll write a little macro to remind you what macros make possible. You've used Clojure's `let` macro several times so far. Although `let` itself is a macro, it's implemented in terms of the `let*` special form, which sets up lexical scope for the symbols named in the binding form. You'll now implement a subset of the functionality of `let` via a macro that generates function calls. This is what you'd like to do:

```
(my-let [x 10
         y x
         z (+ x y)]
   (* x y z))
;=> 2000
```

This should return 2000, because x is 10, y is also 10, and z is 20. Here's the implementation:

```
(defmacro single-arg-fn [binding-form & body]
  `((fn [~(first binding-form)] ~@body) ~(second binding-form)))

(defmacro my-let [lettings & body]
  (if (empty? lettings)
    `(do ~@body)
    `(single-arg-fn ~(take 2 lettings)
       (my-let ~(drop 2 lettings) ~@body))))
```

In case you'd like to refresh your memory on how macros work, please refer back to chapter 7. Although the preceding code is a limited implementation, you still get all the advantages that arise from using functions underneath the covers. For instance, you can do the following:

```
(my-let [[a b] [2 5]
         {:keys [x y]} {:x (* a b) :y 20}
         z (+ x y)]
        (println "a,b,x,y,z:" a b x y z)
        (* x y z))
a,b,x,y,z: 2 5 10 20 30
;=> 6000
```

Notice here that all destructuring forms just work, because underneath the covers, regular functions are at work. Specifically, you're taking each `my-let` binding and setting it up as the single argument to an anonymous unary function. You're essentially converting the `my-let` form into a nested series of such unary functions. Try expanding the macro at the read-evaluate-print loop (REPL) to see the forms generated.

You're not doing any error checking here, but hopefully this example has reminded you how macros work, as well as shown you how to seemingly add features to the Clojure language itself. Use macroexpand-1, macroexpand, and clojure.walk/macroexpand-all to get a hint as to how the my-let does its thing. We're now ready to look beyond the basics.

In this section, we're going to explore three new concepts. The first is that of *anaphora*, an approach of writing macros that utilize intentional variable capture to their advantage. You'll see why they're called anaphoric and how they can be used to add special syntax features to Clojure.

The second concept we'll explore is the idea of moving some of the computation from a program's runtime into its compile time. Some computation that would otherwise be done when the program is already running will now be done while the code is being compiled. You'll see not only where this might be useful but also an example of precomputing decrypting tables.

Finally, we'll look at writing macros that generate other macros. This can be tricky, and we'll look at a simple example of such a macro. Understanding macro-generating macros is a sign of being on the path to macro Zen.

Without further ado, our first stop is Clojure anaphora.

11.2 *Anaphoric macros*

In chapter 7, we talked about the issue of variable capture. As a reminder, variable capture happens when a variable name in a macro expansion (say in a generated let binding) shadows something outside that immediate scope (say in an outer let binding). You saw that Clojure solves this issue in an elegant manner through two processes: the first is that names inside a macro template get namespace qualified to the namespace that the macro is defined in, and the second is by providing a convenient auto-gensym reader macro.

Macros that do their work based on intentional variable capture are called *anaphoric* macros (*anaphor* means a word or phrase that refers to an earlier word or phrase). In this section, we'll do more variable capture but in a slightly more complex manner. To get things started, we'll visit a commonly cited example that illustrates this concept. You'll then build on it to write a useful utility macro.

11.2.1 *The anaphoric if*

Writing the anaphoric version of the if construct is the "Hello, world!" of anaphora. The anaphoric if is probably one of the simplest of its ilk, but it illustrates the point well, while also being a useful utility macro.

Consider the following example, where you first do a computation, check if it's truthy, and then proceed to use it in another computation. Imagine that you had the following function:

```
(defn some-computation [x]
  (if (even? x) false (inc x)))
```

It's a placeholder to illustrate the point we're about to make. Now consider a use case as follows:

```
(if (some-computation 11)
  (* 2 (some-computation 11)))
;=> 24
```

Naturally, you wouldn't stand for such duplication, and you'd use the `let` form to remove it:

```
(let [computation (some-computation 11)]
  (if computation
    (* 2 computation)))
```

You also know that you don't need to stop here, because you can use the handy `if-let` macro:

```
(if-let [computation (some-computation 11)]
  (* 2 computation))
```

Although this is clear enough, it would be nice if you could write something like the following, for it to read more clearly:

```
(anaphoric-if (some-computation 11)
  (* 2 it))
```

Here, `it` is a symbol that represents the value of the condition clause. Most anaphoric macros use pronouns such as `it` to refer to some value that was computed.

Although the anaphoric style can produce very compact and easy-to-read code (that is, if you know what the anaphoric names are), Clojure idiom prefers to allow the user to provide a name to bind, such as in `if-let`. You should prefer this idiom, too, because such code is clearer and allows nested forms easily while being only slightly more verbose. But the anaphoric style is useful in DSLs, especially those designed for non-programmers.

IMPLEMENTING ANAPHORIC-IF

Now that you've seen what you'd like to express in the code, let's set about implementing it. You could imagine writing it as follows:

```
(defmacro anaphoric-if [test-form then-form]
  `(if-let [~'it ~test-form]
     ~then-form))
```

Here's the macro expansion of the example from earlier:

```
(macroexpand-1 '(anaphoric-if (some-computation 11)
                  (* 2 it)))
;=> (clojure.core/if-let [it (some-computation 11)] (* 2 it))
```

That expansion looks exactly like what you need because it creates a local name `it` and binds the value of the `test-form` to it. It then evaluates the `then-form` inside the `let` block created by the `if-let` form, which ensures that it happens only if the value of `it` is truthy. Here it is in action:

```
(anaphoric-if (some-computation 12)
  (* 2 it))
;=> nil
(anaphoric-if (some-computation 11)
  (* 2 it))
;=> 24
```

Notice how you had to force Clojure not to namespace qualify the name `it`. You do this by unquoting a quoted symbol (that's what the strange notation ~'it is). This forces the variable capture. You'll use this technique (and the unquote splice version of it) again in the following sections.

> **NOTE** Remember that when you're using anaphora, you're using variable capture. So although it may be okay that the symbol `it` is captured in this example, that may not always be the case. Watch for situations where intentional variable capture can cause subtle bugs.

Now that you have an anaphoric version of `if`, you'll write a macro that generalizes it a little.

GENERALIZING THE ANAPHORIC IF

Recall the implementation of the anaphoric `if` macro:

```
(defmacro anaphoric-if [test-form then-form]
  `(if-let [~'it ~test-form]
     ~then-form))
```

Note that you built this on the `if-let` macro, which in turn is built on the `if` special form. If you were to remove the hard dependency on the `if` special form and instead specify it at call time, you could have a more general version of this code on your hands. Let's take a look:

```
(defmacro with-it [operator test-form & exprs]
  `(let [~'it ~test-form]
     (~operator ~'it ~@exprs)))
```

So, you take the idea from `anaphoric-if` and create a new version of it where you need to pass in the thing you're trying to accomplish. For instance, the example from before would now read like this:

```
(with-it if (some-computation 12)
  (* 2 it))
;=> nil
(with-it if (some-computation 11)
  (* 2 it))
;=> 24
```

Why would you want to do this? Because now you can have an anaphoric version of more than just the if form. For example, you could create anaphoric versions of and and when, as shown here:

```
(with-it and (some-computation 11) (> it 10) (* 2 it))
;=> 24
```

Or you could do this:

```
(with-it when (some-computation 11)
  (println "Got it:" it)
  (* 2 it))
Got it: 12
;=> 24
```

Try these out at the REPL, and also try versions that use if-not, or, when-not, and so on. You could even go back and define macros like anaphoric-it in terms of with-it, for instance:

```
(defmacro anaphoric-if [test-form then-form]
  `(with-it if ~test-form ~then-form))
```

You could define all such variants (using if, and, or, and so on) in one swoop.

This wraps up our introduction to anaphoric macros. As we mentioned at the start of this section, these examples are quite simple. The next one will be slightly more involved.

11.2.2 *The thread-it macro*

A couple of the most useful macros in Clojure's core namespace are the threading macros—the thread-first macro (->) and the thread-last macro (->>), which we covered in chapter 2. As a refresher, you'll write a function to calculate the surface area of a cylinder with a radius r and height h. The formula is

```
2 * PI * r * (r + h)
```

Using the thread-first macro, you can write this as

```
(defn surface-area-cylinder [r h]
  (-> r
    (+ h)
    (* 2 Math/PI r)))
```

You saw a similar example when you first encountered this macro. Instead of writing something like a let form with intermediate results of a larger computation, the first form is placed into the next form as the first argument, the resulting form is then placed into the next form as *its* first argument in turn, and so on. It's a significant improvement in code readability.

The thread-last macro is the same, but instead of placing consecutive results in the first argument position of the following form, it places them in the position of the last argument. It's useful in code that's similar to the following hypothetical example:

```
(defn some-calculation [a-collection]
  (->> (seq a-collection)
       (filter some-pred?)
       (map a-transform)
       (reduce another-function)))
```

THREADING IN ANY POSITION

Now, although both the thread-first and thread-last macros are extremely useful, they do have a possible shortcoming: they both fix the position of where each step of the computation is placed into the next form. The thread-first macro places it as the first argument of the next call, whereas the thread-last macro places it in the position of the last argument.

Occasionally, this can be limiting. Consider the previous code snippet. Imagine you wanted to use a function written by someone else called compute-averages-from that accepts two arguments: a sequence of data and a predicate, *in that order.* As it stands, you couldn't plug that function into the threaded code shown previously, because the order of arguments was reversed. You'd have to adapt the function, perhaps as follows:

```
(defn another-calculation [a-collection]
  (->> (seq a-collection)
       (filter some-pred?)
       (map a-transform)
       (#(compute-averages-from % another-pred?))))
```

> Notice the anonymous function reader macro, required because of threading order of the thread-last macro

You've seen the use of anonymous functions to create adapter functions such as this before, but it isn't pretty. It spoils the overall elegance by adding some noise to the code. What if, instead of being limited to threading forms as the first and last arguments of subsequent forms, you could choose where to thread them? Clojure 1.5 introduced the as-> threading macro (which you saw in chapter 2) to do just that. You could rewrite the preceding example as follows:

```
(defn another-calculation [a-collection]
  (as-> (seq a-collection) result
        (filter some-pred? result)
        (map a-transform result)
        (compute-averages-from result another-pred?)))
```

> Result of each step will be bound to result.

> You don't need an anonymous function anymore: you just put result in the right place.

IMPLEMENTING THREAD-IT

Just like if-let, as-> requires that you supply a symbol for bindings. You created an anaphoric-if macro that always binds to the symbol it. Now you're going to create a version of as->, called thread-it, which will always bind to the symbol it. With this new macro, you'll be able to do something like this:

```
(defn yet-another-calculation [a-collection]
  (thread-it (seq a-collection)
             (filter some-pred? it)
             (map a-transform it)
             (compute-averages-from it another-pred?))))
```

Before we jump into the implementation, let's add another change to the way Clojure's built-in threading macros work, in that they expect at least one argument. You'd like to be able to call the thread-it macro without any arguments. This may be useful when you're using it inside another macro. Although the following doesn't work

```
(->> )
ArityException Wrong number of args (0) passed to: core/->>
clojure.lang.Compiler.macroexpand1 (Compiler.java:6557)
```

you'd like the macro to do this:

```
(thread-it)
;=> nil
```

Now we're ready to look at the implementation. Consider the following:

```
(defmacro thread-it [& [first-expr & rest-expr]]
  (if (empty? rest-expr)
    first-expr
    `(let [~'it ~first-expr]
       (thread-it ~@rest-expr))))
```

As you can see, the macro accepts any number of arguments. The list of arguments is destructured into the first (named first-expr) and the rest (named rest-expr). The first task is to check to see if rest-expr is empty (which happens when either no arguments were passed in or a single argument was passed in). If this is so, the macro will return first-expr, which will be nil if there were no arguments passed into thread-it or the single argument if only one was passed in.

If there are arguments remaining inside rest-expr, the macro expands to another call to itself, with the symbol it bound to the value of first-expr, nestled inside a let block. This recursive macro definition expands until it has consumed all the forms it was passed in. Here's an example of it in action:

```
(thread-it (* 10 20) (inc it) (- it 8) (* 10 it) (/ it 5))
;=> 386
```

Also, with the way it's implemented, the following behavior is expected:

```
(thread-it it)
CompilerException java.lang.RuntimeException: Unable to resolve symbol: it in
this context, compiling:(NO_SOURCE_PATH:1:1)
```

This happens because you don't start by binding anything to it. You could change this behavior by initially binding it to a default value of some kind. That's all there is to the implementation. It can be a useful macro in situations where the functions (or macros) in a threading form take arguments in an irregular order. Further, as a refinement, or perhaps as another version of this macro, you could replace the let with an if-let. This will short-circuit the computation if any step results in a logically false value like the some-> and some->> macros.

This leads us to the end of the discussion on anaphora. It's a useful technique at times, even though it breaks hygiene because it involves variable capture. As mentioned, you have to be careful while using it, but when you do, it can result in code that's more readable than it would be otherwise.

11.3   *Shifting computation to compile time*

Our next stop is to examine another use case of macros. You're going to make the Clojure compiler work harder by doing some work that would otherwise have to be done by your program at runtime.

11.3.1   *Example: Rotation ciphers without macros*

So far in this book, you've seen several uses of macros and have written several macros yourself. In this section, you're going to see another use of macros, and it has to do with performance. To illustrate the concept, we'll examine a simple code cipher called ROT13. It stands for "rotate by 13 places" and is a simple cipher that can be broken quite easily. But its purpose is to hide text in a way that isn't immediately obvious, so as not to communicate spy secrets. It's commonly used as the online equivalent of text printed upside down (for example, in magazines and newspapers), to give out puzzle solutions, answers to riddles, and the like.

ABOUT THE ROT13 CIPHER
Table 11.1 shows what each letter of the alphabet corresponds to.

Table 11.1   Alphabet rotated by 13 places

1	2	3	4	5	6	7	8	9	10	11	12	13	14	15	16	17	18	19	20	21	22	23	24	25	26
a	b	c	d	e	f	g	h	i	j	k	l	m	n	o	p	q	r	s	t	u	v	w	x	y	z
n	o	p	q	r	s	t	u	v	w	x	y	z	a	b	c	d	e	f	g	h	i	j	k	l	m

The first row is the index for each letter of the alphabet, starting at 1. The second row is the alphabet itself. The last row is the alphabet shifted by 13 places. Each letter on this last row corresponds to the letter that will be used in place of the letter above it in a message encrypted using this cipher system. For example, the word *abracadabra* becomes *noenpnqnoen*.

Decrypting a rotation cipher is usually done by rotating each letter back the same number of times. ROT13 has the additional property of being a reciprocal cipher. A message encrypted using a reciprocal cipher can be decrypted by running it through the cipher system itself. The encryption process also works to decrypt encrypted messages. In this section, you'll implement a generalized rotation cipher by allowing the rotation length to be passed in as a parameter.

GENERALIZED ROTATION CIPHERS

Let's begin the implementation with the letters of the alphabet. Recall that Clojure has a convenient reader macro to represent literal characters:

```
(def ALPHABETS [\a \b \c \d \e \f \g \h \i \j \k \l \m \n \o \p \q \r \s \t
\u \v \w \x \y \z])
```

Let's also define a few convenience values based on the alphabet shown:

```
(def NUM-ALPHABETS (count ALPHABETS))
(def INDICES (range 1 (inc NUM-ALPHABETS)))
(def lookup (zipmap INDICES ALPHABETS))
```

Now, let's talk about your approach. Because you want to implement a generic rotation mechanism, you'll need to know at which numbered slot a letter falls when it's rotated a specific number of times. You'd like to take a slot number such as 14, rotate it by a configurable number, and see where it ends up. For example, in the case of ROT13, the letter in slot 10 (which is the letter *j*) ends up in slot 23. You'll write a function called `shift`, which will compute this new slot number. You can't add the shift-by number to the slot number because you'll have to take care of overflow. Here's the implementation of `shift`:

```
(defn shift [shift-by index]
  (let [shifted (+ (mod shift-by NUM-ALPHABETS) index)]
    (cond
      (<= shifted 0) (+ shifted NUM-ALPHABETS)
      (> shifted NUM-ALPHABETS) (- shifted NUM-ALPHABETS)
      :default shifted)))
```

There are a couple of points to note here. The first is that you calculated `shifted` by adding `(mod shift-by NUM-ALPHABETS)` to the given `index` (and not `shift-by`) so that you can handle the cases where `shift-by` is more than `NUM-ALPHABETS`. Because you handle overflow by wrapping to the beginning, this approach works, for example:

```
(shift 10 13)
;=> 23
(shift 20 13)
;=> 7
```

Now that you have this function, you can use it to create a simple cryptographic tableau, a table of rows and columns with which you can decrypt or encrypt information.

In this case, for ROT13, the tableau would be the second and third rows from table 15.1. Here's a function that computes this:

```
(defn shifted-tableau [shift-by]
  (->> (map #(shift shift-by %) INDICES)
       (map lookup)
       (zipmap ALPHABETS)))
```

This creates a map where the keys are alphabets that need to be encrypted, and values are the cipher versions of the same. Here's an example:

```
(shifted-tableau 13)
;=> {\a \n, \b \o, \c \p, \d \q, \e \r, \f \s, \g \t, \h \u, \i \v, \j \w, \k
     \x, \l \y, \m \z, \n \a, \o \b, \p \c, \q \d, \r \e, \s \f, \t \g, \u
     \h, \v \i, \w \j, \x \k, \y \l, \z \m}
```

Because this cipher is quite simple, a simple map such as this suffices. Now that you have your tableau, encrypting messages is as simple as looking up each letter. Here's the encrypt function:

```
(defn encrypt [shift-by plaintext]
  (let [shifted (shifted-tableau shift-by)]
    (apply str (map shifted plaintext))))
```

Try it at the REPL:

```
(encrypt 13 "abracadabra")
;=> "noenpnqnoen"
```

That works as expected. Recall that ROT13 is a reciprocal cipher. Check to see if it works:

```
(encrypt 13 "noenpnqnoen")
;=> "abracadabra"
```

It does! If you rotate by anything other than 13, you'll need a real decrypt function. All you need to do to decrypt a message is to reverse the process. You'll express that as follows:

```
(defn decrypt [shift-by encrypted]
  (encrypt (- shift-by) encrypted))
```

decrypt works by rotating an encrypted message the other way by the same rotation. This shows how it works at the REPL:

```
(decrypt 13 "noenpnqnoen")
;=> "abracadabra"
```

Great, so you have all the bare necessities in place. To implement a particular cipher, such as ROT13, you can define a pair of functions as follows:

```
(def encrypt-with-rot13 (partial encrypt 13))
(def decrypt-with-rot13 (partial decrypt 13))
```

Now try it at the REPL:

```
(decrypt-with-rot13 (encrypt-with-rot13 "abracadabra"))
;=> "abracadabra"
```

So there you have it; you've implemented the simple cipher system. The complete code is shown in the following listing.

Listing 11.1 A general rotation cipher system to implement things like ROT13

```
(ns clj-in-act.ch11.shifting)
(def ALPHABETS [\a \b \c \d \e \f \g \h \i \j \k \l \m \n \o \p \q \r \s \t
    \u \v \w \x \y \z])
(def NUM-ALPHABETS (count ALPHABETS))
(def INDICES (range 1 (inc NUM-ALPHABETS)))
(def lookup (zipmap INDICES ALPHABETS))
(defn shift [shift-by index]
  (let [shifted (+ (mod shift-by NUM-ALPHABETS) index)]
    (cond
      (<= shifted 0) (+ shifted NUM-ALPHABETS)
      (> shifted NUM-ALPHABETS) (- shifted NUM-ALPHABETS)
      :default shifted)))
(defn shifted-tableau [shift-by]
  (->> (map #(shift shift-by %) INDICES)
      (map lookup)
      (zipmap ALPHABETS )))
(defn encrypt [shift-by plaintext]
  (let [shifted (shifted-tableau shift-by)]
    (apply str (map shifted plaintext))))
(defn decrypt [shift-by encrypted]
  (encrypt (- shift-by) encrypted))
(def encrypt-with-rot13 (partial encrypt 13))
(def decrypt-with-rot13 (partial decrypt 13))
```

The issue with this implementation is that you compute the tableau each time you encrypt or decrypt a message. This is easily fixed by memoizing the shifted-tableau function. This will take care of this problem, but in the next section, you'll go one step further.

11.3.2 *Making the compiler work harder*

So far, you've implemented functions to encrypt and decrypt messages for any rotation cipher. Your basic approach has been to create a map that can help you code (or decode) each letter in a message to its cipher version. As discussed at the end of the previous section, you can speed up your implementation by memoizing the tableau calculation.

Even with memoize, the computation still happens at least once (the first time the function is called). Imagine, instead, if you created an inline literal map containing the appropriate tableau data. You could then look it up in the map each time, without having to compute it. Such a definition of encrypt-with-rot13 might look like this:

```
(defn encrypt-with-rot13 [plaintext]
  (apply str (map {\a \n \b \o \c \p} plaintext)))
```

In an implementation, the tableau would be complete for all the letters of the alphabet, not only for \a, \b, and \c. In any case, if you did have such a literal map in the code itself, it would obviate the need to compute it at runtime. Luckily, you're coding in Clojure, and you can bend it to your will. Consider the following:

```
(defmacro def-rot-encrypter [name shift-by]
  (let [tableau (shifted-tableau shift-by)]
    `(defn ~name [~'message]
       (apply str (map ~tableau ~'message)))))
```

This macro first computes the tableau for `shifted-by` as needed and then defines a function by the specified name. The function body includes the computed table, in the right place, as illustrated in the preceding code sample. Look at its expansion:

```
(macroexpand-1 '(def-rot-encrypter encrypt13 13))
;=> (clojure.core/defn encrypt13 [message] (clojure.core/apply clojure.core/
    str (clojure.core/map {\a \n, \b \o, \c \p, \d \q, \e \r, \f \s, \g \t,
    \h \u, \i \v, \j \w, \k \x, \l \y, \m \z, \n \a, \o \b, \p \c, \q \d, \r
    \e, \s \f, \t \g, \u \h, \v \i, \w \j, \x \k, \y \l, \z \m} message)))
```

This looks almost exactly like the desired function, with an inline literal tableau map. Figure 11.1 shows the flow of the code.

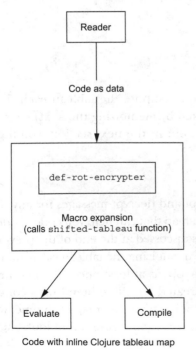

Code with inline Clojure tableau map

Figure 11.1   As usual, the Clojure reader first converts the text of your programs into data structures. During this process, macros are expanded, including the `def-rot-encrypter` macro, which generates a tableau. This tableau is a Clojure map and is included in the final form of the source code as an inline lookup table.

Now check to see if it works:

```
(def-rot-encrypter encrypt13 13)
;=> #'user/encrypt13
(encrypt13 "abracadabra")
;=> "noenpnqnoen"
```

And there you have it. The new `encrypt13` function at runtime doesn't do any tableau computation at all. If, for instance, you were to ship this code off to users as a Java library, they wouldn't even know that `shifted-tableau` was ever called.

As a final item, you'll create a convenient way to define a pair of functions that can be used to encrypt or decrypt functions in a rotation cipher:

```
(defmacro define-rot-encryption [shift-by]
  `(do
     (def-rot-encrypter ~(symbol (str "encrypt" shift-by)) ~shift-by)
     (def-rot-encrypter ~(symbol (str "decrypt" shift-by)) ~(- shift-by))))
```

And finally, here it is in action:

```
(define-rot-encryption 15)
;=> #'user/decrypt15
```

Here, it prints the decrypt function var, because it was the last thing the macro expansion did. Now use the new pair of functions:

```
(encrypt15 "abracadabra")
;=> "pqgprpspqgp"
(decrypt15 "pqgprpspqgp")
;=> "abracadabra"
```

Shifting computation to the compile cycle can be a useful trick when parts of the computation needed are known in advance. Clojure macros make it easy to run arbitrary code during the expansion phase and give the programmer the power of the full Clojure language itself. In this example, for instance, you wrote the `shifted-tableau` function with no prior intention of using it in this manner. Moving computation into macros this way can be quite handy at times, despite how simple it is to do.

11.4 *Macro-generating macros*

Now that you understand what it is to move computation to the compile phase of program execution, you're ready for a new adventure. You'll expand your mind a little as you try to write code that writes code that writes code—that is, you're going to write a macro that writes a macro.

Let's look at an example of a macro that will create a synonym for an existing function or macro. Imagine you have two vars as follows:

```
(declare x y)
;=> #'user/y
```

And if you use the new macro make-synonym

```
(make-synonym b binding)
;=> #'user/b
```

then the following should work:

```
(b [x 10 y 20] [x y])
;=> [10 20]
```

You'll implement the make-synonym macro in this section.

11.4.1   *Example template*

When writing a macro, it's usually easier to start with an example of the desired expansion. Here's what you want to write:

```
(b [x 10 y 20] (println "X,Y:" x y))
```

And for it to work, b should be replaced with binding, resulting in the expansion

```
(binding [x 10 y 20] (println "X,Y:" x y))
```

You could easily solve this if you wrote a custom macro defining b in terms of binding, as follows:

```
(defmacro b [& stuff]
  `(binding ~@stuff))
```

This replaces the symbol b with the symbol binding, keeping everything else the same. You aren't interested in the vars being bound, or the body itself, which is why you lump everything into stuff.

Now that you have a version of b that works as expected, you need to generalize it into make-synonym. The previous code is an example of what the make-synonym macro ought to produce.

11.4.2   *Implementing make-synonym*

You know that make-synonym is a macro and that it accepts two parameters:

- A new symbol that will be the synonym of the existing macro or function
- The name of the existing macro or function

You can begin implementing the new macro by starting with an empty definition:

```
(defmacro synonym [new-name old-name])
```

The next question is, what should go in the body? You can start by putting in the sample expansion from the previous section. Here's what it looks like:

```
(defmacro make-synonym [new-name old-name]
  (defmacro b [& stuff]
    `(binding ~@stuff)))
```

Obviously, this won't work as desired, because no matter what's passed in as arguments to this version of make-synonym, it will always create a macro named b (that expands to binding).

What you want, instead, is for make-synonym to produce the inner form containing the call to defmacro, instead of calling it. You know you can do this using the back-quote. In this case, you'll have two backquotes. While you're at it, instead of the hard-coded symbols b and binding, you'll use the names passed in as parameters. Consider the following increment of the make-synonym macro:

```
(defmacro make-synonym [new-name old-name]
  `(defmacro ~new-name [& stuff]
     `(~old-name ~@stuff)))
```

This is a little confusing, because you have two backquotes in play here, one nested inside the other. The easiest way to understand what's happening is to look at an expansion. So try it at the REPL:

```
(macroexpand-1 '(make-synonym b binding))
;=> (clojure.core/defmacro b [& user/stuff]
       (clojure.core/seq
         (clojure.core/concat (clojure.core/list user/old-name)
                              user/stuff)))
```

To understand this expansion, let's first look at what happens to a backquote when it's expanded:

```
(defmacro back-quote-test []
  `(something))
;=> #'user/back-quote-test
(macroexpand '(back-quote-test))
;=> (user/something)
```

This isn't surprising, because the Clojure namespace qualifies any names unless explicitly asked not to. Now, add a backquote:

```
(defmacro back-quote-test []
  ``(something))
;=> #'user/back-quote-test
```

You've added another backquote to the one already present. What you're saying is that instead of expanding the backquoted form and using its return value as the expansion of the back-quote-test macro, you want the backquoting mechanism itself. Again, to refresh your memory of how backquotes work, refer to chapter 7. Here it is at the REPL:

```
(macroexpand '(back-quote-test))
;=> (clojure.core/seq
      (clojure.core/concat (clojure.core/list (quote user/something))))
```

Because you're using the symbol something as is, Clojure is namespace qualifying, as you'd expect. Now that you know what the backquote mechanism itself is, you can return to the expansion of make-synonym:

```
(macroexpand-1 '(make-synonym b binding))
;=> (clojure.core/defmacro b [& user/stuff]
      (clojure.core/seq
        (clojure.core/concat clojure.core/list user/old-name) user/stuff)))
```

Here, the symbol b gets substituted as part of the expansion of the outer backquote expansion. Because you don't explicitly quote the symbol stuff, it gets namespace qualified (you'll need to fix that soon). To understand what's happening to old-name inside the nested backquote, look at the following:

```
(defmacro back-quote-test []
  ``(~something))
;=> #'user/back-quote-test
(macroexpand '(back-quote-test))
;=> (clojure.core/seq (clojure.core/concat (clojure.core/list user/
      something)))
```

If you compare this to the previous version of back-quote-test and the expansion it generated, you'll notice that user/something is no longer wrapped in a quote form. This is again as expected, because you're unquoting it using the ~ reader macro. This explains why the nested backquote form of the make-synonym macro expands with user/old-name as it does. Again, you'll need to fix this problem because you don't want the symbol old-name but the argument passed in.

Finally, to see what's going on with the unquote splicing and the stuff symbol, look at the following simpler example:

```
(defmacro back-quote-test []
  ``(~@something))
;=> #'user/back-quote-test
(macroexpand '(back-quote-test))
;=> (clojure.core/seq (clojure.core/concat user/something))
```

If you now compare this version of the expansion with the previous one, you'll note that user/something is no longer wrapped in a call to list. This is in line with the expected behavior of unquote splicing in that it doesn't add an extra set of parentheses.

At this point, we've walked through the complete expansion of the make-synonym macro. The only problem is that it still doesn't do what you intended it to do. The two problems identified were that both stuff and old-name weren't being expanded correctly. You'll fix stuff first. Consider the following change to make-synonym:

```
(defmacro make-synonym [new-name old-name]
  `(defmacro ~new-name [& ~'stuff]
     `(~old-name ~@~'stuff)))
```

Here's the expansion:

```
(macroexpand-1 '(make-synonym b binding))
;=> (clojure.core/defmacro b [& stuff]
       (clojure.core/seq (clojure.core/concat
                             (clojure.core/list user/old-name) stuff)))
```

Finally, you'll fix the issue with user/old-name:

```
(defmacro make-synonym [new-name old-name]
  `(defmacro ~new-name [& ~'stuff]
     `(~'~old-name ~@~'stuff)))
```

And here's the expansion:

```
(macroexpand-1 '(make-synonym b binding))
;=> (clojure.core/defmacro b [& stuff]
       (clojure.core/seq (clojure.core/concat
          (clojure.core/list (quote binding)) stuff)))
```

Notice the odd ~'~old-name quoting and unquoting. This evaluates like so: first, ~old-name is expanded, leaving ~'binding (the value of old-name) for the generated macro. Then the outer backquote is expanded, leaving you with 'binding, which finally becomes (quote binding). You have to do this to ensure that the value of old-name isn't resolved until the *generated* macro expands.

To check to see if this is what you expect, compare it with your original template:

```
(defmacro b [& stuff]
  `(binding ~@stuff))
```

This is indeed what you set out to do, and you can test it as follows:

```
(declare x y)
;=> #'user/y
(make-synonym b binding)
;=> #'user/b
(b [x 10 y 20] [x y])
;=> [10 20]
```

Phew, you're finished. That was a lot of calisthenics for three lines of code. We'll wrap up this section with why you even bothered with this somewhat esoteric code.

11.4.3 *Why macro-generating macros*

There are at least two reasons why it's useful to know how to write macros that generate macros. The first is the same reason you'd write any other kind of macro: to create abstractions that remove the duplication that arises from patterns in the code. This is important when these duplications are structural and are difficult to eliminate without some form of code generation. Clojure macros are an excellent tool to do this job, because they give the programmer the full power of Clojure to do it. The fact that code generation is a language-level feature does pull its weight.

Having said this, although writing macros is a common thing to do in a Clojure program, it isn't often the case that a macro generates another macro. You'll probably do it only a handful of times in your career. Combined with the other uses you've seen, such as moving computation to compile time and intentional symbol capture—the few times when you do need macros to abstract patterns out of macros themselves—writing macros to generate macros can lead to a solution that would be difficult without the technique.

The second reason, and the more commonly useful one, for knowing this concept is to drive home the process of macro expansion, quoting, and unquoting. If you can understand and write macros that generate macros, then you'll have no trouble writing simpler ones.

With these topics about macro writing out of the way, we're ready to move on to a couple of examples. In the next section, we'll look at using macros to create domain-specific languages (DSLs).

11.5   *Domain-specific languages*

We're now going to look at explicitly doing something you've been doing implicitly so far. In several chapters, you've written macros that appear to add features to the Clojure language itself. For example,

- In chapter 8, you created a simple object system with most of the semantics of regular object-oriented languages.
- In chapter 9, you created `def-modus-operandi`, which allowed multimethods to be used in a manner similar to Clojure protocols.

These are just a couple of examples of macros helping you present your abstractions as a convenient feature of the language.

In this section, we're going to further explore the idea of wrapping your abstractions in a layer of language. Taking this idea to its logical end brings us to the concept of metalinguistic abstraction—the approach of creating a domain-specific language that's then used to solve the problem at hand. It allows you to solve not only the problem you started out with but a whole class of problems in that domain. It leaves you with a system that's highly flexible and maintainable, while staying small and easier to understand and debug. Let's begin by examining the design philosophy that leads to such systems.

11.5.1   *DSL-driven design*

To design a DSL you must consider two factors: how can the DSL decompose its problem domain into its various parts (the language's "vocabulary"), and how will it facilitate composing those parts back together in expressive ways (its "grammar")?

DESIGN CONSIDERATION #1: DECOMPOSITION

When given the requirements of a software program, the first step in creating a program to satisfy them usually involves thinking about what approach to take. This might end with a big design session that produces a detailed breakdown of the various components and pieces that will compose the final solution.

Top-down decomposition

This often goes hand in hand with the traditional top-down decomposition technique of taking something large and complex and breaking it into pieces that are smaller, independent, and easier to understand.

By itself, this approach has been known to not work particularly well in most cases. This is because the requirements for most systems are never specified perfectly, which causes the system to be redesigned in ways big and small. Many times, the requirements explicitly change over time as the reality of the business itself changes. This is why most agile teams prefer an evolutionary design, one that arises from incrementally building the system to satisfy more and more of the requirements over time.

When such an approach is desirable (and few systems can do without it these days), it makes sense to think not only in a top-down manner but also in a bottom-up way.

Bottom-up decomposition

Decomposing a problem in a bottom-up manner is different from the top-down version. With the bottom-up approach, you create small abstractions on top of the core programming language to handle tiny elements of the problem domain. These domain-specific primitives are created without explicit thought to exactly how they'll eventually be used to solve the original problem. Indeed, at this stage, the idea is to create primitives that model all the low-level details of the problem domain.

DESIGN CONSIDERATION #2: COMBINABILITY

The other area of focus is combinability. The various domain primitives should be combinable into more complex entities as desired. This can be done using either the combinability features of the programming language itself (for instance, Clojure's functions) or by creating new domain-specific constructs on top of existing ones. Macros can help with such extensions, because they can manipulate code forms with ease.

Functional programming aids in the pursuit of such a design. In addition to recursive and conditional constructs, being able to treat functions as first-class objects allows higher levels of complexity and abstraction to be managed in a more natural manner. Being able to create lexical closures adds another powerful piece to your toolset. When higher-order functions, closures, and macros are used together, the domain primitives can be combined to solve more than the original problem specified in the requirements document. It can solve a whole class of problems in that domain, because what gets created at the end of such a bottom-up process is a rich set of primitives, operators, and forms for combination that closely models the business domain itself.

The final layers of such a system consist of two pieces. The topmost is literally the respecification of the requirements in an executable DSL. This is metalinguistic abstraction, manifested in the fact that the final piece of the system that seems to solve the problem is written not in a general-purpose programming language but in a language that has been grown organically from a lower-level programming language. It's often understandable by nonprogrammers and indeed is sometimes suitable for them to use directly.

The next piece is a sort of runtime adapter, which executes the domain-specific either by interpreting it or by compiling it down to the language's own primitives. An example may be a set of macros that translate the syntactically friendly code into other forms and code that sets up the right evaluation context for it. Figure 11.2 shows a block diagram of the various layers described.

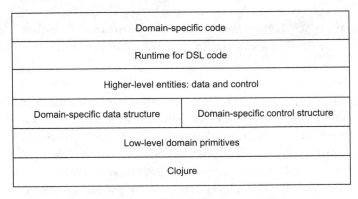

Figure 11.2   The typical layers in a DSL-driven system. Such systems benefit from a bottom-up design where the lowest levels are the primitive concepts of the domain modeled on top of the basic Clojure language. Higher layers are compositions of these primitives into more complex domain concepts. Finally, a runtime layer sits on top of these, which can execute code specified in a DSL. This final layer often represents the core solution of the problem that the software was meant to solve.

It's useful to point out that a domain-specific language isn't about using macros, even though they're often a big part of the final linguistics. Macros help with fluency of the language, especially as used by the end users but also at lower levels to help create the abstractions themselves. In this way, they're no different from other available features of the language such as higher-order functions and conditionals. The point to remember is that the core of the DSL approach is the resulting bottom-up design and the set of easily combinable domain primitives.

In the next section, we'll explore the creation of a simple DSL.

11.5.2 *User classification*

Most websites today personalize the experience for individual users by using users' own data to improve their experience. Amazon, for example, shows users things they might like to buy based on their purchase history and browsing patterns. Other web services use similarly collected use statistics to show more relevant ads to users as they browse. In this section, we'll explore this business domain.

The goal here is to use data about the user to do something special for them. It could be showing ads or making the site more specific to the user's tastes. The first step in any such task is classifying the user. Usually, the system can recognize several classes of users and is able to personalize the experience for each class in some way. The business folks would like to be able to change the specification of the various segments as they're discovered, so the system shouldn't hardcode this aspect. Further, they'd like to make such changes quickly, potentially without requiring development effort and without requiring a restart of the system after making such changes. In an ideal world, they'd even like to specify the segment descriptions in a nice little GUI application.

This example is well suited to our earlier discussion, but aspects of this apply to most nontrivial systems being built today. For this example, you'll build a DSL to specify the rules that classify users into various segments. To get started, you'll describe the lay of the land, which in this case will be a small part of the overall system design, as well as a few functions available to find information about your users.

DATA ELEMENT

You'll model a few primitive domain-specific data elements, focusing on things that can be gleaned from the data that users' browsers send to the server along with every request. There's nothing to stop you from extending this approach to things that are looked up from elsewhere, such as a database of users' past behaviors, or indeed anything else, such as stock quotes or the weather in Hawaii. You'll model the session data as a simple Clojure map containing the data elements you care about, and you'll store it in Redis. You don't need to focus on how you create the session map, because this example isn't about parsing strings or loading data from various data stores.

Here's an example of a user session:

```
{:consumer-id  "abc"
 :url-referrer "http://www.google.com/search?q=clojure+programmers"
 :search-terms ["clojure" "programmers"]
 :ip-address   "192.168.0.10"
 :tz-offset    420
 :user-agent   :safari}
```

Again, sessions can contain a lot more than what comes in via the web request. You can imagine loads of precomputed information being stored in such a session to enable more useful targeting as well as a caching technique so that things don't have to be loaded or computed more than once in a user's session.

USER SESSION PERSISTENCE

You'll need a key to store such sessions in Redis,[2] and for this example :consumer-id will serve you well. You'll add a level of indirection so the code will read better as well as let you change this decision later if you desire:

```
(def redis-key-for :consumer-id)
```

First, you'll define a way to save sessions into Redis and also to load them back out. Here's a pair of functions that do that:

```
(defn save-session [session]
  (redis/set (redis-key-for session) (pr-str session)))
(defn find-session [consumer-id]
  (read-string (redis/get consumer-id)))
```

Now that you have the essential capability of storing and loading sessions, you have a design decision to make. If you consider the user session to be the central concept in your behavioral targeting domain, then you can write it such that the DSL always executes in context of a session. You could define a var called *session* that you'll then bind to the specific one during a computation:

```
(def ^:dynamic *session*)
```

And you could define a convenience macro that sets up the binding:

```
(defmacro in-session [consumer-id & body]
  `(binding [*session* (find-session ~consumer-id)]
    (do ~@body)))
```

The following listing shows the complete session namespace defined so far.

Listing 11.2 Basic functions to handle session persistence in Redis

```
(ns clj-in-act.ch11.session
  (:require redis))
(def redis-key-for :consumer-id)
(def ^:dynamic *session*)
(defn save-session [session]
  (redis/set (redis-key-for session) (pr-str session)))
(defn find-session [consumer-id]
  (read-string (redis/get consumer-id)))
(defmacro in-session [consumer-id & body]
  `(binding [*session* (find-session ~consumer-id)]
    (do ~@body)))
```

---

[2] See http://redis.io. In this chapter we follow the redis-clojure library's API by Ragnar Dahlén (https://github .com/ragnard/redis-clojure), but you should use the newer and better Carmine library for your own projects (https://github.com/ptaoussanis/carmine). The code package with this book contains a redis namespace that mocks enough of the redis-clojure library for you to run the code in this chapter without running a Redis server or using a Redis library.

Now that you've dealt with persisting user sessions, next you'll focus on the segmentation itself.

SEGMENTING USERS

In your application, you'd like to satisfy two qualitative requirements of this segmentation process. First, these rules shouldn't be hardcoded into your application; it should be possible to dynamically update the rules. Second, these rules should be expressed in a format that's somewhat analyst friendly. That is, the rules should be in a DSL that's somewhat simpler for nonprogrammers to express ideas in. Here's an example of something you might allow:

```
(defsegment googling-clojurians
    (and
      (> (count $search-terms) 0)
      (matches? $url-referrer "google")))
```

Here's another example of the desired language:

```
(defsegment loyal-safari
    (and
      (empty? $url-referrer)
      (= :safari $user-agent)))
```

Notice the symbols prefixed with $. These are meant to have special significance in your DSL, because they're the elements that will be looked up and substituted from the user's session. Your job now is to implement def-segment so that the previous definition is compiled into something meaningful.

Syntax of Clojure DSLs

In many programming languages, especially dynamic ones such as Ruby and Python, domain-specific languages have become all the rage. There are two kinds of DSLs: internal and external. Internal DSLs are hosted on top of a language such as Ruby and use the underlying language to execute the DSL code. External DSLs are limited forms of regular programming languages in the sense that they have a lexer and parser that convert DSL code that conforms to a grammar into executable code. Internal DSLs are often simpler and serve most requirements that a DSL might need to satisfy.

Such DSLs are often focused on providing English-like readability, and a lot of text-parsing code is dedicated to converting the easy-to-read text into constructs of the underlying language. Clojure, on the other hand, has its magical reader. It can read an entire character stream and convert it into a form that can be executed. The programmer doesn't have to do anything to support the lexical analysis, tokenizing, and parsing. Clojure even provides a macro system to further enhance the capabilities of textual expression.

This is the reason why many Clojure DSLs look much like Clojure. Clojure DSLs are often based on s-expressions because using the reader to do the heavy lifting of creating a little language is the most straightforward thing to do. The book *DSLs in Action* by Debasish Ghosh (Manning Publications, 2010) is a great resource if you're interested in DSLs in a variety of languages.

You can start with a macro skeleton that looks like this:

```
(defmacro defsegment [segment-name & body])
```

You'll begin by handling the $ prefixes. You'll transform the body expressions such that all symbols prefixed by the $ will be transformed into a session lookup of an attribute with the same name. Something like $user-agent will become (:user-agent *sessions*). To perform this transformation, you'll need to recursively walk the body expression to find all the symbols that need this substitution and then rebuild a new expression with the substitutions made. Luckily, you don't have to write this code because it exists in the clojure.walk namespace. This namespace contains several functions that are useful when walking through Clojure code data structures. The postwalk function fits the bill:

```
(doc postwalk)
-------------------------
clojure.walk/postwalk
([f form])
  Performs a depth-first, post-order traversal of form.  Calls f on
  each sub-form, uses f's return value in place of the original.
  Recognizes all Clojure data structures except sorted-map-by.
  Consumes seqs as with doall.
;=> nil
```

This is what you need, so you can transform your DSL code using the following function:

```
(defn transform-lookups [dollar-attribute]
  (let [prefixed-string (str dollar-attribute)]
    (if-not (.startsWith prefixed-string "$")
      dollar-attribute
      (session-lookup prefixed-string))))
```

You'll need a couple of support functions, namely, session-lookup and drop-first-char, which can be implemented as follows:

```
(defn drop-first-char [name]
  (apply str (rest name)))
(defn session-lookup [dollar-name]
  (->> (drop-first-char dollar-name)
       (keyword)
       (list '*session*)))
```

Now test that the code you wrote does what's expected:

```
(transform-lookups '$user-agent)
;=> (*session* :user-agent)
```

This is a simple test, but note that the resulting form can be used to look up attributes of a user session if the *session* special var is bound appropriately.

Now, use `postwalk` to test your replacement logic on a slightly more complex form:

```
(postwalk transform-lookups '(> (count $search-terms) 0))
;=> (> (count (*session* :search-terms)) 0)
```

That works as expected. You now have a tool to transform the DSL body expressed using the $-prefixed symbols into usable Clojure code. As an aside, you also have a place where you can make more complex replacements if you need to.

You can now use this in the definition of `defsegment` as follows:

```
(defmacro defsegment [segment-name & body]
  (let [transformed (postwalk transform-lookups body)])
```

You've now transformed the `body` as specified by the user of your DSL, and you now need to convert it into something you can execute later. Let's look at what you're working with:

```
(postwalk transform-lookups '(and
                               (> (count $search-terms) 0)
                               (= :safari $user-agent)))
;=> (and
      (> (count (*session* :search-terms)) 0)
      (= :safari (*session* :user-agent)))
```

The simplest way to execute this later is to convert it into a function. You can then call the function whenever you need to run this rule. You used a similar approach when you defined the remote worker framework, where you stored computations as anonymous functions that were executed on remote servers. If you're going to do this, you'll need a place to put the functions. You'll create a new namespace to keep all code related to this storing of functions for later use. It's shown in the following listing.

Listing 11.3 `dsl-store` namespace for storing the rules as anonymous functions

```
(ns clj-in-act.ch11.dsl-store)
(def RULES (ref {}))
(defn register-segment [segment-name segment-fn]
  (dosync
    (alter RULES assoc-in [:segments segment-name] segment-fn)))
(defn segment-named [segment-name]
  (get-in @RULES [:segments segment-name]))
(defn all-segments []
  (:segments @RULES))
```

Now that you know you can put functions where you can find them again later, you're ready to improve the definition of `defsegment`:

```
(defmacro defsegment [segment-name & body]
  (let [transformed (postwalk transform-lookups body)]
    `(let [segment-fn# (fn [] ~@transformed)]
       (register-segment ~(keyword segment-name) segment-fn#))))
```

You now have all the pieces together for your DSL to compile. The following listing shows the complete segment namespace.

Listing 11.4   Segmentation DSL defined using a simple macro

```clojure
(ns clj-in-act.ch11.segment
  (:use clj-in-act.ch11.dsl-store
        clojure.walk))
(defn drop-first-char [name]
  (apply str (rest name)))
(defn session-lookup [dollar-name]
  (->> (drop-first-char dollar-name)
       (keyword)
       (list '*session*)))
(defn transform-lookups [dollar-attribute]
  (let [prefixed-string (str dollar-attribute)]
    (if-not (.startsWith prefixed-string "$")
      dollar-attribute
      (session-lookup prefixed-string))))
(defmacro defsegment [segment-name & body]
  (let [transformed (postwalk transform-lookups body)]
    `(let [segment-fn# (fn [] ~@transformed)]
       (register-segment ~(keyword segment-name) segment-fn#))))
```

Here it is in action, at the REPL:

```clojure
(defsegment loyal-safari
  (and
    (empty? $url-referrer)
    (= :safari $user-agent)))
;=> {:segments
     {:loyal-safari
       #<user$eval3457$segment_fn__3232__auto____3458
     user$eval3457$segment_fn__3232__auto____3458@5054c2b8>}}
```

The definition of googling-clojurians still won't work, because it will complain about an unknown matches? function. You're going to solve this and add more functionality in the next couple sections.

FINE-TUNING: THE POWER OF THE DSL

So far, you've put together the plumbing of the DSL. You can define some DSL code and expect it to compile and some functions to be created and stored as a result. At least three things influence how powerful your DSL can be.

The first is the data inside a user's session. Entities such as $url-referrer and $search-terms are examples of this. These data elements are obtained either directly from the web session of the user, from historical data about the user, or from any other source that has been used to load information into the user's session.

The second factor is the number of primitives that can be used to manipulate the data elements. Examples of such primitives are empty? and count. You've leveraged

Clojure's own functions here, but there's nothing to stop you from adding more. You'll actually be adding a function called matches? to the example shortly.

The final factor is combinability, or how the data elements and the language primitives can be combined to create more complex forms. Here again you can use all of Clojure's built-in facilities. For example, in the previous examples, you used and and >.

In the next section, you'll focus on creating new primitives, and then you'll write code to execute the DSL. Such new primitives will make the DSL more powerful and expressive.

ADDING PRIMITIVES TO THE EXECUTION ENGINE

As you can imagine, matches? is a function. For the purposes of this example here, it can be as simple as this:

```
(defn matches? [^String superset ^String subset]
  (and
   (not (empty? superset))
   (> (.indexOf superset subset) 0)))
```

You can add more functions such as this one, and they can be as complex as needed. The user of the DSL doesn't need to know how they're implemented, because they'll be described as the primitives of the DSL.

Now, let's go ahead and define the remainder of the execution engine. The first piece is a function to load up with the DSL program. Typically, this will be some text either written by a user or generated by another program such as a graphical rules editor. Given that ultimately the DSL is Clojure code, you can use load-string to load it. Consider the following code:

```
(ns clj-in-act.ch11.engine
  (:use clj-in-act.ch11.segment
        clj-in-act.ch11.session
        clj-in-act.ch11.dsl-store))
(defn load-code [code-string]
  (binding [*ns* (:ns (meta #'load-code))]
    (load-string code-string)))
```

Note that the load-code function first switches the namespace to its own (using metadata available on the load-code var) because all supporting functions are available in it. This way, load-code can be called from anywhere, and all supporting functions can be found. It then calls load-string.

The next step is to execute a segment function and to see if it returns true or false. A true value means that the user belongs to that segment. The following function checks this:

```
(defn segment-satisfied? [[segment-name segment-fn]]
  (if (segment-fn)
    segment-name))
```

You now have all the pieces to take a bunch of segment definitions and classify a user into one or more of them (or none of them). Consider the classify function:

```
(defn classify []
  (->> (all-segments)
       (map segment-satisfied?)
       (remove nil?)))
```

The complete source of the engine namespace is shown in the following listing.

Listing 11.5   Simple DSL execution engine to classify users into segments

```
(ns clj-in-act.ch11.engine
  (:use clj-in-act.ch11.segment
        clj-in-act.ch11.session
        clj-in-act.ch11.dsl-store))
(defn load-code [code-string]
  (binding [*ns* (:ns (meta #'load-code))]
    (load-string code-string)))
(defn matches? [^String superset ^String subset]
  (and
   (not (empty? superset))
   (> (.indexOf superset subset) 0)))
(defn segment-satisfied? [[segment-name segment-fn]]
  (if (segment-fn)
    segment-name))
(defn classify []
  (->> (all-segments)
       (map segment-satisfied?)
       (remove nil?)))
```

Now you'll test it at the REPL. You'll begin by creating a string that contains the definitions of the two segments in your new DSL:

```
(def dsl-code (str
  '(defsegment googling-clojurians
     (and
      (> (count $search-terms) 0)
      (matches? $url-referrer "google")))
  '(defsegment loyal-safari
     (and
      (empty? $url-referrer)
      (= :safari $user-agent)))))
;=> #'user/dsl-code
```

Next, you'll bring in your little DSL engine:

```
(use 'clj-in-act.ch11.engine)
;=> nil
```

It's now easy to load up the segment definitions:

```
(load-code dsl-code)
;=> {:segments {:loyal-safari #<engine$eval3399$segment_fn__2833_
```
TRUNCATED OUTPUT

To test classification, you're going to need a user session and Redis running. You can set up a session for testing purposes by defining one at the REPL as follows:

```
(def abc-session {
    :consumer-id "abc"
    :url-referrer "http://www.google.com/search?q=clojure+programmers"
    :search-terms ["clojure" "programmers"]
    :ip-address "192.168.0.10"
    :tz-offset 480
    :user-agent :safari})
;=> #'user/abc-session
```

Now put it into Redis:

```
(require 'redis) (use 'clj-in-act.ch11.session)
;=> nil
(redis/with-server {:host "localhost"}
  (save-session abc-session))
;=> "OK"
```

Everything is set up now, and you can test segmentation:

```
(redis/with-server {:host "localhost"}
  (in-session "abc"
    (println "The current user is in:" (classify))))
The current user is in: (:googling-clojurians)
;=> nil
```

It works as expected. Note that the `classify` function returns a lazy sequence that's realized by the call to `println`. If you were to omit that, you'd need a `doall` to see it at the REPL; otherwise, it will complain about the `*session*` var not being bound.

With this, you have the basics working end to end. Expanding the DSL is as easy as adding new data elements and new primitives such as the `matches?` function. You can also expand the `$attribute` syntax by doing more in the `postwalk` transformation. Before addressing updating rules, you'll add a way to name the abstractions you're defining and allow for segments to be reused.

INCREASING COMBINABILITY

Imagine that you'd like to narrow the scope of the `googling-clojurians` crowd. You'd like to know which of these folks are also using the Chrome browser. You could create a segment as follows:

```
(defsegment googling-clojurians-chrome
    (and
      (> (count $search-terms) 0)
      (matches? $url-referrer "google")
      (= :chrome $user-agent)))
```

This will work fine, but it has the obvious problem that two of the three conditions are duplicated in the `googling-clojurians` segment. In a normal programming language, creating a named entity and replacing the duplicate code in both places with that entity can remove such duplication. For example, you could create a Clojure function and call it from both places.

If you do that, you'll expose the lower-level details of the implementation of your DSL to the eventual users of the DSL. It would be ideal if you could hide that detail while letting them use named entities. Consider this revised implementation of def-segment:

```
(defmacro defsegment [segment-name & body]
  (let [transformed (postwalk transform-lookups body)]
    `(let [segment-fn#  (fn [] ~@transformed)]
       (register-segment ~(keyword segment-name) segment-fn#)
       (def ~segment-name segment-fn#))))
```

The change made here does what you talked about doing by hand. The definition of a segment now also creates a var by the same name. It can be used as follows:

```
(defsegment googling-clojurians-chrome
    (and
      (googling-clojurians)
      (= :chrome $user-agent)))
```

This is equivalent in functionality to the previous definition of this segment, with the duplication removed. This is an example of increasing the combinability of domain-specific entities, where segment definitions are built on top of the lower-level session-lookup primitives, combined with built-in logical operators. Note that because your DSL code is all executed within a single namespace, you have a single namespace going. This could cause problems with name conflicts, and this may need to be addressed, depending on the requirements.

Another example of a language-level construct is in-session, which given a customer ID sets up the execution context for classification. It abstracts away the details of where the session is stored and how to access and load it.

Although this is a small example, we've explored several of the concepts we talked about in the opening discussion. The last step will be to look at how the DSL can be updated dynamically.

DYNAMIC UPDATES

With the DSL, you've exposed a linguistic layer to the code that follows. You also would like to add dynamic updates to the rules. You've already seen that, but we didn't focus on it. Consider again a definition such as this:

```
(defsegment googling-clojurians
    (and
      (> (count $search-terms) 0)
      (matches? $url-referrer "yahoo")))
```

You know that evaluating this code will change the definition of the segment known as `googling-clojurians` (not to mention that it's named incorrectly, because Yahoo! search is being used). But the following code has the same effect:

```
(load-code (str '(defsegment googling-clojurians
    (and
     (> (count $search-terms) 0)
     (matches? $url-referrer "yahoo")))))
```

Notice that `load-code` accepts a string. This DSL code snippet can be created anywhere, even from outside your execution engine. It could be created, say, from a text editor and loaded in via a web service.

Let's take another example by imagining you had a set of remote worker processes that implemented your rule engine to classify users into segments. You can imagine `classify` being implemented using `def-worker`. When sent a request, it will access a commonly available Redis server, find the specified user session, and classify the user into segments. This is no different from what you've seen earlier, except for the fact that this code would run on multiple remote servers.

Now, imagine `load-code` also being implemented as a `def-worker`. In this scenario, not only could you remotely load DSL code, but you could also use `run-worker-everywhere` to broadcast DSL updates across all remote workers. You'd get the ability to update the segmentation cluster in real time, with no code to deploy.

We'll end this section with one last point. We haven't addressed error checking the DSL code so far, and in a production system you'd definitely need to do that. You've also built quite a minimal DSL, and you could certainly make it arbitrarily powerful. Being able to use the full Clojure language inside it is a powerful feature that can be used by power users if so desired. As the capability of the DSL itself is expanded to do more than segmentation, the ability to update running code in such a simple way as described previously could prove to be useful.

11.6 Summary

When most people start out with the Lisp family of programming languages, they first ask about the odd syntax. The answer to that question is the macro system. In that sense, we've come full circle. Macros are special because they make Clojure a programmable programming language. They allow the programmer to mold the core language into one that suits the problem at hand. In this way, Clojure blurs the line between the designers of the language itself and the programmer.

This chapter started with a few advanced uses of Clojure macros. Anaphoric macros aren't used a lot, and they certainly come with their gotchas, but when applied carefully, they can result in truly elegant solutions. Similarly, moving computation into the compile phase of your program seems like something that isn't done often. Certainly, the example we looked at gives only a glimpse into what's possible. It's an important technique, though, that can be effective when needed. Finally, macros that define other macros threaten to send you down the rabbit hole. Understanding such use of the macro system is the only way to true Lisp mastery.

Lisp encourages a certain style of programming. Everyone seems to be talking about domain-specific languages these days, but in Clojure, it's the normal way to build programs. You've written code similar to the behavioral targeting DSL example throughout the book, be it the mocking framework to help you write tests in chapter 10, the object system utility in chapter 8, or the faux protocols library called modus operandi in chapter 9. Some people express concern about the misuse of macros, but the real concern should be an incomplete understanding of the Lisp way.

Conclusion

What you've seen in this book is only the tip of the iceberg. Lisp, and thus Clojure, makes it possible to build systems that can withstand today's demanding requirements. It isn't far-fetched to think that the revival of Lisp will prompt systems that can someday do what you mean. To do that, you'll need more than a few language features or a macro system. You'll need more than DSLs.

You'll need a system that can adapt itself to new and changing requirements. Programmers will need to recognize that evaluators are themselves programs, and they can be built like everything else, allowing new kinds of evaluation rules and paradigms. You'll need programs that watch themselves as they run and modify themselves to improve their output. All this might seem like fantasy, but it's possible. In the words of Alan Kay, the computer revolution hasn't even started yet.[1] And paraphrasing him some more, the way to build systems that can do all this is to play it grand. You have to build your systems grander than you think they can be. A language like Clojure gives you the tools to make this happen.

---

[1] *The Computer Revolution Hasn't Happened Yet*, 1997 OOPSLA Keynote: https://youtu.be/oKg1hTOQXoY.

appendix
Installing Clojure

You have a few options for installing a Clojure compiler and read-evaluate-print loop (REPL) to run Clojure code. (A REPL is a programming language's interactive command line, like a command prompt or terminal shell.) We'll survey some options in this appendix, and you can find more options at Clojure's Getting Started page (http://clojure.org/). But most people will want to install Clojure via the project management tool Leiningen (see section A.3).

In almost every case you'll first need to install Java 1.6 or greater. To check if you have Java installed, open a command prompt and type the following:

```
$ java -version
java version "1.8.0_20"
Java(TM) SE Runtime Environment (build 1.8.0_20-b26)
Java HotSpot(TM) 64-Bit Server VM (build 25.20-b23, mixed mode)
```

If you get an error, or if the first line shows a Java version lower than 1.6, you'll need to follow the instructions to install Java for your platform (https://www.java.com/en/download/help/download_options.xml). Once you have Java installed, you can follow the instructions shown here to install Clojure.

A.1   *Try Clojure*

The easiest way to install something is *not* to install it. Try Clojure (http://www.tryclj.com) is a Clojure REPL you run in your browser. This REPL has two major limitations:

- It runs an older version of Clojure (1.4 as of this writing).
- If you define too many things or wait 15 minutes, your environment is reset. (It's kept if you close your browser window, so you can reopen it without losing your defined vars and functions.)

But if you just want to try some Clojure code, this isn't a bad option. You can follow along with most of the examples in chapters 2 and 3 using nothing more than the Try Clojure REPL.

A.2   Clojure.jar

Clojure is really just some Java code, and Java code is distributed in JAR files. You can download prebuilt Clojure JAR files from http://clojure.org/downloads. Unzip the downloaded file and run the clojure.main entry point to get a REPL:

```
$ java -cp clojure-1.6.0.jar clojure.main
Clojure 1.6.0
user=>
```

The clojure.main entry point has some other command-line options, too:

```
$ java -cp clojure-1.6.0.jar clojure.main --help
Usage: java -cp clojure.jar clojure.main [init-opt*] [main-opt] [arg*]

  With no options or args, runs an interactive Read-Eval-Print Loop

  init options:
    -i, --init path     Load a file or resource
    -e, --eval string   Evaluate expressions in string; print non-nil values

  main options:
    -m, --main ns-name  Call the -main function from a namespace with args
    -r, --repl          Run a repl
    path                Run a script from from a file or resource
    -                   Run a script from standard input
    -h, -?, --help      Print this help message and exit

  Operation:

    - Establishes thread-local bindings for commonly set!-able vars
    - Enters the user namespace
    - Binds *command-line-args* to a seq of strings containing command line
      args that appear after any main option
    - Runs all init options in order
    - Calls a -main function or runs a repl or script if requested

  The init options may be repeated and mixed freely, but must appear before
  any main option. The appearance of any eval option before running a repl
  suppresses the usual repl greeting message: "Clojure ~(clojure-version)".

  Paths may be absolute or relative in the filesystem or relative to
  classpath. Classpath-relative paths have prefix of @ or @/
```

A.3   Leiningen

Leiningen is the standard Clojure project and dependency management tool—almost all Clojure projects are managed using Leiningen. For most people, almost all of their contact with Clojure is actually through Leiningen. If you're not sure what Clojure installation option you need, then it's this one!

If you're familiar with the Java world, you're sure to have come across Maven. This is an open source tool that can simplify dependency management and builds of any Java-based project. Although Maven has become ubiquitous in the Java world, it's known for being somewhat difficult to use, especially when it comes to larger, complex projects.

Luckily, despite Clojure being a Java project itself, you don't have to use Maven directly. Phil Hagelberg (http://technomancy.us) has created the Leiningen project, which uses the best parts of Maven while providing a very clean Clojure interface to end users. In this section, you'll install Leiningen and use it to set up your Clojure project.

Getting Leiningen to work on your computer is trivial. Just follow the instructions on the project's GitHub page: https://github.com/technomancy/leiningen. Once you've finished, you should be able to run the `lein` (short for Leiningen) command from your shell. To get into a Clojure REPL from anywhere, run `lein repl`.

But Leiningen's true power is managing *projects*: Clojure programs and libraries with multiple dependencies, entry points, tests, deployment processes, and the like. Read on to learn the basics of Leiningen project creation and management.

A.3.1 *lein tasks*

Running `lein` will show you a list of available tasks. The simplest one that lets you get started is `lein new`. Running this task creates a skeleton project.clj file, which is the basic configuration file that drives Leiningen, along with a directory structure for a new Clojure project. Here's the set of directories and files created by running `lein new trial`, where `trial` is the name of the project we're creating:

- project.clj
- README.md
- doc/
- src/
- test/

You may have slightly different content in this directory, depending on your exact version of Leiningen. The following shows the contents of the project.clj file we just generated:

```
(defproject trial "0.1.0-SNAPSHOT"
  :description "FIXME: write description"
  :url "http://example.com/FIXME"
  :license {:name "Eclipse Public License"
            :url "http://www.eclipse.org/legal/epl-v10.html"}
  :dependencies [[org.clojure/clojure "1.6.0"]])
```

The file contains a single call to `defproject`, which is part of the `lein` DSL. As you can see, the name of the project is `trial`, and the version number has been set to `0.1.0-SNAPSHOT`. If you're familiar with Maven, you'll know what setting the version of a project to SNAPSHOT means (it just means that this version hasn't yet been released and is perhaps not official). Apart from the name of the project and the version, defproject accepts a number of keyword parameters. The ones shown previously are mostly self-explanatory, but one of interest is :dependencies. This specifies the various libraries (JAR files) that the project depends on and that will be pulled in from a Maven repository (by default, lein looks at the Maven repository hosted at http://clojars.org). Incidentally, you may have a different version of Clojure as your dependency, depending on the latest stable release of Clojure.

A.3.2 lein repl

The next step is to run another lein task called repl. This causes lein to first run a task called deps, which connects to the default Maven repository (and any others that you may specify via the :repositories parameter in your project.clj), and get the dependency JAR files. These will be stored in your home folder, under the .m2 directory.

Once the dependencies have been downloaded, you'll be dropped to a Clojure prompt that's the REPL, with the classpath set up to include all the specified dependencies. This makes it really easy to manage your project's dependencies and their specific versions. The following shows how it looks once the task runs (again, your output may be slightly different). Remember to change directory so you're in the project folder:

```
$ lein repl
nREPL server started on port 58315 on host 127.0.0.1 - nrepl://
     127.0.0.1:58315
REPL-y 0.3.5, nREPL 0.2.6
Clojure 1.6.0
Java HotSpot(TM) 64-Bit Server VM 1.8.0_20-b26
    Docs: (doc function-name-here)
          (find-doc "part-of-name-here")
  Source: (source function-name-here)
 Javadoc: (javadoc java-object-or-class-here)
    Exit: Control+D or (exit) or (quit)
 Results: Stored in vars *1, *2, *3, an exception in *e

user=>
```

At this point, you're up and running at an active Clojure prompt. Next, let's take a look at how to add other dependencies to your Clojure project.

A.3.3 Adding dependencies to a Leiningen project

Larger Clojure programs often need other libraries on which to build functionality. Traditionally, managing such libraries has been a chore, but over the past couple of years, Leiningen has become the default dependency management tool for Clojure projects. As mentioned earlier, it uses Maven repositories as sources for the various libraries (JAR files in the Clojure world). There's a community repository hosted at https://clojars.org, which is the default repository for Leiningen. You can search this repository, and you'll often find what you're looking for if someone has uploaded that library. Of course, you can also upload your own JAR files if you don't find what you're looking for. Further, you can also tell Leiningen to look at other repositories and indeed host your own Maven repository if you'd like.

Here's an example of how you might conveniently add the JSON handling library called Cheshire to your program. You go to https://clojars.org and search for Cheshire, and you'll notice several options. One of them has version 5.4, which is a recent version and one that you'll probably be comfortable with. When you go to the web page for that library, you'll see the Leiningen dependency vector you need to add this to your project. In this case it is

```
[cheshire "5.4.0"]
```

You copy and paste that into the :dependencies section of your project.clj, save the file, and then run lein deps. Leiningen will download the correct JAR file, and you'll have it available to use when you start your REPL the next time.

index

Symbols

` (backquote) 38, 172, 283
^ (meta character) 38
^{} (reader macro) 57
^:dynamic 157
, (comma) 23
; (semicolon) 23, 38
. (dot) operator 12–13
.. (dot-dot) macro 121–122
' (quote) 38
( ) parentheses 9–10, 124
@ (deref character) 38
@ (unquote splice reader
    macro) 174
compile path global var 129
\ (backslash) 38
& (ampersand) 35, 92
# (dispatch character) 38
#( ) reader macro 76, 170
== (double-equals) function 43
- (dash) 131
-> (thread-first macro) 51, 273
->> (thread-last macro) 51, 64,
    273
~ (unquote character) 38, 172
~@ (unquote splice reader
    macro) 174

A

Abstract Windowing Toolkit. *See*
    AWT
ACI (atomic, consistent, iso-
    lated) properties 149
action at a distance 81
actions, defined 150
ad hoc polymorphism
    overview 99–101
    using multimethods
        defmethod macro
            105–106
        defmulti macro
            104–105
        overview 103–104
add-watch function 160
agent-error function 154
agents
    await function 153
    creating 150–151, 159
    defined 144
    dereferencing 159
    errors from 153–154
    mutating
        send function 151
        send-off function 152
    overview 150
    side effects and 161
    validations 154
aget function 125
alength function 125
all-ns function 90
alter function 146–148, 159
ampersand (&) 92
anaphoric macros
    if macro 270–273
    overview 270
    thread-it macro 273–276
and macro 178–179
anonymous functions 76–77
AOT (ahead of time) 126
apropos function 21

ArithmeticException 26, 61
arity of functions 65
arrays, Java, functions for
    124–125
:as keyword 92
as-> (thread-as macro) 52
aset function 125
AssertionError 65
assertions 248–255
assert-true macro 184
assoc function 31–32
assoc-in function 33
atomic, consistent, isolated
    (ACI) properties 149
atoms
    creating 155–156, 159
    defined 144
    dereferencing 159
    mutating
        compare-and-set!
            function 157
        reset! function 156
        swap! function 156
    vars vs. 161
auto-gensym function 175
await-for function 153
AWT (Abstract Windowing
    Toolkit) 125

B

backquote (`) 38, 172, 283
bean function 124
binding, of vars 80–81, 158–159
bottom-up decomposition 287
Bouncy Castle 12

C

case sensitivity 24
catch blocks 60
characters 24
CIL (Common Intermediate
    Language) 7
classes, Java 11–12, 117–118
classes. *See* object system for
    Clojure
clear-agent-errors function 154
Clojure
    functional programming 3–6
    installation 303
    interop
        dot and new operators
            12–13
        Java types, classes, and
            objects 11–12
        threads and
            concurrency 13
    Lisp and 2–3
    on JVM 6–7, 10–11
    overview 1–2
    parentheses 9–10
    significance of name 86
    syntax 7–9, 21–24
    Try Clojure site 302
clojure.test library 220
closed dispatch 100
closures
    data vs. function 201–202
    defined 86
    delayed computation
        and 198–199
    free variables and 197–198
    object system for Clojure
        class inheritance 209–214
        creating instances 203–204
        defining classes 202–203
        defining methods 205–207
        invoking methods 207–208
        objects and state 204–205
        pros and cons of 214–215
        referring to this 208–209
    private data and 199–201
CLR (Common Language
    Runtime) 2
combinability of DSLs 287–288
comment macro 23, 177
comments 23–24
Common Intermediate Lan-
    guage. *See* CIL
Common Lisp 2
commute function 147–148, 159

comp function 72
compare-and-set! function 157
comparison functions 42
compile function 127
compile time, shifting computa-
    tion to 276–281
complement function 71
compute-across function 191
concurrency
    agents
        await function 153
        creating 150–151
        errors from 153–154
        overview 150
        send function 151
        send-off function 152
        validations 154
    atoms
        compare-and-set!
            function 157
        creating 155–156
        reset! function 156
        swap! function 156
    Clojure approach to
        creation functions 159
        deciding which reference
            type to use 161
        immutability by
            copying 143–144
        managed references
            144–145
        mutation 159–160
        mutation, watching
            for 160–161
        overview 143
        persistent data
            structures 144
        references 159
        transactions 160
    futures 162–163
    identities and values
        immutable values 140, 142
        objects over time 140–141
        understanding identity vs.
            state 139–140
    in Java 13
    promises 163
    refs
        alter function 146–147
        commute function 147–148
        creating 145
        ref-set function 146
    state issues
        dirty reads 136
        locking solution 137–138

        lost updates 136
        overview 136
        phantom reads 137
    STM
        ACI (atomic, consistent, iso-
            lated) properties 149
        MVCC (multiversion con-
            currency control) 150
        overview 148–149
        side effects from 155
        transactions 149
    vars
        bindings for 158–159
        creating 157–158
cond macro 40
cond-> (conditional threading
    macro) 53
conditionals
    cond 40
    if 39–40
    if-not 40
    when 40–41
    when-not 41
conj function 28
cons function 34
constantly function 71
:constructors option 131
create-ns function 90
cube-all function 188

D

dash prefix 131
data structures
    characters 24
    keywords 26–27
    lists 27–29
    maps 31–33
    nil 24
    numbers 25–26
    sequences 33–34
    strings 24
    symbols 26–27
    vectors 29–30
deadlock 138
decimal numbers 25
declare macro 177–178
decomposition of DSLs 287
def form 80
:default case 111
defclass function 202
defmethod macro 105–106
defmulti macro 104–105
defn macro 35, 63, 81
defnn macro 183

defonce macro 105, 178
defprotocol macro 235
defrecord macro 240–243
deftest macro 220
deftype macro 244
defwebmethod macro 181–183
delayed computation, closures
    and 198–199
deliver function 164
dependencies, Leiningen
    305–306
deref function 145, 159
derive form 109–110
destructuring
    map bindings 93–95
    overview 91
    vector bindings
        nested vectors 92–93
        overview 91–92
        using & and 92
dirty reads 136
dispatch character (#) 38
dissoc function 31
do form 37–38
:doc key 58, 63
doc macro 20–21, 63
doc-string macro 63
documentation
    apropos function 21
    doc macro 20–21
    find-doc function 21
domain-specific languages. See
    DSLs
doseq macro 46
dosync blocks, STM transaction
    side effects 155
dosync function 147
dosync macro 160
dot operator 12–13
dot special form 120–121
dot-dot (..) macro 121–122
dotimes macro 46
doto macro 122
double-equals (==) function 43
DSLs (domain-specific
    languages) 177
    designing
        combinability 287–288
        decomposition 287
    internal vs. external 291
    user classification through
        data element 289
        dynamic updates 298
        factors affecting power of
            DSL 294–295
        increasing combinability
            297–298
        overview 289, 295–297
        segmenting users 291–294
        user session
            persistence 290–291
duck typing 101
dynamic scope, of vars 81–83

E

equality functions 42
every? function 70
exceptions
    from agents 153
    in Java 60–62
expectations library 248
:exposes option 132
:exposesmethods option 132
expression problem
    data types side of
        defrecord macro 240–243
        deftype macro 244
        reify macro 244
        specifying Java
            interfaces 243–244
    defined 222
    example scenario for
        adding functions 219
        creating base 218
        existing Java codebase
            220–222
        testing code 219–220
    inadequate solutions
        if-then-else 223
        monkey patching 223
        wrappers 222–223
    multimethods as
        solution 223–225
    operations side of
        overview 225–227
        tracking using
            metadata 227–233
    overview 218
    protocols
        defining 235–236
        extend function 237
        extends? function 238–239
        extend-type macro 237
        nil and 238
        overview 234–235
        using 236–237
extend function 237
extend-protocol macro 236
:extends option 131
extends? function 238–239
extend-type macro 237
external DSLs 291
extreme programming. See EP

F

:factory option 132
FileFilter interface 126
filter macro 47
finally clause 61
find-doc function 21
find-ns function 90
"first-class" functions 3
fixed arities 66
floating-point numbers 25
flow control
    conditionals
        cond 40
        if 39–40
        if-not 40
        when 40–41
        when-not 41
    iteration
        doseq and dotimes 46
        filter 47
        for 48–50
        loop/recur 44–45
        map function 46–47
        reduce 47–48
        while 44
    logical functions 41–43
    threading macros
        conditional threading 53
        thread-as 52–53
        thread-first 50–51
        thread-last 51–52
for macro 48–50
Fortran 2
free variables, closures and
    197–198
function composition 70
functional programming
    (FP) 3–6
    closures
        data vs. function 201–202
        delayed computation
            and 198–199
        free variables and 197–198
        private data and 199–201
    higher-order functions
        collecting results of
            functions 187–189
        filtering lists of things
            191–192

functional programming (FP)
  (continued)
  overview 187
  reducing lists of
    things 189–191
  object system for Clojure
    class inheritance 209–214
    creating instances 203–204
    defining classes 202–203
    defining methods 205–207
    invoking methods 207–208
    objects and state 204–205
    pros and cons of 214–215
    referring to this 208–209
  partial application of func-
    tions
    adapting functions
      193–196
    defining new
      functions 196–197
    overview 192–193
functions
  anonymous 76–77
  calling 69–70
  creating 35
  defining 62–65
  general discussion 62
  higher-order
    comp 72
    complement 71
    constantly 71
    creating 73–75
    every? 70
    memoize 73
    overview 70
    partial 72
    some 70
  higher-order functions
    collecting results of
      functions 187–189
    filtering lists of things
      191–192
    overview 187
    reducing lists of
      things 189–191
  keywords 77–80
  logical 41–43
  multiple arity 65
  mutually recursive 67–69
  overloading 100
  partial application of
    adapting functions 193–196
    defining new
      functions 196–197
    overview 192–193

private vs. public 88
recursive 66–67
symbols 78–80
unary 46
variable arity of 35
variadic 66
futures 162–163

G

:gen-class directive 127
gen-class macro 129–131
generics 99
gen-interface macro 129–131
-getCurrentStatus function 131

H

hash maps 79
:hierarchy keyword option 113
higher-order functions
  collecting results of
    functions 187–189
  comp 72
  complement 71
  constantly 71
  creating 73–75
  every? 70
  filtering lists of things 191–
    192
  memoize 73
  overview 70, 187
  partial 72
  reducing lists of things 189–
    191
  some 70
hosted languages 6

I

identities
  immutable values 140, 142
  objects over time 140–141
  state vs. 139–140
if macro 39–40, 270–273
if-not macro 40
if-then-else 223
immutable values
  identities and 140, 142
  via copying 143–144
:implements option 131
:impl-ns option 132
:import key 89
import macro 118
:import option 118

infix macro 180
infix notation 8
:init option 131
–initialize function 131
in-ns function 90
installation
  checking Java installation 302
  Clojure.jar 303
  Leiningen
    adding dependencies to
      project 305–306
    lein repl task 305
    lein tasks 304–305
    overview 303–304
  Try Clojure site 302–303
instance? function 110
integers 25
interfaces, defined 11
internal DSLs 291
interop
  calling Clojure from
    Java 133–134
  calling Java from Clojure
    .. (dot-dot) macro 121–122
    accessing methods and
      fields 119–120
    array functions 124–125
    bean function 124
    creating instances 118–119
    dot special form 120–121
    doto macro 122
    importing Java classes
      117–118
    memfn macro 123–124
    MouseAdapter class
      125–126
    reify macro 126
  compiling Clojure code to
    Java bytecode
    calculator example 126–129
    creating Java classes and
      interfaces using gen-class
      and gen-interface
      129–131
    example generating Java
      classes 131–132
    using Leiningen 132–133
  dot and new operators 12–13
  Java types, classes, and
    objects 11–12
  threads and concurrency 13
into-array function 125
in-transaction values 149
invoke method 134
:io key 56

isa? function 110
ISeq interface 33
iteration
    doseq and dotimes 46
    filter 47
    for 48–50
    loop/recur 44–45
    map function 46–47
    reduce 47–48
    while 44

J

JAR files 221
Java
    calling Clojure from 133–134
    calling from Clojure
        .. (dot-dot) macro 121–122
        accessing methods and
            fields 119–120
        array functions 124–125
        bean function 124
        creating instances 118–119
        dot special form 120–121
        doto macro 122
        importing Java classes
            117–118
        memfn macro 123–124
        MouseAdapter class
            125–126
        reify macro 126
    checking installation 302
    compiling Clojure code to
        bytecode
        calculator example 126–129
        creating Java classes and
            interfaces using gen-class
            and gen-interface
            129–131
        example generating Java
            classes 131–132
        using Leiningen 132–133
    dot and new operators 12–13
    exceptions in 60–62
    primitive types 59–60
    static fields 119–120
    static methods 119
    threads and concurrency 13
    type hints 58–59
    types, classes, and objects
        11–12
java.lang package 11
JavaScript 2
Jetty 12
JIT (just-in-time) compiler 6

Joda Time library 12, 249
JSP (JavaServer Pages) 172
just-in-time compiler. See JIT
JVM (Java Virtual Machine)
    Clojure on 6–7, 10–11
    dot and new operators 12–13
    Java types, classes, and
        objects 11–12
    threads and concurrency 13

K

:keys key 94
keywords 26–27, 77–80

L

lazy-seq macro 189
Leiningen 127, 132–133
    adding dependencies to
        project 305–306
    lein repl task 305
    lein tasks 304–305
    overview 303–304
lein-localrepo plugin 221
let form
    overview 35–36
    scope and 85–86
lexical closures 86–87
lexically scoped variable 80
Lisp 301
    Clojure and 2–3
    syntax 7–9
lists 27–29
livelock 138
:load-impl-ns option 132
loadResourceScript method 134
locks 137–138
logical functions 41–43
loop macro 44–45
loop/recur construct 67

M

:macro key 58
macroexpand function 171
macroexpand-1 function 171
macroexpand-all function 171
macros
    advantages of 176–177
    anaphoric
        if macro 270–273
        overview 270
        thread-it macro 273–276
    and macro 178–179

comment macro 177
declare macro 177–178
defonce macro 178
examples of custom
    assert-true macro 184
    defnn macro 183
    defwebmethod macro
        181–183
    infix macro 180
    randomly macro 180–181
macro-generating macros
    defined 281–282
    example template 282
    make-synonym macro
        implementation
        282–285
    purpose of 285–286
overview 167
rotation cipher example
    276–279
shifting computation to
    compile time 276–281
templates
    generating names
        174–176
    splicing 173–174
    unquote splice reader
        macro (~@) 174
    unquoting 172–173
    using backquote (`)
        macro 172
textual substitution
    example 167–168
time macro 179–180
unless form
    as function 169–170
    as macro 170–171
    overview 168–169
magic variables 19–20
:main option 132
make-hierarchy function 113
make-synonym macro 282–285
managed references 144–145,
    161
map bindings 93–95
maps 31–33, 46–47
mathematical functions 22
Maven repository 305
memfn macro 123–124
memoize function 73
:meta option 154
metadata
    Java primitive types 59–60
    Java type hints 58–59
    overview 56–58

:methods option 131
Midje library 248
mocks
    defined 256
    implementing 260–261
    state management 264–265
    stubs vs. 261–264
monkey patching 223
MouseAdapter class 125–126
multimethods
    ad hoc polymorphism using
        defmethod macro
            105–106
        defmulti macro 104–105
        overview 103–104
    as solution to expression
        problem 223–225
    creating functionality
        without 103
    multiple-dispatch 106–108
    subtype polymorphism using
        building and querying type
            hierarchies 109–110
        overview 108–109
        resolving method
            ambiguities 111–112
        subtypes and multiple-
            dispatch 110–111
        user-defined
            hierarchies 112
multiple-dispatch
    overview 106–108
    subtypes and 110–111
multithreading. See concurrency
mutation
    of agents
        send function 151
        send-off function 152
    of atoms
        compare-and-set!
            function 157
        reset! function 156
        swap! function 156
    of refs
        alter function 146–147
        commute function 147–148
        ref-set function 146
    overview 159–160
    watching for
        add-watch function 160
        remove-watch function 161
mutually recursive
    functions 67–69
MVCC (multiversion concur-
    rency control) 150

N

:name option 131
namespaces
    all-ns function 90
    create-ns function 90
    find-ns function 90
    importing Java classes
        into 118
    in-ns function 90
    ns macro 87–88
    ns-interns function 90
    ns-publics function 90
    ns-resolve function 90
    ns-unmap function 90–91
    overview 87
    reload and reload-all 89–90
    remove-ns function 90–91
    resolve function 90
    using external libraries
        88–89
nested vectors 92–93
new operator 12–13
nil
    as return 187
    overview 24
    protocols and 238
ns macro 87–88
ns-interns function 90
ns-publics function 90
ns-resolve function 90
ns-unmap function 90–91
NullPointerException 24
numbers 25–26

O

object system for Clojure
    class inheritance 209–214
    creating instances
        203–204
    defining classes 202–203
    defining methods 205–207
    invoking methods 207–208
    objects and state 204–205
    pros and cons of 214–215
    referring to this 208–209
objects, changes over time
    to 140–141
objects, Java 11–12
OO (object-oriented) 2
open dispatch 100
operators, absence of 8
ordering-fn function 75
overloading functions 100

P

packages, defined 117
parametric polymorphism 99
parentheses ( ) 9–10, 124
partial application of functions
    adapting functions 193–196
    defining new functions
        196–197
    overview 192–193
partial function 72, 195
pattern matching. See destructur-
    ing
peek function 30
persistence
    defined 144
    persistent data structures 144
    principles of persistent data 4
phantom reads 137
polish notation 21
polymorphism
    ad hoc 99–101
    function overloading as 100
    general discussion 98–99
    multimethods
        ad hoc polymorphism
            using 103–104
        building and querying type
            hierarchies 109–110
        creating functionality
            without 103
        defmethod macro 105–106
        defmulti macro 104–105
        multiple-dispatch 106–108
        resolving method
            ambiguities 111–112
        subtype polymorphism
            using 108–109
        subtypes and multiple-
            dispatch 110–111
        user-defined
            hierarchies 112
    parametric 99
    subtype 101–103
pop function 30
:post key 65
:postinit option 132
:pre key 64
predicate functions 70
prefer-method function 112
prefix notation 8, 21–22
:prefix option 131–132
primitive types, Java 59–60
private functions 88
profilers 12

promises 163
protocols
  defining 235–236
  extend function 237
  extends? function 238–239
  extend-type macro 237
  nil and 238
  overview 234–235
  using 236–237
public functions 88
pure functions 3, 6, 19

Q

quote (') 38

R

race conditions 138
Rails HTML. *See* RHTML
randomly macro 180–181
reader literals 95
reader macros 38–39, 57
read-evaluate-print loop. *See* REPL
recur construct 67
recur macro 44–45
recursive functions 66–67
Redis 290
reduce macro 47–48
refactor mercilessly 255–256
referentially transparent,
    defined 3
refs
  creating 145, 159
  defined 144
  dereferencing 159
  mutating
    alter function 146–147
    commute function 147–148
    ref-set function 146
ref-set function 146
regex (regular expression) 21
reify macro 126, 244
reload/reload-all 89–90
remove-ns function 90–91
remove-watch function 161
REPL (read-evaluate-print
    loop) 19
  documentation in
    apropos function 21
    doc macro 20–21
    find-doc function 21
  for Clojure 17–18
  general discussion 16–17
  magic variables in 19–20

:repositories parameter 305
require 89
reset! function 156
resolve function 90
RHTML (Rails HTML) 172
root binding 80
ROT13 cipher 276
rotation cipher example 276–279
-run function 131
run-tests function 220
RuntimeException 61

S

:safe key 56
scope
  let form and 85–86
  overview 80
  vars
    binding of 80–81
    dynamic scope 81–83
    laziness and 84–85
    thread-local state 84
Selenium WebDriver 12
semicolon (;) 23
send function 151
send-off function 152
sequences 33–34
side-effects 37, 155
software transactional memory.
    See STM
some function 70
sort-by function 74
sorter-using function 74, 76
splicing 173–174
StackOverflowError 67
starvation 138
state issues
  dirty reads 136
  locking solution 137–138
  lost updates 136
  overview 136
  phantom reads 137
  See also concurrency
static fields, Java 119–120
static methods, Java 119
STM (software transactional
    memory) 5
  ACI properties 149
  MVCC 150
  overview 148–149
  side effects from 155
  transactions 149
strings 24
:strs key 95

structural editing 10
structural sharing 4
structural subtyping 101
stubs
  defined 256
  expense finders
    example 256–257
  implementing 257–260
  mocks vs. 261–264
  state management 264–265
subtype polymorphism
  overview 101
  using multimethods
    building and querying type
      hierarchies 109–110
    overview 108–109
    resolving method
      ambiguities 111–112
    subtypes and multiple-
      dispatch 110–111
    user-defined
      hierarchies 112
swap! function 156–157, 161
symbols 26–27, 78–80
:syms key 95
syntax
  case sensitivity 24
  comments 23–24
  do form 37–38
  functions
    creating 35
    variable arity of 35
  let form 35–36
  overview 7–9
  parentheses 9–10
  prefix notation 21–22
  reader macros 38–39
  underscore identifier 36–37
  whitespace 22–23

T

:tag key 58
TDD (test-driven development)
  creating assertions 248–255
  general discussion 247–248
  mocks
    defined 256
    implementing 260–261
    state management 264–265
    stubs vs. 261–264
  organizing tests
    are macro 266
    overview 265–266
    testing macro 266

TDD (test-driven development)
    (continued)
    refactor mercilessly 255–256
    stubs
        defined 256
        expense finders example
            256–257
        implementing 257–260
        mocks vs. 261–264
        state management 264–265
templates, macro
    generating names 174–176
    splicing 173–174
    unquote splice reader macro
        (~@) 174
    unquoting 172–173
    using backquote (') macro 172
this keyword 208
thread-as macro 52–53
threading macros
    conditional threading 53
    thread-as 52–53
    thread-first 50–51, 273
    thread-it 273–276
    thread-last 51–52, 64
thread-local state, of vars 84
threads, in Java 13
throw form 60–62
time macro 179–180
to-array function 125
to-array-2d function 125
top-down decomposition 287
trampoline function 68
transactions, STM 149
Try Clojure site 302–303
try form 60–62

type hints, Java 58–59
types
    Clojure 11
    Java 11–12

U

unary functions 46
unboxed types 59
underive form 109
underscore identifier 36–37
unit testing 219
unless form
    as function 169–170
    as macro 170–171
    overview 168–169
unquote character (~) 172
unquote splice reader macro
        (@) 174
unquoting 172–173
update-in function 33
:use key 89
user classification using DSL
    data element 289
    dynamic updates 298
    factors affecting power of
        DSL 294–295
    increasing combinability
        297–298
    overview 289, 295–297
    segmenting users 291–294
    user session persistence
        290–291
user namespace 17
UUIDs (universally unique
    identifiers) 96

V

:validator option 154
values, in functional
        programming 3
variable arity 8
variable capture 175,
        272
variadic functions 21, 66
vars
    atoms vs. 161
    binding of 80–81
    bindings for 158–159
    creating 157–158
    defined 144
    dynamic scope 81–83
    laziness and 84–85
    thread-local state 84
vector bindings
    nested vectors 92–93
    overview 91–92
    using & and 92
vectors 29–30

W

when macro 40–41
when-not macro 41
while macro 44
whitespace 22–23
wrappers 222–223

X

XP (extreme
        programming) 255